Fodor's EXPLORING

VENICE

FODOR'S TRAVEL PUBLICATIONS

NEW YORK • TORONTO • LONDON • SYDNEY • AUCKLAND

WWW.FODORS.COM

Copyright © Automobile Association Developments Ltd. 1997, 1999, 2001
Maps copyright © Automobile Association Developments Ltd. 1997, 1999, 2001

Published in the United States by Fodor's Travel Publications, Inc.
Published in the United Kingdom by AA Publishing.

ISBN 0-679-00911-6
Third edition

Fodor's Exploring Venice

Author: **Tim Jepson**
Revision Verifier: **Susie Boulton**
Cartography: **The Automobile Association**
Original Copy Editor: **Barbara Mellor**
Revision Copy Editor: **Sarah Hudson**
Cover design: **Tigist Getachew**
Front Cover Silhouette: **AA Picture Library**

Printed and bound in Italy by Printer Trento srl
10 9 8 7 6 5 4 3 2 1

How to use this book

ORGANIZATION

Venice Is, Venice Was
Discusses aspects of life and culture in contempory Venice and explores significant periods in its history.

A–Z
Covers places to visit, including walks and excursions. Within this section fall the Focus On articles, which consider a variety of subjects in greater detail

Travel Facts
Contains the practical information that is vital for a successful trip

Accommodations and Restaurants
Lists recommended establishments throughout Venice, giving a brief description of what each offers

Atlas Section
Comprises ten pages of large-scale, high-quality maps

ABOUT THE RATINGS
Most places described in this book have been given a separate rating. These are as follows:

▶ ▶ ▶   **Do not miss**

▶ ▶   **Highly recommended**

▶   **Worth seeing**

MAPS
To make each particular location easier to find, every main entry in this book has a map reference to the right of its name. This comprises a number, followed by a letter, followed by another number, such as 176B3. The first number (176) refers to the page on which the map can be found, the letter (B) and the second number (3) pinpoint the square in which the main entry is located. The maps on the inside front cover and inside back cover are referred to as IFC and IBC respectively.

Contents

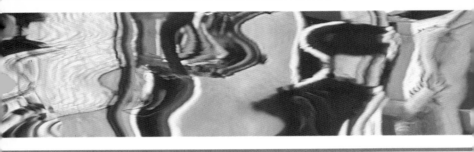

6

Maps

My Venice

My first visit to Venice was a nightmare: the dog days of August, churning crowds, heaving restaurants and, it seemed, not a Venetian in sight—save those taking money from the flood of tourists. Caught up in the human throng, and swept over bridges and down alleys towards the big sights—St. Mark's and the Doge's Palace—I wondered why I was here and how quickly I could leave. In the event I spent a day in a hot and irritated daze, abandoning the city convinced, as the cynics had warned, that Venice was a lifeless husk, a medieval theme park peddling its beauty for profit.

But I was young then, and poorly prepared, believing —naïvely—that Venice would soften the hardest heart, and its charms triumph over crowds and commercialism. This youthful misadventure, sadly, kept me away from Venice for years, which only goes to show how wrong first impressions can be. When I eventually returned it was in April, and this time it was to a revelation: azure skies, empty squares, peaceful canals and, most remarkably, a city with a life of its own. For the first time I saw mothers with children, rubbed shoulders with students, drank with old men in cafés, and chattered at market stalls.

For Venice, I now realize, really is the world's most beautiful city; a city in the genuine sense, one that has spirit, character, and purpose, and whose more subtle charms take time and application to uncover. I was lucky enough to spend several months in the city, and to avoid the busy and debilitating days of high summer. Whenever you come and however long you stay (as long as it's more than a day) it's enough to heed the oldest of guidebook clichés: get off the beaten track, explore the backstreets, and try to meet (or at least mingle with) the locals.

I gave Venice a chance to weave its magic on me and have since made many return visits. I hope the city will make you feel the same.

Tim Jepson

Tim Jepson's love of travel began with a busking trip through Europe, and has since taken him from the drowsy calm of the Umbrian hills to the windswept tundra of the Yukon and far north. Hopelessly in love with Italy—like many a romantic Englishman before him—he has lived in Rome, Venice, and Tuscany, but has plans to leave the warmth of the Mediterranean for the Arctic and the hidden mountains of South America. He has written several guides for the AA, including *Explorer* guides to Italy, Florence & Tuscany and Canada

Venice Is

Venice's beauty, and our reaction to it, are nothing new. The city has been seducing visitors for centuries, taking their money and granting enchantment in return. Yet over the centuries its commercial frenzy and over-familiar charms have made it—in the eyes of some—almost a beguiling cliché.

REACTIONS What is one to make of the world's most beautiful city? It is a question that has vexed visitors to Venice for centuries. D. H. Lawrence considered it "an abhorrent, green, slippery city." To Edward Gibbon it afforded "hours of astonishment and…days of Disgust." For Truman Capote it was like eating "a box of chocolate liqueurs at one go." For most, however, it has been a place of enchantment. Disappointment, a rare response, has tended to be aroused by other people, by the army of tourists with whom one has to share one's pleasures. "There are some disagreeable things in Venice," wrote Henry James, but "nothing so disagreeable as the visitors."

> ❏ "… nothing is like it, nothing is equal to it, not a second Venice in the world." Elizabeth Barrett Browning (1851) ❏

> ❏ "The clichés about Venice are imposed on us because, like most clichés, they are based on true observations which have occurred to some of the greatest and most modest minds alike." Gore Vidal, *Vidal in Venice* (1985) ❏

"No word," agreed Mary McCarthy, "can be spoken in this city that is not an echo of something said before." Yet words are not what Venice invites, nor—in the long run—how we remember her. She is, according to Charles Dickens, "something past all writing of or speaking of—almost past all thinking of." Max Beerbohm went one step further: "I should not," he wrote, "envy the soul of one

CLICHÉ Visitors continue to plague Venice, crowding it to the point of saturation throughout the dog days of summer. Escaping from the crowd, contrary to popular belief, is rarely an option. Tourists seem to come at you over bridges and around corners in every quarter of the city. The visitors, and their endlessly renewable enthusiasms, are the despair of some: "There is nothing left to discover or describe," lamented Henry James, "and originality of attitude is utterly impossible."

10

> ❏ "…somewhere between a freak and a fairytale." Jan Morris, *Venice* (1960) ❏

Venice's Grand Canal, a most beautiful high street

who at first sight of such strange loveliness found anything to say."

A PERSONAL REVELATION For all the crowds, and all the impossibility of first discovery, the spell of Venice remains forever fresh and unbroken. The thrill of that first impression, of that first ride on the Grand Canal, that first view of the mist-shrouded lagoon, is a revelation unsullied by any number of pictures or descriptions. For "nothing in the world," in the words of Dickens, "that you ever heard of Venice, is equal to the magnificent and stupendous reality."

The city, gloriously unchanged since Dickens's day (and before), remains almost impossible to adequately describe or depict. It is a place simply to be seen and enjoyed.

> ❏ "The only way to care for Venice as she deserves it, is to give her a chance to touch you often—to linger and remain and return." Henry James, *Portrait of Places* (1883) ❏

No matter that your pleasure is shared with millions, no matter—for now—that the city is bursting at the seams. Revel in its every pleasure, ignore the crowds, forget the prices. Escape workaday cares, workaday cities: "unlace yourself," in the words of Gore Vidal, "for your own clichés."

True Venetians are a dying breed, their numbers sapped by emigration to mainland Mestre and the arrival of dilettante outsiders. Those who remain, however—if we are to believe other Italians—are still as cultured and cosmopolitan, and as wily and wineloving, as their illustrious and civic-minded forebears.

THE CITY'S EFFECT A city as singular as Venice was always likely to produce singular citizens. In surroundings where, as Goethe put it, "the place of street and square and promenade was taken by water...the Venetian was bound to develop into a new kind of creature." "Like the tide —six hours up and six hours down" runs a Venetian proverb, alluding to the Venetians' swings of character and notoriously mercurial moods. "As among brute beasts," wrote Pius II rather less charitably, "aquatic creatures have the least intelligence, so among human beings the Venetians are the least just and the least capable of humanity."

❏ "The Venetians are grave and dignified, full of ceremonious courtesy; at the same time, they are ironical and quick with retort." Mary McCarthy, *Venice Observed* (1961) ❏

THE INFLUENCE OF HISTORY
The city has touched its citizens in other ways, not least in its fall from power over the centuries. Many claim this accounts for a sardonic strain in the Venetian character. According to Mary McCarthy, Venetians still feel themselves to be chosen, but "chosen in a twofold sense, singled out on the one hand for special favors and, on the other, to be mocked by Fate." This sense of separateness, of being "excluded from the fold of other nations" in the words of Jan Morris, also accounts for the Venetians' occasional wistfulness—"the introspective melancholy pride of a people on their own." The city's historical legacy, and in particular her links with the Orient, perhaps also accounts for the Venetians' penchant for elegance and decoration. Wiliness, cunning and clever speech—all celebrated Venetian traits—may also derive from the city's past, bred from a mercantile acumen accumulated over centuries.

> ❏ "I wish you were here in Venice, there are so many pleasant people…of noble spirit that show me much honor and friendship. On the other hand there are also the most false, lying, thieving rascals that may be found, I think, anywhere in the world." Albrecht Dürer, *Letter* (1506) ❏

Venetians are generally also industrious and hardworking and yet are reputed to enjoy their wine rather more than they should. Today, however, the question is not so much whether Venetians are good or bad, but whether their once unique characteristics are enough to stop the drift away from the city created by their special talents.

CIVICMINDED Venice's past and its lonely singularity perhaps also give rise to the Venetians' instinct for cooperation and their sense of civic pride, not always present throughout Italy. In the past, when the state was all, individual prowess was invariably sacrificed to the common good. Venice has few statues, having long ignored the cult of the individual. These days Venetians still pull together, displaying a unity of purpose sometimes conspicuous by its absence in Rome or Naples. The result is a clean, efficiently run city distinguished by little crime, no vandalism, and a sense of civilized decorum in the streets and squares.

> ❏ "If there is one thing in the world that is unashamedly indolent and lazy, it is the Venetian women of the upper class." Théophile Gautier, *Voyage en Italie* (1857) ❏

OLD AND NEW For all its isolation and introspection, Venice's links with the East and its role as a melting pot of cultures have also given Venetians a reputation for tolerance and cosmopolitan *élan*. Visitors to the city—whose numbers should give Venetians every reason for rudeness —usually find their hosts unfailingly kind and courteous (yet who knows how often they have directed dazed tourists to the Rialto or St. Mark's?).

Venice faces a war on many fronts. She is threatened not only by numbers of visitors, and by floods, subsidence and pollution, but also by a slow bleeding away of her population that may ultimately reduce the city to nothing more than a lifeless husk to be enjoyed by visiting tourists.

14

FACTORIES Of all the 20th-century perils that assail Venice, the factories at nearby Marghera are perhaps the worst. Mainland industries first sprouted in the 1930s, with the laudable aim of bringing work to an increasingly moribund city. By the time of Italy's post-war boom in the 1950s, development was mushrooming out of control. Marghera boasted the country's largest alumina and aluminium plants, one of Europe's biggest petrochemical plants, sprawling shipyards, electrometallurgical, and calcium carbide works, and factories churning out steel, coke, ammonia, fertilizers, and nitric acid.

CORROSIVE BREW Pollutants disgorged by these concerns included phenols, cyanides, salts, chlorine, naphtha, and detergent solvents. The worst of the emissions, however, was sulphur dioxide, a noxious discharge

The chimneys of Marghera's factories rise threateningly above Venice's fragile beauty

which in combination with the damp and salt air of the lagoon spelled doom for the city's stonework. Despite the imposition of more stringent controls, Marghera's factories still pump some 50,000 tons of the gas into the atmosphere every year.

POPULATION The effect of Marghera's factories has not been limited to the environment. Originally it had been thought that Venetians would commute to their new jobs and return to the historic city at night. In practice they chose to move permanently to

the mainland, and in particular to the dormitory town of Mestre. In retrospect, this was a development that should have caused little surprise. A study of 1957, around the time of the greatest exodus, underlined the reasons. Some two-thirds of Venice's houses required radical restoration; a third received only "minimal" light; a quarter had two or more inhabitants per room; only a tenth—in this dampest of cities—had central heating; and 9 percent were uninhabitable (with another 13 percent deemed to be in "bad condition"). Eleven apartments in every hundred received no sunlight at all.

> ❏ "Venice is a moral obligation on the international community."
> UNESCO statement ❏

AN EMPTYING CITY In 1938, when Venice's population was 280,000, Mestre and Marghera had just 50,000 inhabitants; the city's birthrate, meanwhile, at 33 per 1,000, was double the Italian average. Today, Mestre's figure has risen to 200,000, and Venice's has dropped to 60,000. However, the latest census indicates that the population drift away from the center has at last slowed down. About a third of Venetians are over 60. Half the labor force is directly or indirectly involved in the tourist industry. Per capita income, however, is now the lowest in the Veneto, while prices are the highest in Italy. Moreover, homes are increasingly owned by absentee Italians and foreigners.

MISCELLANEOUS PERILS The steady disappearance of Venice's population

is closely linked to another dilemma, namely whether—in the face of ever greater numbers of tourists—the city should forgo its status as a "living" metropolis and become a glorified theme park. Schemes to preserve Venice for Venetians—modern houses, more jobs, a new metro—are often at odds with those aimed at preserving Venice for profit and posterity. And even if these issues are resolved, the more literal perils remain—too many tourists, too much pollution, too many pigeons—as well as that ultimate fate reserved for a city built on water: the relentless and corrosive advance of the elements.

> ❏ **Venice in Peril**, Morley House, 314–322 Regent Street, London W1R 5AB. Tel: 020-7636 6139. Website: www.veniceinperil.org
> **Save Venice Inc**, 216 East 78th Street, New York, NY 10021. Tel: 212/737-3141. Website: www.savevenice.org ❏

Venice's sea-level setting has always made it a watery hostage to the vagaries of wind and tide. Today the area of the city affected by flooding is over three times greater than it was only half a century ago. And yet, contrary to the received wisdom, Venice is not sinking— or at least not any more.

HISTORY OF FLOODING Venice has always been prone to inundation. An early chronicle recalls how in AD 589 "the waters changed their usual course and the whole land took on the appearance of a marsh." In 885 a report spoke of water "invading the whole city, penetrating the houses and the churches." In 1250, according to a contemporary, "the water rose from eight o'clock until midday. Many were drowned in their houses or simply died of the cold." Over the centuries, high tides have continued to cause frequent flooding in the low-lying parts of the city. The most famous deluge was on November 14, 1966, when the city was flooded to a depth of nearly six feet.

❏ "On that single night…our city aged fifty years." The Mayor of Venice on the 1966 flood ❏

DISTURBING THE LAGOON The cause of the floods is simple—high tides, coupled with southeasterly winds, fill Venice and the lagoon to overflowing. Why they have grown worse is more elusive. Some claim the melting of the polar icecaps has raised the level of the Adriatic. Others say the level of the Po basin, of which Venice forms a part, has been sinking. All agree that natural factors have been exacerbated by manmade mistakes. Land reclamation has removed the lagoon's

16

marshes (once a buffer against high tides). Dredging, and the deepening of shipping lanes, has altered tides and currents. And the churning of boats, especially in Venice itself, has led to the erosion of the seabed.

The chief culprit, however, has been the extraction of water to service the factories of Marghera. Bore holes, first sunk in the 1930s, numbered 55 by 1969 and were taking 1.6 million quarts of water *hourly* from the 985 feet of silt and clay underpinning Venice's foundations. The result was to lower the water table and with it the city. Extraction was curtailed—but not stopped—in 1973. But while the water table recovered, Venice— whose subsidence, say experts, is "unrecoverable"—did not.

> ❏ "Venice, lost and won
> Her thirteen hundred years of freedom done
> Sinks, like a sea-weed into whence she rose!"
> Lord Byron, *Childe Harold's Pilgrimage* (1812–1818) ❏

SOLUTIONS Venice first started building sea defences of clay and wicker in the 14th century. The first stone defences were laid between 1744 and 1751, and were repaired in 1846 by the Austrians, who set aside the equivalent of $1.5 million a year for their maintenance. As early as 1501, a conservation body, the *Magistrato alle Acque* (which exists to this day), already conscious of the lagoon's delicate balance, had declared a "zone of respect" around the city in which reclamation and barricades were prohibited.

Laws alone, however, were to prove ineffectual. Today more radical solutions are deemed necessary. After years of discussion, plans to complete a £5 billion flood barrier (called the MOSE project) at the three entrances to the lagoon are still subject to controversy. The project began in 1988, but still awaits final approval. Opposition centers on claims that the system will be inadequate to protect the city for any length of time and that it will disturb the normal daily tides which are essential for flushing the Venetian canals.

Meanwhile, attention has been focused on raising levels of the low-lying zones of the city and on dredging canals.

Part of the MOSE project, designed to save Venice from flooding

> ❏ Other cities make Venice's subsidence look modest. Ravenna has fallen 6 inches, while Mexico City and Long Beach, California, have both sunk a massive 26 feet. ❏

Venice's single road, and with it all the trappings of normal city life, ends in Piazzale Roma. Thereafter people and products must move around on water or on foot. The result, in the words of Chateaubriand, is "une ville contre nature"—"a town against nature."

18

❏ "...streets full of water. Please advise." Robert Benchley, telegram on arriving in Venice (1947) ❏

STREETS AND CANALS Venice may have no roads, but it has no shortage of streets. An estimated 3,000 separate alleys and thoroughfares make up the Venetian labyrinth. If laid end to end, it has been calculated, they would stretch for 125 miles. This is in a city barely 3 miles long and a little over a mile wide—or roughly the size of New York's Central Park. Over 400 bridges link these fractured highways, spanning the 118 islets and 170 canals that form Venice's watery patchwork. Just three cross the Grand Canal, the city's multi-laned main street alive with boats and bluster.

GETTING AROUND On first entering Venice, nothing seems stranger than taking to the water to travel. Yet after a few days, nothing seems more natural or more efficient. And, in the absence of roads, little compares with walking in a carless city, free of fear and fumes (even if some of the car's trappings—traffic lights, one-way streets, and do not enter signs—can still be seen policing boats on the city's canals). And nothing, in the blessed absence of horns and engines, compares with Venice's placid nighttime silence. If you don't enjoy walking (though distances are never great), boats—from water taxis to ponderous *vaporetti*—are on hand to perform the job of getting from A to B.

Supplies for the Rialto market are unloaded beside the Grand Canal

An ambulance prepares to take a patient to hospital; one of the many services adapted to the particular demands of Venice's setting

❑ "White phantom city, whose untrodden streets
Are rivers, and whose pavements are the shifting
Shadows of palaces and strips of sky."
Henry Wadsworth Longfellow, *Venice* ❑

FEEDING THE CITY Venice has other more pressing needs than transport, however, not least of them being the daily task of feeding its water-besieged population. In the past, the Canale di Cannaregio, Venice's chief mainland-facing canal, provided the city's principal aquatic lifeline. All the essentials of daily life once crossed on small boats that plied the lagoon's marked channels. A similar if smaller flotilla still ferries back and forth, but these days most provisions come into the city by less romantic means; by road and rail, or aboard vast and graceless container ships. Early dawn in Piazzale Roma presents a frenzied scene, with supplies being unloaded from trucks on to an armada of waiting boats. These then disappear into the city's furthest reaches, delivering fish to the Pescheria, fruit to the Rialto, and all manner of miscellanea to distant homes and stores.

ESSENTIAL SERVICES Food is only one concern in a roadless metropolis. What of the panoply of pipes beneath a normal city street, or the work of police, fire, and ambulance services; what of garbage, sewage or sudden death? Water, once drawn from wells in the city's squares, or *campi*, now comes from the mainland. Garbage, once scoured from canals by the tides, is now taken by boat to dumps in the lagoon. Sewage, for the most part, winds up in *pozzi neri*, or black wells, the septic tanks whose emptying over the centuries has enriched many a Venetian. The emergency services use the canals like everyone else (few sights are more memorable than a police launch, siren screaming, roaring down the Grand Canal). Coffins, too, float to their final resting place by boat. Venice's waterways are a fact of Venetian life from the cradle to the grave, as indispensable in death as they are in life.

Italians can sometimes appear to treat politics with cynicism and weary distain. For Venice, however, with its unique problems and declining numbers—and therefore fading political voice—the behavior of local politicians is perhaps of more importance than it is in other cities

THE HISTORICAL PERSPECTIVE
Venetians have always been better diplomats than politicians. Blessed with a cast-iron constitution, the city's former republic rarely had to suffer the Machiavellian politics that convulsed much of medieval Italy. Doges came and went, their power carefully circumscribed (see pages 30–33), while individual and factional interests were subjugated to the good of the state. Political energies were instead directed outwards, with a view to furthering Venice's position on the European stage. Trade, and with it the city's well-being, dominated the political agenda.

❏ "It seems to me less difficult to have established this city on the face of the bottomless waters than to have united and led so many different spirits in the same direction; and despite the differing inclinations by which they are moved as individuals to have maintained the body of this republic, its power intact and unshaken." French ambassador (17th century) ❏

A contemporary political rally is held outside the Palazzo Ducale

A NONPLAYER Venice's history of long isolation from the mainstream of Italian politics left it ill-prepared by the 19th century for a role in a unified Italy. Rome, with its weight of historical precedent, was the obvious candidate for the country's capital. Piedmont—and latterly the South —provided the state bureaucracy. The new monarchy, formerly the Dukes of Savoy, hailed from the northwest. Venice, for all its former power, was a nonplayer.

EBB AND FLOW Greater political say returned to Venice after the fall of Mussolini, when more power was devolved to the regions (in an attempt to prevent the rise of another centralized and dictatorial state).

OBIETTIVO! OBIETTIVO! AUTONOMIA AUTONOMIA

At the same time, the city's declining population, and the rise of its mainland satellites, saw power in local politics ebb to the industrial redoubts of Mestre and Marghera. Thus even today, while politicians meet in Venice's gilded salons, their homes—and those of their political supporters—are nearly all on the mainland.

Posters to the right (above), and to the left (left)

A POLITICAL FOOTBALL Venice today faces special political problems. On the one hand, local and regional politicians with their power bases in the Veneto and Mestre (still officially part of Venice) must look to regional and mainland issues to remain in power. The city of Venice, with its tiny and ageing population—and ever-decreasing number of votes—now counts for little in a world where votes are all. On the other hand, the city's international profile provides politicians with myriad PR opportunities, allowing them to ride to prominence on the back of Venice's fame without doing anything to resolve (in fact often exacerbating) the city's problems.

THE WAY FORWARD One way round this dilemma has been to try and separate Venice and Mestre—still

a single municipality—thus helping to elect politicians whose sole concern would be Venice itself. Three referendums, however, have failed to resolve the issue. Another has been the election of politicians dedicated to the Venetian cause. The city's most dynamic mayor for years, the left-wing Massimo Cacciari, resigned in 2000 to stand as a candidate for the Presidency of the Region. However, he failed to overthrow the right-wing administration and another left-wing mayor, Paolo Costa, took his place.

> ❏ "A city...which garners its strength from its armies and its trade but still more from the virtues of its people; which is founded on solid marble but is yet more secure upon the foundations of the unswerving unity of its population, and which, better than the sea, is protected and safeguarded by the sagacity and the wisdom of its offspring."
> Petrarch (14th century) ❏

Pageants and processions are close to the heart of most Italians, but nowhere is the love of grandiose spectacle more marked than in Venice. As well as hosting a world-famous Carnival, the city uses its magnificent natural setting as a backdrop for a series of unique festivals and historical regattas.

CARNEVALE Venice's Carnival takes its name from the Latin *carnem levare* or *carne vale*—the "farewell to meat." Some claim to trace its Venetian origins as far back as 1094, but most scholars see its beginnings in the *Compagnie de' Calze*, or "Stocking Companions" of the 15th century. These were private clubs whose members identified themselves with different colored hose—red stockings for one group, yellow for another. Dedicated initially to boat races and social dalliance, the clubs eventually took to competing in masked balls on *Martedì Grasso*, the prelude to Lent.

From these humble beginnings was born the Carnival, a festival which, far from being a farewell to flesh, evolved into an excuse for all manner of carnal indulgence. By the 18th century, the festival's heyday, carousing began on December 26 and continued for two months (in time, some of the festivities were to continue for six months). The festival faded slightly after the fall of the Republic, and again under Fascism, when the wearing of masks in public was made illegal. Festivities were started once more in 1979 (by a group of non-Venetians) and soon received the enthusiastic backing of the city authorities. Proceedings these days last just ten days, but the event has become so vast—and so commercialized—that Venice frequently has to be "shut" during this time owing to the sheer weight of numbers.

> ❏ "…all the world repaire to Venice to see the folly and madnesse of the Carnevall; the women, the men, persons of all conditions disguising themselves in antiq dresses, with extravagant musiq and a thousand gambols…'tis impossible to recount the universal madnesses of this place during this time of licence." John Evelyn, *Diary* (1646) ❏

PLAGUE FESTIVALS Two similar festivals commemorate Venice's deliverance from plague. The Festa del Redentore, which takes place on the third Sunday in July, celebrates the end of the 1576 epidemic, while the Festa della Salute marks the end of the 1630 outbreak and is held on November 21. In both cases a pontoon of boats carries worshippers to services of thanksgiving in the

The color of Carnevale

23

> ❏ On April 25, the feast day of St. Mark, the city's patron, it is the custom for Venetian men to send a single red rose to their beloved. ❏

Salute and Redentore (churches built to commemorate the passing of the plagues). During the Festa del Redentore, the more spectacular of the two, Venetians take to their boats for a traditional picnic on the water. Fireworks round things off, after which it is customary to row to the Lido to watch the sunrise.

REGATTAS Venice's finest pageants take place, not surprisingly, on water. The Regata Storica, held on the first Sunday in September, is a grandiose showcase for the talents of the city's boatmen and women. A vast armada of beautifully decorated craft, their crews decked out in period dress, travels in colorful procession down the Grand Canal. Races are then held, the most fiercely contested being that between rival gondoliers, who equip themselves with special gondolas for the occasion.

The Regata Storica *(historic regatta) is held on the Grand Canal on the first Sunday in September*

The feast of La Sensa, which takes place on the Sunday after Ascension Day, is a resurrected—and watered down—version of the Marriage to Sea (see page 99). It is accompanied by the rather more impressive Vogalonga, or "Long Row," during which any crew, in any boat, can compete in a 20-mile race to Burano and back. Other *regate* include the Regata della Befana (January 6), the Regata di San Zanipolo, for young gondoliers (third week in June), the Regata di Pellestrina (first Sunday in August) and the Regata di Burano (third week in September).

> ❏ Venice's famous international art exhibition, the Biennale, is held every odd-numbered year from June to September at venues throughout the city. The annual Venice Film Festival takes place on the Lido in late August and early September. ❏

Nothing, at first glance, could be more absurd than this city whose watery position seems to defy all apparent logic. Closer acquaintance, however, reveals it as an eminently sensible piece of townplanning, and a place that might even prove a model for cities of the future.

CARS AND BUSES Venice's most obvious absurdity, the fact that it is built on water, strikes you from the moment you enter the lagoon. The second, that it has no streets, occurs to you as you line up at the Tronchetto or Piazzale Roma. A third emerges in the Tronchetto itself, the largest parking lot in Europe—in a city that has no cars of its own. Other absurdities dawn more slowly. Where else can you wait for a bus at a bus stop that bobs gently up and down in the water? And where else, when the bus arrives, does the conductor tie it up with a seaman's knot?

Not so absurd Take a closer look at more conventional cities, however, and they, too, begin to seem absurd. Venice's *vaporetti* may be slow, but they are no slower than buses grid-locked in rushhour traffic. Her canals

The traghetto *operating between the Pescheria and Santa Sofia*

may be tortuous, but no more so than streets jammed with double-parked cars. And the city is a stranger to smog. Silence, rather than sirens, fills the night. No mugger waits in a dark-ened alley. Traffic jams are unheard of. Venice's drawbacks, if that is what they are, begin to appear minimal—even desirable—when set against those of modern cities. Who knows, perhaps when the car finally supplants people, planners may once again look to the absurdities of Venice as they plan the cities of the future?

> ❏ "There is no more magnificent absurdity than Venice. To build a city where it is impossible to build a city is madness in itself; but to build there one of the most elegant and grandest of cities is the madness of genius."
> Alexander Herzen, *My Past and Thoughts* (1867) ❏

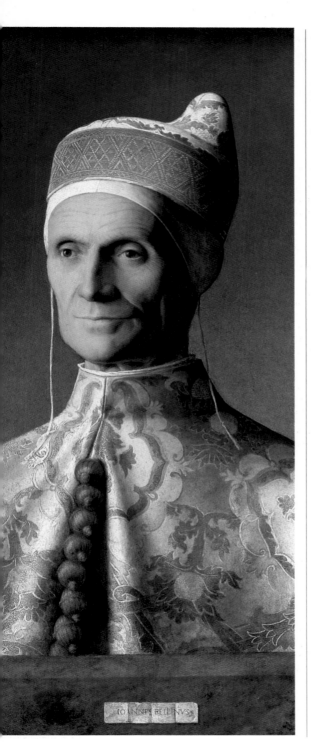

IO ANNES BELLINVS

Venice was

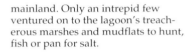

During the centuries-long rule of the Roman Empire, Venice remained no more than a series of sparsely inhabited mudflats scattered across a lost lagoon. Only during the Dark Ages, as barbarian tribes descended on Italy's mainland cities, did people begin to seek refuge on its island redoubts.

THE FIRST VENETIANS Venice's first inhabitants, according to her earliest chroniclers, rose like nymphs from the sea. Later historians claimed the city was settled by pioneers from the Baltic or Babylon, or from Illyria and the coast of Brittany. In fact her earliest visitors were probably the Venetii, or Henetti, an Indo-European tribe who drifted into northeast Italy in about 1000 BC. Most of them established farming and trading communities on the mainland. Only an intrepid few ventured on to the lagoon's treacherous marshes and mudflats to hunt, fish or pan for salt.

ROME By the time of the rise of Rome in the 2nd century BC, most of the region had been absorbed into Roman *Venetia*, a flourishing imperial outpost dotted with colonies such as Aquileia, Padua, Verona and Altinium. Vital roads crisscrossed the area, pushing north and east to the empire's European margins. The lagoon's lonely sandbanks remained all but deserted, however, home only to a few brave itinerants and the occasional fisherman.

> ❏ "No city ever had more undistinguished beginnings. Venice started life as a funk-hole —a refuge for frightened men."
> John Julius Norwich, *Venice* (1990) ❏

BARBARIAN HORDES With Rome's demise, Venetia found itself in the front line of resistance to the hostile tribes who descended on the empire from the north. The earliest incursions occurred around AD 375, prompting the Emperor Theodosius to divide the empire in two, in a belated attempt to impose order on a rapidly unraveling dominion. A Western Empire was established, centered on Ravenna, and this was mirrored by an increasingly autonomous Eastern Empire ruled from Byzantium—later Constantinople.

A fanciful 19th-century depiction of Attila the Hun

The move simply served to delay the inevitable. In 402 Alaric the Goth sacked Aquileia and its neighbors, prompting refugees from the ravaged cities to flee to the lagoon. The exodus provides partial historical justification for the (probably mythical) date of Venice's foundation, traditionally set at midday on March 25, AD 421 (a Friday and not by coincidence, the Feast Day of the Virgin Mary, a vision of whom is said to have guided the people of Altinium to a safe sanctuary in the lagoon).

Madonna and Child in Torcello's cathedral of Santa Maria Assunta; Jan Morris thought the church the "noblest memorial of the lagoon"

FIRST TOWNS In 453 Aquileia was sacked again, this time by Attila the Hun, who thus precipitated the first major evacuation of the mainland colonies to the lagoon (Goths and Huns were primarily horsemen, ill-equipped to venture onto mud and water). Each city gravitated to a separate safe haven: Paduans to Malamocco and Chioggia, Aquileians to Grado, and the Altinese to Burano and Torcello. By 466, when the lagoon boasted 12 settlements, the new colonies were already electing "maritime tribunes" to coordinate policy and action.

CONSOLIDATION By 476, and the Western Empire's demise, Italy had become a Gothic kingdom ruled by Theodoric. In 553 the Goths fell to a resurgent Eastern Empire, ruled from Byzantium by the Emperor Justinian. The task of occupying the lagoon was given to Narses, Justinian's leading general, who reputedly built a church to St. Theodore on the future site of St. Mark's (as a tribute to the lagoon's villages, whose ships had helped to recapture Ravenna). In 568, another northern tribe, the Lombards, descended on northern Italy, prompting a larger—and this time permanent—exodus of refugees to the lagoon's nascent villages.

> ❏ "Venice was founded in misfortune...The early chronology of Venice is hazy and debatable, and nobody really knows what happened when, if at all."
> Jan Morris, *Venice* (1960) ❏

Over the course of three centuries, the villages of the lagoon coalesced into a single city, Civitas Venetiarum. Despite its theoretical allegiance to Byzantium, the new city underlined its independence by electing a single leader, and bolstered its prestige with one great symbolic act—the theft of the body of St. Mark from Alexandria.

> ❏ "This race did not seek refuge in these islands for fun, nor were those who joined later moved by chance; necessity taught them to find safety in the most unfavorable location."
> Goethe, *Italian Journey* (1786–88) ❏

MYTHICAL FIRST LEADER As the Lombards consolidated their power on the mainland, two key events contrived to bring Venice—still a confederation of dispersed settlements—into sharper focus. The first was the election of a single leader, designed to unify the islands in the face of the Lombard threat. According to myth this occurred in 697, at a meeting convened by the Patriarch of Grado (the region's leading churchman). Paoluccio Anafesto emerged as the first "doge," a corruption of the Latin *dux*, meaning "leader."

THE FIRST DOGE The Venetians' first leader was probably in fact elected in 726, in the aftermath of an unpopular decree promulgated by Leo III, Emperor of the Eastern Empire, which ordered the destruction of Christian icons throughout the empire and sparked revolts across Byzantine Italy. In the anarchy that followed, towns and garrisons

Paoluccio Anafesto, the "first" doge

that owed allegiance to Byzantium seized the chance to assert their independence and proclaim their own leaders. Among them were the towns of the lagoon, which elected one Orso Ipato as doge, a role he carried out from the now-vanished island colony of Heraclea.

CHARLEMAGNE AND PEPIN The second spur to Venice's birth was the arrival in 752 of the Franks, a northern-based race invited into Italy by the papacy in order to rid the peninsula of the Lombards. Under their leader Pepin the Short, followed by his son Charlemagne, the new arrivals conquered and claimed dominion over much of northern Italy. It was left to Charlemagne's son, another Pepin, to sail against the lagoon towns, which were still proving resistant to their new overlords. Malamocco was quickly taken, prompting the Venetians to regroup under Doge Angelo Participazio around the more easily defended islands of the Rivus Altus, the present-day Rialto. After a six-month siege Pepin was forced to retreat; the Venetians had for the first time presented a united front and so triumphed against a common enemy.

THE NEW CITY Following Pepin's withdrawal, the Venetians moved their seat of government to the Rivus Altus, which in its position at the heart of the lagoon had proved almost impervious to

A 9th-century medal struck in honor of Doge Candiano

attack. Following the move the central islands became the focus of a new city, known as the Rivus Altus until about the 12th century, then as Civitas Venetiarum, and eventually as Venetia.

DEFINING MOMENT After his son's humiliation, Charlemagne signed the treaty of Aix-la-Chapelle with the Byzantines, thus recognizing Venice as a dukedom within the Eastern Empire. In the event the treaty counted for little, for Venice and its satellites—already semi-autonomous—moved quickly to assert their *de facto* independence. As the city began to benefit from trading concessions in the East, its theft of St. Mark's relics in 828 (see page 61) raised its spiritual stock to unprecedented heights. A defining moment in the city's history, the heist marked its symbolic departure from Byzantium as well as coinciding with the genesis of two buildings that were to stand as emblems of the state for centuries to come—the Palazzo Ducale (started in 814) and the Basilica di San Marco (begun in 829).

> ❏ "…who in their right mind would build a village, far less a town or city, on a cluster of soggy shoals and sandbanks rising from a malarial, malodorous lagoon?" John Julius Norwich, *Venice* (1990) ❏

29

The lion of St. Mark (here on the Torre dell'Orologio in Piazza San Marco), ubiquitous symbol of Venice

From 726 to 1797 Venice was ruled by a total of 120 doges, who in the city's formative years enjoyed almost unlimited powers. Later incumbents were more circumscribed, but the office never lost its cachet nor its symbolic and constitutional importance.

EARLY DOGES Designated *primus inter pares*, or "first among equals," Venice's first doges were presented to the people—in theory their electors—with the words: "This is your Doge, if he pleases you." In practice, early incumbents took few pains to please. Usually powerful patrician figures, they were men (never women) whose rule was virtually despotic, able to negotiate in their own right with foreign rulers, choose most of their officials (and often their successors), and decide personally on matters of justice, war, and peace.

Early doges tended to suffer more calamitous fates than their successors. Of 50 doges up to 1172, no less than 20 were murdered, banished, mutilated, or deposed. Three were exiled to Constantinople, three were assassinated, one fled and became a saint, four were deposed, four abdicated, one was executed, and four were judicially blinded over a brazier of hot coals.

CHANGING HABITS
Laws to restrict the doges' powers were tightened in the 10th century, when Pietro Candiano's attempts to make the doge-ship hereditary led to widespread rioting. Henceforth doges were prevented from naming their co-regents, and in 1044 decrees were issued preventing nepotism and the naming of successors. From about 976 a distinct body, the *Senato*, evolved to

> ❏ "Out of the Great Council... 9 were picked by lot to elect 40 electors, who had to be chosen by a majority of at least seven. The 40 drew lots to see which 12 would elect 25 more by a majority of at least seven. These 25 then drew lots to see which 9 would elect 45 by a majority of at least seven. Finally, these 45 drew lots to choose 11, who would vote for 41 electors, who would elect the doge by a majority of at least 25."
> Mary McCarthy, *Venice Observed* (1961) ❏

supervise the doges' activities, a trend that culminated in the mid-12th century with the doges' election by the *Maggior Consiglio* (see page 32).

ELECTING A DOGE The methods of election involved Byzantine complexities (all designed to prevent cliques or individuals exerting undue influence). Before the process could even start the youngest member of the *Maggior Consiglio* was ordered into Piazza San Marco to fetch a passing Venetian boy. The child's job was then to pick names from a hat during the

Part of the collection of doges' artifacts housed in the Museo Correr

30

labyrinthine process that followed (see box). Once chosen, doges ruled for life, which is one reason why nominees were invariably elderly. Old men, it was felt, would have less time to accrue powers (the average age on election of doges between 1400 and 1600 was 72).

> ❏ "He looks like the grandpapa of the whole race." Goethe on Doge Paolo Renier, *Italian Journey* (1786–88) ❏

RESTRICTED FUNCTIONS By about the 13th century, the doge's role was similar to that of a modern day state president. Restrictions on his behavior were numerous: he could not open letters or meet envoys in private; he was forbidden to hold office or own property outside the

Catena's portrait of the commanding figure of Doge Andrea Gritti. He wears the ring which symbolizes the wedding of Venice to the sea

Republic; and his children had to seek the *Consiglio's* consent to marry (sons were forbidden to leave the Republic). Censors read his letters, both incoming and outgoing; his family was barred from public office; and he was prevented from maintaining personal connections with foreign heads of state. He was forbidden to commission or improve public buildings, and the only gifts he was allowed were rosewater, herbs, flowers, and balsam. By 1694, when Silvestro Valier was elected, the office had become almost a charade: the new incumbent, a gambler and dilettante, was selected (according to one contemporary report), simply "because he was decorative."

While the doge served as Venice's head of state, the jobs of government, maintaining law and order, and the day-to-day running of the Republic, were left to a number of carefully balanced state institutions whose members were drawn from the city's patrician ruling class.

THE *MAGGIOR CONSIGLIO* As the doges' powers decreased, legislative power in the Republic passed to the *Maggior Consiglio*, or "Great Council." Founded in 1172, this initially drew together 35 members of Venice's leading noble families. By 1297 its numbers had grown to 500, prompting an act known as the *Serrata del Maggior Consiglio* (literally the "Closing of the Great Council"). Henceforth only names listed in the act were eligible for Council membership. In 1315 the list was superseded by the *Libro d'Oro*, or *Book of Gold*, a closed register of leading families, which confirmed patrician status and—for males over 25—eligibility for election to the *Consiglio* and other offices of state. A new constitution, together with a civil and criminal code, was issued at the same time, and all remained virtually unaltered for 500 years.

❏ Although no family was ever dropped from the *Libro d'Oro*, the register was reopened—against all earlier vows—in the middle of the 17th century. The reason, as so often in Venice, was financial. Short of cash, the state agreed to admit new families on payment of 100,000 ducats (ca$1 million today). ❏

THE *SENATO* The other key roles in the legislature were taken by the *Senato* and *Collegio*. While drawing much of its 60-strong membership from the *Consiglio*, the former also contained members from most of the state's other institutions (notably the *Zonta*, which was made up of

Top: the façade, Palazzo Ducale
Below: Sala del Maggior Consiglio

six patricians from the *Consiglio*, five from the provinces, and five representatives of the religious orders). Its function was, in effect, that of a parliament, deciding on matters of war and peace, appointing state officials, and supervising the committees responsible for day-to-day government business.

The *Collegio*, by contrast, was a form of supercommittee, comprising the doge, his six chief councillors, the three chairmen of the *Zonta* and the three magistrates responsible for the courts of justice. It met foreign envoys, negotiated with the papacy, acted as a court of appeal, and prepared bills for presentation to the *Senato*.

LAW AND ORDER The *Quarantia*, Venice's key judicial body, was formed in 1179 as a 40-man court of appeal (*quaranta* means forty). By the 14th century, it had evolved into a number of separate bodies responsible for all criminal and civil actions in the Republic. The *Avvogardi*, created at about the same time, was a three-man constitutional court, responsible for checking the legality of decisions taken by the *Senato*, *Consiglio* and other state bodies. Venice's most feared body,

and its most powerful institution, was the Council of Ten, founded in 1310 to deal with insurrection. Inquisition, court, and state police rolled into one, it enjoyed almost unlimited powers and the names of its members were kept secret (though the Ten were supplemented by the doge, one of the *avvogardi* and six councillors). No one was beyond its reach, not even the doge: Doge Marin Falier was executed on its orders in 1355.

Gabriele Bella's 18th-century depiction of the Sala del Consiglio dei Dieci in the Palazzo Ducale

CIVIL SERVANTS Almost as notorious, in their way, were the *cattaveri*, or tax assessors, the most notable of the myriad civil servants required to run the state machine. Less feared were the *provveditori*, the state's bureaucratic footsoldiers, responsible for a wide range of day-to-day administration. Finally there were the little-used *censori*, or censors, charged with rooting out cheating and corruption in the elections for state offices.

> ❏ "The state is all; it is for the individual unconditionally to serve the state. No other person may rise above the others, no cult of personality will be tolerated..." from the Constitution of the Republic ❏

For much of its thousand-year existence, Venice's wealth and power were built on its dominance of trade and territory in the lands of the East. From its first tentative gains in the Adriatic, the city extended its influence into the eastern Mediterranean, eventually acquiring the largest medieval empire in the western world.

34

EXPANSION The first stirrings of Venice's imperial ambitions began within years of St. Mark's relics arriving in the city. In 866 the Venetian fleet moved against Comacchio, a rival trading outpost south of the lagoon. In 932 the town was sacked completely. Pirates in the Adriatic, who had long harried Venetian shipping, were defeated in 1000 by Doge Pietro Orseolo II. This last expedition—commemorated ever after in the ceremony of the "Marriage to the Sea" (see page 99)—not only destroyed rebel bases on the Dalmatian coast, but also brought much of Dalmatia within the Venetian domain.

The "Marriage to the Sea" ceremony

THE NORMANS Expansion in the southern Adriatic was more problematic. Here the Normans held sway, their imperial designs on Byzantium inevitably at odds with Venice's own. In 1081 the Byzantine emperor, alarmed at the Normans' aggressive intentions, asked Venice for help. Vast naval battles—from which Venice was to emerge victorious—raged between the two powers for four years. Its shipping lanes secure, the city then

established itself as the protector of a demoralized Byzantine Empire. It also extracted trading concessions from a grateful emperor, enshrined in the "Golden Bull" of 1082, exempting Venetian traders from all taxes and tolls in Byzantine territories.

THE CRUSADES The Crusades, the first of which was proclaimed in 1095, provided further opportunities for financial and territorial gain. The city's fleet, now the swiftest and most efficient in the Mediterranean (see pages 112–114), came to dominate trade to the Holy Land. Hard cash, rather than religious faith, was the motivation behind Venetian involvement, however. Fighting remained anathema to the Republic, for the sound reason, in the words of John Julius Norwich, that as "a merchant republic, her interest was always in peace…she infinitely preferred doing business with the Saracens to killing them."

The Fourth Crusade All this changed during the Fourth Crusade, proclaimed in 1199, when—for a short while at least—Venice seemed moved by genuine religious sentiment (though financial considerations soon became paramount once more). Venice's contract was to equip and ferry

an army of 4,500 knights, 4,500 horses, 9,000 squires, and 20,000 infantry. The fee, to include provisions for a year, was 85,000 silver marks, or about 18 ounces of silver, for every man transported.

THE SACK OF CONSTANTINOPLE

When the Crusaders gathered at Venice in 1202 their leaders found themselves unable to pay, and in the horsetrading that followed Venice exacted favors in lieu of cash. The first was the quelling of a rebellion in Zara, a town that had risen against the Venetian yoke. The second was the sack of Constantinople, which the Crusaders ravaged—on the flimsiest of pretexts—in 1204. Not only were hundreds of (Christian) inhabitants slaughtered, but the Venetians also made off with the accumulated treasures of a 900-year-old empire.

AN EMPIRE Much of this empire was then divided up; thus Venice acquired most of its dominions, including the Peloponnese, Crete (and later Cyprus), the Ionian islands, the Thracian seaboard, much of the Greek mainland, and a string of staging posts stretching from the lagoon to Palestine and the Black Sea. In 1261 Marco Polo and others extended these to China, India, and Southeast Asia.

Knights leaving for the Crusades

Venice first entered the tangled world of Italian politics as a tentative measure to secure its trade routes into western and northern Europe. Eventually it continued its expansion on to terra firma *for more imperialistic ends, accumulating a mainland empire that was to remain intact until the arrival of Napoléon.*

THE MAINLAND THREAT Venice's empire in the East inevitably brought it into conflict not only with powers that had vested interests there—the Greeks and Saracens—but also with other seafaring cities such as Pisa and Genoa. Most of these conflicts could be confined to the sea—battles against the Genoese, in particular, raged for much of the 13th and 14th

36

Top: Venetian influence reached the Dolomites in the 15th century
Below: the Villa Foscari on the Brenta Canal

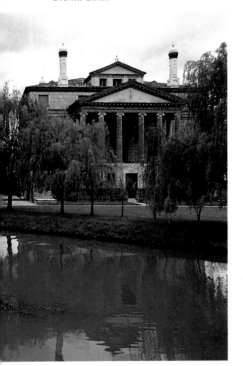

centuries—allowing Venice to stand aloof from the conflicts that condemned the Italian mainland to centuries of civil strife.

Venice's trade with northern Europe depended almost as much on its Italian hinterland as on its mastery of the Mediterranean. Control of, or at least free access to, the waterways of northern Italy, not to mention the Alpine passes into France and Germany, became legitimate areas of Venetian concern. Preoccupation with the mainland increased during the 14th century, when the rise of powerful families (the Visconti in Milan and Scaligeri in Verona) threatened the balance of northern Italian power.

> ❏ *Coltivar el mare e lasser star la terra*—"cultivate the sea and let the land alone."
> Venetian proverb ❏

SECURING THE MAINLAND Venice's first forays into the murky world of Italian alliances and counter-alliances began in 1338, when it sided with Florence and a league of Lombard cities against the Scaligeri. Quickly victorious, the city gained nearby Treviso along with Castelfranco and Conegliano, all major mainland towns on strategic routes to the north. The surrender of Feltre, Belluno, Bassano, and Vicenza followed, together with the defeat of Padua and Verona—two of the most powerful cities of the time—in 1406. Udine and the Friuli, previously ruled by Hungary, tumbled into Venetian hands in 1420, doubling the size of the mainland empire and taking its borders to the foothills of the Alps.

WORDS OF WARNING Once Venice had secured its hinterland, many felt further expansion for its own sake could only lead to envy, suspicion, and eventual disaster. Foremost among these was Doge Tommaso Mocenigo, who in 1423 called the city's chief magistrates to his deathbed to warn against the territorial ambitions of his likely successor, Francesco Foscari. Venice, he pointed out, was at the height of its powers: richer than any other European city, dominant in the Mediterranean, unequaled in the size of its fleet, and unparalleled in the efficiency with which it ran its affairs at home and abroad. Further expansion was not only unnecessary but might prove positively dangerous. If the young Foscari were elected, he warned, "the man who has ten thousand ducats will have a thousand; the man who has two houses will have one; you will spend

The lion of St. Mark lords it over the Piazza delle Erbe in Verona

your silver and gold, reputation, and honor. Instead of being master in your city, you will be at the mercy of your troops, your military men, and captains."

MAINLAND EMPIRE Mocenigo's warning went unheeded, and within a fortnight of his death Foscari was elected doge. He was to remain in the post until 1457 when, at the age of 84, he was forced to abdicate by the Council of Ten. During his reign Mocenigo's prophecies were fulfilled, as Venice's meandering expansionist policy secured her the likes of Bergamo, Brescia, Cremona, and Ravenna, and huge fees were paid to mercenary soldiers, or *condottieri*, in particular Carmagnola, Gattamelata, and the infamous Bartolomeo Colleoni (see pages 152–153). The costs to Venice, however, were as much political as financial, as the eventual extent of her power aroused the ire of other Italian and European powers—with ultimately disastrous consequences.

37

Few cities can equal Venice's artistic riches, a patrimony whose thousand-year history began with Byzantine-influenced icons and mosaics. While later artists belatedly adopted Gothic and Renaissance ideas, they never abandoned the city's particular preoccupations with color, light, and atmosphere.

EARLY ART Venice took its artistic lead from Byzantium, with which it shared close commercial ties, turning to eastern-influenced mosaics for inspiration in the churches of Torcello and the fledgling Basilica di San Marco. Byzantium also provided the wherewithal for the Pala d'Oro, the great jewel-encrusted screen in St. Mark's, commissioned by Doge Falier from workshops in Constantinople in 1105. Eastern influences lingered on for two centuries, Venetian art remaining until the 14th century the province of icon-painters, glassmakers and mosaicists.

❏ "How does one recognize Venetian paint? By a brilliance of color, some say…by a greater luminosity, say others…By the subject matter, many would confess, meaning the milky-breasted goddesses of Titian, Tintoretto, and Veronese, or the views of Guardi and Canaletto. I would say it identifies itself…by an enhanced reality, a reverence for the concrete world." Mary McCarthy, *Venice Observed* (1961) ❏

Torcello cathedral's 12th-century mosaic depicts the Last Judgement

❏ "Venice…was not like other cities. Her encircling sea protected her not only from the armies of the West but from its cultural influences." John Julius Norwich, *Venice* (1990) ❏

FIRST PAINTERS
Byzantine influences also prevailed among Venice's earliest painters. Paolo Veneziano, for example, active between 1320 and 1358, showed such a strong affinity with the stylized narrative, gilding and enamel-like color of mosaics and Byzantine icons that he was commissioned to paint the cover for the Pala d'Oro. At the same time he introduced the polyptych, or panel painting, to Venice, the finest of these being his *Coronation of the Virgin* (1354–1358), in the Accademia.

None of Veneziano's work nor that of his (unrelated) namesake, Lorenzo Veneziano (active ca1357–1372), displayed any great debt to the pioneering work of Giotto, who had painted his frescoes in nearby Padua some 50 years before (see page 216), thus reflecting an insularity and self-sufficiency that was to linger among Venetian painters for centuries.

Lorenzo's work did begin to depart gently from Byzantine convention, however, notably in his adoption of lighter colors, three-dimensionality, and tentative characterization.

INTERNATIONAL GOTHIC Venice's Byzantine tradition was eventually married to Gothic art through the offices of International Gothic, a style most seductive to the Venetians by virtue of its detailed and decorative approach. Introduced to the city by its greatest exponents, Gentile da Fabriano (ca1370–1427) and Antonio Pisano, called Pisanello (ca1397–1455) —who painted frescoes (now lost) in the Palazzo Ducale—

its influence continued to resonate in the works of Jacobello del Fiore (ca1370–1439) and Michele Giambono (ca1420–1462). Another major artist of the period, Antonio Vivarini (ca1419–1476), founder of a family workshop, also painted in the style, often in collaboration with his brother-in-law, Giovanni d'Alemagna (d.1450).

❏ "Since our eyes are educated from childhood on by the subjects we see around us, a Venetian painter is bound to see the world as a brighter and more joyful place than most people see it." Goethe, *Italian Journey* (1786–1788) ❏

THE EARLY RENAISSANCE Much as Venice had languished behind the rest of Italy in its lingering fondness for Byzantium, so it was slow to adopt the tenets and techniques of the Florentine Renaissance. Andrea del Castagno, a pioneering Florentine, visited Venice in 1442 (see page 188), but was almost completely ignored. Even artists who belatedly embraced the new ways— notably Alvise Vivarini (ca1445–1505) and Jacopo Bellini (ca1400–1470)— transformed them into paintings that remained true to Venetian traditions.

Top: mosaics from the Basilica di San Marco
Left: Stefano Veneziano's late 14th-century Coronation of the Virgin

Venetian art reached its peak in the 16th century with the sublime works of Bellini and the towering figures of Titian and Tintoretto. It then surrendered its artistic supremacy to Rome, re-emerging in the 18th century with a final flowering of rococo splendor.

RENAISSANCE GENIUS The first and perhaps the greatest of Venice's true Renaissance painters was Giovanni Bellini (1430–1516), the son of Jacopo, whose altarpieces in the Frari, the Accademia and elsewhere are among the city's most beautiful works of art. Luminous and contemplative, his works adopted the oil-painting techniques of the Sicilian artist Antonello da Messina (introduced into Venice in 1476), and often contained carefully constructed architectural settings—notably arched and pillared frames—to enhance their effect.

HISTORY PAINTINGS Giovanni's brother, Gentile Bellini (ca1429–1507),

Top and below: from the Sala del Maggior Consiglio, Palazzo Ducale

❏ "All Venice was both model and painter, and life was so pictorial that art could not help becoming so." Henry James, *Portrait of Places* (1883) ❏

was better known for his history paintings, or *istorie*, a genre whose popularity in Venice dated from the mosaic narratives of San Marco. Ten or more painting cycles were commissioned between 1475 and 1525, the heyday of the Venetian Renaissance, often by religious and charitable confraternities known as *scuole* (see pages 190–191). Gentile's most famous work is the *Procession of the Holy Relic in Piazza San Marco* (see page 56), now in the Accademia, part of a cycle painted for the Scuola di San Giovanni Evangelista.

One of Venice's most likeable artists, Vittore Carpaccio (ca1465– 1527), was also a painter of *istorie*, the finest of which are in the Scuola di San Giorgio (see pages 200–202) and the St. Ursula cycle painted for San Zanipolo, now in the Accademia (see pages 58–60). Charming and lyrical, the cycles were also crammed with incidental detail, providing invaluable social and documentary records of 16th-century Venetian life.

THE HIGH RENAISSANCE

Less well-known but no less accomplished painters like Lorenzo Lotto (1480–1556) and Cima da Conegliano (ca1459–1517) painted in the shadow of the greats of Venice's Renaissance. None, however, has puzzled posterity as much as Giorgioda Castelfranco (1477–1511), a mysterious painter, known as Giogione. His brief life—probably cut short by plague—was as enigmatic as his most famous painting, *The Tempest* (see page 53).

Prodigious where Giorgione was parsimonious, Titian (Tiziano Vecellio, d.1576) was among the greatest painters of any age, renowned for a robust style, brilliant color, and virtuoso technique. Masterpieces in the Frari and Accademia aside, however, he is badly represented in his home city, unlike his rival Tintoretto (Jacopo Robusti, 1512–1594), whose gargantuan and dynamic paintings are found in many Venetian churches and galleries. Paolo Veronese (Paolo Caliari, 1528–1588), while less turbulent than Tintoretto, shared his contemporary's love of huge canvases, not to mention his penchant for visual games—notably the juggling of perspective and viewpoints—in a quest for drama and effect.

BAROQUE AND ROCOCO After Titian and Tintoretto, artistic pre-eminence shifted to Rome, home to the baroque, a style that found comparatively little favor in 17th-century Venice. In the following century, however, the city's artists reveled in the ripe sensuality of rococo. The genre's almost decadent qualities and dazzling coloring were taken up by painters such as Ricci, Piazzetta, and Tiepolo. Venice's artistic dotage was marked by Antonio Canal, better known as Canaletto (1697–1768), and Pietro Longhi (1702–1785), both of whom painted often frivolous or idealized documentary portraits of their native city.

41

The Accademia's Madonna and Child Enthroned *by Paolo Veronese*

❏ "I hated almost all the Venetian painters, who are of the flesh and yet do not know that the most lovely flesh is that through which the soul shines…[they] were never purely young and never beautifully decadent, but always in a tawdry and sensual middle-age."
Rupert Brooke, *Letters* (ed. 1968) ❏

No enemy in Venice's thousand-year history succeeded in taking the city by storm. During the Republic's last three centuries, however, the insidious effects of declining trade, the rise of the Turks, and the combined forces of other European countries reduced her from a world power to a provincial backwater.

THE TURKS While no single cataclysm caused the Republic's decline, several events stand out on the path to its eventual demise. The first was the fall of Constantinople, captured by the Ottoman Turks in 1453. By this time the Turks, who had been virtually unheard of until 1300, had already seized Asia Minor, Bulgaria, Serbia, and much of the eastern Balkans, and had a force of over a thousand galleys and a million men-at-arms. Expansion of this order inevitably threatened Venice, whose own empire and trade routes were soon in the firing line.

❏ In 1478 the Turks came so close to Venice that the fires of ravaged towns in nearby Friuli could be seen from the city's bell towers. ❏

LOST EMPIRE They were to remain under threat for over three centuries. Venice's triumphs in this period were few, the most notable being at Lepanto in 1571, the largest naval battle ever fought in the Mediterranean. For the rest the story was one of gradual and ever greater losses. In 1479, after a 15-year war, she lost Euboea; in 1499 she relinquished the Peloponnese; in 1571 she surrendered Cyprus (after a 22-year siege); and in 1669, after 465 years of Venetian occupation, she handed over Crete, her last significant overseas colony. She was still fighting, though to no avail, in 1718, when the Treaty of Passarowitz (signed under Austro–Turkish pressure) forced her to cede the last of her eastern outposts.

❏ "Venice spent what Venice earned." Robert Browning ❏

NEW WORLDS Venice lost trade not only to the Turks, but also to the emerging markets of the New World. Vast reservoirs of wealth remained beyond Venetian reach, the Americas' huge spoils falling to Spain, Portugal and—to a lesser

extent—England and France. Worse was to come in 1498, when Vasco da Gama's discovery of the Cape route to the East removed Venice's trading primacy at a stroke. Merchants now had a quicker and more convenient route to the Orient. Not only were they spared the pirate-infested seas of the Mediterranean, but they could also avoid having to move goods across land in the Middle East (Venice had long argued for the building of a Suez canal to surmount this last problem, centuries ahead of its eventual construction).

MAINLAND WARS While Venice was being humbled by the Turks, she was also having to wage crippling wars to retain her mainland empire (see page 37). These came to a head in 1508, when virtually every state in Europe, jealous of the Republic's power, allied against her in the League of Cambrai. The League's prime mover,

> ❏ "No other nation ever died in such feverish hedonism." Jan Morris, *Venice* (1960) ❏

the Emperor Maximilian, described the Venetians as "conspiring the ruin of everyone," calling on all concerned to put out "like a common fire, the insatiable cupidity of the Venetians and their thirst for domination." This was duly achieved in 1509, when Venice's mercenary army was swept aside at the Battle of Agnadello. Only intense wrangling within the League prevented the Republic's complete dismemberment. Venice's power and freedom of action, none the less, would henceforth be increasingly subject to European sanction.

At Lepanto, on the coast of western Greece, the Turks outnumbered the Venetians in ships, but not firepower

Despite Venice's decline, and her eventual occupation by France and Austria, during her dotage the city would have continued to present a dazzling face to the world. She was still producing painters and architects, still building churches (the Salute was begun in 1631) and still ranked as one of Europe's foremost banking and financial centers.

EUROPE'S PLAYGROUND No longer a player on the European political stage, in the 17th and 18th centuries Venice became Europe's playground. Florians opened its celebrated doors in 1720, the sumptuous Fenice opera house was built in 1790, and the wealthy—in particular the feckless and fun-loving—flocked to the gaming tables, flophouses and endless festivals of an ever more decadent city. No wonder, then, that in this enervated state

La Fenice opera house

Venice found itself quite powerless, unable to resist the inexorable rise of France and of Napoléon.

THE REPUBLIC'S FALL By 1797 the French had already taken much of the Italian mainland. All they required was a pretext to invade Venice. This duly came in April 1797, when a French frigate, the ironically named *Libérateur d'Italie*, sailed through the Porto di Lido without

Venice's permission. No such liberty had been taken for five centuries. Her dignity badly dented, Venice shelled, boarded, and looted the ship. Even more provocatively, the French commander was killed. Napoléon, claiming that the Venetians were "dripping with French blood," declared war on Venice on May 1, 1797.

Weak, and with little stomach for a fight, Venice was served with an ultimatum on May 9 demanding the dissolution of the Republic. On May 12, the *Maggior Consiglio* met for the last time, agreeing by 512 votes to 30 (with five

> ❏ "*Io non voglio più Inquisitori, non voglio più Senato; sarò un Attila per lo Stato Veneto*" – "I want no more Inquisitors, no more Senate: I will be an Attila for the Venetian state." Napoléon ❏

abstentions) to bring about its own demise. In a gesture that has entered Venetian folklore, the last doge, Lodovico Manin, then handed his valet the ducal cap, symbol of the thousand-year-old Republic, saying "Take it, I shall not be needing it again."

THE FRENCH OCCUPATION The French tenancy was short-lived, lasting only—in the first instance—until October, whereupon Venice was ceded to Austria. Between 1805 and 1810, however, a period that saw the symbolic destruction of the ducal crown and other emblems of the old

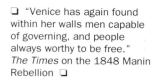

> ❏ "Venice has again found within her walls men capable of governing, and people always worthy to be free."
> *The Times* on the 1848 Manin Rebellion ❏

Napoléon Bonaparte

Republic, the city became part of Napoléon's new "Kingdom of Italy." No fewer than 50 religious houses and 40 palaces were demolished, and the shipyards of the Arsenale were deliberately wrecked. Some 20,000 or more art treasures were also looted and taken to France, including the *quadriga*, the Basilica's famous bronze horses (many great Venetian paintings remain in the Louvre in Paris to this day).

AUSTRIA

Napoléon's defeat at Waterloo in 1815 saw Venice surrendered again to the Austrians, with whom it remained for most of the next 50 years. Although they were much hated, the new occupiers proved better land-lords than the French. Buildings were restored, some

of the more unhygienic canals were filled in, and, most importantly, a causeway was built to link Venice to the mainland. Finding themselves reduced to poverty, however, many Venetians were forced to sell off treasured possessions (the years after the Republic's fall saw an estimated 96 percent of Venice's artistic patrimony lost to the city).

DANIELE MANIN Venice's historical swan-song came in 1848, when the city joined the wave of rebellions against the Austrian yoke then sweeping Italy. Under their leader, Daniele Manin, the reproclaimed Republic and its people stood defiant for 15 heroic months, withstanding—among various other assaults—the world's first aerial bombardment (bombs were dropped from balloons floated over the lagoon). Inevitably hunger and disease at last forced an honorable surrender. Final liberation from occupation, and subsequent integration with a united Italy, came in 1866, when Austria was defeated by Bismarck and the Prussians at the Battle of Sadowa.

Daniele Manin (1804–1857), the lawyer who led the heroic, but unsuccessful, uprising against the Austrians. At one stage the Venetians blew a hole in the newly built causeway

Venice's integration with a united Italy brought a measure of new prosperity. Renewed decline following World War I was arrested by the proliferation of industry on the mainland, a development which turned out to be a mixed blessing for the modern city.

THE 19th CENTURY The late 19th century saw a swing in Venice's fortunes. Modest economic success in the rest of the country was echoed in the city, where flour mills appeared on the Giudecca, lace was made in quantity on Burano, and the old furnaces on Murano again produced glass for export. Trade was given a further boost, although a temporary one, by the opening of the Suez Canal in 1869. Shipbuilding, in the doldrums after the Austrian occupation, returned to the Arsenale's yards. Tourism, meanwhile, descended on Venice anew, as the Lido and its bathing establishments became Europe's most fashionable resort.

An early 20th-century family in a peaceful Piazza San Marco

❑ Venice's civilian casualties in the two world wars numbered around 200, most of whom, it is claimed, walked into canals during the blackout and were drowned. ❑

WORLD WAR I Venice's despised former masters returned to haunt her during World War I, when Austrian troops pushed almost to the borders of the lagoon. Some 620 shells fell on the city, though with little serious damage. Shipbuilding was dealt a deathblow, however, as Venice's proximity to enemy positions saw commissions moved to Genoa and Naples in 1917, a calamity from which the Arsenale never recovered.

THE 1930s Like much of Italy, Venice quickly embraced Fascism after the war (it was the second city in which organized Fascist gangs appeared), and the city became a nationalist *cause célèbre*: "We are not and will not be," swore the poet d'Annunzio, a Fascist favorite, "a museum or hostelry… a sky painted Prussian blue for honeymoon couples." Partly to reduce the city's dependence on tourism, new industrial initiatives were started on the mainland at Porto Marghera. Fears for Venice's future were being voiced even as the first tracts of lagoon vanished under cement. *The Times* warned British visitors that as they approached Venice they would see "docks and factories in the course of construction…a new industrial port destined to raise Venice once more to a position of primary importance among the ports of the Mediterranean."

WORLD WAR II Venice survived World War II largely unscathed, despite its hinterland's growing industrial importance. Many of its Jewish inhabitants, however, were murdered in Nazi concentration camps. Liberation, when it came (in 1945), gave rise to endless tall stories. One has the British arriving in gondolas (and being overcharged for the privilege). Another has the Allies racing to liberate the best hotels (a race won by a pair of frontline New Zealand tanks). Crossing a flyover on the mainland, so another story goes, advancing Allied troops reported seeing the Germans retreating at full tilt on the road beneath them.

POSTWAR CONUNDRUM Marghera's industrial complex grew beyond all expectations in the post-war boom.

With it came a mass exodus to the mainland, compounding Venice's growing problems of pollution with those of depopulation and urban decay (see pages 14–17). The great

The Basilica di San Marco looks out over a city left almost untouched by two world wars

flood of 1966 brought the city's worsening predicament to the world's attention. Countless schemes are currently afloat to preserve the city as more than the "thinking person's Disneyland," though it is in the emerging markets of central Europe—which could again restore Venice to trading prominence—that long-term salvation may lie.

❑ Two-thirds of Venice's population was evacuated during World War I. The front-line trenches came so close to the city that barrage balloons could be seen from the top of the Campanile. ❑

Looking from the water-front by the Piazzetta towards the Salute

EXPLORING Venice's 118 islands, over 400 bridges and 170 canals are divided into six ill-defined districts, or *sestieri*. Three lie west of the **Grand Canal** (San Polo, Dorsoduro, and Santa Croce), and three east (San Marco, Castello, and Cannaregio). In theory the arrangement seems labyrinthine; in practice it is slightly easier to navigate than it may appear. Distances are short, and several key "streets" wend through the maze to link key areas. The **Rialto** and **Piazza San Marco** provide central points of reference.

The best way to see individual attractions is in self-contained clusters. Study the map to sort out the main sights, and which other sights are close to them: the Frari, Scuola di San Rocco, San Polo, and San Pantalon, for example, make a convenient morning's outing. Bear in mind that only three bridges cross the Grand Canal, so plan itineraries carefully to avoid unnecessary walking. Also learn to use the little ferry services, or *traghetti,* that crisscross the Canal (see page 242).

STARTING OUT See anything in Venice on your first morning, but not Piazza San Marco, the Doge's Palace or the Basilica di San Marco. Start instead with something smaller, something whose crowds and razzamatazz are not going to turn you against the city at the first acquaintance. Then move to the bigger draws; to the two key galleries, the **Accademia** and **Collezione Guggenheim**; to the two major churches, **Santi Giovanni e Paolo** and **Santa Maria Gloriosa dei Frari**; and to the two finest *scuole*, the **Scuola di San Rocco** and **Scuola di San Giorgio degli Schiavoni.** Leave time for the eclectic collections of art and artifacts in the **Ca' d'Oro** and the Correr; and the lovely churches of Santa Maria dei Miracoli, San Giacomo dell'Orio, and San Giovanni in Bragora.

ONE-OFFS Some of Venice's best moments come not in a relentless gallery-by-gallery route march, but in quieter and more incidental moments away from the usual sights. Thus at some point you should take a boat (the No 1)

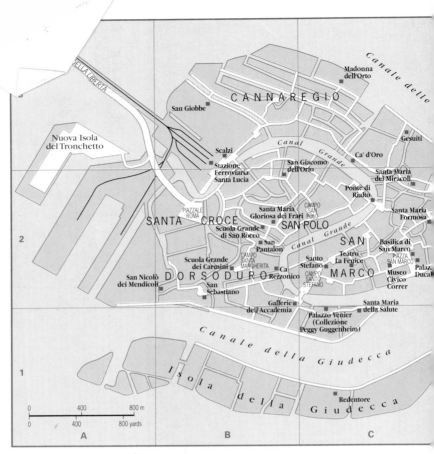

THE GRAND CANAL

To see the Grand Canal, or *Canalazzo* as Venetians call it, board *vaporetto* No 1 at the railroad station (*Ferrovia*) and disembark at San Zaccaria. Aim for one of the prized seats at the front or back of the boat. Some 200 palaces and ten churches line the Canal's banks, 46 side canals enter it, and 48 alleys run down to its edge.

TOO MANY CHURCHES

"There are 107 churches in Venice, and nearly every tourist feels he has seen at least 200 of them; for the guides and guidebooks presuppose an unflagging whiplash of energy in their victims…"
Jan Morris, *Venice* (1960)

along the Grand Canal just for the ride. Or you should see the **Rialto markets** at the crack of dawn before the crowds arrive. An ice cream or cappuccino in a square is a good way to enjoy the city's quieter side: **Campo San Polo**, **Campo Santo Stefano** and **Campo Santa Margherita** are three of the best. Little in Venice beats an aerial view of the city, but avoid the hordes cramming into the Campanile and enjoy the better vista from the top of **San Giorgio Maggiore**. Finally, see a different side of Venice by walking to its fringes; to the gardens of the **Biennale** in the east, or to the curiously moribund quarter around **San Nicolò dei Mendicoli** in the west.

EXCURSIONS After a while in Venice you might want to explore further afield. This might simply mean taking a boat to the **Giudecca**, the narrow island strip that curves across the skyline south of the city. Or it might involve a longer trip to the **Lido**, a vast sandspit that forms part of Venice's outer defences on the edge of the lagoon. Once a wild and windswept shore, these days it is a busy mixture of hotels, beaches, and modern housing. Unless you want to swim, there is little reason to come here.

VENETIAN WORDS

Understanding some of the words peculiar to Venice can add to your enjoyment of the city. A _campo_, from the Italian for "field," is a square (Venice has only one "piazza" Piazza San Marco); a small square is a _campiello_ or _campazzo_; _rio_ means canal; _rio terrà_ is a canal that has been filled in; _piscina_ is a pool or turning basin for boats that has been filled in to become a square; _calle_ means street; _ruga_ is an important street or one lined with shops; _fondamenta_ and _riva_ mean a wide street running along a canal; _corte_ is a courtyard or dead-end alley; _ramo_ (from the word for "branch") is a short street or the extension of another street with the same name; a _salizzada_ means a paved street (once rare); and a _sottoportego_ is an arcade or arched passage under a building.

51

Left: Venice and its sestieri
Below: the Rio della Pietà, though it could be almost any one of Venice's backwaters

Head instead for **Murano**, only seven minutes by boat from the city. Most people come for its glass, which has been made on the island since the 13th century, but there are also a couple of fine churches and Italy's only glass museum to while away the time. Although it is not as appealing as more distant islands (see below), consider making this a self-contained trip, perhaps with a stopoff on the way back at the old island cemetery of San Michele to see its church.

Burano and **Torcello**, 40 minutes from Venice, can also be seen together. Despite their distance from the city—which means you need to allow at least a morning for the trip—the islands are less than five minutes apart. They can also be visited using the same special boat ticket (see page 241). The trip out here is a pleasure in itself, offering lovely views back to Venice and a fascinating firsthand look at the lagoon. Torcello, with its incomparable church and tranquil scenery, is by far the more magical place (though try to arrive on the first boat to avoid the crowds). Burano has a fishing-village atmosphere, still (just) untainted by the big summer crowds. Known primarily for its lace, it also has a charming museum and streets full of brightly colored houses.

MARTYRS

Carpaccio's strange painting in Room 2 was commissioned in 1512 as an ex-voto following a plague epidemic. Crammed with countless crucified figures, it is based on the legend that 10,000 Roman soldiers, having defeated an army of Armenian rebels, were then betrayed by their leaders and condemned to death on the trees of Mount Ararat. The right foreground shows the King of Persia pronouncing the sentence.

EARLY FAME

Giovanni Bellini's *Madonna and Saints* in Room 2 was mentioned in the *Cronaca di Marin Sanudo*, a chronicle of 1493, in which it was acknowledged as one of the city's greatest paintings within just eight years of its completion.

▶▶▶ Accademia, Gallerie dell' 276A2

Porta dell'Accademia; Canal Grande (Quay: Accademia; Vaporetti 1, 82)
Open: Tue–Sun 8:15–7:15, Mon 8:15–2.
Admission: expensive

The Accademia was founded in 1750 as the city's art school. It moved to its present site in 1807, garnering much of its permanent collection from churches and religious houses recently suppressed by Napoleonic decree. Its new home occupies one such church, **Santa Maria della Carità** (designed by Bartolomeo Bon), along with portions of Palladio's unfinished **Convento dei Canonici Lateranensi** (1561) and the 13th-century **Scuola della Carità** (oldest of Venice's six *Scuole Grandi*; see pages 190–191). As the city's premier art gallery it contains a feast of Venetian paintings, but a feast with several second-rate courses you would be well advised to skip. Its central portions, for example, are particularly unappetizing, and deserving of less time than the two great painting cycles that form the gallery's memorable climax.

Avoid Sunday if possible (it is the gallery's busiest day) and arrive early in summer to avoid the inevitable lines. Only 300 visitors are admitted to the gallery at a time.

Rooms 1–5 The beautiful blue-gold ceiling of the Accademia's first room, once part of the Scuola della Carità, almost overshadows the paintings below, a medley of Byzantine-tinged works distinguished by their radiant colors, rigid Madonnas and stern-faced saints. The most dazzling is the *Coronation of the Virgin* (ca1345) by Paolo Veneziano, an influential early painter who helped Venetian art develop from mosaic to the painted polyptych. The city's painting was moved further away from its Byzantine roots by Lorenzo Veneziano (an

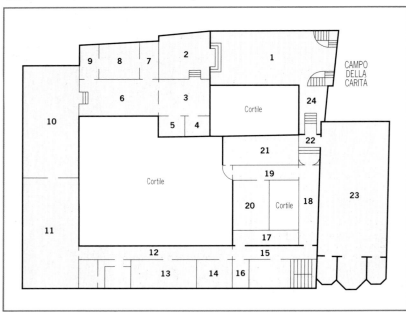

apprentice of Paolo, but no relation), whose grand *Annunciation* near the exit displays a livelier treatment of faces and figures than is evident in the more stylized rendering of his namesake.

Lorenzo's tentative steps away from Byzantium have become a leap by **Room 2**, a treasure trove of 15th- and 16th-century altarpieces. Of these the most beguiling is Carpaccio's *Presentation of Jesus in the Temple*, and the most grisly—also by Carpaccio—*The Ten Thousand Martyrs of Mount Ararat* (see panel on page 52). Both the *Presentation* and two of the room's other highlights—Basaiti's *Agony in the Garden* and Giovanni Bellini's masterful *Madonna and Saints* (ca1485)—originally hung in San Giobbe (see page 139). The Bellini's coffered background once corresponded exactly to the frame and architectural setting of its original surroundings, for which reason there are those who think it should be returned, damp or no damp, to the church from which it came.

Venetian artists' supposed mastery of light and color is hardly in evidence in **Room 3**, where Sebastiano del Piombo's *Sts. Bartholomew and Sebastian* is one of a group of gloomy and leaden paintings. More cheerful are **Rooms 4** and **5,** tiny areas which contain the gallery's most famous works. Mantegna's brightly colored *St. George* (1466–1467), perhaps part of a larger painting, is here, along with Piero della Francesca's strange *St.*

ALLEGORIES
Giovanni Bellini's five small paintings were probably designed for a piece of furniture (possibly a mirror), though their exact meaning is disputed: some claim they should be seen in pairs, one representing virtuous love and its reward, the other anguish and vain illusions (with the blindfolded Nemesis as an accompaniment). Others see them as symbolizing Slander or the Burden of Sin (the men with the shell); Sensuality or Perseverance (the two male figures); Prudence (the naked woman with a dish); Virtue (the blindfolded figure); and Inconstant Fortune (the woman in a boat).

RELICS
There are three orders of holy relics. The most efficacious are a saint's physical remains (toes, tongues, bones)—one reason why the body of St. Mark was so important to the Venetians. Next come clothes and objects worn or used by the saint; third are pieces of cloth that have been brushed over a saint's remains. If you visit Padua and its basilica you will see the faithful press their hands and faces against St. Antony's tomb, anxious to be imbued with the benefits imparted by his bones inside.

Jerome, whose green pigments have decayed to a curious burnt brown. The room also contains several paintings by Giovanni Bellini, an artist greatly influenced by Piero, the loveliest of them a *Madonna and Child with Saints*. Note the yellow light that bathes its protagonists' faces, and the distinctive positions of the various half-figures: both elements suggest an affinity with Leonardo da Vinci, who was in Venice in March 1500, close to the date of the painting.

Bellini also dominates **Room 5** with a *Pietà* (ca1505), a series of *Allegories* (see panel), and three versions of the *Madonna and Child*. The city in the *Pietà* is made up of Vicenza's tower and duomo, Cividale's Natisone, and Ravenna's Sant' Apollinare. The most striking Madonna is the *Madonna of the Red Cherubim*, distinguished by a wonderfully ugly Child and a diabolic-looking circle of winged heads above the Virgin. More striking still is Venice's most famous painting, Giorgione's *Tempest* (ca1500), the most iconographically enigmatic work in Italian art. No one has the remotest idea what it means, unlike the artist's neighboring canvas, *Col Tempo* ("With Time"), an allegory of old age and the passing of time.

Rooms 6–8 No room of Venetian paintings is without some charm, but these rooms represent a definite falling off of interest. In the main they feature lesser works that pave the way for the High Renaissance masterpieces to come. The better paintings include Paris Bordone's *Fisherman Presenting St. Mark's Ring to the Doge* (Room 6), Lorenzo Lotto's pale-faced *Portrait of a Gentleman* (Room 7), and Palma Vecchio's *Holy Family and Saints* (Room 8).

The Translation of the Body of St. Mark *by Tintoretto (ca1560)*

Rooms 10–11 After passing through the bookshop in Room 9, Rooms 10 and 11 kick off the Accademia's roster of High Renaissance masterpieces with Veronese's luxuriant *Supper in the House of Levi* (1573). Painted for the refectory of San Zanipolo (see pages 146–151), the work was originally intended as a *Last Supper*, but after protests from the Inquisition—who objected to its "buffoons, drunkards, Germans, dwarfs and similar indecencies"—Veronese was forced to change its title (while leaving the content resolutely unaltered). The painter, incidentally, is the figure in green in the center on the left.

Two paintings by Tintoretto in Room 10 prove almost equally eye-catching. The first, the iconoclastic *Miracle of the Slave* (1548), shows St. Mark dropping head first to intercede at the execution of a slave who had disobeyed his master in order to visit the saint's shrine. The second, the *Translation of the Body of St. Mark* (ca1560), with its grinning camel and bubbling clouds, features the most surreal content and extraordinary composition of any picture in the gallery. Titian's equally febrile *Pietà* (ca1576), painted when the artist was over 90, was probably intended for the painter's own tomb in the Frari. Titian is said to have scoured and heaped the paint on to the canvas not only with brushes but also with his bare hands. He has also painted himself as the red-cloaked figure (Nicodemus) to the right of Christ. The arched niche to the rear pays homage to his master, Giovanni Bellini, whose paintings frequently used the same frame-like device—most notably in the Madonnas of San Zaccaria and the Frari.

The gallery's long corridor and most of the adjacent rooms collect together paintings by Venice's less-talented 18th-century artists. **Room 17** is the best, thanks to the Accademia's only painting by Canaletto, Rosalba Carriera's milky-skinned portraits, and Pietro Longhi's fascinating sequence of scenes from everyday Venetian life. Among the last, look out in particular for the *Farmacista* (Pharmacy), noteworthy for its painful-looking oral examination and the evil brew being boiled up in one corner. You might also want to hunt out Longhi's *Family of Luigi Pisgni* across the corridor, described in the Accademia's commentary as a "masterpiece of European portraiture," but in truth one of the worst paintings in this or any other gallery.

The Miracles of the True Cross The eight paintings in Room 20 describe the *Miracles of the True Cross* (1494–1510), part of a cycle by a variety of artists painted for the Scuola di San Giovanni Evangelista. Each of the

Bellini's Madonna and Child with St John and a Female Saint

55

PARTISAN RELIC
The fragment of "True Cross" responsible for the *Miracles of the True Cross* was presented to the Scuola di San Giovanni by Philippe de Mézières on his return from Jerusalem in 1369. Mézières, a member of the Scuola, was the chancellor of Cyprus to the confraternity's then *Guardian Grande*, Andrea Vendramin. It is perhaps no coincidence that the relic should show itself remarkably biased. Of the eight wonders depicted in the paintings, six directly involved members of the Scuola. Stranger still, two featured Andrea Vendramin as their main beneficiary. One shows him saving the reliquary; the other, Perugino's *The Deliverance of Andrea Vendramin's Ships*, has since been lost.

56

THEN AND NOW

Piazza San Marco is not all it should be in Bellini's *Procession of the Holy Relic*. The campanile, for example, has wandered over to the right, occupying a site that now contains the Procuratie Nuove; the Torre dell'Orologio—started a year before the painting was executed—has since been completed on the Basilica's left; the flagstaffs have wooden pediments and are missing their lions; and all but one of the Basilica's mosaics have since been replaced.

pictures contains a cornucopia of anecdote, the detail often consigning the miracle of each scene to the painting's periphery. As such, the cycle survives as both a work of art and a priceless document of Venetian social history.

The cycle proceeds clockwise from the door, starting with Giovanni Mansueti's *Miracle in Campo San Lio*. The picture describes a miracle that took place in 1414, when the Scuola attempted to bury one of its members who had disparaged the confraternity's prized relic (see panel on page 55). As the funeral cortège entered San Lio the reliquary became so heavy that no one could carry it into the church. The relic had to be substituted, thus shaming the unfortunate corpse, a dishonor witnessed by onlookers in every one of the Campo's windows. No detail was too small for Mansueti, who even included a little scrap of paper (on the house on the extreme left) saying *Casa da fitar ducati 5* (House for rent, 5 ducats).

In Lazzaro Bastiani's following picture, *The Relic is Given to San Giovanni*, Philippe de Mézières is shown presenting the relic to Andrea Vendramin, the Scuola's *Guardian Grande* (see panel). Bastiani imagines the scene in and around the church of San Giovanni, parts of which have now been modified or destroyed (though the Scuola —located just beyond the Frari—still possesses its precious relic). The jury is still out on the meaning of the next panel, Benedetto Rusconi's *Miracle of Santa Croce*, but its most likely subject is the recovery of Alvise Finetti's four-year-old son after falling from a ladder in 1480.

No doubts surround Gentile Bellini's glorious *Procession of the Holy Relic in Piazza San Marco*, an almost photographically exact reproduction of St. Mark's and its piazza as it appeared in 1496 (the date of the painting). The miracle concerned Jacopo de' Salis, a Brescian merchant, who was in Venice on business when he heard that his son had fractured his skull. Next day, by chance, was the annual Feast of St. Mark, so as the Scuola carried its reliquary in procession he knelt down to pray for his son's recovery (in the painting he is the red-cloaked figure just visible behind the relic). He returned home to find his son had been cured the day after the procession. As in the other pictures, however, Bellini is less concerned with the miracle than with Venice itself. The painting's foreground shows the annual procession of the major *scuole* (filing in from the left with their reliquaries), and that of the doge and his entourage (shown streaming in on the right from the Palazzo Ducale's Porta della Carta).

Miracles can be wrought not only by a holy relic, but by objects that have come into contact with saintly or otherwise sanctified substances (see panel on page 54). Thus in the next picture, *The Healing of Pietro de' Ludovici*—again set in San Giovanni—Gentile Bellini depicts Ludovici being cured merely by touching a candle close to the reliquary. A miracle of a different order takes place in Bellini's famous *Miracle of the Cross at Ponte San Lorenzo*, where the relic has been accidentally knocked into a canal while being paraded to San Lorenzo. In an unlikely looking scene, white-robed brothers of the Scuola are shown trying to salvage the reliquary, their vestments flowing out behind them in the green waters of the canal. The relic saves them the trouble, however, floating miraculously to the surface, where it is held in triumph by the Scuola's *Guardian Grande*, Andrea—later Doge Andrea—Vendramin.

In Mansueti's *Cure of the Daughter of Benvegnudo di San Polo*, Benvegnudo's daughter, paralyzed since birth, is cured by touching three candles brought by her father from the reliquary's altar. The poor girl herself, however —little more than a pictorial afterthought—finds herself tucked away in her crib in the top right of the painting. The protagonist again takes a back seat to incidental detail in Carpaccio's *Miracle of the Possessed Man*, in which the miraculously cured lunatic is closeted away on the first floor of the building on the left. Instead, it is washing that dominates the scene, together with a positively industrial cluster of chimneys on the painting's right. Equally

PORTRAITS
As well as incidental details such as the Moor and great forest of chimney pots, Gentile Bellini's view of Ponte San Lorenzo contains a portrait of the ex-Queen of Cyprus, Caterina Cornaro (the figure front left wearing blue robes and white veil). The five kneeling figures on the right may be members of the painter's family or leading members of the Scuola: Bellini himself is believed to be the figure fourth from the left.

57

The Miracle of the Cross at Ponte San Lorenzo *(1500) by Gentile Bellini*

ST. URSULA

Carpaccio's cycle tells the story of Ursula, daughter of the Breton King Maurus, and her proposed marriage to Hereus, son of the English King Conon. It was agreed that the ceremony would take place on two conditions: first, that Conon wait three years, and second, that he convert to Christianity and accompany Ursula on a pilgrimage to Rome. Neither demand seemed too onerous, except that the pilgrimage was to be made in the company of 11,000 virgins, and that the whole party was to be massacred at Cologne on their return from Rome.

Carpaccio's Departure for Rome, *from the St. Ursula cycle*

prominent is the bridge at the center, the old Ponte di Rialto (built in 1458), still bearing the raised central portion that collapsed into the Grand Canal in 1524.

The St. Ursula Cycle Hard on the heels of Room 20's *Miracles* comes the Accademia's other famous cycle, Vittore Carpaccio's nine-canvas sequence of paintings portraying episodes from the *Life of St. Ursula* (ca1490–1496). Painted for the Scuola di Sant'Orsola at San Zanipolo, it describes the story of the unfortunate St. Ursula (see panel), mixing together a dazzling narrative technique with a wealth of contemporary documentary detail.

The cycle starts on the long wall opposite the entrance with the *Arrival of the English Ambassadors*. Three distinct events spread across the one painting, each separated from its neighbor by a painted pillar. From left to right are depicted the arrival of the English ambassadors; their presentation to Maurus; and Ursula in her room replying to her father (with Ursula's nurse pensively awaiting developments at the foot of the stairs). Many of the incidental figures are probably members of the Scuola di Sant'Orsola. In the next picture, the *Conditions of Marriage*, Ursula dictates to a scribe the terms of her marriage, against a backdrop including the Palazzo Ducale.

Several scenes are again rolled into one in the *Return of the Ambassadors*, which depicts the ambassadors' return to

England and the presentation of Ursula's conditions to King Conon. Note Carpaccio's fanciful portrait of England, especially the Italianate arch under which Conon receives his emissaries. Note, too, the menagerie of animals—the monkey in particular—a Carpaccian trademark. The figure in red by the canal (next to the child playing the violin) is the *Scalco*, a musician retained by the doge to accompany foreign ambassadors. The towers on the left are probably based on those of Venice's Arsenale (see pages 112–114).

The *Departure for Rome* features no fewer than four episodes (divided into pairs by the painting's flagpole). On the left Hereus addresses his father and supporters and the engaged couple meet for the first time; on the right the pair salute the King and Queen of Brittany and depart for Rome (in something that looks suspiciously like a Venetian galley). In the remaining scenes Carpaccio pokes fun at "London" (the city on the left), using ruined ships and symbolic gray-brown monochromes to suggest a city sunk in barbarism. The marble-bedecked city on the right (the Breton capital), by contrast, is shown as a civilized metropolis founded on idealistic humanist principles. The latter's palace owes something to Venice's Ca' d'Oro, while its towers are those of the 15th-century Venetian forts at Rhodes and Candia (present-day Iráklio on Crete).

The cycle's simplest and most enchanting panel, the *Dream of Ursula,* shows Ursula contemplating the gory

RO●●
Room 23, ●
old church of the
is often closed, but ha●
several excellent
paintings. Among them
are works by Giovanni
Bellini (and his
workshop), Alvise and
Bartolomeo Vivarini, Carlo
Crivelli, and Gentile
Bellini. Room 24, the dark
and beautifully coffered
albergo of the former
Scuola della Carità, is
home to Titian's
Presentation of the Virgin
(1534–1538) and Antonio
Vivarini's fine triptych on
the stairs. Further works
by Venetian Masters are
in the top-floor Quadreria.
These can be visited
as part of the guided
tour on Saturday at
11 AM or on Tuesday
afternoon by reservation
(tel: 041 713498).

...e St.
...eight
...tro
Lt ...d been paid
the . amount to
design and construct an
entire *church* (Santa
Maria dei Miracoli). Extra
funds for the paintings
came from the Loredan
family, also members of
the Scuola, whose coats-
of-arms were added to
two of the canvases.

CONFUSED STORY

Ursula's story, like many
saints' legends, is heavy
with myth. In some
versions she is a Cornish
princess, and sails to
Brittany for her marriage
with 11,000 virgins and
60,000 serving women.
In 9th-century accounts,
however, Ursula had only
five, eight, or eleven
companions. The figure of
11,000 probably came
from a misrepresentation
of XI MV in an early
manuscript, expanded to
Undecim Millia Virgines
(11,000 virgins) instead
of the intended *Undecim
Martyres Virgines* (11
virgin martyrs). In 1155,
however, the higher figure
received credence when a
huge collection of bones
was found in a mass
grave at Cologne, scene
of Ursula's supposed
martyrdom (though many
were the bones of men
and children).

...at awaits her (though some suggest the dream is she had as a child, when she dreamed she would ...evote her life to God). Note the soft dawn light, accompanied by the annunciate angel, creeping slowly into the bedchamber. In the next picture, the *Arrival in Rome*, Carpaccio paints the first of the 11,000 virgins streaming from their boats to meet Pope Cyriac (Rome is suggested by the presence of the Castel Sant'Angelo in the background). The Pope's procession files in from the right, a device perhaps deliberately echoed by Bellini's *Procession of the Holy Relic* in Room 20 (painted three years later).

No Carpaccio is complete without a dog, and another one pops up in the *Arrival at Cologne*. Not a virgin is in sight, however, as Carpaccio introduces a martial element that anticipates Ursula's martyrdom in the adjacent *Massacre and Funeral of St. Ursula*. Ursula was foolish enough to disembark with her homeward-bound virgins at Cologne, then under siege by the Huns, who turned their attention from the city to the explicit virgin-by-virgin massacre depicted on the painting's left-hand side (a painted pillar separates the carnage from Ursula's funeral to the right). Ursula herself, who refused to save her life by marrying the son of the Hun ruler, is shown about to be dispatched by a particularly dashing bowman. Her funeral takes place outside the city, overseen by bishops, Dominican monks, and members of the Scuola for whom the cycle was painted. In the final picture, the *Apotheosis* (on the end wall), Ursula and her companions find their eventual reward in heaven.

▶▶▶ Basilica di San Marco   277F3
Piazza San Marco
Open: daily, summer 9:30–5, winter 10–4:30. Those not attending services are requested to restrict visits to Sun 2–4:30. The interior of the basilica is usually illuminated daily 11:30–12:30, Sat afternoons, all day Sun and feast days. Admission free to the main body of the church. Admission charge to the Loggia dei Cavalli, the Sanctuary and Pala d'Oro, and the Treasury.
Venice's most famous building was for centuries the doge's private chapel, the tomb of St. Mark and a powerful symbol —despite its religious function—of the power and autonomy of the Venetian state. Only in 1807 did the French make it the city's cathedral (replacing San Pietro di Castello), yet for almost a thousand years it was the city's spiritual heart, accumulating the decorative fruits of a millennium to emerge as the most exotic hybrid of western and Byzantine architecture in Europe. There are many surveys which claim that the vast proportion of visitors to Venice see Piazza San Marco, its Basilica, and nothing more. Yet few seem concerned to explore the Basilica in any depth, being either indifferent to its beauty or intimidated by its size and complexity. While the crowds detract from the pleasure of anyone who *does* want to enjoy the building, and the famous mosaics are almost too bewildering to contemplate (see page 71), the main sights in and around the church are not as intimidating as they first appear.

St. Mark Venice's tenuous link with St. Mark began during the Evangelist's return to Rome from Aquileia, an important Roman outpost in the northern Adriatic. Dropping anchor in the lagoon—he never set foot in what was to become Venice—he was visited by an angel who greeted him with the words: *"Pax tibi Marce, evangelist meus. Hic requiescet corpus tuum"* ("Peace be with you Mark, my Evangelist. Here shall your body rest"). Centuries later this divine prediction was adopted—or invented—by the Venetians to lend spiritual legitimacy to Venice, whose humble beginnings hardly squared with its inhabitants' inflated view of their city. In 828 it was wheeled out again, this time to justify the theft of Mark's body from Alexandria, a defining moment in Venice's history.

Specific details of this heist are hazy. Some accounts say two Venetians were involved, others three; some that it was accomplished with the help of local priests, others that it was a scheme executed by Venice alone. In the standard version, the custodians of Mark's body were worried by the King of Alexandria, who had been ransacking the saint's tomb for treasures to furnish his palace. Afraid of further desecration, they agreed to help the Venetians steal the body, hiding the corpse under a consignment of pork to smuggle it past the Muslim guards. As the tomb was opened, according to one chronicler, "an odor spread through the city, so sweet that had all the spice shops of the world been in Alexandria it would not have been enough to scent it so." After a perilous voyage, when Mark miraculously saved the day during a storm, the boat reached Venice and the body was presented to Doge Giustiniano Participazio. Mark was promptly declared the city's patron saint, usurping the lackluster and less prestigious St Theodore (see panel on page 62).

Building St. Mark's The first basilica, a hastily built chapel inside the Doge's Palace, was replaced in 832 by a church-cum-mausoleum modeled on Constantinople's Aya Sofya and Church of the Twelve Apostles (the latter was the imperial mausoleum of Byzantium, home to the tombs of

OPINIONS

"This church is in my opinion much too dark and dismal." John Evelyn, *Diary* (1645);

"...low in structure, very somber, in miserable taste, both within and without ..." Charles de Brosses, *Letter* (1739);

"...[a place] that belongs to a pre-Christian Christianity, to a Church founded before religion existed." Théophile Gautier, *Voyage en Italie* (1852);

"...like a warty bug out for a stroll." Mark Twain;

"...so quiet and sad and faded and yet all so brilliant and living." Henry James;

"St. Mark's as a whole, unless seen from a distance or at twilight, is not beautiful...it is better not to look too closely, or the whole will begin to seem tawdry, a hodge-podge..." Mary McCarthy, *Venice Observed* (1961).

61

Often hiding one part or another beneath scaffolding, the Basilica here shows its intended face to the Piazza San Marco

ST. THEODORE

Little is known of Venice's first patron saint. Probably a 4th-century Greek soldier-martyr, his cult was particularly strong in the East, hence Venice's readiness to drop him in favor of St. Mark (part of the city's attempts to assert its independence from Byzantium). St. Theodore had a reputation as a miracle-worker, refused to worship idols and died after a harrowing series of tortures. Relics were transported to both Venice and Chartres, and his legend is depicted in the mosaics of the Basilica and in the stained glass at Chartres. By the 10th century, however, his story had become so convoluted that two St. Theodores were celebrated (both soldiers), one a general, the other a recruit.

Constantine and the first Eastern emperors). This was replaced in turn in 978, two years after rioting destroyed the original building. Further reconstruction was initiated by Doge Domenico Contarini in 1063 (who demanded the new chapel should be "the most beautiful ever seen"), and continued under Doge Domenico Selvo between 1071 and 1084. The church, consecrated in 1094 by Doge Vitale Falier, retained the Greek cross plan of the earlier churches, suggesting a continuing nod—in the architectural sphere at least—to the influence of Byzantium. In the political arena, however, Venice's autonomy was underlined in the same year when the Basilica was declared the official "church of state" in the presence of Emperor Henri IV.

Falier's building, though roughly the one you see today, was yet to acquire the nine centuries' worth of decorative embellishment that was to turn it, in Ruskin's words, into a "treasure heap...a confusion of delights." The bulk of this decoration, a "treasury of bits" as Henry James called it, came as loot from the Fourth Crusade (1204), although work on the mosaics (a notable Byzantine skill) started in about 1100, evidence of the Oriental influence that dominated the Basilica's decoration long after the waning of Byzantium's political influence. Marble facing was added to the brickwork in 1159, while the sculptural work on the upper facades dates from the end of the 14th century.

The north facade The Basilica's exterior is not as intimidating a prospect as the interior, but to enjoy its principal features without keeling over still requires a measured approach. The best plan of attack is to start on the north facade (facing the Piazzetta dei Leoncini) and work your way around to the south facade, alongside the Palazzo Ducale.

Detail from one of the Basilica's mosaic-inlaid arches

The rather grubby frontage of the north facade, built in the first half of the 13th century, was among the last areas of the Basilica to be completed. The center of the first arch contains a relief of the *Twelve Apostles*, a 7th- or 8th-century Byzantine work in which the Apostles (symbolized by lambs) worship the throne of the Last Judgement. A small 10th-century relief between the first two arches depicts Alexander the Great's mythical attempt to reach heaven on a chariot chained to two griffins (note the pieces of liver attached to the spears, designed to spur the griffins on). The 13th-century doorway to the left is the **Porta dei Fiori** (Door of Flowers), flanked by carved arches that frame a lovely Nativity. The porphyry monument to its left is the tomb of Daniele Manin (d.1857, see page 45).

The main facade On the front of the Basilica, the left-hand door, the **Porta di Sant'Alipio**, boasts the exterior's only original mosaic, the *Translation of the Body of St. Mark to the Basilica* (1260–1270). It features both the earliest known representation of St. Mark and the first image of the Basilica (the bronze horses are already in place). The 14th-century bas-reliefs below, in yellow sandstone on a green marble background, depict the symbols of the Evangelists. The figures and panels forming the door's architrave are either 5th-century works or a 13th-century pastiche. The mosaics over the remaining doors are 18th- or 19th-century copies.

The Romanesque carvings above the central (third) door are the exterior's highlight. The innermost arch, begun between 1220 and 1240, has fighting figures on its outer face, and the earth, oceans, and seven pairs of animals on its underside; the central arch's outer face depicts virtues and beatitudes, its inner the signs of the Zodiac and labors of the months; the outer arch (ca1265) shows Christ and the prophets, and a collection of Venetian trades below (including a nail-biting architect—see panel).

The south facade The facade facing the Piazzetta di San Marco was originally the principal gateway and ceremonial entrance to the Basilica—it was the frontage visitors would see first as they approached from the sea. The original door, its large arched outline still visible, was blocked off in 1504 during the building of the interior's Cappella Zen (see page 71). The jutting walls on the right, hard up against the Palazzo Ducale, form part of the Treasury (see page 70), and may have been the area of the Palazzo Ducale first used to display St. Mark's body. The marbles and fragments of relief (*plutei*) date from the 9th to 11th centuries. The pair of free-standing columns, from 5th-century Syria, came either from Constantinople after the Fourth Crusade, or from the church of St. Saba in Acre (in present-day Israel) following Venice's defeat of the Genoese there in 1256. The smaller column at the corner, the **Pietra del Bando**, is probably from Acre (see panel on page 65).

Stand back from the facade to glimpse the tiny mosaic Madonna between the arches in the galleried upper facade. According to the 19th-century writer Augustus Hare it "commemorates the remorse of the Council of Ten for the unjust condemnation of Giovanni Grassi (1611), pardoned ten years after his execution. He swore that the senators who condemned him would all die within the year, and they all obliged him." Two votive lamps burn to either side, once lit, claims Hare, at an execution, when the condemned man, before mounting the

NAILBITER

According to myth, the lame man chewing his knuckles on the main facade's central portal is the Greek architect hired to help design the Basilica of 1063. At one point he tumbled off scaffolding surrounding the church, either in dismay because the Senate had criticized his work, or in a transport of delight brought on by the beauty of his architecture. Venetians favor the former, claiming he is biting his fingers in a frenzy of fury.

The horses from the main facade of the Basilica di San Marco

63

scaffold, would turn to the mosaic and cry *"Salve Regina."* Venetian tradition, by contrast, claims they commemorate either the wrongful execution for murder of a young boy in 1507, or a vow made by an old sailor lost at sea and eventually saved by the Madonna.

The interior Entering the main body of the Basilica, you first reach an entrance hall (or narthex) whose six shallow domes glitter with some of the interior's oldest and more intelligible mosaics (see plan on page 66). The first arch to your right shelters Venice's oldest funerary monument (1), the **Tomb of Doge Vitale Falier** (d.1096), who consecrated the Basilica in 1094. On the floor in front of the central door sits a red porphyry slab (2), traditionally held to be where the Venetians forced the Emperor Barbarossa to kneel in homage to Pope Alexander III in 1177. Before entering the interior proper, take the narrow stairs (3) signed by the central door to the Loggia dei Cavalli.

The Loggia dei Cavalli: apart from a tremendous view of the facade and the Piazza below, the loggia has long been home to four great gilded horses, one of the city's most valued treasures and the only *quadriga* (four-horse chariot team) to have survived from classical antiquity. The horses *in situ* these days are copies: the originals, controversially removed for safekeeping in 1979, are now displayed beneath a brick-lined cupola in a small upstairs museum (*Open* daily 9:30–4:30. *Admission: inexpensive*). Their origins are hazy, no one being quite sure whether they are Greek or Roman, or whether they date from the 4th century BC or the 3rd century AD. The weight of opinion leans towards Roman provenance and a date somewhere in the 3rd century: all that is known for certain, however, is that they came to Venice from Constantinople in 1204. Fifty years later they were languishing in front of the Arsenale, and might have been lost altogether had not an anonymous Florentine ambassador saved them for posterity. Once installed in the basilica, they quickly became one of the city's best-known symbols. Napoléon, who stole them in 1797, had them hitched to a chariot in Paris (in the place du Carrousel), where they remained for 18 years. The

Far left: the main facade of the Basilica

The Basilica's horses were replaced by copies in 1979

65

Basilica di San Marco

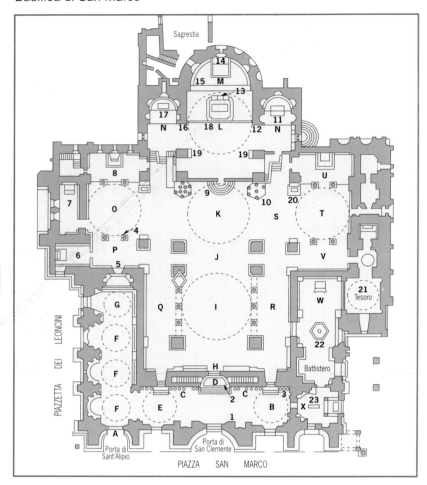

Key to mosaics

A arrival of the body of St. Mark (1260)

B Genesis and Creation (1230)

C from the life of Noah (first and second arch); Sts. Alipio and Simon (third arch)

D Madonna with Apostles and Evangelists (1065)

E Abraham (dome) and four prophets (tondi)

F from the life of Joseph

G from the life of Moses

H Christ, the Virgin Mary and St. Mark

I Dome of the Pentecost (12th century)

J betrayal of Christ, Crucifixion, Marys at the tomb, descent into limbo, Doubting Thomas (between domes)

K Dome of the Ascension (13th century): concentric circles depict the Ascension, Virgin with two cherubim and the Apostles, virtues and beatitudes, evangelists, four allegories of the holy rivers

L Dome of Emmanuel

M Christ Pantocrator (1506) and the four patron saints of Venice (1100)

N from the lives of Sts. Mark and Peter

O acts of St. John the Evangelist (12th century)

P life of the Virgin and infant Christ (13th century)

Q miracles of Christ (13th century); five mosaic tablets

of Christ and four prophets (wall of north aisle 1210–30)

R the Virgin, Agony in the Garden (13th century); five mosaic tablets of the Virgin and four prophets (wall of south aisle)

S from the life of Christ (arch between the dome and nave)

T (dome) mosaics of Sts. Leonard, Clement, Blasius and Nicholas (13th century)

U parables and miracles of Christ (13th century)

V *Inventio* (rediscovery) of the body of St. Mark

W from the lives of Christ and St. John the Baptist (14th century)

X from the Life of St. Mark (13th century, but restored)

Venetian sculptor Antonio Canova, who made his name in Paris, was partly instrumental in having them returned—minus the medallions that used to hang round their necks.

The **north transept**: the order in which people are herded round the Basilica changes from time to time. Usually you enter not by the central door into the nave, but via a door on the left that takes you into the north transept. The first thing you notice, after the breathtaking overall impression, is a beautifully carved 12th-century Greek marble stoup (4). Above the door behind you curves a lovely carved arch (5) framing a 13th-century mosaic of the Madonna. The **Cappella della Madonna dei Mascoli** (6) takes its name from a confraternity of male (*mascoli*) worshippers who adopted the chapel in 1618 (Venetian folklore claims the name derived from the fact that pregnant women came here to pray for male offspring). The marble-cased Gothic altar (1430) on the wall has statues of the Madonna and Child with Saints by Bartolomeo Bon. The vault's mosaics (1430–1450), one of Italy's most important cycles of its age, depict the Life of the Virgin and represent one of Venice's earliest Renaissance works (probably based on drawings by Jacopo Bellini and the Tuscan artist Andrea del Castagno).

The often barred **Cappella di Sant'Isidoro** (7) was built in 1354 by Doge Andrea Dandolo (whose tomb lies in the Baptistery; see page 70). Its statues and mosaics relate to the life of Isidoro, a 3rd-century martyr whose remains were stolen by the Venetians from Chios in 1125 and

The interior is usually illuminated between 11:30 and 12:30 each day, on Saturday afternoons and all day Sunday

CLEVER CASTING
The Basilica's famous horses are unusual in being made from a bronze that consists almost entirely of copper. This made them more difficult to cast but easier to gild. The horses' collars conceal a join, either caused by the statues having been cast in two halves, or because they were cut in two in 1204 to make them easier to transport from Constantinople. It is thought the partial gilding and scratches on the horses' surface were deliberate, and were probably added to help catch the sun's rays.

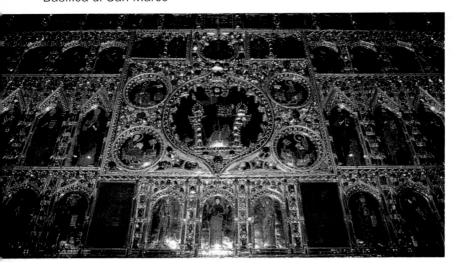

68

Once on show only for religious ceremonies, the Pala d'Oro is now on permanent display

THE PALA D'ORO
The Pala d'Oro's 157 enameled plaques and roundels are embellished with 15 rubies, 38 chiseled figures, 100 amethysts, 300 sapphires, 300 emeralds, 400 garnets, 1300 pearls, and 200 miscellaneous stones.

hidden for two centuries for fear of confiscation. Venice also stole the tiny icon that takes pride of place in the adjacent **Cappella di Madonna di Nicopeia** (8). The city's most venerated image, the icon is considered the Protectoress of Venice, and was once carried into battle by Byzantine emperors. It dates at least from the 12th century, and was brought from Constantinople in 1204.

The **Sanctuary** and **Pala d'Oro** (*Open* daily 9:30–4:30, Sun 2–4:30. *Admission: inexpensive*): now move across the church, passing the great iconostasis or rood screen (9), whose eight shadowy columns support a vast silver and gold cross (1394) by Marco Benato, and marble statues of the Virgin, St. Mark and the Apostles (1394) by Jacobello and Pier Paolo dalle Masegne. The pulpit (10) on its right was where a new doge was traditionally presented to the people after his coronation. It was also the spot where the basilica's relics were displayed on feast days (see panel page 70). To its right is the entrance to the Sanctuary, and to the interior's most famous sight, the jewel-encrusted Pala d'Oro. As you walk to the ticket desk notice the **Cappella di San Clemente** (11) straight ahead, whose simple altarpiece is also by the dalle Masegne brothers, and the fine Gothic tabernacle (12) behind the ticket desk itself.

Behind the high altar, the reputed resting place of St. Mark, stands the **Pala d'Oro** (13), or "screen of gold," perhaps the finest piece of medieval gold and silverware in Europe. Commissioned in Constantinople by Doge Pietro Orseolo I in 976, it was further embellished by Byzantine craftsmen in 1105, and reset in 1209 to accommodate jewels seized during the Fourth Crusade. The oldest fragments—dating from 976—are the circular gold and enamel plates around the rim. Much of the more intricate work, however, is almost impossible to make out, with the many Biblical figures and countless religious scenes forming an indecipherable confusion of gilt and glitter.

Facing the screen stands an **altar** (14) framed by six fine columns, two of which are made of a strange translucent alabaster. To its left is the **door** (15) to the sacristy (usually shut), crafted by Sansovino in 1546, its frame decorated with portraits of Titian, Aretino, Palladio, Veronese and the Sansovino brothers. Moving around to the front of the high altar, the left-hand pier contains a sculpted tabernacle (16) by the dalle Masegne brothers. The altar of the **Cappella di San Pietro** (17), glimpsed to the left, features a 14th-century relief of St. Peter and two kneeling procurators.

Walking back in front of the high altar, note the four ancient alabaster columns (18) of the altar's *baldacchino*, each carved with striking if incomprehensible scenes from the lives of Christ and the Virgin. A debate rages as to their age, some critics claiming they are 5th-century Byzantine works, some that they are 13th-century Venetian pieces, and others that they were brought to Venice by Doge Pietro Orseolo II in the 10th century. The eight statues on the marble balustrade (four on each side) represent the four Evangelists, sculpted by Sansovino in 1522, and the four Patriarchs, added by Paliari between 1608 and 1614. The painting on the altar (on the back of the Pala d'Oro) is an early 15th-century work attributed to Michele Giambono. Turning to face down the nave there are two singing galleries (19) to the right and left, each decorated with bronze reliefs by Sansovino (1537–1544) depicting the miracles and martyrdom of St. Mark.

A VENETIAN ST. PETER'S
Venice's adoption of a saint that gave her spiritual legitimacy and historical prestige matched the legitimacy claimed by Rome and the papacy through the shrine and church of St. Peter. Where the pope was the natural successor to St. Peter, the doge, in effect, became the successor to St. Mark. This led to a degree of religious autonomy and to clashes between Venice and the papacy. Venetian bishops were appointed by the Senate; priests were elected by ballot (and had to be Venetian by birth); the Inquisition was a branch of the state; and the Patriarch of Venice could convene a synod only with the doge's permission.

69

Mosaics in the narthex (vestibule)

The narthex contains 13th-century mosaics such as that of Noah and the Flood

RELICS

John Moore, an 18th-century English visitor, mentions some of the hundreds of holy relics owned by the Basilica: "...eight pillars from Solomon's temple at Jerusalem; a piece of the Virgin Mary's veil, some of her hair, and a small portion of her milk; the knife used by Christ at his last supper; one of the nails of the cross, and a few drops of His blood." These, he said, were only a "few of the most valuable."

The Treasury (*Open* Mon–Sat 9:30–4:30, Sun 2–4:30. *Admission: inexpensive*): moving into the main body of the church, look for the pillar from which St. Mark's body miraculously "reappeared" in 1094 (see panel on page 71). This is commemorated by a square of marble inlay on the left-hand of two pilasters round the corner from the small altar (20). In the opposite corner of the transept a door leads to the tiny but priceless collection in the Basilica's Treasury (21). Europe's finest collection of early Byzantine silverware, it was even finer until 1797 when Napoléon melted enough exhibits to produce 55 ingots of gold and silver. The "Throne of St. Mark," left of the turnstile, was carved in Alexandria and presented to the Patriarch of Grado by Emperor Heraclius in 630. The room's thick walls may have belonged to a 9th-century tower of the original ducal palace.

The Baptistery: (*rarely open*) although dominated by a baptismal font (1546) by Sansovino (who is buried near by), the Basilica's Baptistery (22) is known for Giovanni de' Santi's tomb of Andrea Dandolo (d.1354), the last doge to be buried in the Basilica. Dandolo commissioned the vault's Byzantine-tinged mosaics, which describe scenes from the lives of Christ and John the Baptist, and the sending out of the Apostles into the world: note the lunette's fashionably garbed Salome—in clingy red dress and white tassels—dancing with the Baptist's head. The granite slab at the altar, traditionally the stone from which Christ delivered the Sermon on the Mount, probably came from Tyre in 1126.

The Cappella Zen: *(rarely open)* from the Baptistery walk through to the chapel (23) named after Giambattista Zen (d.1501), a cardinal who left a fortune to the state on condition that he was buried in St. Mark's. Unlike Bartolomeo Colleoni, who made a similar request but was snubbed (see pages 152–153), the Senate blithely sealed off part of the Basilica to provide the requisite chapel (previously this corner of the church had opened on to both the narthex and the Piazzetta outside). The high altar's *Madonna of the Shoe* (1506), a sculpture by Antonio Lombardo, alludes to the story of the peasant who gave his shoe to the Virgin (who then turned it into gold as a mark of heavenly gratitude). The marbles and verde-antiques on the walls are reputed to be the stolen gravestones of Byzantine emperors.

Mosaics Mosaics swathe almost every interior surface of the Basilica (and parts of the exterior), covering nearly 40,000 square feet with a bewildering variety of gold-tinged narratives. The earliest date from the 12th century, dependent on the traditions of Byzantium for inspiration, but new mosaics and restoration work on the originals continued until as late as the 18th century. Mosaics in later centuries were often based on sketches by leading artists, among them Titian, Tintoretto, and Veronese. Trying to make sense of all the individual scenes and episodes is difficult, but it is well worth trying to identify some of the older or more striking of the mosaics (notably the domes of the Pentecost and Ascension: see the plan on page 66 and the accompanying panel). Most of the mosaics in the narthex depict Old Testament scenes, a deliberate counterpoint to the New Testament episodes in the main body of the church. If you are going to spend any time looking at the mosaics, it is worth bringing a pair of binoculars.

MISLAID ST. MARK
St. Mark's remains are supposed to reside beneath the Basilica's high altar. In fact they were probably destroyed during the fire that devastated the church in 976. They were certainly missing when Doge Falier came to consecrate the new basilica in 1094. A service was held to invoke divine help in relocating the mislaid saint. As it proceeded a wrenching sound was heard from one of the Basilica's pillars, and as the congregation looked on, first a hand, then an arm, and eventually the saint's entire body burst from the crumbling column.

FIRST IMPRESSIONS
John Ruskin describes St. Mark's interior: "Under foot and over head, a continual succession of crowded imagery, one picture passing into another, as in a dream; forms beautiful and terrible mixed together—dragons and serpents, and ravening beasts of prey, and graceful birds that in the midst of them drink from running fountains and feed from bases of crystal..."
The Stones of Venice (1851–1853)

71

EATING AND PAINTING

Burano has long been an artists' colony. Paintings of the so-called Burano School hang in Da Romano, a historic old restaurant in Burano's main street at Via Galuppi 221 (*Closed* Tue and Sun afternoons; tel: 041 730030). The restaurant instigated the Burano art prize in 1947. At Via Galuppi 371 is the slightly cheaper Ai Pescatori, which also has many devotees (*Closed* Mon; tel: 041 730650). Cheapest of all, and in the best position (with tables overlooking the canal opposite the fish market) is Al Gatto Nero, Fondamenta della Giudecca 88 (*Closed* Mon; tel: 041 730120). It, too, is lined with paintings, but takes its name from Derek, quite possibly the largest cat in the world.

PRACTICALITIES

A day trip to Burano makes an ideal accompaniment to Torcello (see pages 206–207). To reach both islands take the hourly boat No 12 from the Fondamente Nuove. A special *Biglietto Itinerario* allows unlimited use of the routes connecting the islands of the northern lagoon for 12 hours. Travel time to Burano is 40 minutes. Most boats call at Burano first before crossing to Torcello (5 minutes away). If you are continuing to Torcello, be sure to board the right boat—not one returning directly to Venice (via Murano) or continuing to Treporti and Punta Sabbioni.

The colorful houses of Burano

►► Burano, Isola di 271B3

Burano is known for its lace and brightly colored houses, and is one of the most popular day trips on the lagoon from Venice. These days much of its lace is machinemade, a pale imitation of the intricate *punti in aria* that for centuries made the island's output the most prized in Europe (see below). The jaunty houses, however, and the salty tang of a genuine fishing community, more than make up for the air of commercialism—and there is a lovely little museum if you want to see *bona fide* examples of the lace that brought the island its fame.

The island Like many outposts on the lagoon, Burano has probably been inhabited since Roman times. Refugees from the mainland fled here in the 7th century, naming their new sanctuary Boreana, perhaps after the *bora*, the cold northeasterly wind that blows into Venice from the Balkans. It was this same wind, coupled with the island's distance from the lagoon's marshier reaches, that spared Burano the malaria-infested fate of Torcello (malaria takes it name from the Italian for "bad air"—*mal aria*). Despite the island's medieval prosperity, much of it generated by the export of lace, little survives today to suggest a period of any great glory. The only "sight," bar the lace museum (see below) and a wonderfully lopsided campanile, is a *Crucifixion* (second altar on the left) by G. B. Tiepolo in Burano's main church, San Martino (located in the piazza at the top of the main street).

Be sure to wander the handful of streets, whose brilliantly colored houses make them as attractive as any in Venice itself. According to legend the colors were painted by fishermen's wives to help their husbands identify their homes when far out at sea. Also make a point of finding

The distinctive weaving and stitching techniques of Burano's lace may derive from the methods used to make and repair fishing nets

SHARED STITCHES
Burano lace has seven main stitches. Each woman specialises in one stitch, which means that most work passes through several hands before it is completed.

73

HAIR COLLAR
Burano lace was particularly well received in France. Louis XIV once ordered a collar woven from white human hair, no thread being fine enough to meet the requirements of his design.

the old marble stalls of the fish market (in Fondamenta della Pescheria), and walk to the island's grassy fringes to enjoy views of Venice and the shoreline's old world vignettes of beached boats and half-painted gondolas.

Lace Although Venetian women of all social classes made lace using bobbins from at least the 15th century, it was the development of the stitch known as "Burano point"— an infinitesimally intricate and refined lace—that made the island both famed abroad and the main center of Venetian production. The new technique removed the need for a canvas backing, allowing the lace to be stitched on to a piece of parchment which could later be removed. The lace was thus able to stand alone—hence *punti in aria*, or "points in air."

By the 19th century, however, Burano's output had been almost obliterated by foreign competition. In 1872, when a school was opened to preserve the tradition, only one woman, it is said—Cencia Scarpariola— still remembered the lacemakers' old secrets. Matters improved, and within a few years seven factories employing 5,000 people were again operating around the lagoon.

Today the outlook is once again fairly bleak. The school is still running as a cooperative, but has just ten members, while only an estimated 30 older women on the island still make real Burano lace. A few work in the **Scuola dei Merletto** (opposite San Martino in the main square), sitting on special stools and bent over stitches almost invisible to the naked eye (note the distinctive round cushions with their backing of green paper, used because it is easier on the eye). The scuola houses a wonderful museum (*Open* Apr–Oct, Wed–Mon 10–5, Nov–Mar, Wed–Mon 10–4. *Admission: moderate*) filled with some breathtaking older pieces, chief among them a wedding veil that took 30 women seven hours a day over two years to complete. In the back room are teaching boards displaying enlarged examples of Burano's distinctive stitches.

The Ca' d'Oro by Friedrich Nerly (1807–1878)

▶ ▶ Ca' d'Oro (Galleria Franchetti)   272B2

Calle di Ca' d'Oro; Canal Grande (Quay: Ca' d'Oro; Vaporetto 1)

Souvenir stands and speedboats aside, it is almost possible to believe you see Venice as it has always been; the notion that you are walking in a miraculously preserved medieval fossil is one of the city's greatest charms. In truth, time has wrought a host of changes, with dilapidated palaces and plundered paintings often leaving only a ghost of the beauty that would have seduced a medieval onlooker. Nowhere is this more apparent than in the Ca' d'Oro, or "House of Gold," whose name derived from its external gilding, long since scoured clean by centuries of wind and rain.

A similar loss has been suffered in the interior, ravaged over the years by a succession of architects and ignorant owners. Restoration between 1969 and 1984 saved the building from total ruin, but at the cost of almost completely stripping away its medieval ambience. What remains is a bland shell, a surprisingly lackluster setting for one of the city's more rewarding galleries. The building's "inner spirit," in the words of Gore Vidal, "has fled along with its creators."

The palace (*Open* Tue–Sun 8:15–7, Mon 8:15–2. *Admission: moderate*) The first building on the present site, the Palazzo Zeno, was bought in 1420 by the Procurator Marino Contarini, who commissioned from Marco d'Amadio alterations designed to create the most

ENTRANCE
Entry to the Ca' d'Oro is by a side door in a nondescript alley leading from the Ca' d'Oro landing stage. Water afforded the palace's best approach, and the land side of the buildings is not as ornate. The Ca' d'Oro facade, battered by the elements and the vibrations of the *vaporetti*, underwent years of restoration. Happily the intricate architectural detail has been preserved.

ostentatious palace on the Grand Canal. Lombard crafts-men employed in the work's early stages were later replaced by Venetian artisans under the command of Giovanni and Bartolomeo Bon. The mélange of architects and workmen produced a variety of decorative detail that makes the palace's exterior—even without its gilding—Venice's finest Venetian-Byzantine monument after San Marco. Contarini's aspirations were principally satisfied by the facade, an almost literal reflection of its owner's wealth that used the costliest decorative finishes of the day—gilt, cinnabar red, and ultramarine blue.

Contarini's Ozymandias-like ambition was inevitably undone by time: the roof's golden pinnacles were rubbed clean by the elements, the vermilion of its floral tracery washed over the years into the waters of the Grand Canal. Few subsequent owners lavished either care or money on the palace, leaving it a virtual ruin by the time it was bought by the Russian Prince Troubetskoy in 1847. Things deteriorated further when Troubetskoy gifted the palace to Maria Taglioni, one of the greatest ballerinas of her time but not, sadly, one of its greatest interior decorators. The architectural abuse she visited on the interior justifi-ably provoked Ruskin's ire (see panel). Baron Franchetti bought the palace in 1894, leaving both it and his private art collection to the state in 1916. It was opened to the public in 1927.

Each of the gallery's two floors is divided into an open plan space—the palace's former *portego*—and a large room off to the left and three smaller ones to the right (plus access to a loggia at the Grand Canal end of each *portego*). On the **first floor**, a polyptych by Antonio Vivarini greets you at the top of the stairs, a detailed *Crucifixion* flanked by 12 tiny and exquisitely detailed vignettes. In front of it stands the headless torso of a knight in chain mail, one of several fragments from an anonymous 14th-century *Massacre of the Innocents*. On the right as you turn into the main hall is a fascinating, waxy-hued *paliotto*, a three-dimensional work in alabaster made in England during the 16th century. Removed from the church of Santa Caterina in Venice, it shows *Scenes from the Life of St. Catherine*, with Sts. Zita and Dorothy in narrow panels at either side.

Straight ahead, in a little chapel specially built by Franchetti, is the gallery's high-light, Andrea Mantegna's *St. Sebastian* (1506). One of the painter's last works (it remained unfinished at his death), it shows a heavily arrowed and slightly squashed St. Sebastian, patron saint of the sick, a popular talisman in plague-torn Venice (see pages 176–177). Notice the guttering candle in the painting's bottom right-hand corner, a symbol of Mantegna's famously pessimistic view of life. Its symbolism is underlined by the Latin inscription at the saint's feet, which reads "Only the Divine is eternal, all else is but smoke."

As you turn into the *portego*, the right wall features a lively pair of 15th-century

BALLETIC WRECKER
Among other "restor-ations" to the Ca' d'Oro, Maria Taglioni wrecked its great staircase, sold its well, disposed of its floor tiles and threw away many of its exterior marbles. John Ruskin, present as the work progressed, was incensed by the proceedings: "You cannot imagine," he wrote, "what an unhappy day I spent yesterday before the Casa d'Oro, vainly attempting to draw it while the workmen were hammering it down before my face…fancy trying to work while one sees the cursed plasterers hauling up old beams and dashing in old walls and shattering the moldings, and pulling barges across your gondola bows…"
Letter (1845)

75

A ceramic jug of Venetian origin dating from the 15th or 16th century

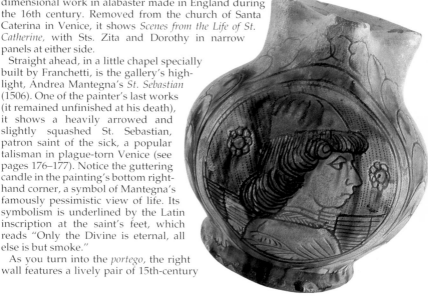

TIME'S RAVAGES
"Everything here is ruinous, on the point of crumbling into the water that floats this poor, worn city on its surface. The facades of the palaces are ravaged by time, stained by humidity, eaten up by the leprosy which destroys stone and marble."
Guy de Maupassant,
Gil Blas (1851)

Hercules wrestling with Achelous
*by Stefano Maderno
(1576–1636)*

busts by Tullio Lombardo: an almost modern-looking couple, the man sporting a self-satisfied smirk, the woman an indiscreetly plunging neckline. To their left stand six fine bronze reliefs, the work of Andrea Briosco, known as Il Riccio (1470–1532). The four most detailed panels represent episodes from the story of the True Cross, the fifth is a tabernacle door, the sixth a scene showing *St. Martin Sharing his Cloak with a Beggar.*

The three rooms off to the right contain cases full of medals, an art form that became popular during the Renaissance but makes for dull viewing today. Pisanello, who is heavily represented here, virtually invented the genre, borrowing heavily from old Roman coins for his images and ideas (typically a portrait on one side and an emblem or narrative scene on the other). Giovanni Bellini also experimented with the form, but here his medals take second place to a painting, the *Madonna degli Occhi Belli* (Madonna of the Beautiful Eyes).

Other paintings in these rooms are mainly obscure Venetian offerings, the exception being Carpaccio's *Annunciation* and *Death of the Virgin* in the second room, part of a cycle intended for the Scuola degli Albanesi.

Back across the *portego,* the large room on the left features walls full of Florentine and Sienese paintings, a rather disconcerting sight in a Venetian context. The best are a detailed *Flagellation* by Luca Signorelli, Andrea di Bartolo's *Coronation of the Virgin* (near wall) and two panels in the left corner by Biagio d'Antonio da Firenze. One of Biagio's panels describes *Scenes from the Life of Lucrezia,* notably her funeral and the graphically illustrated suicide precipitated by her rape. Part of a wedding chest, the picture was intended as a warning to brides, its somewhat harsh moral suggesting suicide was the only honorable option for a woman of "compromised" virtue. The scene to its right, *Hercules at the Crossroads,* depicts Hercules torn between the figures of Vice and Virtue. Removed from a *desco da nozze,* a tray used to display wedding gifts, its story symbolized the marital choices available to husbands, choices with less traumatic consequences for those that erred.

An attractive, but desperately worn, 15th-century staircase leads up from the gallery store to the **second floor** and a roomful of Flemish tapestries. Such wallhangings were far more fashionable (and expensive) than paintings in 16th-century Venice, casting an interesting light on some of the other works in the room: a *Venus* by

Titian, Van Dyck's *Portrait of a Gentleman* (1622–1627), and Tintoretto's *Portrait of the Procurator Nicolò Priuli*. The four busts in the corners of the room are by Alessandro Vittoria: three of them are portraits of procurators: the fourth, less flattering (notice the crow's feet), depicts Benedetto Manzini, a local parish priest.

The second floor *portego* is devoted to ravaged frescoes by Pordenone, removed from the church of Santo Stefano (see page 179), but clearly not removed soon enough, their wrecked state is another reminder of the riches lost to Venice over the centuries. Still more deteriorated frescoes, the work of Titian and Giorgione (the latter's only definitively documented work) fill the open-plan space at the hall's far end. They were removed from the Fondaco dei Tedeschi, one in 1937, the rest as late as 1967. The rooms off to the right are given over to Flemish and other northern European paintings, as anomalous in their Venetian context as the Tuscan works downstairs.

The Procurator Nicolò Priuli *by Jacopo Tintoretto*

▶ **Ca' Pesaro (Palazzo Pesaro)**   272A2
Fondamenta Mocenigo; Canal Grande (Quay: San Stae;
Vaporetto 1)
Museo d'Arte Moderna: (*closed for restoration*)
Museo Orientale: *Open: Tue–Sun 8:15–2.*
Admission: moderate

One of the Grand Canal's more impressive palaces, the
Ca' Pesaro is better known as the home of Venice's
Museo d'Arte Moderna (Museum of Modern Art). Its
top floor also contains the **Museo Orientale**. In many ways
the palace, bought as three separate buildings by the
Pesaro family in 1628, is more interesting than either of
the two museums. Leonardo Pesaro began the job of
joining the three buildings together between 1650 and
1682, employing Baldassare Longhena, one of the
period's foremost architects, to carry out the conversion.
The result is one of the high points of Venetian baroque,
renowned for the *chiaroscuro* effects of its Grand Canal

The magnificent
17th-century facade of
the Ca' Pesaro

78

facade and the decorative caprices of its *putti* and its lively grotesques.

By the 19th century, the palace had passed to the Duke of La Masa, a Veronese aristocrat, and in 1889 it was left to the city by his widow, Felicità Bevilacqua La Masa. Before her death, Felicità created a foundation designed to provide struggling Venetian painters with studio and exhibition space. Subsequently, the city subverted her wishes, and in 1902 installed a gallery in the palace to accommodate works bought from the Biennale.

Although a few foreign names creep in—Klimt, Klee, Kandinsky, Ernst, Matisse—the bulk of the gallery is given over to 19th- and 20th-century Italian painters and sculptors, including such names as Giorgio Morandi, known for his still-life etchings and strange sculpted clergymen; Filippo de Pisis, a purveyor of fine townscapes and winsome Venetian scenes; Guglielmo Ciardi, popular for his views of the lagoon; and Medardo Rosso, whose seven wax heads form one of the gallery's highlights.

Much of the Museo Orientale's collection was presented to Venice by Austria, by way of an apology for the incendiary bombs dropped on the city during World War I. As a peace offering it left something to be desired, for little in the potpourri of arms, armor, sculpture, paintings, and musical instruments will appeal to anyone but fans of Chinese and Japanese artifacts. Its most interesting exhibits are Japanese paintings, bronzes, and lacquerwork.

► Ca' Rezzonico—Museo del Settecento Veneziano   *276A3*

Fondamenta Rezzonico Barnaba; Canal Grande (Quay: Ca' Rezzonico; Vaporetto 1)
Closed for restoration

Although currently closed for restoration, the Ca' Rezzonico is one of the few palaces where you are usually able to penetrate the sumptuous facade, rather than offering no more than tantalizing glimpses of interior splendor as you chug slowly past on some heavily laden *vaporetto*. Despite its extenal promises, its interior comes as something of a disappointment: a stripped-down and melancholy palace-turned-museum. Designed to reflect the décor and style of 18th-century Venice, its trappings and art collection (bar a few Tiepolo frescoes and Longhi vignettes) are often third rate. Few of the exhibits are native to the palace, many having been brought from elsewhere or made in the last few years to double for unavailable originals.

The Venetian Procurator Filippo Bon commissioned the palace in 1667 from the leading baroque architect Baldassare Longhena, who managed to complete only the first floor and *piano nobile* before his death in 1682. Bon's subsequent ruin brought work to a halt, the half-finished palace remaining covered by a temporary wooden roof for 70 years. In 1751 the shell was sold to the Rezzonico family, a *nouveau riche* clan whose architect, Giorgio Massari, completed the building in 1756. After the death of the last Rezzonico in 1810, and a string of mostly forgotten owners—Robert Browning's son among them—the palace was bought by the state and opened as a museum in 1936.

PALAZZO MOCENIGO
The Mocenigo family produced no fewer than seven doges and had many palaces (see page 88). One of their palaces lies close to Ca' Pesaro at San Stae 1992 (*Open* Tue–Sat 10–5. *Admission: moderate*). Rooms on the piano nobile, furnished with 18th-century frescoes, portraits of Mocenigo worthies and Murano chandeliers, give some idea of wealthy patrician life in the last phase of the Serenissima.

The elaborate costumes on display come from the Study Center of the History of Fabrics, and Costumes, in the same building, open only for temporary exhibitions. A combined ticket to the Palazzo Mocenigo grants admission to other civic museums (see Palazzo Ducale, page 118).

79

PALATIAL ASSURANCE
Henry James described the Ca' Rezzonico as "thrusting itself upon the water with a peculiar florid assurance, a certain toss of its cornice which gives it the air of a rearing seahorse." *The Grand Canal* (1892)

GREEDY PLEASURES
The 18th century was, according to a famous phrase of the time, a period when "Venetians did not taste their pleasures, but swallowed them whole." One contemporary, observing the wild abandon of the time, said of Venice that "the men are women, the women men, and all are monkeys."

From the collection of the Ca' Rezzonico

THE REZZONICO

Giambattista Rezzonico bought his way into the Venetian nobility in 1687 by contributing 100,000 ducats to the state treasury (a sum then equivalent to two percent of the Republic's annual income). He gave another 60,000 ducats to charity.

First floor The museum's collection spreads over three floors and around 30 rooms, but is not as intimidating a prospect as it sounds, for the exhibits are well labeled and the highlights few. The ballroom at the top of Massari's staircase provides a fine opener, thanks mainly to its *trompe l'œil* and mammoth chandeliers. The furniture here and elsewhere in the palace is the work of Andrea Brustolon (1662–1735) notable for his extravagant style and exquisite craftsmanship. Prize for the most gaudy piece goes to the console table, featuring Hercules, two river gods, and three slaves shackled by carved chains.

When walking out of the ballroom to the right, the first highlights are the ceiling frescoes of Giambattista Tiepolo in the second room, the **Sala dell'Allegoria Nuziale**, painted to celebrate the dynastic marriage of Ludovico Rezzonico and Faustina Savorgnan in 1758. The main panel shows Fame trumpeting the union, the happy couple borne by Apollo, no less, who guides the Chariot of the Sun towards the Rezzonico family crest. The next room has noted but insipid pastel portraits by Rosalba Carriera, and is followed by a roomful of 17th-century Flemish tapestries and a pretty green-yellow lacquered door, one of the few pieces of décor from the original palace (such lacquerwork was highly fashionable in 18th-century Venice).

The last room on this side, the **Sala del Trono**, or Throne Room, was named after the throne used during a visit to the palace by Pope Pius VI in 1782. It also has another Tiepolo ceiling, *The Allegory of Merit*. The *portego*, or main hall, contains more Brustolon furniture, four busts by Tiepolo and a wonderfully spooky *felze*, one of the cabins fitted to gondolas for winter travel.

Second floor Little in the remaining rooms on the first floor is really worth seeing, so take the stairs from the *portego* to the second floor, where the corresponding *portego* is arranged as a gallery. Its pride and joy is a pair of paintings by Canaletto, two of only a handful still on public display in Venice. Explore the rooms off to the right, where the bedroom and its closet provide one of the palace's few insights into the realities of 18th-century life. The contents of the 18th-century toiletry-bag—a great array of silver accoutrements of largely unfathomable function—are particularly fascinating.

Other rooms on this side of the *portego* contain pictures by Francesco Guardi, including his celebrated views of the Ridotto's gambling rooms and the high society high jinks practised in the convent of San Zaccaria (see pages 186–188). Equally well known is Pietro Longhi's hornless *Rhinoceros*, captured on canvas during its famous 18th-century visit to Venice. It is one of the 34 fascinating pictures by the artist on this floor. Back across the *portego*, the Harpsichord Room is noteworthy for two pretty painted chests and a pair of mauve-colored wardrobes.

The final rooms contain the museum's pictorial highlight, a sequence of satirical frescoes, painted between 1793 and 1797, by Giandomenico Tiepolo, removed from the painter's family home near Mestre. Best known is the large panel of the *New World*, in which Tiepolo pokes fun at the follies of fashion, its well-dressed crowd symbolically turning its back on the viewer and the "Old World" to enjoy a peepshow of scenes from the New. Tiepolo himself forms part of the scene, depicted as the figure looking through a magnifying glass in the right-hand corner (his father is next to him). The playful scenes of the last suite feature the prancing figure of Pulcinella, a Neapolitan clown adopted by the Venetians as a Carnival character.

Third floor Previous restoration had kept the Ca' Rezzonico's upper story closed for years, though what was done with the time is hard to see. All it now offers—bar some marvelous views of the city—are a handful of puppets (you will see better in many Venetian store) and an entire 18th-century pharmacy, whose appeal is spoiled by being antiseptically displayed behind glass.

ROBERT BROWNING
The English poet Robert Browning died in the Ca' Rezzonico in 1889 while visiting his son, Pen, who had bought the palace with the help of his wealthy American wife. Browning, poignantly, had hoped the palace would be "a corner for my old age." After lying in state in the ballroom for two days, he was transported to San Michele, and thence to Westminster Abbey. A plaque on the palace's Grand Canal facade records his death.

REZZONICO POPE
Two years after the Ca' Rezzonico's completion, Giambattista Rezzonico's son, Carlo, Bishop of Padua, was elected Pope Clement XIII. Carlo was not a model pope, notorious for his nepotism and old-maidish prudery. It was he, for example, who covered the Vatican's vast collection of classical statues with judiciously placed fig leaves.

A gondola's felze *allowed clandestine liaisons—not unusual in 18th-century Venice*

Walk

The Accademia to Piazza San Marco (pages 276–277)

Take Rio Terrà A Foscarini left of the Accademia and follow it to the church of the Gesuati. Then follow Fondamenta delle Zattere to Santa Maria della Salute. Return to the Accademia via San Gregorio and the Guggenheim museum.

Explore the **Gesuati**, which contains a ceiling fresco by G. B. Tiepolo and paintings by Tintoretto and Piazzetta. Look out for the Pensione Calcina on the Zattere, marked with a plaque recording John Ruskin's presence there in the last century. Beyond lies a large children's home (the Casa di Rieducazione), previously the **Incurabili**, one of four foundling hospitals in Venice famed for their music (see pages 144–145). Wonderful views unfold across to San Giorgio Maggiore and the Giudecca as you approach the tip of Dorsoduro, the Punta della Dogana. The derelict

buildings here are the old custom house (*dogana*) and the **Magazzini del Sale**, the Republic's former salt warehouses. Round the corner you encounter the **Salute** (see pages 171–173), one of the city's most distinctive landmarks. On the way back to the Accademia, notice the **Palazzo Dario**, among the Grand Canal's most beautiful palaces, visit the **Guggenheim** (see pages 94–95) and browse in the wonderful paper shop at Fondamenta Venier 721.

Cross Ponte dell'Accademia and turn left after the former church of San Vidal on Calle Fruttarol. At San Samuele and the Palazzo Grassi take Calle delle Carrozze and Salizzada San Samuele to Campo Santo Stefano.

San Vidal (San Vitale) is now a private gallery, but above the high altar it retains a noted Carpaccio painting, *San Vitale and Saints*. Resist Campo Santo Stefano for the moment and make a detour to **San Samuele**, Casanova's parish church, and the **Palazzo Grassi**, a palace restored by Fiat as an exhibition space. At Calle Corner Crosera, just before Piscina San Samuele, note the shoe carved on number 3127, site of the old shoemakers' Scuola. **Santo Stefano** is a

Left: the Zattere, looking towards Palladio's Il Redentore on the Giudecca Right: a bas-relief of a fortress adorning the facade of Santa Maria del Giglio

quiet church with fine tombs and paintings (see pages 178–179). Leave time for refreshment at Paolin, producers of some of the city's best ice cream. The café's outside tables make a fine place from which to watch the street life on one of Venice's nicest squares.

Leave Campo Santo Stefano on Calle del Spezier and continue on Calle dei Zaguri to Santa Maria del Giglio. Make a detour north to the Fenice and San Fantin before returning to Calle Larga XXII Marzo on Calle delle Veste.

Santa Maria del Giglio, also known as Santa Maria Zobenigo, has a Tintoretto over the high altar and an extraordinary range of lovingly displayed saints' relics. The five statues on the facade represent the Barbaro brothers, who paid for the church's overhaul from 1680 to 1683. Note, too, the facade's strange reliefs, depictions of fortresses that featured in the brothers' military careers. The famous Gritti hotel abuts the church's *campo*, and there is a fine old-fashioned bar, Haig, in the square's southwest corner. Follow the map carefully to arrive in front of the **Fenice**, Venice's opera house and principal theater (see page 96). Note **San Fantin**, a Renaissance church built by Sansovino and Scarpagnino, and then return to Calle Larga XXII Marzo, home to some of the city's most elegant stores.

After San Moisè turn right on Calle del Ridotto, turn left at the waterfront and wander through the Giardinetti Reali before confronting Piazza San Marco.

The facade of **San Moisè** is one of the most extravagant pieces of baroque in the city. Look for the grotesques, in particular the strange camel, carved in 1668. Turn right after the church, where an alley leads past the site of

the old **Ridotto**, once among Venice's most notorious casinos. It was closed by the Senate in 1774 "in order to stamp out…vice in its principal seat." A pleasant walk along the waterfront passes **Harry's Bar**, Venice's most famous drinking establishment, and the **Giardinetti Reali**, a welcome patch of green before Piazza San Marco's milling crowds.

83

Taking the sun in the Giardinetti Reali

▶▶ Campanile 277F3

Piazza San Marco (Quay: San Marco; Vaporetti 1, 52, 82)
Open: daily 9:30–7:30; shorter hours in winter.
Admission: moderate

Venice's loftiest building (at 323 feet) was supposedly
founded in 912 on April 25, the feast day of St. Mark. In its
earliest incarnation it served as both a lookout for the
harbor (then contained in what is now the Piazzetta
below) and a bell tower for the basilica. Its bronze-
sheathed summit was also designed to catch the sun's
rays and act as a daytime beacon. Galileo demonstrated
his telescope to the Doge from its belfry, while Goethe
enjoyed his first view of the sea from the platform below.
Emperor Frederick III once rode to the summit on
horseback, and the bells provided an accompaniment to

*Beneath the rubble lies
the only casualty of the
1902 collapse of the
Campanile—a cat,
called Mélampyge
after Casanova's dog*

*The current
tower is almost
identical to its
predecessor*

the lives of ordinary Venetians for almost a
thousand years (see panel on page 244).

Collapse For centuries, refinements
to the Campanile were made, the
most extensive being those of
Bartolomeo Bon between 1511
and 1514. Despite these tinkerings,
few Venetians ever doubted the
tower's stability, trusting to foundations reputed to fan out beneath
Piazza San Marco in an enormous
star-shaped bulwark.

In fact, the tower had long been
growing weaker, corroded by salt
water, buffeted by wind and
rain, and—thanks to its height
and inviting bronze tip—struck
repeatedly by lightning (its lightning conductor, fitted in 1793,
was one of the earliest in
Europe). Worse still, the fabled
foundations were only 65 feet

deep. Nemesis arrived in July 1902, soon after a crack was discovered in the tower's side. Bands in the piazza were quickly forbidden to play, and the firing of the noon cannon was canceled—all to no avail, for on July 14 at 9:52 AM, in front of a watching crowd, the tower toppled gently to the ground.

While Sansovino's Loggetta was devastated, the basilica escaped miraculously unscathed, apparently saved by the pillar at the corner of the Palazzo Ducale (the fact that Bon's angel had landed intact at the Basilica's door had already been taken as a good omen). The tower's great bell, the Marangona, also survived (the other bells did not), as did six shirts ironed by the custodian's wife the previous day. The only casualty was the keeper's cat, crushed when it foolishly returned to finish its breakfast.

A meeting of the town council was convened that evening and, despite protests about cost (and claims by some that the piazza was improved without the tower), it was decided, in a phrase that has entered Venetian folklore, to rebuild the Campanile *dov' era e com' era*—"where it was and how it was." On April 25, 1912, exactly a thousand years after the tower's foundation, a new Campanile was inaugurated. It was 600 tons lighter and had an extra 1,000 piles, but otherwise it was identical to the original. At a celebratory banquet that evening, six honored guests wore the shirts rescued almost ten years earlier.

Viewpoint No trip to Venice is complete without enjoying the view from the Campanile. In times past entry was allowed only at high tide, a measure designed to prevent spies from surveying the channels of the lagoon (take note, incidentally, of the instruments at the tower's base, which give an interesting record of the tides and high water levels around the city). Most of Venice spreads out below you, with views extending to the distant Alps on clear days.

On a crisp winter's day the snowy peaks of the Alps are visible from the Campanile

LEANING TOWERS
In the 16th century, Venice had 200 church towers—today there are 170. Thirty have fallen down, and some of those remaining have an alarming list.

CAMPANILE CAGE
Venice punished wayward priests, clerics and other "persons of scandalous behavior" by imprisoning them in a cage, or *cheba*, dangling from a window halfway up the Campanile. The sight became one of the city's chief tourist attractions. Some inmates were released after a few days; some stayed there a year or more; and some enjoyed one of the world's most beautiful views before execution. Denied any means of replying to the tourists and occasional tormentors below, prisoners were inclined, according to a popular 16th-century poem, to *pissarli adosso*, or "piss on them from above."

Canal Grande

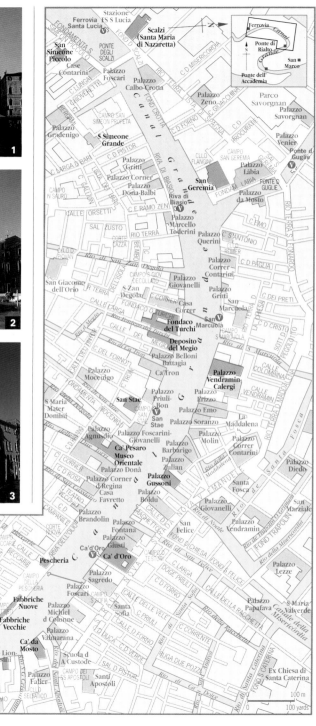

▶▶▶ Canal Grande 276C4

Ferrovia to the Rialto The green-domed **San Simeone Piccolo** (1), built in 1738 as an imitation of Rome's Pantheon, is notable as a concert venue. The **Ponte degli Scalzi**, one of only three bridges across the canal, was raised in 1934 to replace the iron bridge built by the Austrians in 1860. To its left stands the **Scalzi** (see page 189), a church designed in 1656 by Longhena, who also planned Santa Maria della Salute.

Whereas the Scalzi escaped demolition during the construction of the station, the old church of Santa Lucia was not so lucky. When it was destroyed during the 1860s, its prize relics, those of St. Lucy, a 4th-century martyr, were moved to **San Geremia**, whose rear extension abuts the canal on the corner of the Canale di Cannaregio. The walkway opposite, the **Riva di Biasio**, recalls the eponymous butcher, beheaded between the Palazzo Ducale's Piazzetta columns for selling human flesh as pork.

The multi-arched **Fondaco dei Turchi**, among the canal's oldest palaces, was clumsily restored in the 19th century. Now the Natural History Museum, it was a headquarters for Ottoman (*Turchi*) traders between 1621 and 1838. Immediately to its left is the plain **Deposito del Megio**, the Republic's old granary, once kept permanently stocked in readiness for siege or famine. Opposite is one of the canal's masterpieces, Mauro Coducci's **Palazzo Vendramin-Calergi** (4), better known as the winter home of the Casino. Richard Wagner occupied a 15-room suite here during his last months. When he died in February 1883, his body was taken to the station by gondola at dead of night for subsequent burial in Bayreuth.

The 1709 baroque facade of **San Stae** (2) overshadows the red-fronted building to its left, the **Scuola dei Battiloro e Tiraoro**, built in 1711 for jewelers specializing in drawn and beaten goldware (from *tirare*—to draw or pull). Two palaces down stands the redoubtable **Ca' Pesaro** (3) (see page 78), Longhena's last project. The **Palazzo Gussoni Grimani della Vida** (5) opposite was once covered in Tintoretto frescoes. Its most notable resident was Sir Henry Wotton, England's consul between 1614 and 1618, known for his observation that an ambassador was "an honest man sent to lie abroad for his country."

The **Ca' d'Oro**'s (7) gilt-covered facade must once have been the canal's most ravishing sight (see pages 74–77). Less hallowed, but equally colorful in its way, is the **Pescheria**, a neo-Gothic fish market built in 1907 on a site where fish stalls have been set up for over 600 years. The irregular 13th-century arches of the **Ca' da Mosto** (6) belong to the canal's oldest palace, propping up a building that in 1432 was the birthplace of Alvise da Mosto, the explorer who discovered the Cape Verde islands. Almost opposite are the long arcades of the **Fabbriche Nuove** (ca1550) and **Fabbriche Vecchie di Rialto**, heavy-handed market buildings designed by Sansovino and Scarpagnino respectively. The last building before the Rialto is the **Palazzo dei Camerlenghi**, the Republic's old treasury, whose water-level chamber was a debtors' prison. Opposite stands the **Fondaco dei Tedeschi**, once home not only to medieval German (*tedeschi*) merchants, but also to Hungarian, Austrian and other central European traders. It is now the main post office.

Ponte di Rialto to the Ponte dell'Accademia The **Palazzo Loredan** and **Palazzo Farsetti** now form Venice's town hall, though the latter was once home to the sculptor Antonio Canova. **Palazzo Grimani** (12) (ca1560), currently the city's appeals court, was reputedly built to humiliate the owner of the **Palazzo Papadopoli** opposite. He had forbidden his daughter to marry Grimani because he was too poor. Grimani promptly built a palace whose windows were larger than the Papadopoli's main portal. One of **Palazzo Benzon**'s habitués was the racy Contessa Querini Benzon, head of Venice's leading 19th-century salon, where she "entertained" the likes of Byron and Canova. Coducci's nearby **Palazzo Corner-Spinelli** (13) (1490) slightly pre-dates his more imposing Palazzo Vendramin (the Casino), while anticipating the Renaissance elements that were his trademark (such as the facade of San Zaccaria, see pages 186–188).

The tracery of the **Palazzo Bernardo** (8) ranks among the canal's finest, and like much of Venice's Byzantine-Gothic work was copied from the Palazzo Ducale. It is followed a short way down by the **Palazzo Barbarigo della Terrazza**, named after its roof terrace, a rare commodity on the canal's crowded frontage. The Barbarigo family owned a huge art collection until the 1850s, when poverty forced them to sell it to the Russian tsars. (It is now in the Hermitage in St. Petersburg.)

The Mocenigo family, who produced seven doges, was, by contrast, rarely so financially embarrassed. They owned no fewer than four palaces on the curve of the canal's sharpest bend, the Volta del Canal. One, the **Palazzo Mocenigo** (14), served as lodgings for two years to Lord Byron, his dog, fox, wolf, and monkey. Byron's guests included the fiery Margherita Cogni, who responded to Byron's rejection by attacking him with a knife and leaping into the canal. Byron also took to diving into the canal, but more for acts of bathing bravado. Giovanni Mocenigo, an earlier occupant, entertained the alchemist Giordano Bruno here in 1592, eager to discover his secrets. Later he betrayed him to the papacy, which had him burnt as a heretic in Rome's Campo dei Fiori. His ghost is said to haunt the **Palazzo Mocenigo Vecchio**.

Another of the great Venetian families, the Foscari, was responsible for the **Ca' Foscari** (9), one of Ruskin's favorite Gothic buildings. Commissioned in 1437 by Francesco Foscari (at 34 years Venice's longest serving doge), it was used to put up Henri III of France during his memorable visit to the city in 1574. The adjacent **Palazzo Giustinian** (see page 93) belonged to one of the city's oldest families, who claimed descent from the Roman Emperor Justinian. Wagner lived here for seven months in 1858, contemplating suicide before deciding to concentrate on *Tristan and Isolde*. Two doors down is Longhena's **Ca' Rezzonico** (10) (see pages 79–81), and almost opposite, the **Palazzo Grassi**, the canal's last major palace (1748–1872), restored in 1984 as an exhibition space. Tiny **Palazzo Falier** is known for its rare covered balconies, while the **Palazzo Giustinian-Lolin** (11) to its right is one of Longhena's earliest works (ca1623). *Vaporetti* empty at the **Accademia**, (see pages 52–60), before hurrying under the wooden **Ponte dell'Accademia**, the canal's final bridge. Built in 1932, it replaced an iron bridge built by the Austrians in 1854.

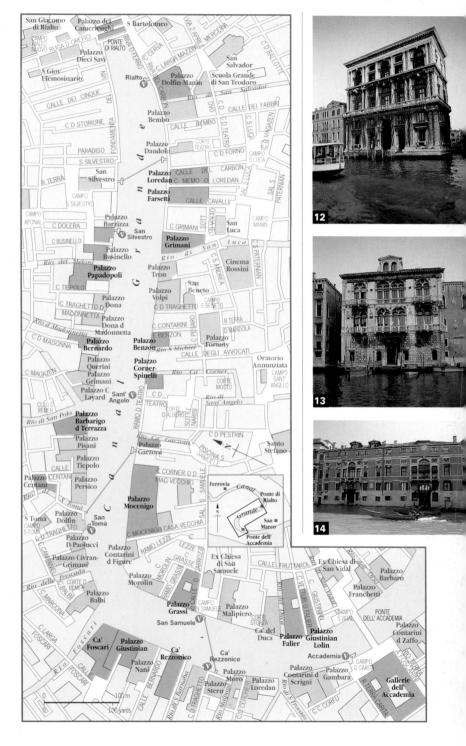

Canal Grande

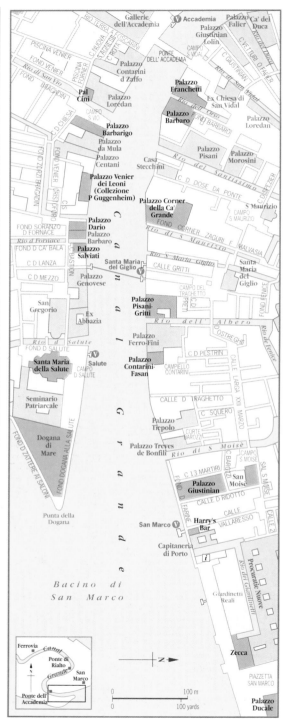

Gallerie dell'Accademia
Accademia
Palazzo Falier
Ca' del Duca
Palazzo Giustinian Lolin
PISCINA VENIER
FOND VENIER
Rio di San Vio
FOND BRAGADIN
PONTE DELL' ACCADEMIA
CAMPO S VIDAL
Palazzo Contarini d Zaffo
Pal Cini
Palazzo Loredan
Palazzo Franchetti
Ex Chiesa di San Vidal
Palazzo Loredan
Palazzo Barbarigo
Palazzo Barbaro
Palazzo da Mula
Palazzo Centani
Casa Stecchini
Palazzo Pisani
Palazzo Morosini
Palazzo Venier dei Leoni (Collezione P Guggenheim)
Palazzo Corner della Ca' Grande
S Maurizio
CAMPO S MAURIZIO
FOND CORNER ZAGURI F MALVASIA
Palazzo Dario
Palazzo Barbaro
Rio di S Maurizio
Santa Maria del Giglio
Palazzo Salviati
Santa Maria del Giglio
CALLE GRITTI
Palazzo Genovese
CAMPO DEL TRAGHETTO
Palazzo Pisani-Gritti
San Gregorio
Ex Abbazia
Rio dell' Albero
Palazzo Ferro-Fini
C D PESTRIN
Palazzo Contarini-Fasan
Santa Maria della Salute
Salute
CAMPIELLO CONTARINI
CALLE D TRAGHETTO
C SQUERO
Seminario Patriarcale
Palazzo Tiepolo
Dogana di Mare
Palazzo Treves de Bonfili
Rio di S Moisè
C 13 MARTIRI
San Moisè
Palazzo Giustinian
CALLE D RIDOTTO
Punta della Dogana
San Marco
Harry's Bar
CALLE VALLARESSO
Capitaneria di Porto
Procuratie Nuove
Bacino di San Marco
Giardinetti Reali
Zecca
PIAZZETTA SAN MARCO
Ferrovia
Ponte di Rialto
San Marco
Ponte dell'Accademia
Palazzo Ducale
100 m
100 yards

Ponte dell'Accademia to San Marco The **Palazzo Franchetti** (19), the first notable building after the Ponte dell'Accademia, was built in the 15th century but over-restored in the 1890s. It is quickly overshadowed by beautiful gardens on both banks, and then by the **Palazzo Barbaro** (20), a 15th-century palace bought in 1885 by the Curtis family. Artlovers and aesthetes, this Boston dynasty entertained countless writers and artists (among them Browning and Henry James, who set *The Wings of a Dove* in the palace). Monet and Singer Sargent had studios here, and Cole Porter was another guest.

The **Palazzo Barbarigo** (15) is easily identified, if only for its bright, modern mosaics (it is owned by a glass company). A little way down stands the truncated **Palazzo Venier dei Leoni**, better known as the home of the Guggenheim collection (see pages 94–95). Notice the single story that lends the palace its alternative name, the *Nonfinito* (Unfinished). Rumor has it that work was never completed thanks to pressure from the owners of Sansovino's massive **Palazzo Corner della Ca' Grande** (21) opposite (begun in 1545). Had it been finished, the *Nonfinito* would have been the largest palace on the canal. The Corner family, however, reputedly objected to the project on the grounds that it would block their sunlight. In truth, the Venier family probably ran out of money, partly, perhaps, after running up huge debts at the Casino.

The precariously leaning **Palazzo Dario** (16) is among the most charming of the canal's palaces. Built in the 1480s, it was probably designed by Pietro Lombardo, whose use of colored marbles is repeated in his master-piece, **Santa Maria dei Miracoli** (see page 170). It has long been believed to be cursed, a notion bolstered by the suicide in the 1990s of its owner, Raul Gardini, an Italian businessman implicated in Italy's 1993 bribes scandals. Two doors and a canal down is the **Palazzo Salviati**, another mosaic-covered building, and is owned by the famous Murano glass firm, Salviati.

Soon after appears the **Palazzo Pisani-Gritti**, a leading hotel that has hosted Ruskin, Hemingway, and countless latter-day honeymooners and VIPs. Almost opposite is Longhena's magnificent **Santa Maria della Salute** (see pages 171–173), commissioned to commemorate the passing of a plague epidemic and now one of Venice's great setpieces. A pontoon of boats is laid across the canal here during the Festa della Salute on November 21 each year. Opposite rises the **Palazzo Contarini-Fasan** (22), traditionally identified with Desdemona, a Venetian woman destroyed by her husband's jealousy and the model for Shakespeare's heroine. She probably did in fact exist—though she never lived in this palace.

Strictly speaking, the Grand Canal ends as it enters the Bacino di San Marco. Boats continue, however, and some of Venice's most famous sights now come into view. Across the water the Giudecca appears to the right, tipped with the magnificent **San Giorgio Maggiore** (see pages 140–141). In front of it, capping the end of the canal's right bank, is the **Dogana di Mare** (17), the old custom house, readily identified by its bronze globe. Before reaching the **Zecca** (18) and the Palazzo Ducale, look out for Harry's Bar and the **Palazzo Giustinian** (now the Hotel Europa), once host to Verdi and Proust, among others.

With their grandeur and decorative variety, the Venetian palaces, particularly those of the Grand Canal, are among the city's chief architectural glories. While their facades reflect the changing taste of the times, the buildings' basic design and function barely altered for over 500 years.

92

ONE-SIDED VIEW
"Venice is not made to be seen in the round. Its architecture is stage architecture, caring little ...for principles and concerned mainly with 'effects'." Mary McCarthy *Venice Observed* (1961)

FULL OF HOLES
In 1985, when divers made a detailed inspection of Venice's foundations, they said that they resembled Swiss cheese.

GOETHE ON VENICE
"Architecture in Venice," wrote the German poet, "rises out of its grave like a ghost from the past." *Italian Journey* (1786)

The Palazzo Giustinian in the 19th century (see opposite)

Foundations Building a city suspended over mud and water has always presented special problems. In the 6th century the chronicler Cassiodorus described how the Venetians built their houses "like seabirds' nests, half on sea and half on land." Vast numbers of piles still support Venetian buildings, sunk anything up to 100 feet deep to rest on the *caranto*, the layer of sand and clay that underpins most of the city's 118 islands (only the high tannin content of the piles stops them from rotting). Where the caranto proved too deep, barriers were erected while the site was drained and consolidated. A base known as the *zattaron* was then laid, a sandwich of larch timbers cemented with a mixture of rubble and brick. Over this went a layer of Istrian limestone, a water-resistant material which protected the buildings above from damp and mold.

Floors The precarious nature of Venice's foundations meant that few buildings could exceed three or four storys. Where they did, the result was often collapse—as with the Campanile—or a perilous lean. A palace's ground floor (the *piano terra*) usually had a gate opening on to a canal and a broad entrance hall, or *andron*, that ran the width of the building. The former allowed for deliveries and arrival by gondola, the latter for access to a walled garden or courtyard to the rear.

A grand staircase climbed up to the *mezzanino*, a labyrinth of small rooms used as offices, libraries, or living quarters. Above it lay the *piano nobile*, the grandest of the living areas, composed of suites of rooms arranged around the *portego*, a broad corridor that ran the entire width of the building. Like the *andron*, it gave access to rooms, but also encouraged cooling breezes during the dogdays of summer. The humbler story above was reserved for relatives or children. Above this again were the servants' quarters, storage rooms, and the kitchens, the last built at the top of houses to restrict damage in the event of fire. Roofs were usually laid with Roman-style pantiles, arranged on gently sloping timbers and hollow bricks. Stone gutters, or *gorne*, collected rainwater and fed it directly into a well. A few roofs still retain platforms (*altane*), once used by women to bleach their hair (see panel on page 111).

Facades A palace's waterfront facade was invariably the most elaborate (see panel) and rear facades, courtyards, and high-walled gardens were usually dreary by comparison. Facades were often the only part of a palace built or faced with stone (which as well as being costlier than brick was also heavier, and therefore a burden on foundations). Frontages were often rendered, either in pale gray (*rovigno*), or the more distinctive brick red known as *pastellone*. All were punctuated by large windows and balconies, markers for the *portego* and *piano nobile* within. Until about 1475 most were uniformly decorated, usually with Gothic filigree that owed much to the tracery of the Palazzo Ducale. After 1480 decoration changed markedly, as owners sought to emulate the round-arched windows, decorated pillars, and multi-colored roundels of the Palazzo's new east wing. Thereafter décor became increasingly individual, spawning the variety of grilles, capitals, pediments, friezes, and so forth that constitute the palaces' greatest glory. Palazzo Contarini del Bovolo, with its spiral staircase, is a stunning example.

Above: the Palazzo Giustinian by night
Below: typical Venetian windows

Chimneys An early type of Venetian chimney was the "inverted bell," designed to trap sparks and reduce the threat of fire. These were later replaced by the "cube" chimney, ringed by vents and topped by an elaborate cap. The Renaissance adopted the more stolid "obelisk" style.

*Peggy and one of her
many canine friends*

PET LIONS
The Palazzo Venier dei
Leoni takes its name from
the Vernier family's habit
of keeping exotic animals,
and lions (*leoni*) in particular, chained in the
palace's courtyard.

PEGGY GUGGENHEIM
Born in New York in
1898, copper heiress
Peggy Guggenheim fell in
love with avant-garde art
at an early age. Moving to
Europe in 1921, she
opened the Guggenheim-
Jeune Gallery in London
1938, collecting and selling work around Europe
until the outbreak of war.
Forced to return to the
U.S., she opened the Art
of This Century Gallery in
1942 (primary source of
the Venetian collection)
and embarked on a short-
lived marriage to the
painter Max Ernst. She
returned to Venice in
1949, becoming an
honorary citizen of the
city. She died in 1979.

▶▶ Collezione Peggy Guggenheim
(Palazzo Venier dei Leoni)
276C2

*Fondamente Venier or Calle S Cristoforo; Canal Grande
(Quay: Salute; Vaporetto 1; or Accademia; Vaporetti 1 or 82)
Open: Apr–Oct, Wed–Mon 10–6, Sat 10–10;
Nov–Mar, Wed–Mon 10–6 (Admission: expensive).*
Although only a few moments apart, the Accademia and
the Guggenheim, Venice's two most visited galleries,
offer the chance to view two collections whose outstand-
ing paintings could scarcely have less in common. After
the medieval sublimities of the Accademia, the
Guggenheim, created by the American heiress Peggy
Guggenheim, contains one of Europe's most important
collections of 20th-century art.

Palazzo Venier dei Leoni Before hurrying from the
Guggenheim's knitted wire gates to the gallery proper,
take a moment or two to reflect on its setting, the oddly
modern-looking Palazzo Venier, begun in 1749. Never
completed, hence its curiously truncated single story (and
its nickname, the *Nonfinito*, or Unfinished), it was
designed to house the Venier, one of Venice's most
illustrious families (a dynasty that since its ennoblement
in 1297 had furnished the city with three doges, including
the redoubtable Sebastiano, commander-in-chief of the
Christian fleet at the Battle of Lepanto).
Guggenheim was not the palace's first eccentric owner
(see panel), nor, for that matter, was this its first brush with
a woman inclined to the avant-garde. Earlier
this century the building

PEGGY GUGGENHEIM COLLECTIO
THE SOLOMON R. GUGGENHEIM FOUNDATION

belonged to one Marchesa Luisa Casati, a Milanese patron, socialite, and high priestess of the eccentric. A committed partygiver, she hosted bacchanals for the leading Futurists which involved spraying the palace's garden with lilac paint (plants and all), and filling it with apes, Afghan hounds, and gold-sprayed naked "slaves." Dressed by Russian ballet designer Basket, she liked to drift among her guests leading a pair of leopards, tangoing all the while to the accompaniment of a nude pianist.

No such *divertimenti* brighten up the garden today, which none the less remains a delightful place, filled with light, trees, statues, and birdsong. This may be the largest area of green shade you have seen for a while, one of the reasons for its great charm. The unexpected pleasure of so much space offers a little insight into the nature of Venice itself, whose cramped intimacy, the garden makes you realize, is quickly taken for granted. Sculptures here include works by Henry Moore, Paolozzi, Giacometti, and others, while on the south side the New Wing (1994) contains the museum store, a café overlooking the gardens, and space for temporary exhibitions.

The collection The Guggenheim is a museum with a high word-of-mouth reputation, particularly among American visitors. The collection itself, however, while of the highest quality, is not extensive, and the gallery's appeal has much to do with the charm of its setting (notably the garden) and the collection's sprightly and highly polished presentation.

Guggenheim's taste—which was both faultless and far-ranging—moved her to acquire representative works from virtually every modern art movement this century. Thus the collection's paintings are both varied and well chosen, but also display some particular strengths, notably in the first room on the right of the main entrance, where canvases by Salvador Dali, Max Ernst, and René Magritte are the most striking of the gallery's many Surrealist works. Cubism is represented by Picasso and Braque, Constructivism by Mondrian, Malevich, and Pevsner, English modernism by Francis Bacon, and the Americans by de Kooning, Pollock, Rothko, Still, and others. There are sculptures by Calder (a delicate silver bedhead in Peggy's former bedroom), Brancusi and Giacometti (gracing the garden), and works by Italians (notably Futurists such as Balla and Boccioni) and Venetians, such as Vedova, Tancredi, and Santomaso. Probably the most memorable work, however, is Marino Marini's startling *Angel of the Citadel*, provocatively placed facing the Grand Canal, so that his outstretched arms, and more to the point, his prominent erection, seem to be welcoming the staid world of Venice into the contemporary artistic fold.

CANINE CHUMS
Peggy Guggenheim took her adopted city to heart, even to the extent of indulging in Venetian women's apparently insatiable passion for small dogs. Her own grave at the rear of the garden is overshadowed by that of her canine pals—Carpaccio, Madam Butterfly, Sir Herbert, *et al*, whose headstone reads "Here Lie My Beloved Babies."

A provocative pose: Marino Marini's Angel of the Citadel

VIVA VERDI!

One way in which 19th-century opera-goers demonstrated their dislike of the Austrian occupation was to shout "Viva Verdi!," as the composer's name formed an acronym for *Vittorio Emanuele, Re d'Italia* (Victor Emmanuel, King of Italy). Another way was to shower the stage with bouquets of red, white, and green flowers (the colors of the Italian flag), or with flowers tied with ribbons corresponding to the Austrian flag—which the singers could then trample and kick contemptuously aside.

The interior of La Fenice —dramatic in its own right

▶ Fenice (Teatro La) 276C3

Campo San Fantin; Calle delle Veste (Quay: San Marco; Vaporetti 1, 82). Currently closed for restoration.

Although secondary to San Carlo in Naples, and currently outclassed by Milan's La Scala, Venice's La Fenice nonetheless still occupies a place among the first rank of Italian opera houses—or will do when it is rebuilt, for the entire building was gutted by fire (some believe deliberately) in 1996.

For a long time the city's leading theater, La Fenice takes its name from events at San Benedetto, Venice's principal opera house before it was gutted by fire in 1774. Bitter wrangling broke out between the old theater's managers and its owners, the Venier family: when the dispute was settled in the latter's favor, the disgruntled managers built their own theater, naming it La Fenice ("The Phoenix") to recall the resurrection of both company and opera house.

Gian Antonio Selva's neoclassical plan for the new theater, chosen from a total of 29 submitted, met with little approval on its realization in 1792. By the time the Fenice burned down for a second time, however (in 1836), the Venetians had grown used to their theater, and the building was rebuilt by Selva's pupils as a virtual copy of the original.

Since its inauguration, the theater has seen many moments of glory, including the first performances of Rossini's *Tancredi* (1813) and *Semiramide* (1823), Verdi's *Rigoletto* (1851), Stravinsky's *The Rake's Progress* (1951), and Benjamin Britten's *The Turn of the Screw* (1954). Verdi, despite a close association with the Fenice, suffered the indignity of boos and whistles at the opening of *La Traviata* (1853), a first night which even the composer described as a fiasco. Irate Italians were incensed at the production's poor singers and modern dress, but took particular exception to the absence of the anti-Austrian, pro-*Risorgimento* sentiments that infused Verdi's other operas—features that proved great crowdpleasers during the years of the hated Austrian occupation (see panel).

Marble deception: the Gesuiti's arresting trompe l'œil

WARMING SAINT
"In this dreary sanctuary is one of Titian's great paintings, *The Martyrdom of St. Lawrence*, to which ...you turn involuntarily, envious of the Saint toasting so comfortably on his gridiron amid all that frigidity." W D Howells, *Venetian Life* (1881)

► **I Gesuiti (Santa Maria Assunta)**   273D3
Campo dei Gesuiti (Quay: Fondamente Nuove; Motoscafi 41, 42, 51, 52). Open: daily 10–12, 5–7
As a religious order who liked to impress, the Jesuits (*Gesuiti*) can hardly have been pleased with the location of their church, whose huge facade appears rather forlorn in its peripheral and dilapidated surroundings. The shock troops of the Counter Reformation, they preferred the scale and richness of their churches to dazzle onlookers. Although firm papal favorites, they shared an uneasy relationship with Venice, where the Republic was neither cowed by the papacy nor influenced by its pronouncements ("Venetians first, Christians second" was a popular motto). Never was papal impotence more manifest than during the Interdict of 1606, when Rome excommunicated Venice and Venice expelled the Jesuits in retaliation.

By the time the order came to seek a home, the Republic had forbidden the building of new churches. The response, a typically sharp piece of Jesuitical maneuvring, was to buy an old church, destroy it, and then graft on an entirely new fabric (work was completed between 1715 and 1729). Its interior is one of the dankest spots in Venice, every corner weighed down by gloom and stillness. Just one feature stands out: the remarkable spread of marble *trompe l'œil* that covers most interior surfaces. It is best seen in the pulpit on the left, whose solid stone is carved to resemble pelmets, tassels, drapes, damask, carpets, and curtains in a masterpiece of decorative eccentricity.

Two interesting paintings lurk amidst the stonework: Tintoretto's *Assumption of the Virgin* (left transept) and Titian's *The Martyrdom of St. Lawrence* (first chapel on the left; see panel).

KITSCH MASTERPIECE
Little in Venice is as magnificently kitsch as the Gesuiti's high altar, "so baroque," in the words of Hippolyte Taine, "that one cannot help laughing." (*Voyage en Italie*, 1866). Its lumpish mix of heavy twirled columns and huge bulbous dome were paid for by the church's patrons, the Manin family, who were also responsible for producing Venice's lily-livered last doge. Several members of the family are interred beneath the altar.

Lido

LAWRENCE ON THE LIDO

"This was a holiday-place of all holiday-places. The Lido, with its acres of sun-pinked bodies or pyjamaed bodies, was like a strand with an endless heap of seals come up for mating. Too many people in the piazza, too many limbs and trunks of humanity on the Lido, too many motor-launches, too many steamers, too many pigeons, too many ices, too many cocktails, too many manservants wanting tips, too many languages rattling, too much sun, too much smell of Venice, too many cargoes of strawberries, too many silk-shawls, too many huge, raw slices of watermelon on stalls: too much enjoyment, altogether far too much enjoyment!"

D H Lawrence, *Lady Chatterley's Lover* (1928)

Once, the long curving sandspit (*lido*) that protects Venice from the open sea was a wild and windswept shore; years later its bathing establishments made it the height of 19th-century chic; these days it is nothing but a recreational refuge. It would be hard now to imagine Byron galloping on horseback along its empty dunes, or Thomas Mann's von Aschenbach installed in the *belle époque* splendor of the Grand Hôtel des Bains. Any romantic echoes it once had are drowned by the trundling of traffic, cheek-by-jowl beach facilities, residential housing, and big summer crowds. If you want an island adventure, visit Torcello; if you want a break from Venice, visit Padua or Verona; come to the Lido only if you want a beach, and only then if you are prepared to pay for the privilege and don't mind water of dubious cleanliness.

If you are curious, it is at least easy to get here, with car ferries running from the Tronchetto and regular *vaporetti* and *motoscafi* (Nos 1, 6, 52, 82) operating from San Zaccaria near San Marco. All boats dock at Santa Maria Elisabetta, from where buses run to several points on the island. If you want to explore further afield, bikes can be rented from several outlets. If you want to swim or lie on the beach, you will need to pay to enter one of the hotels or private *stabilimenti* that have a monopoly on most of the island's sand. Prices are high, but your money buys you the use of changing facilities, bars and showers, and usually guarantees clean and well-groomed sand. If you balk at the prices, there is a stretch of public beach (the *spiaggia comunale*) at the end of the main road that links the quays to the Lido's southern shore (roughly ten minutes' walk). The sand here, however, is likely to be pretty grimy.

You can play golf and tennis on the Lido, or go horseback-riding, parachuting, and claypigeon shooting, but otherwise it offers very little in the way of conventional

A 1918 postcard of the Lido; it had enjoyed its heyday before World War I

sightseeing. You might choose to visit the Casino or Palazzo del Cinema, two architectural dinosaurs of Fascist vintage, the latter used during August and September as the headquarters of the Venice Film Festival. The curious or the committed film buff might pass the Grand Hôtel des Bains, used as a setting in both the book and film of Thomas Mann's *Death in Venice*. Like its near neighbor, the Grand Hôtel Excelsior, it stands as a monument to the halcyon summers of the Lido's pre World War I heyday. The Lido's only "sights" are San Nicolò, an unexciting church, and a view across the water to the Fortezza di Sant'Andrea, once one of the lagoon's principal defensive bastions.

Marriage to the Sea One of Venice's most famous ceremonies, the Marriage to the Sea, took place for centuries close to the Lido's shores. It began on Ascension Day in the year 997 (1000 in some versions), when Doge Pietro Orseolo II set sail to attack Dalmatia, among the first dominions of Venice's fledgling empire. In its earliest form it was probably no more than a libation before battle. In time, though, it came to symbolize both Venice's naval power and the city's special relationship with the sea. After much on-shore pomp and ceremony, the doge would sail with his retinue into the lagoon. From the doge's barge, the *Bucintoro*, he would then drop a golden ring into the sea with the words: *"Desponsamus te, mare, in signum veri perpetuique dominii"* ("We espouse thee, O sea, in sign of our real and perpetual dominion over thee"). Divers then competed to find the ring, the winner—if any—earning relief from "all the burdens to which dwellers in the republic are subject." Doge and company would retire for a service in San Nicolò and then return for further carousing in the Palazzo Ducale.

Luchino Visconti's Death in Venice *starred* Dirk Bogarde

RIDING ROMANTICS
In his poem *Julian and Maddalo*, Shelley recalls riding on the still-pristine Lido with Byron (Maddalo):
"I rode one evening with
  Count Maddalo
Upon the bank of land
  which breaks the flow
Of Adria towards Venice: a
  bare strand
Of hillocks, heaped from
  ever-shifting sand,
Matted with thistles and
  amphibious weeds,
Such as from earth's
  embrace the salt ooze
  breeds,
Is this; an uninhabited
  sea-side,
Which the lone fisher,
  when his nets are dried
Abandons; and no other
  object breaks
The waste, but one dwarf
  tree and some stakes
Broken and unrepaired,
  and the tide makes
A narrow space of level
  sand thereon,
Where 'twas our wont to
  ride while day went
  down."
Percy Bysshe Shelley,
Julian and Maddalo
(1818)

Madonna dell'Orto's magnificent Gothic facade dates from the 15th century

CAMPO DEI MORI
This sleepy campo, just south of Madonna dell'Orto, may take its name from the Moorish merchants who traded on the *fondaco* near by, or from three brothers—Robia, Sandi and Alfani Mastelli—who left the Peloponnese (*Morea*) and its civil war to settle in Venice in 1112. The square contains three Moorish statues, two of which are embedded in the brothers' former *palazzo*, and a fourth—with a distinctive iron nose—known as Sior Antonio Rioba. Naive new arrivals in the city were told to "call" on Sior Antonio, and anonymous denunciations of the state were signed with his name and left pinned at his feet.

PAINTERS' PORTRAITS
The carriers of the calf in Tintoretto's *Making of the Golden Calf* have been tentatively identified as Giorgione, Titian, Veronese, Tintoretto (fourth from the left), and Sansovino (pointing on the right).

PAINTER'S PENANCE
A far-fetched legend—doubtless coined to explain Madonna dell'Orto's many Tintorettos—claims the painter was once forced to take refuge in the church. His crime was apparently to have added cuckold's horns to a portrait of a doge rejected by its sitter. The doge agreed to forgive the insult in return for Tintoretto decorating the church, expecting the commission to keep him quiet for several years. In fact it took him only six months.

►► Madonna dell'Orto   272B5
Fondamenta della Madonna dell'Orto (Quay: Madonna dell'Orto; Motoscafi 41, 42, 51, 52)
Open: Mon–Sat 10–5. Admission: inexpensive

Although Madonna dell'Orto is smaller than its near rivals, the Frari and Giovanni e Paolo, its Gothic facade—a vision of terracotta-hued brick and white Istrian marble—is the city's prettiest, while its airy interior is home to numerous fine paintings, not least several large canvases by Tintoretto, who is buried here with his son and daughter (this was the family's parish church).

The first church on the site was founded in 1350 by Fra Tiberio da Parma, head of the Umiliati order, and dedicated to St. Christopher, patron saint of travelers. It was rededicated to the Madonna in 1377, a change of heart inspired by a miracle-working statue of the Virgin found in an adjacent vegetable garden (*orto*).

St. Christopher still dominates the facade, his 15th-century statue above the portal attributed to the Florentine Nicolò di Giovanni. It was commissioned by the Scuola dei Mercanti (the Merchants' Guild), whose altar to the saint (their patron) lay inside the church. Perfectly suited to both Venice and merchants, Christopher was invoked against water, tempest and plague, and sudden death.

The elegant doorway, a Renaissance-tinged work by Bartolomeo Bon, marks a departure from the facade's predominantly Gothic flavor (most noticeable in the windows' filigree Gothic tracery). The niche statues, the work of the dalle Masegne brothers, represent the Apostles. Up above, the campanile's onion-shaped dome —a city landmark—bears clear witness to the Byzantine influence that infuses much Venetian achitecture.

Renovations in the interior have repaired the hack restoration work of the 19th century, a period that saw the church's pavement tombs ripped up and the wholesale demolition of the organ, once considered among the finest in Europe. The nave's Greek marble columns have also been stripped of their overpainting and returned to their pristine pearl-gray state (though they still lean alarmingly). In 1993, thieves stole Giovanni Bellini's great *Madonna and Child* from the first chapel on the left. A photograph and empty frame are its only memorials.

As a result the church's highlights now start with Cima da Conegliano's *St. John the Baptist* of 1493 (first altar on the right). Tintoretto's dramatic *Presentation of the Virgin* (1551) stands above the door at the end of the right nave, guarding the entrance to the dim and picture-choked Cappella di San Mauro. Here you can see the chubby Madonna responsible for the church's 14th-century rededication, a clumsily restored statue attributed to Giovanni de' Santi.

Back in the main church, the chapel to the right of the choir contains the **tomb of Tintoretto** and his children Domenico and Marietta (both of whom were also painters), marked by a simple slab and a bust of the artist. A wall separates him from two of his finest paintings, the choir's colossal *Last Judgement* and *The Making of the Golden Calf*. Four of the five *Virtues* to the rear are also by Tintoretto (the central figure, *Faith*, is unattributed). The artist completed the works free of charge, asking only for the cost of his materials. The apse's *Beheading of St. Paul* and *Vision of the Cross to St. Peter* are also by Tintoretto; the *Annunciation* is by Palma Giovane. The Cappella Contarini features yet another Tintoretto, the altarpiece of *St. Agnes Raising Licinius*.

CRITICAL GUSH

John Ruskin considered Tintoretto's *Last Judgement* the finest interpretation of the subject in Italian art, describing it as "...the river of the wrath of God, roaring down into the gulf where the world has melted with its fervent heat, choked with the ruin of nations, and the limbs of its corpses tossed out of its whirling, like water-wheels. Bat-like, out of holes and caverns and shadows of the earth, the bones gather, and the clay heaps heave, rattling and adhering into half-kneaded anatomies, that crawl and startle, and struggle up among the putrid weeds, with the clay clinging to their clotted hair, and their heavy eyes sealed by the earth-darkness."
Works (1904)

101

The church contains works by Tintoretto— as well as his earthly remains

PRACTICALITIES

Murano is just seven minutes by boat from Venice. Take the No 42 from the Fondamente Nuove (or board it at San Zaccaria or Piazzale Roma) and disembark at the Colonna quay. Then cross the Canal Grande di Murano at the end of the Fondamenta, bearing right on Fondamenta Cavour, which bends left to bring you to the Museo Vetrario and SS Maria e Donato. Murano can also be reached by boats 12 and 13. *Biglietti turistici*, valid for 12 hours, are available for the Laguna Nord, Murano, Burano and Torcello.

The church of Santi Maria e Donato on Murano was controversially restored in the 19th century

▶▶ Murano, Isola di   *271A3*

History Although settled during Roman times, the largest of the lagoon's islands first rose to prominence during the barbarian invasions of the 6th century. By the 10th century, Ammurianum was a prosperous trading center, and by 1276 it had become a virtually autonomous enclave within the Republic. It went on to mint its own coins, employ its own police force, and even to produce its own *Libro d'Oro*. Greater fame and still greater prosperity arrived in 1291, when Venice's glass furnaces were moved here as a precaution against fire (see pages 104–105).

Fondamenta dei Vetrai While Murano is not as appealing as Burano or Torcello, it is not as commercialized as most commentators often make out. After stepping off the boat, wander the kitsch-filled glass shops of the **Fondamenta dei Vetrai**, noting the lion-topped column by the second bridge, the Ponte Ballarin, Murano's symbolic center and the point from which government proclamations were read.

At the end of the Fondamenta stands **San Pietro Martire** (*Open* daily 8–noon, 1:30–6:30), a Dominican Gothic church begun in 1363 but rebuilt after a fire in 1474, and remodeled again in 1511. Remarkable at first glance for its marvelous Murano chandeliers, it is more famous for Giovanni Bellini's *Madonna and Child with Doge Barbarigo and Sts. Mark and Augustine* (1488), framed by damp-stained

The map shows the island of Murano with the following labeled features:

Campo Sportivo, Canale di Santa Maria, Cimitero Nuovo, Santa Maria degli Angeli, FOND SEBASTIANO VENIER, Canale degli Angeli, CAMPO S BERNARDO, CALLE CONTERIE, Canale di San Donato, C. DEL CONVENTO, FOND SEB SANTI, Cimitero, San Matteo, Rio San Mateo, SS Maria e Donato, Museo Vetrario, FOND LORENZO RADI, Venier, FONDAMENTA CAVOUR, Rio FOND, Sacca Serenella, Palazzo Da Mula, PONTE VIVARINI, Canal Grande, Museo, RIO DEI NAVAGERO, Palazzo Trevisan, Serenella, Canale Serenella, San Pietro Martire, FOND A COLLEONI, FOND MANIN, FOND ANDREA, Navagero, Canale Ondello, FOND SERENELLA, C.LLE BERTOLIN, FONDAMENTA dei VETRAI, Rio dei VETRAI, FONDAMENTA V GARIBALDI, FOND S GIOV DEI BATTUTI, Campo S Stefano, Faro, Colonna

0 200 400 m
0 200 400 yards

walls above the second altar on the right. On the opposite (north) wall, on the third and fourth altars respectively, are Veronese's *St. Agatha in Prison* and *St. Jerome in the Desert*. The door here leads right to the Sacristy Museum, well worth a look for its tremendous wooden carvings (1652–1656), an almost life-size collection of panels representing characters such as Caesar, Nero, Socrates, Pythagoras, and Pontius Pilate. (*Open* as main church. *Admission: inexpensive*).

Santi Maria e Donato (*Open* daily 9–noon, 4–6) Across Murano's main canal lies the **Museo Vetrario** (see page 105) and the nearby Santi Maria e Donato, the main reason, glass aside, for visiting the island. Founded in the 7th century, the church was restored in the 9th century and almost completely rebuilt in 1125, after the bones of St. Donatus, Bishop of Eurorea, were brought here from Cephalonia by Doge Domenico Michiel. Although overrestored, its interior and arcaded apse are still striking, particularly the latter, which was orientated towards the main canal to make it the first thing seen on arrival by sea.

The interior's beautiful mosaic floor (1141) is almost equally eye-catching, with its swirling patterns scattered with strange symbols and curious little narratives in glass. The apse mosaic, a lovely lone Madonna on a field of gold, is also from the 12th century. Behind the altar, just visible between its two columns, are a stacked set of bones, reputedly part of a dragon killed by St. Donatus with nothing more than a well-aimed gob of saintly spit. Elsewhere note the 6th-century gray marble pulpit on the left, and the relief in the north aisle of St. Donatus (dated 1310), a work commissioned by Donato Memo (then governor of Murano), who is shown kneeling alongside his wife.

The 12th-century mosaic floor of Santi Maria e Donato

Glass-making in the Venetian lagoon can be traced back to Roman times, but only acquired its special renown when Venice's foundries were moved to the island of Murano in 1291. Today the centuries-old tradition is as strong as ever, with glass of every size, shape, and color available in stores all over the city.

POISON
Murano glass was said to be so fine that it would break on coming into contact with even the smallest drop of poison.

GLASS DAGGER
Murano glass was used in the "Venetian dagger," one of the Middle Ages' nastiest weapons. Much loved by Venice's secret police, it consisted of a razor-sharp blade of glass, sheathed in metal, which when sunk into a victim's body would snap off at the shaft. The unfortunate's skin would close over the glass, leaving a wound apparently no more than an innocent graze at the point of entry.

Winged goblets of contemporary design from Murano

Murano glass Within years of achieving its glass-making monopoly, Murano became one of Europe's major centers of production, its glass being one of only a handful of home-produced commodities available to Venice for export. Special privileges accrued to its craftsmen as a result, including the right to wear swords, and immunity from the imprecations of the Ten (whose spies were forbidden to set foot on the island). Following a decree of 1376, glassblowers' daughters were allowed to marry the sons of Venetian patricians and enter the *Libro d'Oro* (unlike other cross-class marriages), while any male offspring of the union became eligible to sit on the *Maggior Consiglio*. So jealous was Venice of its trade secrets, however, that any Murano worker who set up a business in a rival city was declared a traitor and might be hunted down by state assassins (though in practice records show exiles trading quite happily, suffering no more than the sequestration of their Venetian assets and the brief imprisonment of their families).

Types of glass Murano began to export glass on a large scale in about the middle of the 14th century, specializing first in mirrors, on which it maintained a European monopoly for centuries. It then developed enameled glass (*smalto*), mostly in dark colors, and crystalline glass, noted for its extraordinary transparency. Later it invented aventurine, which used gold flux, and rediscovered *milfiori* ("a thousand flowers"), an ancient technique that involved mixing strands of colored and transparent glass. It also became known for a series of colored glasses (such as chalcedony) designed to resemble gemstones. These became so indistinguishable from the real thing that a decree was issued outlawing the manufacture of false gems.

Other innovations included a *ghiaccio*, which replicated the rough surface of ice; *graffitto*, in which motifs were scratched on to the glass's surface; *stellaria*, a glass threaded with copper crystals; *filigrana*, in which white glass was laid in patterns over a plain base; a milky glass called *lattimo* (from *latte*, meaning milk); and a blend of clear glass and *lattimo* known as *latticino*.

Decline Murano's decline began at the turn of the 16th century, when foreign glassmakers began to unravel the secrets of its prized crystalline glass. During the 17th and 18th centuries it also began to be overtaken by the innovations of producers in northern Europe. It was unable, for example, to compete with the new crystal glass coming out of Bohemia, or to produce a glass suitable for the popular cutting and faceting techniques being pioneered elsewhere. Even its famous mirrors, while as fashionable as ever, were superseded by ground glass mirrors from France. Terminal decline was arrested only in the 19th century, thanks principally to the work of families such as the Salviati, still one of the island's leading producers.

Glass Museum (*Open* Thu–Tue 10–4:30 (3:30 in winter), *Admission: moderate*) The Museo Vetrario, Italy's only glass museum, combines the history of glass-making on Murano, with a collection of antique exhibits that make an antidote to the more kitsch offerings of the island's modern-day producers. Housed in the gaunt 17th-century Palazzo Giustinian, the old bishops' palace, its ground floor contains fragments of Roman and foreign glass, a prelude to the displays on the first floor that describe how glass is made and contain some of the earliest surviving examples of Murano glass. The star turn is the famous Barovier Marriage Cup (1470–1480), a beautiful blue bowl of enameled glass decorated with portraits of the bride and groom, a hunting scene and a lovely turquoise fountain.

The Barovier Cup was created for a 15th-century Venetian wedding

SOMETHING IN THE AIR
Medieval writers struggled to explain the superiority of Murano glass: "... altho' one should transplant a Glass Furnace from Murano to Venice herself," wrote one, "or to any part of the Earth besides, and use the same materials, the same Workmen, the same Fuel, the self-same Ingredients every way, yet they cannot make Crystal Glass in that perfection, for beauty and lustre, as in Murano: Some impute it to the quality of the circum-ambient Air...o'er the Place..." James Howell, *Familiar Letters* (1621). Modern research attributes the glass's superiority to soda ash imported from Syria, which by 15th-century standards was of immensely high quality.

Walk

A circular walk from the Rialto (pages 272–273)

Start from the Ponte di Rialto. Walk north on Ruga degli Orefici, visiting San Giacomo and San Giovanni Elemosinario. Turn left on Ruga Vecchia San Giovanni and then right on Calle della Donzella and Calle dei Boteri to reach San Cassiano.

The **Rialto bridge** (see pages 134–135) leads directly into the lively market area wedged into the streets to the north. Picturesque **San Giacomo**, known for its pretty clock and five-columned portico, is reputedly the oldest church in the city (see page 135). **San Giovanni Elemosinario**'s high altar contains a fine Titian, *San Giovanni Giving Alms* (1545), while in the chapel to its right is a painting by Pordenone of St. Catherine and the plague saints Roch and Sebastian. **San Cassiano**, once the focus of Venice's red-light district (see page 159), has a *Crucifixion, Resurrection* and *Descent into Limbo* by Tintoretto.

Take Calle del Campanile and the Riva dell'Olio to see the fish markets of the Pescheria, then take the traghetto to Santa Sofia. Turn left on to the Strada Nova and look into San Felice before doubling back to turn left at Campo dei Testori. Follow Calle Larga Doge Priuli and Fondamenta Santa Caterina to the Gesuiti.

After walking on the Riva dell'Olio, which takes its name from the oil once unloaded here, cross the Grand Canal by boat and see the **Ca' d'Oro** (see pages 74–77). **San Felice** has a painting of St. Demetrius by Tintoretto (third altar on the right). Crossing the bridge to the Fondamenta Santa Caterina, look to the left for a delightful view of the church of Santa Maria Valverde across the Canale della Misericordia. The area around the **Gesuiti** (see page 97) is somewhat forlorn, but the church

is worth a look for its extraordinary *trompe l'œil* marble and Titian's dark *Martyrdom of St. Lawrence*. Depending upon the time available you might take a boat to Murano (see pages 102–105) from the Fondamente Nuove to the north. The journey takes seven minutes.

Thread through the maze of streets southeast of the Gesuiti to reach San Canciano. Walk to Santa Maria dei Miracoli via Campo Santa Maria Nova. Cut back to Campo Santi Giovanni e Paolo via Calle Larga Giacinto Gallina.

San Canciano is a dull church in one of Venice's nicer, less-visited, corners. The church of the **Miracoli** is a tiny jewel, its marbled facades beautifully complemented by an intimate interior (see page 170). **Santi Giovanni e Paolo** is one of Venice's largest churches, crammed with outstanding tombs and funerary monuments (see pages 146–151). To its left is the old **Scuola Grande di San Marco** (now a hospital), fronted by one of the city's most attractive facades. Verrocchio's equestrian statue of the mercenary general Bartolomeo Colleoni commands the adjoining square (see pages 152–153).

Take Fondamenta Dandola from Campo Santi Giovanni e Paolo and turn left on Fondamenta Sanudo to Campo di Santa Marina. Take Calle Scaletta from the corner of the campo and follow the alleys west to Salizzada San Giovanni and San Giovanni Crisostomo. Return to the Ponte di Rialto via Campo San Bartolomeo.

Pop into Corte Seconda il Milion, a little courtyard by the Teatro Malibran, to see the plaque that records the site of Marco Polo's house (see pages 203–205). **San Giovanni Crisostomo**, an often overlooked Renaissance church, is best known for a painting of *Seven Saints* (1508–1511) by Sebastiano del Piombo (on the high altar) and Giovanni Bellini's outstanding last work, *Sts. Christopher, Jerome, and Louis of Toulouse* (right aisle).

The Rialto was the only bridge across the Grand Canal until the 19th century

106

Many of the museum's
exhibits will mean more if
you already know a little
about the city, so you may
wish to visit the museum
towards the end of your
stay in Venice. Then, for
example, you can
compare the naval section
with the Museo Storico
Navale, or perhaps better
understand the collection
of ducal costumes in the
context of the festivals or
ceremonies for which they
were worn.

▶▶ Museo Civico Correr   277E3

*Procuratie Nuove; Piazza San Marco (Quay: San Marco;
Vaporetti 1, 82)*
*Open: daily Apr–Oct 9–7, Nov–Mar 9–5. Admission: expen-
sive (joint ticket with Palazzo Ducale—see page 118—and
other city museums)*

The collection The Correr is a relatively overlooked
museum, yet it contains the finest art gallery in the city
after the Accademia, and a fascinating assortment of
well-displayed artifacts that cover some of the most
interesting aspects of Venice's long history. Founded by
Teodoro Correr, a Venetian worthy, its collection was
left to the city in 1830 and opened to the public in
1922 as the "Museum of the City and the Civilization of
Venice." The highly enjoyable exhibits fill up over
50 rooms on two floors of the Palazzo Reale, the first

floor devoted to the Neoclassical Rooms and Venetian Civilization, the second to the Picture Gallery and the Museo del Risorgimento (currently closed for restoration). The Museo Archeologico (see page 133) and the Libreria Sansovina (see page 132–133) can be accessed from the first floor beyond the section on Venetian Civilization. The museum's entrance is at the western end of the Piazza di San Marco, up the grand staircase that once led to the state rooms of the Ala Napoleonica.

First floor The neo-classical galleries of the first floor make an ideal setting for the works of the sculptor Antonio Canova. The main gallery displays plaster-casts representing episodes from the Homeric poems and Plato's *Phaedo*, as well as a self-portrait. The gallery ends with the cast of Paris, with peculiar black studs used as points of reference by assistants marking up blocks of marble in readiness for the Master. Taking center stage in the Throne Room (Room 4) is one of Canova's earliest masterpieces, a wonderful group showing Daedalus fixing a pair of flimsy wings to Icarus' arms (carved in 1779 when the sculptor was just 22). Rooms 6–18 are devoted to Venetian life and culture. The first two focus on the doge, with portraits, paintings of processions, rituals, and historic events in the lives of the doges. Venice and the Sea are the themes of Rooms 12 and 13. A rare 18th-century watercolor by Antonio di Natale (left wall) shows a plan of the Arsenale in the 18th century, a time when secrecy shrouded the shipyards. Room 14 has an interesting collection of plans, including the astonishingly accurate aerial view of Venice of 1497–1500 by Jacopo de' Barbari, reproductions of which are in print stores all over the city (the original wood block from which it was printed is in the same room). On the wall opposite is G. B. Arzenti's vast painted view, complete with one of the doges' ceremonial boats (the *Bucintoro*) in the right foreground. Armory, trophies, and loot taken from the Turks are followed by four rooms displaying an extensive collection of miniature Renaissance bronzes.

The remaining rooms focus on the *Bucintoro*, Venetian Festivals, and Arts and Trades. Don't miss the little case devoted to footwear. Here you can admire some of the

MUSEO DEL RISORGIMENTO
This small but well-presented museum on the Correr's third floor contains a wealth of memorabilia relating to Venice's 19th-century struggle against the Austrians, and especially the revolt of Daniele Manin and the city's subsequent journey towards integration with a united Italy. From one of its windows there is a beautiful view of San Giorgio Maggiore.

DOGE'S DUCKS
Until the 16th century the oaths taken by doges at their coronation bound them to present each of Venice's noble families with five ducks on New Year's Day. By 1521 the city's swollen aristocracy demanded some 9,000 ducks annually, a quota it became increasingly difficult to fill in one fell swoop. The doges began instead to issue small silver medals, or *oselle*, from the Venetian dialect word for "bird" (*uccello* in Italian). Their design altered from year to year, usually to take account of a notable event in the Venetian calendar.

109

Far left: Doge Giovanni Mocenigo models a ducal hat—known as a corno *—in a portrait by Gentile Bellini*

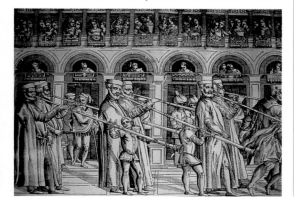

Left: the procession of the royal cortège

Canova's Daedalus and Icarus

famous clogs (*zoccoli* or *ciapine*) which so excited the interest of early visitors. Many speculated on the function of these peculiar elevated shoes, one pair of which on display here is well over 18 inches tall. Thomas Coryat, writing in 1608, described them as so common "that no woman whatsoever goeth without them." They were, he wrote, "a thing made of wood, and covered with leather of sundry colours, some with white, some redde, some yellow...Many of them are curiously painted...so uncomely a thing (in my opinion) that it is a pitty this foolish custom is not cleane banished and exterminated out of the citie." He also reported that the more noble a woman, the higher her clogs, and that "wives and widowes that are of any wealth, are assisted by men or women when they walke abroad, to the end they may not fall." John Evelyn, writing in the 1640s, also observed that women had to "set their hands on the heads of two matron-like servants or old women to support them." The clogs, he suggested, were to prevent infidelity, invented to keep women "at home, it being very difficult to walke with them." Like many, he found the fashion laughable. The footwear, he said, made Venetian women "*mezzo carne, mezzo ligno*" (half flesh, half wood) adding that "'tis ridiculous to see how these ladys crawl in and out of their *gondolas* by reason of their *choppines*, and what dwarfs they appeare when taken down from their wooden scaffold." Richard Lassels, a Catholic priest visiting Venice in 1654, felt the wearing of clogs, on the whole, "was good policy, and a pretty ingenious way either to clog women absolutely at home by such heavy shoes; or at least to make them not able to go farre, or alone, or invisibly." In fact, the fashion probably had less to do with preventing immorality and more to do with circumventing the sumptuary laws that forbade long trains. By wearing high shoes women could add huge amounts of material to their dresses and still comply with the law that allowed hems to reach only as far as their "heels."

Second floor Although the Correr's art gallery contains fewer well-known works than the Accademia, its best paintings—especially the earlier 14th- and 15th-century works—can easily stand comparison with any others in the city. Its most popular picture is Carpaccio's *Two Women* (1507, see page 158), a masterful study of ennui, known for many years as *The Courtesans*, due to its protagonists' plunging necklines and boudoir-like surroundings. Both décor and décolletage, however, were common features of the rooms and costume of the period (see panel opposite): the women are now thought to be portraits of a mother and daughter. Note the painting's wealth of incidental detail, especially the shoes (see above), and the women's teased blonde hair. The latter was a prized commodity in Renaissance Venice, but not one that habitually dark- or auburn-haired Venetian

ANTONIO CANOVA
At the age of 19, under the auspices of his first patron, Giovanni Falier, Antonio Canova (1757–1822) was already regarded as Venice's finest sculptor. After a plethora of commissions he left the city for Rome, where the influence of British artists led him to abandon his early naturalistic style. Within ten years his international reputation was established, and many considered him the greatest sculptor since classical times. Only his heart is buried in Venice (in the Frari); his tomb is in Possagno in the Veneto.

women were born with (see panel opposite). Much of the hair sported by Venetian women was in fact false, having been bought from peasants who sold swags of their hair from poles in Piazza San Marco.

The ladies share their little room with *St. Peter the Martyr*, also by Carpaccio, an unlikely companion, given that he was a Dominican zealot murdered with the skull-splitting cleaver clearly visible in the painting. The following room contains another often reproduced work, again attributed to Carpaccio, *The Man in the Red Hat* (also attributed to Lorenzo Lotto).

Other paintings to look out for include works by Alvise Vivarini and the Bellini brothers, a beautiful *Madonna* (1525) by Lorenzo Lotto, a tiny *Pietà* (1468) by Cosmè Tura, and another *Pietà* (1475–1476) by the Sicilian painter Antonello da Messina. Among the most influential painters to visit Venice, Antonello bequeathed to the city's artists some of the Tuscan influences and oil-painting techniques he had acquired during his apprenticeship (the latter partly learned from studying some of the Flemish painters represented elsewhere in the gallery). The *Pietà*, however, is the only one of his paintings still in Venice.

Visits end with the Museo del Risorgimento, covering the history of Venice from the fall of the Republic in 1797 up to its annexation with the unified kingdom of Italy in 1866.

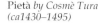

Pietà *by Cosmè Tura (ca1430–1495)*

From galleys to gondolas, the Lido to Lepanto, Venice would have been nothing without its boats. And without the Arsenale, long the world's largest shipyard, it would have been unable to build the galleys and merchantmen that formed the cornerstone of its maritime empire.

SEEING THE ARSENALE

Plans have been in place for years to turn the Arsenale into a museum or cultural center, but for the foreseeable future it seems certain to remain closed to the public, and *motoscafi* no longer take the route through the Canale dell'Arsenale. You can, however, glimpse its interior though the marvelous gateway at Campo dell'Arsenale.

112

This anonymous 16th-century painting suggests the huge scale of Venice's shipyards

Words and dates *Arsenale* comes from the Arabic *darsina'a*, meaning "house of industry," though when the word entered the language, or when the city's first shipyards saw the light of day, remains a mystery. Some form of centralized yard probably existed as early as 1102, but as late as 1320, when a building on the present site is first documented, much of the Republic's state shipping was still being built at private workshops (*squeri*) around the city. Even at this early stage, however, the importance of Venice's shipping was such that the state laid down construction specifications, and during times of crisis was able to pressgang freelance carpenters and caulkers to work in government yards.

Expansion During the 14th century, the Arsenale turned to the construction as well as the repair of ships, and in time established a state monopoly on the light galleys, or *galere sottili*, that formed the backbone of the Venetian fleet. The Republic also controlled the yard's merchant ships (the *da mercati*), which—though leased to traders—remained in state ownership, ready to be fitted for war in times of emergency.

By 1420, 300 different shipping companies were registered at the yards, and between them were responsible for over 3,000 vessels of 200 tons or more, and able to call on a workforce of over 16,000 men—equivalent to

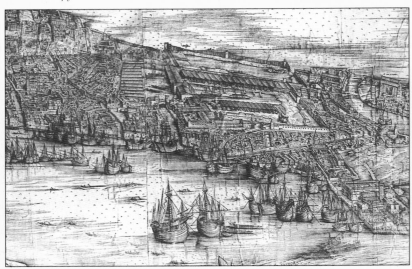

the population of most Italian towns of the period. In a city almost unique at the time for having no major fortifications, the Arsenale's great walls and battlemented towers were also the nearest Venice came to a fortress. It even had its own water supply, kept perpetually pure, it was alleged, by two rhinoceros horns thrown into its well to ward off evil spirits.

Workers As cogs in Venice's most vital industry, the Arsenale's workers, or *arsenalotti*, were considerably more circumscribed than the city's lesser artisans. Then as now, the yard was a proscribed area (see panel), its three-mile outer wall penetrated by just one gateway from land and sea. Workers were privy to classified information, and as such had to undergo security checks, which proved so effective that the Republic managed to keep its shipbuilding techniques secret until 1550. During the last days of the Republic, by contrast, corruption was so rampant that it is estimated that enough wood disappeared from the yards annually to build ten complete galleys.

As a reward for their loyalty, the *arsenalotti* were regarded as an industrial élite, not only receiving some of the city's highest wages, but also enjoying privileges that included crewing the *Bucintoro* (the doge's ceremonial boat) and serving as pallbearers at state funerals. They formed the guard of honor during the election of a new doge, and had the job of carrying the new incumbent around Piazza San Marco after his inauguration. They were also renowned firefighters, formed a reserve naval corps, stood guard over the *Maggior Consiglio* (see page 32), and enjoyed free or low-rent accommodation in specially built houses near the Arsenale (some of the earliest model houses).

Modern methods The workers in the Arsenale were arranged in teams, much as on a modern shop floor, each gang consisting of 15 caulkers, 12 carpenters, six sawyers, two manual laborers and a handful of

The entrance to the Arsenale in 1740

ARSENALE LIONS
Four lions line up in front of the Arsenale's Porta Magna, diminishing neatly in size from left to right. They replaced the famous bronze horses that stood here before they were removed to the Basilica di San Marco. The two on the right date from the 6th century BC and were probably pilfered from Delos (the left-hand one was installed to celebrate the recapture of Corfu in 1716). The larger pair were stolen from Athens in 1687 by Francesco Morosini after the successful campaign in Morea (the Peloponnese).

The Arsenale

The imposing gateway to the Arsenale

THE ARSENALE GATE

Remarkably few people walk the short distance from the Museo Navale and Riva degli Schiavoni to see the Porta Magna, the Arsenale's magnificent main gateway. Built by Antonio Gambello in 1460, and based on a drawing by Jacopo Bellini, it was the first monument in Venice to abandon the Gothic tradition in favor of newer Renaissance idioms. In its basic form it copies a Roman triumphal arch, though the principal columns are 12th-century Venetian-Byzantine originals. Much of the sculpture was added subsequently. Note that the book of the Venetian lion above the gate is closed, perhaps because its traditional message of peace (*Pax tibi...*) was deemed unsuitable for the Arsenale's martial purpose.

apprentices. Production line techniques allowed a phenomenal output, with one squad being able to turn out a good-sized *da mercato* every three months. Standardized parts, such as masts, spars, pulleys, and rowing benches, also meant that ships could be repaired, converted, or brought out of reserve at immense speed. In 1570, for example, when Cyprus was threatened by the Turks, 100 galleys were produced in just two months (a rate of more than one a day). And in 1574, when Henri III visited Venice, he was shown a keel being laid in the morning which by evening had been built, equipped, and made ready for the open sea. Such was the superiority of Venetian ship-building that fully half the ships arraigned against the Turks at the Battle of Lepanto were constructed in the Arsenale's yards.

Decline Even during the Arsenale's 15th-century heyday, developments such as the opening up of the Americas, the growing power of the Turks, and Vasco da Gama's discovery of a new trade route to the East all signaled the end of Venice's maritime supremacy. In just 40 years between 1560 and 1600 the volume of merchant shipping registered at the Arsenale halved, and by 1755 the yards had even been forced to abandon Venice's traditional galleys in favor of British-designed 30-, 40-, and 70-gun frigates.

Napoléon turned his destructive ire on the Arsenale in 1798. He burned the docks, sank the last *Bucintoro*, and made off with the Venetian fleet in an attempt to invade Ireland (when this failed he returned the ships to the Mediterranean, where they were promptly sunk by Nelson at the Battle of Aboukir). The equally reviled Austrians rebuilt the docks, which remained operative until 1917, when they were destroyed again, this time, ironically, by the Venetians themselves, who were desperate to prevent them from falling into the hands of the approaching Austrians. These days the yards belong to the Italian navy, their old sheds and canals now a trifle sad and overgrown.

14

►► Museo Storico Navale 275F1

Riva San Biagio (Quay: Arsenale; Vaporetto 1; Motoscafi 41, 42)
Open: Mon–Fri 8:30–1:30, Sat 8:30–1, closed Sun. Admission:
inexpensive (includes admission to the Padiglione)

Venice's Museo Navale is not only one of the world's largest displays of maritime ephemera, but is also among the most enjoyable of all the city's museums. A rambling collection places Venice and the sea, its inseparable ally, into a vividly presented historical context. See the main museum first, arranged over four floors of a former granary, and then walk a couple of minutes down the Fondamenta dell'Arsenale to see the boats housed in the Arsenale's old oarmakers' shed, the **Padiglione delle Navi** (see panel). This will also give you a chance to look at the Arsenale's main gateway (see panel on page 114), just across the canal from the Padiglione.

The **ground floor** opens with miniature manned torpedoes, moving on through models of Venetian forts and a bristling collection of cannon, mortars, and machine-guns. The **first floor** starts with the bell used in the Arsenale from 1597 to 1910 to mark the beginning and end of each working day, progressing through rooms of instruments, fragments of boats and a vast range of models, some of the most interesting of which are the oar-driven galleys, or *triremi*, that formed the core of the Venetian fleet.

More models scatter the **second floor**, along with uniforms, medals, flags, pendants, paintings and diagrams, unexploded bombs, (from the Austrian bombardments of 1915) and more. Save some time for the room on the **third floor** given over to gondolas. A shimmering collection of shells awaits on the mezzanine above, together with fine views on to the Arsenale and a display devoted to the unexpectedly close links between the maritime traditions of Venice and Sweden.

PADIGLIONE DELL...

On no account miss wonderful collection boats or its evocative setting. The vast old oarmakers' shed contains painted fishing boats from the lagoon, numerous gondolas, a *sagomo a invaso* (the molding cradle used to build gondolas), the boiler of an old steamer (which looks like the guts of some iron dinosaur) and—best of all—the beautiful black and yellow funeral barge used until 1940 to take the coffins of *arsenalotti* to San Michele from San Biagio. San Biagio, the Venetian navy's chapel, is the church immediately to the right of the main museum.

PRODUCTION LINE

During the Middle Ages the Arsenale was one of the city's principal tourist attractions. One 15th-century Spanish visitor, who felt there was "nothing finer in the world," described the yard's production line techniques: "...there is a great street on either hand with the sea in the middle, and on one side are windows opening out of houses of the arsenal ...out came a galley towed by a boat, and from the windows they handed out to them, from one the cordage, from another the bread, from another the arms, and from another the ballistas and mortars, and so from all the sides everything which was required, and when the galley had reached the end of the street all the men required were on board, together with a full complement of oars, and she was equipped from end to end." Pero Tafur, *Travels and Adventures* (1435–1439)

A scale model of the Bucintoro, *the doge's barge*

No single sight more immediately conjures up an image of Venice than the gondola. A perfect mesh of function and design, it has evolved over centuries, and continues to seize the imagination of visitors prepared to endure stratospheric prices and sub-standard serenading in order to share in one of the world's great romantic adventures.

FACTS AND FIGURES
All gondolas are 35.65 feet long and 4.66 feet wide. The right-hand side is 9 inches longer than the left. Each weighs 1540lbs and comprises 280 separate components. The hull is protected by seven coats of paint. Eight types of wood are used in their construction: elm, oak, fir, lime, larch, walnut, cherry, and mahogany. A ninth, beech, is used for the oar.

Origins The first documentary reference to gondolas occurs in 1094, in a decree designed to regulate the wide range of flat-bottomed boats rowed across the lagoon (though a few scholars claim a lineage dating from 697). According to a Venetian poem, they were created when a crescent moon tumbled from a starlit sky to shelter a pair of dewy-eyed lovers. Less romantic commentators claim they have Turkish origins, others that they originated in Malta. Some say the word came from the Greek for cup or mussel, others that it was the name given to Charon's ferry of the dead.

In truth the gondola probably evolved gradually, slowly adapting itself to the special needs of Venice's shallow and sharply angled waterways. In the 13th century, for example, a gondola was a 12-oared, iron-pronged boat; by the 15th century it was smaller and had gained a cabin, or *felze*; a few years later it had acquired such a wealth of ornamentation—silk cushions, gilded prows and carving-choked hull—that a sumptuary law was introduced in 1562 to curb the rampant and ruinously expensive ostentation.

The Venetian gondola; an expensive but comfortable means of transport

Far right: the ferro of a gondola, as much a symbol of Venice as the lion of St. Mark

Mystery Following this legislation, gondolas became a uniform black, their only decoration a curly tail, a *hippocampus* (seahorse) on each side, and the mysterious, multi-pronged *ferro* on the front. Its six prongs facing ahead traditionally represent Venice's six *sestieri* (neighborhoods), although some have only five prongs. The single prong facing fore symbolizes the Giudecca, Piazza San Marco, Cyprus, or the Doge's Palace. The trumpet-shaped blade signifies, according to preference, a lily, the sea, the doge's hat, a Venetian halberd, or the Ponte di Rialto. The *ferro's* origins may lie in a judicial axe, part of a Roman galley, or a symbol once found on Egyptian funerary barges. Its original purpose, if any, may have been to balance the boat, to gauge the height of bridges, or to act as decoration. The metal strip along a gondola's stem, by the way, is said to represent either the Grand Canal or the "History of Venice."

The present The refinement that gave the gondola its present appearance was added as late as the 19th century, when a small boatyard near San Sebastiano began to build boats with one side longer than the other. The resulting shape, with its lop-sided lean and distinctive asymmetry, served to counter the weight of the gondolier and, where necessary, to accommodate two or more rowers. The flat-bottomed hull enables boats to navigate shallow canals and be freed easily from mudbanks, allows greater speed and, as gondolas have no keels, provides a pivot that permits boats to turn sharply on their axis. As a result, only two spots in Venice are said to be beyond the gondola's reach: one near the Fenice, the other close to San Stae.

The future There were some 10,000 gondolas in the 16th century; today there are only a few hundred, together with a handful of subsidized boatyards. Only four or five new boats are made annually, most of them bought by foreigners. A gondolier must also make his living in only a few months. While summer takings are high, winter pickings are virtually non-existent (bear this in mind as you bemoan the price of your gondola ride). Boats may also have to be cleaned every three weeks, and can warp beyond repair in less than five years, whereupon they are either pensioned off as *traghetti* across the Grand Canal, or burned in the glass furnaces of Murano.

FORCOLA
The gondola's sensuously curved oar rest, or *forcola*, is made from a solid piece of walnut. Its cradle, which is oiled and carved to suit each individual gondolier, allows the oar to be used in at least eight different positions.

STANDING UP
According to tradition gondoliers stand up because the Venetians are by nature a watchful race. In fact by standing they are better able to survey the water and Venice's treacherous mudflats, and can use their oars like punting poles in the shallower canals.

DOGE CALIMERO

Palazzo Ducale

SPOT THE JOIN
The two wings of the Palazzo Ducale—one facing the water, the other the Piazzetta—appear virtually identical at first glance. In fact they were built in two phases, from 1340 to 1419 and 1422 to 1460. By looking at the seventh column on the Piazzetta side, which is fatter than the rest, you can see where the two portions were joined.

MAILING ADDRESS
Even today, almost 300 years after the fall of the Republic and the last doge, the Palazzo Ducale is still the city's premier building—at least in the eyes of the post office: its address is 1 San Marco.

▶▶▶ Palazzo Ducale (Doge's Palace)   *277F3*

Piazzetta San Marco (Quay: San Zaccaria; Vaporetti 1, 82; Motoscafo 52)
Open: daily Apr–Oct 9–7 (last admission 5:30), Nov–Mar 9–5 (last admission 3:30). Admission: expensive

Opinions on the Palazzo Ducale (or Doge's Palace) have rarely wavered, invariably lauding the thousand-year-old home of Venice's erstwhile rulers and countless functionaries of state. For John Ruskin it was the "central building of the world," for Henry James "the loveliest thing in Venice," a place where all the city's "splendid stately past glows around you in a strong sea-light." For the modern visitor, however, much of the palace may prove a disappointment. While the exterior, a masterpiece of Italian Gothic, is captivating, the interior has been much restored over the years. Room follows room in an almost identical parade—like "so many small cupboards containing yet more cupboards," in the words of Gore Vidal. All are beautifully decorated, yet the overall effect is somewhat lifeless, a sense of real history emerging only when you enter the prisons at the end of the tour.

However, the palace is unmissable, and a visit is not as intimidating as the building's size and fame might suggest. As a rough plan, you should first wander around the exterior, take in the features of the inner courtyard, and then tackle the interior, where a clear itinerary guides you from room to room. Finally, be sure to take a turn around the outer loggia, a wonderful belvedere for the Piazzetta, San Marco, and the Riva degli Schiavoni.

History The first ducal palace, built in 814, was a dour fortress constructed on one of the few clay redoubts to poke above the lagoon's atmosphere of mud and marsh. Entered by drawbridge, and guarded by water on all sides, its massive fortifications were to prove no defence against two catastrophic fires in 976 and 1106. By 1419 the palace was in its third incarnation, only a few foundations having survived from the earlier buildings.

Around 1340, when work began on a hall for the *Maggior Consiglio*, the palace—at least on its seaward side—began to take on its present appearance. Three years after the hall's completion (in 1422) the Senate decided to bring the rest of the building up to scratch, or to create, as they put it, a "more noble edifice." To this end, part of the old palace was destroyed and a new facade was continued on the Piazzetta frontage to match the 1419 building (see panel). The courtyard and interior, which had grown rapidly as the machinery of state expanded, were both rebuilt by Antonio Rizzo after a fire in 1483 (see panel on page 119). Work was more or less completed by 1550.

In 1574 and 1577, fire again gutted much of the interior, threatening the building with collapse and destroying masterpieces by some of Venice's greatest painters. Plans were drawn up to rebuild the palace completely, with Palladio, who proposed a High Renaissance folly, earmarked as architect. In the event, the plan was abandoned, and a more modest restoration entrusted to Antonio da Ponte, the engineer responsible for the Ponte di Rialto (see pages 134–135). Another restoration project ensued in the 1880s, a huge scheme that involved replacing many of the exterior columns and their beautifully carved capitals.

The Ponte della Paglia and the magnificent exterior of the Palazzo Ducale

The exterior Although the Palazzo's interior may disappoint, there is no denying the glory of its exterior, among the most beautiful of Italy's Gothic buildings. Architectural daring accounts for much of its impact, turning convention on its head by putting the building's bulk (the upper story) above rather than below the pair of lighter multi-columned loggias. Some have seen the arrangement as a symbol of Venice itself, a city built on piles, with the loggias' columns representing a prop for the great edifice of state.

Porta della Carta The main entrance to the palace has the mysteriously named Porta della Carta (see panel), on the Piazzetta (the public entrance is now the Porta del Frumento on the Riva degli Schiavoni). A magnificently flamboyant Gothic gateway (1438–1443), it was designed by Bartolomeo Bon and commissioned by Doge Francesco Foscari, the figure nestling alongside the lion of St. Mark (the portal, incidentally, contains a total of 75 lions). His

RIZZO'S RIP-OFF
During Antonio Rizzo's restoration of the Palazzo Ducale in 1496 it was discovered that not only had he spent 80,000 ducats and completed only half the work, but also that he had embezzled some 12,000 ducats in the process. As a result he was forced to flee to Emilia-Romagna, dying soon after in Foligno.

The Archangel Michael on the corner of the Palace

RED COLUMNS

The two red columns on the Palazzo's Piazzetta facade were reputedly stained crimson by the blood of criminals, whose tortured bodies were stretched out between them before execution. Sentences of death were proclaimed here, and Filippo Calendario (d.1355), one of the palace's master builders, was hanged and quartered between the pillars for his part in the Marino Falier conspiracy.

PORTA DELLA CARTA

The name of this gate— the Gate of Paper—may derive from the archives that were kept near by, from the clerks' stall set up here, or from the petitioners who would wait outside to hand their requests to members of the palace's many councils.

kneeling position supposedly symbolizes the obsequious attitude of the individual to the state. The other statues represent Temperance, Fortitude, Prudence, and Charity.

Much of the gate was originally gilded and painted, a decorative veneer now lost along with the original statues of Foscari and his lion (the present sculptures are 19th-century copies). The originals were smashed as symbols of state oppression in 1797, an act of vandalism carried out by the city's chief stonemason. Keen to show his loyalty to the Napoleonic regime, his herculean aim was to remove all the lions of St. Mark from the city. His hammer spared the little red cluster of embracing knights, or tetrarchs, on the left, a group of mysterious origin (see panel). The **Pietra del Bando**, the stump of a column on the corner of the basilica (behind you on the left), was used to proclaim the laws of the Republic (see panels on pages 65 and 134).

To enjoy the building in the first instance, dodge the people and pigeons and walk to the **Ponte della Paglia** (Bridge of Straw), located at the end of the palace's waterfront facade. On the way note the too-squat pillars (36 in all), whose lower reaches have been buried over the centuries as the sea level has risen (there are five pavements below the level of the present piazza). Note, too, the handsome Islamic-inspired patterning of the stonework, a mixture of Istrian stone and pink Veronese marble. The elaborate window at the center of the facade, topped by a statue of Justice (1579), dates from 1404.

Sculpture At the bridge you can jostle with photographers and other visitors for a view of the **Ponte dei Sospiri**, or Bridge of Sighs, of which you will see the inside later. For the moment, look up at the sculpture on the corner of the palace, the first of three thematically linked carvings, one on each of the palace's three corners. The first, above you to the left, shows *The Drunkenness of Noah* (with the Archangel Raphael above); the second, on the palace's far corner, depicts *Adam and Eve* (with the Archangel Michael); the third, near the palace's entrance, portrays *The Judgement of Solomon*.

The first two pieces you will see are by anonymous Venetian sculptors: the third, probably carved after its neighbors (ca1410), has recently been attributed to the great Sienese sculptor Jacopo della Quercia. All three works had a didactic purpose, representing Compassion (Noah's sons are shown covering their father's nakedness), Severity (the expulsion of Adam and Eve from Paradise), and Justice (the wisdom of Solomon). Noah represents human frailty, while the Archangel Michael symbolizes the protection of humanity from temptation.

Courtyard Enter the palace on the lagoon side which brings you into the courtyard. Walk across the courtyard to the **Scala dei Giganti**, or Giants' Staircase (1484–1501). Designed by Antonio Rizzo, it was named after Sansovino's large statues of *Mars and Neptune* (1567), symbols of Venice's mastery of land and sea. Doges were crowned at its summit after a service in San Marco, when the *Maggior Consiglio*'s youngest member would hand the incumbent the gem-studded ducal crown (the *zogia* or *beretta*): the eldest then placed it on the new doge's head. Thereafter, the hat was only worn during Easter mass at San Zaccaria (see pages 186–188).

On the left is the recently restored **Arco Foscari**, started by Bartolomeo Bon and finished by Antonio Rizzo. It is famed for its statues of *Adam* and *Eve*, bronze copies of two marble originals now kept in the palace (see page 125). The figure of Eve so seduced a 16th-century Duke of Mantua that he offered the Venetians her weight in gold in return for the statue, but they refused.

Scala d'Oro and State Apartments Sansovino's **Scala d'Oro** (1538–1550), the "Golden Staircase," takes you up several flights of stairs to the palace's second floor. In the past this was a route allowed only to the doge, his council, and special guests. The gilt stuccoes (1558) en route are by the ubiquitous Alessandro Vittoria. Though stripped of furniture on the orders of Napoléon, the **State Apartments** on the first floor are notable for their elaborate chimney pieces and richly carved ceilings. The finest example is the **Sala degli Scarlatti**, with a chimney designed by Tullio and a relief of the Virgin and Doge Leonardo by Lombardo (over the door). The adjacent **Sala dello Scudo** has two large 18th-century maps showing the territories of the Venetian Republic and the regions visited by Marco Polo. At the top of the stairs is the **Atrio Quadrato**, little more than a landing, is notable only for Tintoretto's ceiling fresco of *Justice Presenting Doge Priuli with the Sword and Scales* (ca1564), the first of the palace's countless canvases lauding Venice and its achievements. Next comes the start of the tour proper, the **Sala delle Quattro Porte**, a room which rather unceremoniously doubles as the palace's gift store.

The mysterious tetrarchs at the entrance to the Palazzo Ducale

Sala delle Quattro Porte The "Room of the Four Doors" was where foreign guests and ambassadors waited to meet the doge and his council, doubtless suitably breathless and humbled after their haul up the stairs. Its ceiling and general decorative plan are by Palladio, the badly scratched ceiling frescoes by Tintoretto (the latter's various buxom women symbolize cities subdued by Venice). The vast painting on the long wall opposite the entrance illustrates the sort of show Venice could put on for its distinguished visitors: this one was for the young Henri III of France, who is said never quite to have recovered from his Venetian sojourn. The easel painting at the room's far end, Tiepolo's *Venice Receiving the Homage of Neptune*, is best seen when the itinerary brings you back this way.

Sala dell'Anticollegio One of the three most interesting rooms at the palace, the Anticollegio acted as an inner waiting room for visiting foreign worthies. The finest of the paintings are four works (1577–1578) by Tintoretto (two on each of the door walls). Although painted as a collective meditation on concord, each mythological scene also served to glorify an aspect of the Venetian state. Thus *The Marriage of Bacchus and Ariadne* represents Venice's marriage to the sea, portraying the starry crown of supremacy above; *Vulcan's Forge* shows Vulcan and the Cyclops forging weapons for Venice; *Mercury and the Three Graces* symbolizes the city's material wealth balanced by beauty; while *Minerva Dismissing Mars* suggests the victory of wisdom over strength.

The best of the other paintings is Veronese's grand *Rape of Europa*, a work that despite its dubious subject matter was described by Henry James as "the brightest vision that ever descended on the soul of a painter." It was also one of many pictures in the palace taken to Paris by Napoléon and later returned.

Sala del Collegio Among the palace's most beautiful rooms, the Collegio was the meeting place of the *Collegio* and its inner cabinet, the *Signoria* (see panels). The most striking work is Veronese's superb ceiling cycle (ca1577). Its subjects, once again, are the ideals of the Venetian state. Other fine pictures include Tintoretto's vast *Doge Andrea Gritti and the Virgin* (above the entrance door), and Veronese's still larger canvas above the throne, *Doge Sebastiano Venier Offering Thanks to Christ for the Victory at Lepanto*.

Sala del Senato Rooms now come thick and fast, starting with the "Hall of the Senate," the spot where the Senate held its twice-weekly meetings (see panel). Crossing back through the Sala delle Quattro Porte, you enter the **Sala del Consiglio dei Dieci**, home to the Council of Ten, head of Venice's infamous secret police. Established in 1310, this much-feared body had become a permanent institution by the end of the century. For all its dread reputation, though, the council's job was mainly to watch over powerful citizens, ensuring that none threatened the integrity of the state. Its deliberations were held in secret, unlike those of other government bodies, a circumstance which naturally aroused suspicion and bolstered its

The Scala d'Oro

123

THE *COLLEGIO*
This body presided over the *Senato* and formed the Cabinet of the Venetian government. Chaired by the doge, it consisted of six ducal councillors, the three heads of the *Quarantia* (the judiciary), and the 16 *Savi* (special senators with responsibilities for military, maritime, and government affairs). It met foreign ambassadors, dealt with the papacy, acted as the supreme court, and prepared bills to be debated by the Senate.

THE *SIGNORIA*
The highest executive body was an inner sanctum of the *Collegio*, itself an inner cabinet. It consisted of the doge, the six ducal councilors, and the three heads of the *Quarantia*. Members were elected from the *Maggior Consiglio*, and renewed three at a time. None was supposed to be related to the doge, whom they had to observe as well as work with.

Far left: the sumptuous ceiling of the Sala dell'Anticollegio

Palazzo Ducale

BROGLIO
The Palazzo's arcade takes its name from *broglio*, originally a meadow, or a place to walk. It was here that members of the *Maggior Consiglio* met to buy the votes of impoverished nobles known as the *barnabotti* (so called because many of them used to live in the cheap lodgings around Campo San Barnaba). This gave rise to the Italian (and now English) word *imbroglio* (an entanglement) and to the English "to embroil."

PLAQUE
While Venice was ever slow to praise its famous men, it has always been quick to condemn, especially where this served to remind citizens of the fate that awaited less than faithful servants of the state. Hence the prominence of the plaque in the Palazzo's arcade recording the banishment of Girolamo Loredan and Giovanni Contarini for having abandoned the fortress of Tenedos to the Turks, "with grievous injury to Christianity and their country."

THE SENATE
Venice's upper house (created in 1255) was a select band garnered from the *Maggior Consiglio*. The number of its incumbents varied over the years between 60 and 300. Members, who had to be over 30, served for a year and were unique in the Venetian hierarchy in being the only candidates eligible for re-election. They debated policy, filled the top civil servant posts, and recommended candidates to be vetted by the *Maggior Consiglio* for higher office.

sinister reputation. As late as 1850, long after the Republic's fall, its records remained under lock and key in the state archives. The Council of Ten, incidentally, actually numbered 17, for the inquisitors were always supplemented by the doge and the *Collegio's* six ducal councillors. The room's ceiling paintings are by Veronese, their centerpiece a copy of a work stolen by Napoléon and now displayed in the Louvre.

Sala della Bussola This room, next door to the Sala del Consiglio dei Dieci, was an antechamber for those waiting to see the Ten. Just to the right of the exit door is a small safe-like hole in the wall, one of the city's several Bocche dei Leoni (lions' mouths), into which Venetians could drop accusations against fellow citizens (see panel on page 125). The innocuous-looking door protruding from the corner of the room led to the Sala dei Tre Capi, a three-man court of inquisition selected from the Ten (to deal with cases of espionage and high treason). From here a passage led to the Sala dei Inquisitori, or torture chamber, and finally to the prisons. There was no right of appeal against a sentence passed by the Ten: anyone unlucky enough to wind up in any of these rooms, so rumor had it, was as good as dead.

Armeria After a brush with the latent violence of the Venetian state, it is fitting that you come next to the

palace's armory, four fascinating rooms filled with armor and over two thousand pieces of assorted weaponry. A signed but slightly disorientating route then takes you down a floor via the Scala dei Censori, along the lobby of the Andito del Maggior Consiglio (where members of the *Maggior Consiglio* assembled during breaks in business), and past the Sala della Quarantia Civil Vecchia. The last was a civil court that consisted of 40 members, hence the name, from the Italian *quaranta*—"forty." Then comes the Sala Guariento, named after a faded fresco by the Paduan artist Guariento. The veranda beyond is home to Arco Foscari's original *Adam* and *Eve*, copies of which are displayed in the courtyard.

Sala del Maggior Consiglio Little in Venice is as large as the hall of the *Maggior Consiglio*, a room whose size seems still more extraordinary in a city where space is so often at a premium. One reason for its scale was to impress, another was to accommodate Venice's lower house, whose membership by the 16th century had swollen to 2,500 (though in practice fewer than half its members bothered to show up). Built between 1340 and 1355, it was among the earliest parts of the present palace, but suffered particularly badly in the fire of 1577.

Of the present canvases, only Tintoretto's gargantuan *Paradiso* (ca1588–1592) could hold a candle to its illustrious forebears. The largest oil painting in the world (at

Walls and ceiling of the Sala del Senato are heavily laden with gilt

BOCCHE DEI LEONI
These little sealed boxes, or "lions' mouths," were dotted around medieval Venice to encourage Venetians to denounce one another to the Council of Ten. Any anonymous denunciations were rejected, and each accusation had to be backed up by two witnesses. Even then, the Ten had to decide by a five-sixths majority that the matter pertained to state security. Unfounded denunciations were punished, but those denounced were never told the identity of their accuser.

Palazzo Ducale

The Bridge of Sighs (in the foreground) reputedly took its name from the sighs of condemned prisoners being led to the dungeons

HOME COMFORTS

To read Casanova's description of his cell in the *Piombi* it is a wonder he ever tried to escape: "What are called 'the leads' are not gaols," he wrote, "but small furnished lock-ups, with barred windows, at the top of the ducal palace, and the inmate is said to be 'under the leads' because the roof is covered with sheets of lead over the larch-wood beams. These…make the rooms cold in winter and very hot in summertime. But the air is good, you get enough to eat, a decent bed and everything else you need, clothes, and clean laundry when you want it. The Doge's servants look after the rooms and a doctor, surgeon, an apothecary and a confessor are always on hand."
Mémoires (1826–1838)

ITINERARI SEGRETI

These highly recommended guided tours begin daily except Wednesday at 10 AM and noon and last 90 minutes. The 20 places on each tour must be reserved two days in advance by calling 522 4951. Although the commentary is in Italian and the charge is expensive, the itinerary is fascinating, visiting the *Piombi*, torture chamber, Sala dei Tre Capi, the old ephemera-filled attics, and the labyrinthine offices of the Venetian civil service.

1,500 square feet), it was painted free of charge when the artist was 72 and depicts the regiments of the saved (500 figures in all), arranged as described in Canto XXX of Dante's *Paradiso*. Tintoretto was also commissioned to paint the frieze of Venice's first 76 doges below the ceiling, best known for the black veil marking the spot destined for the executed Marino Falier. The sequence, unfinished at Tintoretto's death, was completed by his son Domenico.

The room's only other noteworthy paintings are the two large ceiling ovals: Veronese's *Apotheosis of Venice* (above the tribune), painted in 1588 just before the artist's death, and (at the room's opposite end) Palma Giovane's *Venice Welcoming the Conquering Nations.*

Two rooms lead off the Sala to the rear, the small Sala della Quarantia Nuova, a civil court for expatriate Venetians, and the larger Sala dello Scrutinio beyond. The latter was used to count the votes during the election of a new doge, a process that usually took five days, but on one famous occasion in 1615 lasted 24 days, with 104 ballots. Another frieze depicts the last 44 doges; seven were painted by Tintoretto, the rest taken from life by later painters.

Ponte dei Sospiri The palace's atmosphere changes dramatically beyond the Sala del Maggior Consiglio, as the splendor of the state rooms suddenly gives way to the dark corners and dank passageways of the prisons. The shift occurs even before you enter the Ponte dei Sospiri, or Bridge of Sighs (1600), which despite its considerable fame turns out to be little more than a corridor. Lord Byron was responsible for a lot of the romantic nonsense surrounding the bridge, a link between the palace and its prisons reputedly named after the sighs of the condemned men led across it. Only petty criminals were being incarcerated in the dungeons by the time it was built, however, a rather disappointing state of affairs that caused W. D. Howells to call the bridge a "pathetic swindle" and Ruskin, blunt as ever, to describe it, in equally unflattering terms, as "a work of no merit, and of late period...owing the interest it possesses chiefly to its pretty name, and to the ignorant sentimentalism of Byron."

Prisons The cells beyond have also been talked up over the centuries (see panels), but these, too, were late additions to the palace, constructed in the 17th century. Though doubtless none too comfortable, they were probably not a patch on the palace's more feared dungeons, the *Pozzi*, or "Wells." In 1611 the English visitor Thomas Coryat described the cells as "a very fair prison, the fairest absolutely that I ever saw...I think there is not a fairer prison in all Christendome." Casanova's equally luxurious cells under the eaves, by the way, part of the "Leads," or *Piombi* (see pages 128–129), can be seen only on the *Itinerari segreti*, (see panel).

When the infamous prisons were opened in 1797 they were found to contain just four common criminals, one of whom pleaded with the French to be allowed to stay there. He eventually died from a celebratory excess of cakes and chocolate. Shelley, by contrast, claimed there was just one inmate, and he was so old he could barely speak.

Recrossing the Bridge of Sighs, the route takes you through the *Avogaria*, the offices of the *Censori* (censors), where state prosecutors prepared trials, and the Salla dello Scrigno, where strict records were kept of the ranks (nobility and citizens) to which Venetians belonged, and finally to the Milizia da Mar, the powerhouse of the fleet.

As you walk back round the palace looking at the sculptures, be sure to take in the capitals on the top of each pillar, many of which are beautifully carved with allegories of the vices and virtues. Some are 15th-century originals, the others obvious 19th-century copies. Their job was the edification of strollers in the arcade, or *broglio*, a favorite place to meet, chat, and perhaps hatch the occasional *imbroglio*—from which the word derives (see panel on page 124). When you turn the corner (on to the palace's Piazzetta side) look out for the seventh capital down, a hard-hearted story in stone of courtship, marriage, honeymoon, childbirth, and infant mortality. Three pillars further on, stand back to admire the upper loggia, where there is a distinctive pair of red columns (see panel on page 120). Close by, on the wall, is a much-faded plaque with a tale to tell (see panel on page 124).

TORTURE
Venice was among the first states to abolish torture (in about 1710). In its day, though, it was much used. Because the Ten's chambers were so close to the palace's offices, "interrogations" were carried out at dusk to avoid upsetting civil servants. The rooms were designed to face west, so that the setting sun would dazzle the victim and allow his tormenters to remain anonymous in the room's shadows. Waiting victims were kept in adjacent wooden cells, in the hope that their companions' screams would loosen their tongues without the need for further encouragement.

The cells of the Palazzo Ducale

"The chief business of my life," wrote Casanova, "has always been to indulge my senses; I never knew anything of greater importance." Although history remembers him as one of the world's great libertines, the Venetian-born son of an actor was also an ecclesiastic, alchemist, writer, musician, soldier, spy, diplomat, and inveterate traveler.

NOCTURNAL PRANKS
"We often spent our nights roaming through different quarters of the city, thinking up the most scandalous practical jokes and putting them into execution. We amused ourselves by untying gondolas...We often woke midwives and made them dress and go to deliver women who, when they arrived, called them fools. We routed priests from their beds and packed them off to pray for the souls of people in perfect health...In every street we relentlessly cut the bell cord hanging at every door; and when we found a door open...we groped our way upstairs and terrified all the sleeping inmates by shouting at their bedroom doors."
Mémoires (1826–1838)

TYPICAL VENETIAN
"Casanova had the true Venetian temperament: cool, ebullient, and licentious." Mary McCarthy, *Venice Observed* (1961)

PRISON VISITS
Casanova's cell in the Palazzo Ducale was an essential port-of-call for many 19th-century visitors. Lord Byron reputedly spent a day recarving the graffiti on its walls, which were being worn smooth by the touch of visitors' fingers.

Early life Casanova was born on April 2, 1725. Destined for the priesthood from an early age, he spent his formative years in Venice in the seminary of St. Cyprian. Proving immune to the joys of cloistered life, however, he was expelled from his studies for constant philandering and sexual self-indulgence. After a brief period in the service of a Catholic cardinal he became a musician, working as a violinist by day and pursuing a life of dissolution by night. His nocturnal pranks (see panel) are described, along with countless tales of love and conquest, in his 12-volume posthumously published autobiography, the *Mémoires de J. Casanova de Seingalt* (1826–1838).

Prison Casanova's infantile follies saw him banished from Venice for five years, during which time he joined the Masonic Order in Lyon (in 1750), and traveled between Paris, Dresden, Prague, and Vienna. Returning to Venice in 1755 he was promptly sentenced to five years' imprisonment in the Palazzo Ducale's *Piombi*. Sorcery formed part of the charges against him, a quite feasible accusation given Casanova's interest in alchemy and the black arts. His earliest memory, he claimed, was of a Venetian witch, surrounded by black cats, mixing potions and wailing incantations over him to cure a childhood nosebleed. Giovanni Manuzzi, the "pious spy" employed by the Inquisition to tail him, was also clearly scandalized by his somewhat "un-Christian" behavior. After detailing assignations with women of every rank, vast sums lost at gambling tables, and a generous intake of food and liquor, his report concludes that in "conversing with and becoming intimate with the said Casanova, one sees truly united in him misbelief, imposture, lasciviousness, and voluptuousness in a manner to inspire horror."

Great escape On October 31, 1756, after 15 months in prison, Casanova effected his escape, an episode of considerable daring if his vaunting *Mémoires* are to be trusted (though there are those who believe he became an Inquisition spy and was allowed to escape). Making a hole in the ceiling of his cell, he clambered across the prison rooftops, eventually forcing his way into the Palazzo Ducale. Here, scratched and bleeding, and, in his own words, looking like "a man of quality who had been beaten up in a brothel," he waited to be seen by late-night strollers in the Piazzetta. Duly spotted, and his presence reported to the night-watchmen, he was released in the mistaken belief he was a visitor who had

simply been locked in. The Inquisition, investigating the breakout, sentenced the prison governor to spend ten years in his own jail.

Final years Making his way to France by way of Munich, Casanova introduced Paris to the lottery (1757) and soon established a reputation among the city's aristocracy for financial acumen. When his skills deserted him, however, he was forced to flee France to escape an army of angry creditors. Assuming the name Chevalier de Seingalt, he traveled to Germany and Switzerland (where he met Voltaire), before returning to Rome and Florence (from where he was again expelled). He then moved to London, St. Petersburg and Berlin, where he was offered a government post by Frederick II. Moving to Warsaw, he became embroiled in a scandal following a duel and was forced to flee to Spain. In 1774, almost 20 years after his escape, he was allowed back to Venice, working as a spy for the Inquisition until a libel suit forced him from the city for good. He spent his last years (1785–1798) working as a librarian for a Bohemian count.

A scene from Federico Fellini's 1976 film version of Casanova's life starring Donald Sutherland

EQUIPPED FOR LOVE
Casanova describes a suite he has rented for the purposes of seduction: "...everything seemed to be calculated for love, pleasure, and good cheer. The walls were covered with small squares of china, representing little Cupids and naked amorous couples in all sorts of positions, well calculated to excite the imagination...Next to it was an octagonal room, the walls, the ceiling, and the floor of which were entirely covered with splendid Venetian glass, arranged in such a manner as to reflect on all sides every position of the amorous couple enjoying the pleasures of love..."
Mémoires (1826–1838)

Piazza San Marco

277E3

NAPOLÉON'S VIEW

"The most beautiful drawing-room in Europe, for which it is only fitting that the heavens should serve as ceiling."

Little has changed in the piazza in the past century

▶▶▶ Piazza San Marco

Only at dawn, dead of night, or in the depths of winter is Piazza San Marco somewhere to be enjoyed rather than endured. Only then can you escape the rampaging school parties and verminous pigeons that blight its every corner. The square's apologists say it has always been thus, teeming with traders or tourists, the sort of throng that has congregated on Venice's social, religious, and political heart for a thousand years. Diehards still sit at its elegant cafés, ducking the guano, but were Napoléon to return today he might revise his famous opinion (see panel).

Nevertheless, it remains unmissable, if only for the buildings on its flanks—the Basilica di San Marco, Palazzo Ducale, Campanile, and Museo Correr—and the medley of lesser monuments all easily seen in a few minutes' stroll.

COSMOPOLITAN SQUARE

A 17th-century Englishman called the piazza "the fairest place in the city...for here is the greatest magnificence of architecture to be seene, that any place under the sunne doth yeelde. Here you may see both all manner of fashions and attire, and heare all the languages of Christendome...it is a market place of the world." Thomas Coryat, *Coryat's Crudities* (1611)

The Torre dell'Orologio

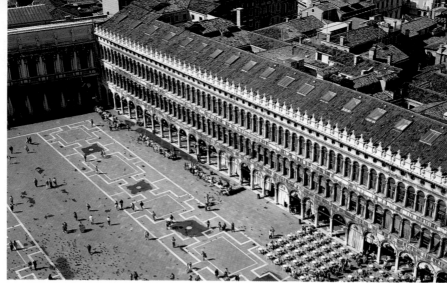

History The piazza is at the city's lowest point and started life as a marshy islet known as the Morso. In time it was drained by a canal (the Rio Batario) and planted with fruit trees belonging to the nuns of San Zaccaria (see pages 186–188). Long before the building of the Palazzo Ducale it was the site of a lighthouse (the first "campanile") and churches dedicated to San Teodoro (the city's first patron saint) and San Geminiano. The latter was built in the 6th century by one of the Emperor Justinian's generals in gratitude for Venice's support against the Goths.

The square's 1,000-year transformation began in 829, when San Zaccaria sacrificed its orchard to make way for the Basilica di San Marco. In the 12th century, Doge Sebastiano Ziani drained the Rio Batario, created the arcades of the Procuratie, and rebuilt San Geminiano opposite San Marco. The 16th century saw the restoration of the Campanile, Zecca, and San Geminiano, and the demolition of buildings such as the old Orseolo hospice (deemed "too old and ugly") to make way for the Loggetta and Libreria Sansoviniana. Napoléon razed the city's 14th-century granaries (the Granai di Terranova) to accommodate the Giardinetti Reali (reputedly to provide him with a better view), while his stepson, Eugène de Beauharnais (the "Viceroy of Italy"), destroyed San Geminiano to provide the Ala Napoleonica with a state ballroom.

Torre dell'Orologio The piazza's clock (1496–1499) was designed by Mauro Coducci (with Pietro Lombardo), probably as an adjunct to the Procuratie Vecchie (see below). *Horas non numero nisi serenas*, claims its legend—"I number only happy hours"—though it also records the signs of the zodiac and phases of the moon. The two bronze figures who strike the hours, known as "moors" after their dark patina, were cast in the Arsenale in 1497. The intricate mechanism was the fruit of three years' labor by Emilian craftsmen Paolo and Carlo Ranieri. Venice rewarded them with a generous pension, though jealous rival cities put about the rumor that they had been blinded to prevent them carrying out similar work elsewhere.

The view of the piazza from the Campanile

131

PEACE PIAZZA
Despite long connections with the politics of the city, after World War II all parties agreed unanimously never again to hold rallies or demonstrations in Piazza San Marco.

PIGEONS
Like them or loathe them, the piazza's pigeons are inescapable. Some say they are descended from birds released by the doge each Palm Sunday (echoing Noah's release of a dove from the ark): those that were subsequently caught were eligible for eating; those that escaped acquired permanent immunity. Others claim they arrived in the city with the first 5th-century refugees, or that they bred from the carrier pigeons that brought news of Constantinople's capture in 1204. Some say they are descended from a pair of birds given by an Oriental king to cheer up a melancholy dogaressa.

Piazza San Marco

Procuratie The arcaded Procuratie Vecchie and Nuove on the north and south sides of the piazza were built to house the offices of the *Procuratie*, among the highest officials of the old Republic. Created in the 10th century, their tasks included the running of government offices, the upkeep of San Marco, and supervising the wealth that accrued to the basilica through private and public gifts. There were four officials in the 13th century, six in 1319, and nine in 1442. Each shared with the doge and grand chancellor the distinction of being the only state representatives elected for life. On election they gave bread to the poor, and wine to the gondoliers—to symbolize the propriety with which they would administer the public purse—and threw lavish parties for the nobility.

Fire destroyed their earliest offices, the Procuratie Vecchie, which were rebuilt ca1500 by Mauro Coducci and completed (after another fire) by Bartolomeo Bon and Jacopo Sansovino in 1512. Work on the Procuratie Nuove, commissioned to relieve overcrowding, started under Scamozzi (1582–1586), who copied Sansovino's adjacent library; it was completed by Longhena between 1616 and 1640. Offices still occupy both wings of the Procuratie, together with the **Museo Correr** (see pages 108–111) and the Museo Archeologico. The former is entered via the **Ala Napoleonica**, which closes the piazza's western end, built in the early 19th century over San Geminiano.

Columns The area in front of the Palazzo Ducale is known as the Piazzetta. On its waterfront, the **Molo**, stand two granite columns, one topped with the lion of St. Mark, the other with St. Theodore and a crocodile-cum-fish-cum-dragon (no one knows what it is or what it means). Both were brought back from Tyre in 1170; a third figure fell into the Bacino while it was being unloaded and has never been found. The problems encountered in raising the columns were such that the doge—according to legend—agreed to grant the wish of anyone who managed to surmount them. In the end they were erected by Niccolò Barattieri, the engineer responsible for the Rialto's wooden bridge, who claimed as his prize the right to open a gaming table between the columns. As gambling was then banned in the city, the doge kept his word but also declared the pillars a place of public execution, thus hoping to discourage gaming.

Whatever the truth of the legend, dicing became rife between the pillars, perhaps because the area—which was Venice's official "gateway"—had the status of a "free zone." It also remained a place of execution, for which reason Venetians still consider it unlucky to walk between the columns. Hanging or decapitation were the favored methods of dispatch, though bonfires and guillotines were also used, and in 1405 three traitors were buried here head first.

Libreria Sansoviniana (or Biblioteca Marciana) and **Museo Archeologico** Venice's state library was built around two literary bequests, one from Petrarch, who left his library to Venice in 1362 (it was later "lost"), the other, in 1468, a collection of 1,000 manuscripts from the great humanist, Cardinal Bessarione. The building, designed by Sansovino in 1537, was considered among the greatest works of the day. Palladio thought it "perhaps the richest and most ornate building to be created since the times of ancient Greece and Rome." Its prestige was somewhat diminished, however, when its vaulted ceiling crashed to the floor, a failing that saw Sansovino jailed by the incensed authorities. Only the impassioned pleadings of influential friends, Titian among them, secured his release. He was subsequently forced to redesign and rebuild the vaults at his own expense. The library's main hall is sumptuously decorated with paintings by Tintoretto, Veronese, and others. Titian's fresco *Wisdom* adorns the anteroom ceiling.

The adjoining **Museo Archeologico** is seldom visited, but contains an impressive collection of Greek and Roman statuary. Both the library and museum are accessed via the Museo Correr (pages 108–111).

The Zecca Venice's original 9th-century mint (*zecca*) was moved from the Rialto to its present site in the 13th century. Its current home, Sansovino's first major Venetian commission (1537–1545), was one of the few buildings in the city to be constructed entirely of stone (as a precaution against fire). Most Venetian buildings, by contrast, sport timber frames behind stone facades. The first Venetian ducat was minted in 1284. In 1540 the ducat became a *zecchino*, which with the Florentine *fiorino* became the cornerstone of trade and exchange across Europe.

Far left and below: the lion of St. Mark and St. Theodore on their columns in the Piazza San Marco

There are few Venetian sights can be as vivid or colorful as the bustling food markets of the Rialto, whose chaotic but appealing mixture of tourists, traders, and gossiping locals can barely have altered in almost a thousand years.

SHYLOCK TO BASSIANO
"I will buy with you, talk with you, walk with you, and so following: but I will not eat with you, drink with you, nor pray with you. What news on the Rialto?" Shakespeare, *The Merchant of Venice*

GOBBO DI RIALTO
The hunchbacked (*gobbo*) stone figure in the corner of Campo San Giacomo was carved by Pietro da Salo in 1534. Bent under the weight of the stairs above, the statue has been seen as an allegory of the heavy taxes heaped on the Venetians over the centuries. Certain mis-creants were once made to run a gauntlet of blows whilst careering from Piazza San Marco to the Gobbo. Next to it stands the Pietra del Bando, a pink granite column, which—like its counterpart in Piazza San Marco—was used for the reading of state proclamations.

Venice's best market for fruit, vegetables, and fish—all unloaded from the nearby Grand Canal

TAX ON TRADE
It has been estimated that a quarter of all the Republic's annual revenues came from taxes levied on goods entering the city.

Market place Venice's commercial heart is almost as old as the city itself. Some of the lagoon's first settlers were attracted to its high banks, or *rivo alto*, among the driest and most easily defended redoubts amid the marsh and mud. By the 11th century, when San Marco emerged as the city's political forum, the Rivoaltus had become its commercial heart. The first private banks appeared in 1157, followed by Europe's first state bank, the Banco di Piazza, in 1161. Soon came tax collectors, magistrates and the other offices of state connected

with commerce and maritime trade. Something of the commercial cornucopia that made this the "world's market" survives in today's Erberia (fruit and vegetable) market (*Open* Mon–Sat 7–1), and in the still more fascinating fish stalls of the Pescheria (*Open* Tue–Sat 7–1).

Ponte di Rialto "It deserves to be reputed the eighth wonder of the world," wrote the 16th-century traveler Fynes Moryson of the Rialto bridge. Arguably Venice's most famous monument, this is the last in a long line of bridges at one of the city's pivotal points. The first, a simple pontoon, appeared around 1172. The second, a wooden span built in 1260, disappeared during a revolt in 1310. Its successor collapsed under a wedding procession in 1444. Carpaccio's famous picture in the Accademia shows how the next version looked (complete with drawbridge). In 1524 the Senate decided to commission a stone bridge, though it was another 33 years before Palladio, Sansovino, Vignola, Scamozzi, and even Michelangelo submitted plans. Eventually, however, it was Antonio da Ponte's controversial single-arched plan which was adopted. Begun in 1588, the bridge took just three years to complete, making light of the site's instability (the foundations required some 12,000 piles) and the difficulty of constructing its high central span (essential to allow the passage of state galleys).

San Giacomo di Rialto (*Open* daily 10–noon) Also known affectionately as San Giacometto ("Little Giacomo"), this tiny church is reputed to be the oldest in Venice, founded in the same year as the city (AD 421). Its more likely date of birth was 1071, about the same time as the Rialto's markets took root. It was much remodeled in 1531 and 1601. Before exploring the interior note the inscription on the apse, a medieval injunction aimed at the markets' stall-holders: "Around this temple," it reads, "let the merchant's law be just, his weights true, and his promise faithful." The facade's lovely 24-hour clock, notoriously unreliable, dates from the 14th century. In the past it has stuck for such long periods that art historians have been able to date various Venetian scenes from its fused hands. The lean-to portico is now one of only two surviving examples in the city (the other is at San Nicolò dei Mendicoli).

Inside, the Greek cross plan of the first church survives, apparently retained on the direct orders of the doge, who worshipped here on Ash Wednesday. The only other early fragments are the six columns, filched from some ancient Greek building, and their decorative foliage, added in 1097.

The clock on San Giacomo di Rialto has long been the least reliable in the city

FESTA DEL REDENTORE

Few Venetian festivals survived unscathed after the fall of the Republic. The Feast of the Redentore, celebrated each third Sunday in July, is one that did. Started to commemorate the end of the 1577 plague, it used to be a three-day affair: Friday would see a lay celebration, Saturday a procession across the water, and Sunday a day of general carousing. Nowadays Saturday evening is rounded off with a fusillade of fireworks, and it has become the tradition for anyone with a boat to take it out and spend the entire night on the lagoon with friends.

▶ Il Redentore   50C1

Campo del Redentore (Quay: Redentore; Vaporetto 82; Motoscafi 41, 42)
Open: Mon–Sat 10–5. Admission: inexpensive

Palladio secured three of Venice's most prominent sites for his trio of Venetian churches, lining up San Giorgio Maggiore, the Zitelle, and the Redentore at intervals along the Giudecca. Only San Giorgio, however, is really worth a visit for its own sake (see pages 140–141), leaving the Redentore—"an antiseptic fane that no one loves" in the words of Jan Morris, "small and contemptible" in those of Ruskin—as a church best seen during a longer visit to the Giudecca.

One of the city's five plague churches, the Church of the Redeemer (*Redentore*) was commissioned in 1577, some time after the worst of this particular outbreak of pestilence had passed (taking as many as 40,000 Venetians with it). Palladio was personally chosen as the church's architect by Doge Alvise Mocenigo, having already begun to make a considerable impact on the city skyline with San Giorgio Maggiore (started 11 years earlier). Crossing to the Giudecca on a pontoon of boats, the doge laid the first stone on July 21, 1577 (the feast day of the Redeemer), instigating a three-day *festa* that continues with no-holds-barred abandon to this day (see panel).

Palladio's church of Il Redentore

CLASSICAL COPY

William Beckford described Redentore as "A structure so simple and elegant, that I thought myself entering an antique temple..."
Italy (1780)

The facade borrows heavily from classical temples, Rome's Pantheon in particular, the antique allusions continuing inside, where Palladio's chief inspiration was the monumental structures of Rome's great bathhouses. The nave's paintings, none of them very good, are all clearly labeled, but your task here (not an easy one) should be to find the sacristan and ask to see the **sacristy**. It is on the choir's right, and full of canvases such as Veronese's *Baptism of Christ* and a *Virgin and Child* by Alvise Vivarini. The room's gallery of waxworks, all lolling heads and rolling eyes, is a collection of eminent Franciscans modeled in the 18th century.

▶ San Francesco della Vigna

275E4

Campo San Francesco della Vigna
(Quays: Celestia, Motoscafi 41, 42, 51, 52)
Open: daily 7–noon, 3–7

San Francesco is one of Venice's more moribund and dispiriting churches: a prominent bell tower and a handful of paintings (one of them a gem) are the only sightseeing beacons—though Palladio's facade, when and if it is restored, may one day draw the architectural faithful.

According to tradition the church's somewhat shabby neighborhood was close to the spot where an angel appeared to St. Mark announcing the lagoon would form his final resting place (see page 61). This holiness by proxy, so the story goes, prompted the building of a chapel on the site. The first recorded building, however, appeared in 1253, when a local vineyard (*vigna*) was given to the Franciscans by Marco Ziani, son of Doge Pietro Ziani. Work on the present church began in 1534 under Sansovino, though its current appearance is the result of countless alterations, not least the facade added by Palladio between 1562 and 1572.

Inside, to the left of the door on the west wall, is a triptych attributed to Antonio Vivarini, and to the right, an ancient but crumbling Byzantine relief. Moving down the right nave, the first chapel features a *Resurrection* (left wall) dubiously attributed to Giorgione, and the fourth a *Resurrection* (1588) thought to be by Veronese. The best of the paintings, however, and surprisingly little-known, is Antonio da Negroponte's sumptuous *Madonna and Child* (ca1450), on the right-hand wall of the right transept.

Make a point of tracking down the church's tombs, the most famous of which, in the fifth chapel on the left, is that of Marco Barbaro, renowned for his unsporting battlefield behavior (see panel). Also look for Doge Andrea Gritti, buried on the right side of the choir immediately after the steps. A licentious friend of Sansovino (he laid the new church's foundation stone), he was an accomplished general and linguist and a notorious womanizer and glutton. He died on Christmas Eve 1538 after eating too many eels.

Other points of interest include the pleasing choir, the gray marble reliefs by Pietro Lombardo (in the chapel to the left of the choir) and the delightful cloister off the left transept. As you leave, the fifth chapel on the left has a *Sacra Conversazione* (1562) by Veronese, and the second chapel three bronze *Saints* by the prolific Alessandro Vittoria.

MARCO BARBARO
Barbaro by name, barbarous by nature, the Barbaro took their family crest, a red circle on a white field, from the heroics of Marco Barbaro, an admiral who during the Battle of Ascalon cut off the hand of a Moor who had seized his ship's flag. He then killed him, unravelled his turban to make a banner, and traced a red circle on it with the blood from his bleeding stump. The dripping pennant was then flown from the masthead as an emblem of triumph.

San Francesco della Vigna's campanile was built between 1571 and 1581

137

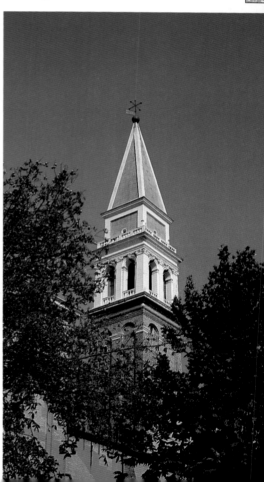

San Giacomo

San Giacomo dell'Orio and its 13th-century campanile

TIGHT FIT

Venice's narrowest street, so it is said, is the 33-inch-wide Ramo Salizzada Zustro, located just west of Campo dell' Orio, off Calle delle Savie.

NAMES

Several ideas have been advanced as to how San Giacomo and its *campo* came by their name. Some say *orio* derives from a laurel tree (*lauro*) that once grew in the square, others that it came from *luprio*, meaning a piece of dry land in the midst of a swamp. More far-fetched theories see its source in *lupo*, after the wolves that might have prowled the area in some mythical past. Others suggest the name was originally San Giacomo del Rio (St. James of the River), a simple device to distinguish it from its namesake on the Rialto.

SAN GIOVANNI EVANGELISTA

Not far from San Giacomo, *en route* for the Frari, stands the Scuola Grande di San Giovanni Evangelista. Once among the city's richest *scuole*, it was responsible, among other things, for commissioning the great *Miracles of the True Cross* cycle now in the Accademia. The main hall and splendid double stairway by Caducci (1480) can be visited on guided tours on Sunday and Monday 10–4. Anyone, however, can enjoy its stunning archway, one of the most beautiful sights in the city, designed by Pietro Lombardo in 1481. The eagle in the lunette is the symbol of St. John (San Giovanni).

▶▶ **San Giacomo dell'Orio**   *281E1*
Campo San Giacomo dell'Orio (Quay: San Stae; Vaporetto 1)
Open: Mon–Sat 10–5. Admission: inexpensive
Venice has many fine churches, but few where you feel any tangible sense of antiquity. San Giacomo, however, with its dark corners and ancient fragments, feels as venerable inside as its 9th-century foundation suggests.

The church was built on marshy ground, hence the ship's keel ceiling, dating from the 14th-century and designed to help reduce the building's weight (dark and pitted with age, it is now one of the nicest such ceilings in the city). The scheme proved only partially successful, as you can see from the lilt of the sunken Byzantine-era apse outside. The sidewalk, by contrast, has been raised so many times its columns are now little more than curiously stunted pillars. Two of the columns are obvious intruders, one red, the other a rare piece of green *verde antico*. Both were plundered by the Venetians during the Fourth Crusade.

The church has not only great intrinsic charm, but also some fine works of art, starting with two early 16th-century *Prophets* by the west door (glance up at the organ here) and a great clover-shaped stoup of Greek marble. The wooden *Madonna and Child* to its right is a fine Tuscan work. Round the corner a wall from the 9th-century church has been exposed (much of the earliest church was rebuilt in 1225, and a broad transept grafted on to the old Byzantine basilica around 1500).

The church's best piece is Lorenzo Lotto's high altarpiece, a *Madonna and Four Saints* (1546). It was among the last works he painted in Venice before leaving the city in a huff over pay and conditions. Note Lorenzo Veneziano's nearby *Crucifix*, the pair of redoubtable Lombardesque crosses set into the wall, and the rare little Byzantine *Madonna* protruding from the apse's left pier. The old and new sacristies left and right of the apse are crammed with paintings, the best of them Veronese's ceiling panels in the latter.

▶ **San Giobbe**   280B4

Campo San Giobbe (Quay: Tre Archi; Motoscafi 41, 42, 51, 52)
Open: Mon–Sat 10–noon, 4–6
Admission: free

In Venice—forever prone to pestilence of one form or another—at least three saints were called into service against the plague: Sebastian, Roch, and Job (*Giobbe*), whose proverbial suffering made him a character the Venetians instinctively warmed to as a source of comfort and relief.

The first shrine to the luckless prophet was raised in the 14th century, tucked away off the Canale di Cannaregio, now a sleepy backwater but once Venice's gateway to the mainland. In 1450 a Franciscan church was built on the site, designed by Antonello Gambello and financed by a stream of salvation-seeking donations. One of the most generous came from Doge Cristoforo Moro (d.1471), whose contribution secured him and his wife a beautifully fashioned tomb slab in front of the church's high altar.

In 1471 Pietro Lombardo added the fine doorway and its statues of Sts. Job and Francis (above) and Sts. Louis, Antony and Bernard of Siena below. The wandering St. Bernard, an eminent Franciscan, had preached at the earlier shrine, and it was to honor his canonization (in 1450) that the new church was created (he was also its co-dedicatee). Lombardo was also responsible for the best of the rather melancholy interior, notably the *putti*-filled reliefs supporting the cupola and the carved chancel arch and its flanking chapels.

Less accomplished, but infinitely more eye-catching, are the colossal crowned lions midway down the south wall, adornments to the tomb of a 17th-century French ambassador, the extravagantly named Renato de Voyer de Palmy Signore d'Argeson (d.1651). The nave's second altar contains a painting of the *Vision of Job*, unexceptional but for its magnificent frame, once paired with an altarpiece by Giovanni Bellini now removed to the Accademia (see page 53). The unusual **Cappella Martini** across the nave (second chapel on the left) was created for silk-weavers from Lucca, hence its glazed roundels and distinctive majolica, both the work of the Tuscan-based della Robbia family. The recently restored sacristy off the right nave has a fine ceiling and a triptych of the *Annunciation and Sts. Michael and Antony* (1445) by Antonio Vivarini and Giovanni d'Alemagna.

MONKISH VANDALS
The bells of San Giobbe's oratory reputedly so annoyed the monks of a neighboring foundation that they crept out one night and destroyed its campanile; they then had to rebuild it at their own expense.

PLAGUE AND PROPHETS
Venice has five churches built to celebrate the passing of plagues or the saints who protected against them: the Redentore, San Giobbe, San Rocco, San Sebastiano, and Santa Maria della Salute. It also followed the Greek Orthodox habit of dedicating churches to Old Testament prophets—Job, Moses (San Moisè), and Samuel (San Samuele).

139

THREE ARCHES
The Ponte dei Tre Archi, close to San Giobbe, is the only bridge in Venice with more than one arch.

ST. BERNARD
San Giobbe's co-dedicatee, St. Bernard, is the patron saint of advertizing, owing to his dictum on rhetoric which advised preachers to keep things "short, sharp and to the point."

The lions from the ambassador's tomb

TRAINS

San Giorgio might have looked very different: when the mainland causeway was built in 1846 there were plans to bring trains across to the Giudecca on an elevated line that was to end in a busy terminus alongside the church.

WHITE IS RIGHT

"Of all colors," wrote Palladio, "none is more proper for churches than white, since the purity of the color...is particularly gratifying to God."
Andrea Palladio, *I Quattro Libri* (1570)

The carved choir impresses through its sheer scale

▶▶ San Giorgio Maggiore   51D1

Isola di San Giorgio Maggiore (Quay: San Giorgio; Vaporetto 82)
Open: daily 9:30–noon, 2:30–6. (4 in winter)
Admission to the campanile: inexpensive

Like the Salute, whose facade it partly mimics, Palladio's San Giorgio Maggiore fixes the eye from San Marco and the Riva degli Schiavoni, its panoramic place on the Venetian skyline almost as important as the building itself. Your most abiding memory of the church, however, is likely to be the breathtaking view from its bell tower, a panorama that surpasses the vista from St. Mark's more famous and more visited Campanile (see pages 84–85).

The first church here was founded in 790, its position doubtless as irresistible then as it is today, and this was joined by a Benedictine monastery in 982. Both buildings were destroyed by an earthquake in 1223, the monastery being rebuilt in 1443, the church having to wait until Palladio's arrival in 1565. The campanile (1791) replaced an earlier tower that collapsed in 1774, leaving, as one contemporary put it, "a dismal vacancy among the marvels." The little lighthouses, dating from 1828, were built after Napoléon dissolved the monastery and declared the island a "free port." Most of the monastery complex, restored after World War II, is now used as a conference and exhibition space.

The architectural subtleties of Palladio's facade, a harmonious interplay of line and space, borrow heavily from ancient pagan temples, using such classical devices as a triangular pediment and four-columned portico as its centerpiece, with smaller half-pilasters and pediments to either side to front the aisle. (Aisles were absent from the single-naved basilicas Palladio took as his model, and his solution to this potential problem is part of the building's genius.)

The ancient world also provided inspiration in the interior, a space Goethe found austere and spiritually cleansing, but which to modern eyes can seem a little empty. Light is introduced by broad, high windows, a device borrowed from old Roman *terme*, or bathhouses. A little might perhaps have been induced to fall on Jacopo Bassano's famous *Adoration of the Shepherds* (1582), a painting whose crepuscular gloom is lit only by a sickly glow emanating from the infant Jesus (second altar on the right). Far better are the paintings in the chancel: Tintoretto's *The Fall of Manna* and *The Last Supper*, the latter among the most lauded of his pictures. Both were painted in the last year of the artist's life.

Other well-labeled works by Tintoretto and his school lie scattered around the walls, but the only thing worth seeing before heading for the campanile is the superb **choir** (1594–1598), tucked away behind the high altar and its bizarre bronze orb. Few of the stalls, which depict *Scenes from the Life of St. Benedict*, have much in the way of individual delicacy, but in their carving and overall effect they are staggering. Note in particular the jockey-like cherubs riding seahorses in front of each stall, and the pair of bronzes on the balustrade of *Sts. George and Stephen* (1593) by Niccolò Roccatagliata.

Palladio's San Giorgio

EARLY-MORNING EYESORE

Every morning, John Ruskin woke in his room in the Hotel Danieli to see San Giorgio Maggiore across the water. It was not a sight he enjoyed. "It is impossible," he wrote of the church, "to conceive a design more gross, more barbarous, more childish in conception, more servile in plagiarism, more insipid in result, more contemptible under every point of rational regard." *Works* (ed 1904)

UNREASONABLE SUCCESS

Although Henry James thought San Giorgio an "ugly Palladian church," he also considered it "a success beyond all reason …a success of position, of color, of the immense detached Campanile… so grandly conspicuous, with a great deal of worn, faded-looking brickwork… a kind of suffusion of rosiness." *Venice* (1882)

RED PRIEST

The font used to baptize Vivaldi stands at the start of San Giovanni's left aisle. A great orange marble affair, it was fashioned from a salvaged Gothic capital and topped with a fading, gilt-covered canopy. On the wall to its right are copies of the original baptismal document, dated May 6, 1678. A plaque on the left of church's beautifully simple facade records the event, describing Vivaldi as the *prete rosso* (red priest), a nickname that referred to either his red hair or the red uniform he wore.

▶▶ San Giovanni in Bragora 275E2

Campo Bandiera e Moro (Quay: Arsenale; Vaporetto 1; Motoscafi 41, 42)
Open: Mon–Fri 9:30–11, 5–7, Sat 9–11

San Giovanni deserves to be known as more than the spot where Antonio Vivaldi was baptized, for not only is it one of Venice's oldest churches, founded in the 8th century (and rebuilt in 1090 and 1475), but its lovely and intimate little interior also contains a marvelous potpourri of paintings, relics, and icons as well as the font used to baptize the young Vivaldi (see panel).

The church's name derives—depending on whom you believe—from *brágora*, which means "market place"; from two dialect words, *brago* (mud) and *gora* (stagnant canal); from the Greek *agora*, meaning "town square"; from *bragolare* (to fish); or from the region in the Middle East that yielded the relics of John the Baptist, to whom the church is dedicated (note the well in the *campo* outside, which has a fine head of the Baptist).

The church's paintings start on the right (south) wall with a triptych to the left of the first chapel by Francesco Bissolo

and a (better) *Madonna and Saints*, which is by Bartolomeo Vivarini. Between the two, above the confessional, is a small Byzantine Madonna. The gaudy second chapel contains the relics of St. John the Almsgiver, brought to Venice from Alexandria in 1247 (note the blackened face and gnarled hands poking out of the sleeves). The fine relief above the sacristy door is somewhat overshadowed by the paintings to either side, Alvise Vivarini's *Risen Christ* (1498) to the left, and Cima da Conegliano's *Constantine and St. Helena* (1502) to the right. The latter has a view of Cima's home town, Conegliano, together with its Palazzo del Podestà, which was damaged by a collapsing tower in 1501.

Cima was also responsible for the church's pictorial highlight, *The Baptism of Christ* (1494), its beautiful frame offset by the high altar's extravagantly stuccoed vaults. Full of limpid blues and winged, multicolored heads, each floating

Above: the font in which Vivaldi was baptized
Far right: The Baptism of Christ by Cima da Conegliano

on its cloud, it is the finest of the painter's many attempts to evoke an idealized northern Italian landscape. Less grandiose, but no less lovely, are two paintings on the wall of the left (north) aisle: a small *Head of the Saviour* by Alvise Vivarini, and Bartolomeo Vivarini's enchanting *Madonna and Child* (1478), to the right of the second chapel.

From Vivaldi and Monteverdi to the crooning of off-key gondoliers, Venice has always been a city steeped in music. Church choirs, opera, and four grand conservatories brought it fame throughout Europe during the 17th century, a period that can still be relived through the many recitals in its present-day churches and concert halls.

DEAD BABIES

A Spanish visitor explains the reasons for founding the Pietà: "In times past, there were few weeks, or even days, when the fishermen did not take dead babies from their nets, and this, they say, came from the fact that the merchants were so long separated from their wives. These...became pregnant, and with intent to save their reputations threw the offspring out of the window into the sea...The rulers...took counsel together and founded a great and rich hospital, very finely built, and placed in it a hundred wet nurses to suckle the babes..." *Pero Tafur, Travels and Adventures, 1435–1439*

Antonio Vivaldi, by an unknown artist

Excellence

"When I search for a word to replace that of music," wrote Nietzsche, "I can think only of Venice." The Englishman Thomas Coryat, visiting San Rocco in 1608, heard "Musicke...so good, so delectable, so rare, so admirable, so superexcellent, that it did even ravish and stupifie all those strangers that never heard the like." In 1739 the French diplomat, Charles de Brosses, wrote that "never am I in want of music here, for there is scarcely an evening on which there is not a concert." Another Frenchman, Jean Jacques Rousseau, claimed never to have heard anything as "voluptuous and affecting" as Venetian music, declaring it unequaled in the "richness of its art, the excellence of the voices, the justness of the execution [and] the exquisite taste of the vocal part."

The *Ospedali*

Much of Venice's musical success sprang from four foundling hospitals, or *Ospedali*, state orphanages founded during the 15th century (see panel), whose orphaned girls received a musical training as part of their state-funded upbringing. By the 18th century their fame and prestige were such that one, La Pietà, had Vivaldi as its head, and parents were passing their children off as orphans in order to gain entry to their choirs and orchestras. "Every Sunday or feast day," wrote Edward Wright, a 17th-century visitor, "in the chapels of these hospices, concerts of vocal and instrumental music are given by the young girls of the institution." The girls played all the instruments, from organ to oboe, but were otherwise allowed out in public only twice a year (and only then with their instructors). Marriage provided the only other means of escape.

Antonio Vivaldi

Venice's most famous composer was born in 1678, the son of a violinist in the orchestra of San Marco. Brought up for the priesthood and ordained in 1703, Vivaldi none the less decided to concentrate on a musical career, teaching the violin at La Pietà for almost 40 years. The girls' resident orchestra enabled him to create an abundance of

orchestral compositions, amongst them the 454 concertos on which his fame largely rests (of these 230 were written for violin and orchestra, 40 for bassoon, 25 for cello, 15 for oboe, and 10 for flute). Vivaldi helped establish the classic three-movement concerto, and to form the fast–slow–fast plan of the concerto's three movements (he also wrote some 50 operas, now mostly forgotten). Although praised at the height of his career (during the 1720s), his music's passion and lyricism were also criticised by contemporaries as eccentric. By the 1730s his star had waned, de Brosses being "much surprised" in 1739 to find "he is not much appreciated here, where everything depends upon the fashion of the day." In 1740, seeking pastures new, he left Venice for Vienna, but died, unlamented, in 1741. He received only a pauper's funeral.

Claudio Monteverdi Venice's other great composer, by contrast, was buried with full pomp in the Frari. Born in Cremona in 1567, Monteverdi became *maestro di cappella*, or master of music, at the Basilica di San Marco in 1613. Having cut his teeth on the madrigal, a form in which music was matched to the mood of the words, it was only a short step to producing his first opera (*Orfeo*, in 1607), a work which with the subsequent *Ulisse* (1641) and *Poppea* (1642) can be said to have virtually invented the modern opera. He also revitalised music in the basilica, creating a body of often highly innovative church music (notably the *Vespers* collection in 1610).

In Santo Stefano

CATERWAULING
Mark Twain was far from entranced by his gondolier's singing: "I stood it a while. Then I said: 'Now, here, Roderigo Gonzales Michael Angelo, I'm a pilgrim, and I'm a stranger, but I am not going to have my feelings lacerated by any such caterwauling as that... I will accept the hearse under protest...but here I register a dark and bloody oath that you shan't sing. Another yelp, and overboard you go.'"
The Innocents Abroad (1869)

Claudio Monteverdi

The imposing entrance to San Zanipolo; the columns on either side are from a lost church on Torcello

MENDICANTS

Mendicants were members of the Franciscan, Dominican, and Augustinian orders thrown up by the religious revival in Italy in the 13th century. Unlike earlier orders, such as the Benedictines, they worked among common people, seeking to preach to the masses and relieve the suffering of the poor and sick. Their churches were large and simple, in line with their desire to reach as many people as possible. In Venice the Dominicans built San Zanipolo; the Franciscans the Frari and San Francesco della Vigna; the Augustinians Santo Stefano; the Carmelites Santa Maria del Carmelo and the Scalzi; and the Servites Santa Maria dei Servi.

NOCTURNAL FANCY

When the Dominicans first arrived in Venice in 1224 they lived in tents under the portico of San Martino, a church close to the Arsenale. Ten years later Giacomo Tiepolo (doge from 1229 to 1249) was prompted by a dream to donate a swampy area of the lagoon to the order as a site for a new church. In his vision, he heard a voice saying, "I have chosen this place for my ministry," and saw the marsh covered in flowers, with white doves circling above with the sign of the Cross on their heads.

▶▶▶ Santi Giovanni e Paolo (San Zanipolo)   *274C5*

Campo Santi Giovanni e Paolo (Quay: Rialto; Vaporetti 1, 82)
Open: Mon–Sat 9–noon, 2:30–6, Sun 3–6

Venice's word-mangling dialect renders Santi Giovanni e Paolo as San Zanipolo, the colloquial name for a church whose only Venetian rival is the similarly Gothic and gargantuan Santa Maria dei Frari across the city (see pages 160–167). Where the latter is the more beautiful building, and home to more ravishing paintings, San Zanipolo's appeal centers on its tremendous tombs—25 doges are buried here—and on surroundings that include Verrocchio's great **Colleoni statue** (see pages 152–153) and the magnificent facade of the **Scuola Grande di San Marco** (see panel on page 147).

It was one man's dream, according to legend, that persuaded the Republic to make over an area of swamp for the first San Zanipolo (see panel). A church was founded on the site in 1246, but demolished in 1333 to make way for the present building, completed in 1390 and consecrated in 1430. Its utilitarian design—large and simple—was intended to match the Dominicans' mendicant aspirations, chief of which was a huge public space to preach to large congregations (see panel).

As a result the church's facade is somewhat plain and is overshadowed by its surroundings, in particular by the dazzling confection of the adjacent Scuola Grande di San Marco. A few of its trappings, however, give pause for thought, notably the enclosed chapel housing the Bellini brothers' tombs (see panel) and the main portal, adorned with a pair of Byzantine reliefs and six Greek marble columns from a (now vanished) church on Torcello. The four tombs built into the facade include the grave of Doge Giacomo Tiepolo (d.1249), the visionary whose dream supposedly inspired the church (it is the most ornate of the four, immediately to the left of the door).

Inside, some stained glass and a handful of paintings aside, your main task is to traipse around a progression of tombs and monuments, an occasionally wearying procession relieved by the stories attaching to some and the outstanding sculptural work of others.

What to see

1. Monumento al Doge Giovanni Mocenigo (d.1485) The Mocenigo family managed not only a dynastic stranglehold on the church's rear (west wall), every piece of statuary here being devoted to a member of the family, but also a monopoly on the skills of Pietro, Antonio, and Tullio Lombardo. Some of the finest Venetian sculptors of their day, the trio were responsible collectively and individually for five separate tombs in the church: this one is the work of Pietro's son, Tullio.

2. Monumento al Doge Alvise Mocenigo (d.1577) Alvise's tomb is a large room that twists around the main door, its best features the rather incidental pair of saints by Pietro Lombardo, hidden in niches.

3. Monumento al Doge Pietro Mocenigo All three members of the Lombardo family were responsible for

BELLINI BROTHERS
Two of Venice's finest painters, Gentile and Giovanni Bellini, are buried in the Cappella di Sant' Orsola, located outside San Zanipolo between the apse and the door to the right transept. Now a closed chapel, in the past it formed part of the Scuola di Sant'Orsola.

SCUOLA GRANDE DI SAN MARCO
Now a hospital, but once the wealthiest of all Venice's *scuole* (see pages 190–191), the Scuola di San Marco retains one of Venice's most captivating facades. Begun in 1487 by Pietro Lombardo and Giovanni Buora, its upper levels were finished eight years later by Mauro Coducci, the architect also active in the nearby churches of Santa Maria Formosa and San Zaccaria.

147

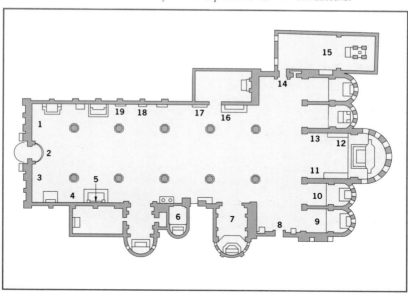

Santi Giovanni e Paolo (San Zanipolo)

The motto on Pietro Mocenigo's tomb reads Ex Hostium Manibus *(from the hands of my enemies)*

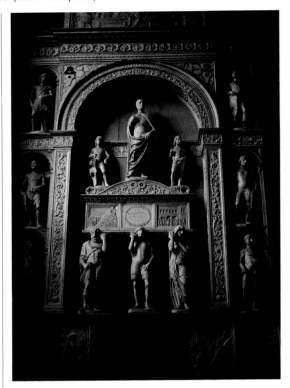

SKINNED ALIVE
Marcantonio Bragadino was a Venetian general captured, tortured, and executed by the Turks in Cyprus in 1571. After a siege lasting 11 months the Turks reneged on a promise of safe passage for him and his officers. The men were butchered and Bragadino had his nose and ears cut off and was brutally tortured. He was threatened with execution three times, each time the executioner withholding his blade at the last moment. Laden with earth, he then had to parade for ten days in front of the Turkish positions, halting to kiss the ground each time he passed in front of the Pasha's encampment. He was also left to hang from the yard-arm of a ship for hours at a time. Finally he was chained to a stake and slowly skinned alive in front of the Pasha. His peeled skin was stuffed with straw, and after suffering numerous indignities returned to Venice. The general's death was avenged at the Battle of Lepanto by Doge Venier, whose bronze statue stands in San Zanipolo's north transept (14).

this tomb (1476–1481), one of the church's undoubted masterpieces. A heroic piece of bombast, it was designed to glorify Pietro (d.1476) while paying little more than lip-service to the religious niceties. The base contains two reliefs depicting the Labors of Hercules, using a pagan story in a Christian context in a typically Renaissance conceit. The Doge, a high and haughty figure, poses inside a triumphal arch (another classical allusion) supported by three figures representing the three ages of man. Reliefs on the sarcophagus recall episodes from the Doge's life, while the Latin motto inscribed at its center— *Ex Hostium Manibus*—suggests that defeated enemies and the spoils of war may have effectively paid for the tomb. The monument's religious elements, such as they are, remain stranded near the summit—a relief of the *Resurrection* with the Virgin and Mary Magdalene at Christ's sepulchre.

4. Monumento al Marcantonio Bragadino (d.1571) One of the most stomach-turning episodes in Venice's history distinguishes this monument (see panel). The large dark urn contains the yellowing and neatly folded skin of Marcantonio Bragadino.

5. St. Vincent Ferrer Giovanni Bellini's lovely polyptych, an early work (ca1465), shows St. Vincent Ferrer (with Sts. Christopher and Sebastian), a preacher of the hellfire and damnation school known chiefly for his enthusiastic promotion of religious persecution in Spain. The effigy below is of the Blessed Tommaso Caraffini, confessor and biographer of St. Catherine of Siena (see panel on page 150).

6. Cappella della Madonna della Pace This chapel takes its name from the miracle-working Byzantine Madonna over the altar, an icon brought to Venice in 1349. It is more remarkable, however, for the over-the-top tombs stacked around its entrance, grandiloquent monuments to two obscure 17th-century doges, Bertuccio (d.1658) and Silvestro Valier (d.1700). Valier, an inveterate gambler, bought his way into the nobility for the bargain sum of 20,500 ducats. According to one contemporary report he was elected doge simply "because he was decorative." The tomb alongside contains Silvestro's wife, the legendary Elisabetta Querini (d.1708), who scandalized Venetian society by insisting on a coronation (though the ceremony had been outlawed 50 years previously) and by having medals struck bearing her own effigy. She so raised the blood pressure of her husband after one argument that she is said to have caused the heart attack that killed him. John Ruskin summed up her monument in a typically robust burst of vitriol (see panel).

DOGARESSA VALIER
John Ruskin described Elisabetta Valier's tomb as "a consummation of grossness, vanity, and ugliness—the figure of a large and wrinkled woman, with elaborate curls in a stiff projection round her face, covered from shoulders to her feet with ruffs, furs, lace, jewels, and embroidery...[the monument] deserving attentive study as exhibiting every condition of false taste and feeble conception."
Works, Vol. XI (1904)

7. Cappella di San Domenico Giambattista Piazzetta, tutor to G B Tiepolo and founder of the Accademia, executed the lascivious frescoes in the vault, a view of *St. Dominic in Glory* (1727) showing the saint rising heavenwards in the company of a small orchestra and a forest of fleshy thighs. The six big bronze reliefs on the left, scenes

The Cappella della Madonna della Pace

Santi Giovanni e Paolo (San Zanipolo)

CATHERINE OF SIENA

One of Italy's two patron saints (Francis is the other), Catherine (1347–1380) earned Europe's gratitude by persuading the popes to return to Rome from Avignon. The youngest of 25 children, she spent much of her life prostrate on wooden boards, wrapped in a hair shirt, or climbing stairs on her knees (uttering a Hail Mary on each step). Bits of her body are scattered all over Italy—a foot in San Zanipolo, skull in Siena, ribs in Rome.

NO NUDES

Tullio Lombardo's monument to Andrea Vendramin originally included two fine nude figures of Adam and Eve. Both were removed in deference to 19th-century moral scruples and replaced with less titillating statues. The figure of Adam is now in New York's Metropolitan Museum of Art.

The tomb of Doge Michele Steno, one of 25 doges to be buried within San Zanipolo

from the *Life of St. Dominic* (1720), are the work of the Bolognese sculptor Giuseppe Mazza. Beside the chapel is a minute shrine bearing the foot of St. Catherine of Siena, a tiny blackened relic preserved in a golden Gothic reliquary (see panel).

8. Transetto (south transept) The best paintings in San Zanipolo after Bellini's *St. Vincent* appear as you turn the corner into the right transept. From right to left around the walls, they are Alvise Vivarini's *Christ Carrying the Cross; The Coronation of the Virgin*, attributed to Cima da Conegliano and Giovanni Martini da Udine; Lorenzo Lotto's wonderful *St. Antoninius Pieruzzi Giving Alms to the Poor* (1542) (Pieruzzi, who died in 1459, was Archbishop of Florence) and the age-darkened *Christ between Sts. Peter and Andrew* by Rocco Marconi. Lotto asked only his expenses and a tomb in the church in return for his painting, but was eventually driven from Venice by petty jealousies among the city's painters. He was eventually buried in Loreto, in the Marche. The transept's stained glass (1473), among the city's finest, was designed by Bartolomeo Vivarini (Alvise's father), and made at Murano. The dog-eared chair below is the throne used by doges when they visited the church.

9. Cappella del Crocifisso Apart from two bronzes by Alessandro Vittoria (difficult to see against the altar's black marble), the only point of interest here is the tomb (on the right wall) of Sir Edward Windsor, a Catholic exile from Elizabethan England who died in Venice in 1574.

10. Cappella della Maddalena The monument on the right of this chapel is the *Tomb of Admiral Vettor Pisani,* whose victory against the Genoese at Chioggia in 1380 (when he was mortally wounded) was vital in preserving Venice's supremacy at sea and thus its future prosperity. The tomb was restored and reconstructed in 1980, on the 600th anniversary of its occupant's death.

11. Monumento al Doge Michele Morosini This lovely tomb is a Venetian Gothic-Byzantine hybrid that John Ruskin described as "the richest monument of the Gothic period in Venice." Its occupant reigned for just four months before succumbing to the plague in 1382.

12. Monumento al Doge Andrea Vendramin (d.1478) Dazzling white marble and sheer size distinguish this tomb, a fine work by Antonio and Tullio Lombardo. Ruskin ruffled Venetian feathers when he demanded a ladder to clamber over the sculpture, anxious to prove the Lombardi had failed to finish the parts of the statuary invisible from below. When his suspicions were confirmed he condemned the Lombardi's lapse as an act of "intellectual and moral degradation."

13. Monumento al Doge Marco Corner (d.1368) This tomb's graceful Madonna (the central one of its five figures) was carved in Pisa by the early Tuscan master, Nino Pisano. Often described as the finest Gothic sculpture in Venice, its tiny size and high position unfortunately make it almost impossible to study in any detail.

14. Transetto (north transept) The walls here belong to the Venier family, one of the city's oldest and most eminent patrician clans. From right to left, they contain the tombs of Doge Sebastiano Venier (d.1578), commander of the fleet at the Battle of Lepanto; Doge Antonio Venier, who died in 1400 (above the door); and Antonio's wife, Agnese, and daughter Orsola.

15. Cappella del Rosario This chapel was created to commemorate the Battle of Lepanto, which took place on the feast day of the Madonna of the Rosary, or *Rosario*. Ravaged by fire in 1867, it lost masterpieces by Titian and Bellini that had been stored here awaiting restoration. A copy of the Titian, the *Martyrdom of St. Peter*, can be seen to the left of Doge Marcello's tomb (19 below). The chapel's best pictures are Veronese's ceiling panels, transplanted here from the demolished church of the Umiltà.

16. Monumento a Palma Giovane (d.1628) The painter Palma Giovane designed his own monument (above the sacristy door), adorning it with busts of himself, Titian, and Palma Vecchio. The three fragments of fresco to the right depict *Three Saints* (1473), parts of a polyptych by Bartolomeo Vivarini.

17. Monumento al Doge Pasquale Malipiero (d.1462) This eye-catching and excellent piece—showing Pasquale recumbent under a vast canopy—is a youthful work by Pietro Lombardo. The sculptor's first undertaking in the church, it was also among Venice's earliest Renaissance tombs.

18. Monumento al Doge Tommaso Mocenigo A tomb (ca1425) in a transitional Gothic-Renaissance style sculpted by Pietro Lamberti and Giovanni di Martino.

19. Monumento al Doge Nicolò Marcello (d.1474) In this outstanding tomb, Pietro Lombardo has abandoned the Gothic canopy of his nearby monument to Malipiero (17)—sculpted some 15 years earlier—in favor of a work more firmly rooted in Renaissance tradition. The final altar to its left has a statue of San Girolamo (1576) by Alessandro Vittoria.

The tomb of Doge Marco Corner

FAKE FUNERALS
From the 15th century, all the funerals of the doges took place in San Zanipolo. Doge Giovanni Mocenigo, however, was buried privately in a family vault before the state funeral in 1485. Mocenigo died of plague, which for health reasons meant his body had to be replaced with a dummy stuffed with straw and a wax mask. Thereafter, all dogal cadavers were replaced by fakes.

CAMPO SAN ZANIPOLO
The little square outside the church of Santi Giovanni e Paolo was known until the 19th century as the Campo delle Maravege, or "Square of Marvels." This may be because of the many extraordinary events said to have occurred there—though history does not relate what they were—or as a result of its beautiful building.

BIZARRE BAROQUE
Leave Santi Giovanni e Paolo and go east on Salizzada SS Giovanni e Paolo to the Ospedaletto, or Santa Maria dei Derelitti, a hospice and church whose extraordinary facade (1662–1674) was built by Baldassare Longhena. A baroque masterpiece, the frontage was deliberately intended to shock and impress; its various motifs—lions, grotesques and giant heads—all carved on an excessively grand scale. The building was originally conceived as a home for the aged, and for destitute, and orphaned children—one of several such institutions in the city (see page 144).

"I do not believe," wrote John Ruskin of Verrocchio's statue of Bartolomeo Colleoni, *"that there is a more glorious work of sculpture existing in the world."* Henry James thought it *"incomparable, the finest of all mounted figures,"* while Hugh Honour felt the horse, at least, had *"a sense of lively, powerful movement hard to parallel in Western art."*

VASARI ON VERROCCHIO

"Andrea smashed the legs and head of his model and returned in a rage to Florence. When the Signoria heard what had happened they gave him to understand that he had better not return to Venice or they would cut off his head. To this Andrea wrote in reply that he would take good care not to return, for once they had cut off a man's head they had no way of replacing it, certainly not one like his: whereas he would have been able to replace the head of the horse, and with something more beautiful at that." Vasari, *Lives of the Artists* (1550)

The man Given the praise lavished on his statue, it is ironic that the man who inspired Venice's sculptural *nonpareil*, the *condottiere* Bartolomeo Colleoni, should have been a mercenary soldier of less than dazzling character. "Somewhat dim," observed Honour, "distinguished neither as a general nor as a personality." Born in Bergamo, Colleoni started his military career in Naples, aged 19, and entered Venetian service in 1431 under another great mercenary, the famous Gattamelata (himself honored with an equestrian statue in Padua). After spells working for Milan (the city imprisoned him for his pains), he went over to the Venetian cause in 1455, tempted by the only thing that could guarantee the loyalty of a medieval mercenary—a gargantuan salary. Life thereafter was something of a vacation, largely because he was called upon to fight only once in the 20 years up to his death.

With few biographical details to detain them, historians over the centuries have been less concerned with Colleoni's exploits than with the origin of his name, which is a corruption of *coglioni*, or "testicles," a play on words of which the mercenary was inordinately proud (*coglioni* featured conspicuously on his emblem). The English traveler Thomas Coryat, writing in 1611, repeated a story—put about by Colleoni himself—that "Bathelmew Coleon…had his name from having *three* stones, for the Italian word Coglione doth signifie a testicle."

152

The scam On Colleoni's death in 1475 Venice was pleased to discover that its faithful servant had left the bulk of his vast fortune—some 100,000 ducats—to the state. They were rather less happy to find that the bequest was dependent on them raising a statue of the *condottiere* in Piazza San Marco. Never keen to encourage the cult of the individual, the Republic was prevented by law and precedent from commemorating any single man in the city's most prominent square. At the same time the Venetians were desperate for the money, and so came up with the notion of building a monument not in *Piazza* San Marco, but in *Campo* San Marco, a small square in front of San Zanipolo.

The statue All except Colleoni, who could hardly complain, were happy with the compromise, and in 1481 the Senate awarded a commission for the statue to the Florentine sculptor Andrea Verrocchio. No sooner had Verrocchio finished modeling the horse, however, than word reached him that the Senate was considering giving the task of completing the figure to another artist (one Vellano of Padua, who had been involved with Donatello's statue of Gattamelata in Padua some 20 years earlier). Verrocchio promptly broke the heads and legs off his horse and returned to Florence in a huff. The Senate, never quick to forgive, forbade him to return on pain of death, an injunction the sculptor seems to have met with equanimity (see panel on page 152).

Once peace had been made, Verrocchio returned to finish the work in 1488—only to die of a chill soon after, leaving the sculpture half-finished. Work was completed in 1496 by Alessandro Leopardi, a local artist (famous for San Marco's flagpoles), and the final result, in the words of J. A. Symonds, was a "joint creation of Florentine science and Venetian fervor" (*History of the Renaissance*, 1875–1886). It was not a portrait (it is unlikely that either artist had ever set eyes on Colleoni), but rather it represented an idealized picture of a medieval warrior, vividly bringing to life, in Hugh Honour's words, "the distant world of fifteenth-century Italy in all its brilliance and brutality."

Top left: 15th-century warriors
Above and far left: Colleoni dominates the small campo by San Zanipolo

A RUM BUNCH

"It is a monument less to an individual than to a whole class of men, the most mercenary captains of all time—proud, treacherous, money-grubbing, rapacious, chivalrous only to those who could reward chivalry with hard cash or to those of their own kind from whom similar treatment was expected by the code of thieves." Hugh Honour, *The Companion Guide* (1965)

JOINT EFFORT

"To Verrocchio, profiting by the example of Donatello's 'Gattamelata,' must be assigned the general conception of this statue; but the breath of life that animates both horse and rider, the richness of detail that enhances the massive grandeur of the group, and the fiery spirit of its style of execution were due to the Venetian genius of Leopardi." J A Symonds, *History of the Renaissance* (1875–1886).

Walk

San Marco to the Arsenale
(pages 274–275)

Start in Piazza San Marco. Take Merceria dell'Orologio (beneath the clock tower) to Calle Fiubera and turn right to San Zulian. Then follow Calle degli Arditi and Calle Cassellaria to reach Campo Santa Maria Formosa.

San Zulian, or San Giuliano, rebuilt by Sansovino in 1553, is known for the figure over its door, one Tommaso Rangone. The man who funded the church's rebuilding, he wished to be remembered for his scholarship, and is shown surrounded by books and globes. Inside are a *Pietà* by Veronese (first altar on the right), ceiling frescoes by Palma Giovane, and Giovanni da Santacroce's *Coronation of the Virgin*. **Santa Maria Formosa** has a pair of dilapidated facades and a couple of good paintings (see pages 156–157). Campo Santa Maria Formosa is one of the city's livelier squares.

Take Ruga Giuffa (the southeastern corner of Campo Santa Maria Formosa) then the second right, Calle dei Mercanti, and follow it to Calle della Chiesa and Campo Santi Filippo e Giacomo. Turn left along Salizzada San Provolo to Campo San Zaccaria.

A touching little bas-relief above an arch ushers you into Campo San Zaccaria, whose church of that name contains Giovanni Bellini's majestic altarpiece (left aisle) and a little "museum" off the right aisle with more fine paintings (see pages 186–188).

Retrace your steps down Salizzada San Provolo and take the first right, Campo San Provolo. Follow Fondamenta dell'Osmarin to the bridge across Rio dei Greci. Turn right into the little lane that leads to San Giorgio dei Greci, and the Museo Dipinti Sacri Byzantini (Byzantine Art Museum, also known as the Icon Museum) next door.

San Giorgio dei Greci is the mother church of Venice's Greek community, which at its 16th-century peak numbered some 4,000 people. Looked down on by its topsy-turvy tower, the church dates from 1539. The interior, though small, is most striking, thanks mainly to the icon-covered iconostasis, or rood screen, that dominates its altar wall. The work of a 16th-century Cretan artist, it incorporates Byzantine fragments from the 12th century. The next-door building is a small museum housing an excellent collection of 16th-, 17th-, and 18th-century icons.

Left: In the Sant'Elena Gardens

Return to the canal and recross the bridge to follow Fondamenta di San Lorenzo. Turn right into Campo San Lorenzo. Take Calle di San Lorenzo on the right-hand side of the Campo. Turn left at the canal, cross the bridge, and turn left to meet Salizzada Santa Giustina. Turn left on Fondego del Te Deum to San Francesco della Vigna.

The Rio di San Lorenzo was the site of the miracle in Gentile Bellini's famous painting in the Accademia, *The Miracle of the Cross at Ponte San Lorenzo* (see page 57). **San Lorenzo** was the burial place of Marco Polo (though his remains were lost during restorations). **San Francesco della Vigna** sits in unprepossessing surroundings (see page 137), but is worth seeing for its Palladio-designed facade and outstanding paintings.

Return to Salizzada Santa Giustina and turn left. Turn right on Salizzada San Francesco. Continue down Salizzada delle Gatte and then turn right into Campo delle Gatte. Take Calle dei Furlani to San Giorgio degli Schiavoni. Turn left along Fondamenta dei Furlani to Campo San Antonin. Turn left on Salizzada San Antonin and continue to Campo Bandiera e Moro.

Be certain to stop at **San Giorgio degli Schiavoni** to see Carpaccio's charming fresco cycle (see pages 200–202). **San Giovanni in Bragora**, Vivaldi's baptismal church, has a deceptively plain frontage but is encrusted inside with paintings and lovely decoration (see page 142).

Take the alley to the left of San Giovanni in Bragora, Calle del Preu, and then the second left, Calle del Prestin. At Campo San Martino follow the canal east to the entrance to the Arsenale (see pages 112–114). Cross the canal and follow Fondamenta dell'Arsenale to the Museo Storico Navale (see page 115). Either return to San Marco on Riva degli Schiavoni, or extend the walk by following Via Garibaldi to explore the gardens of Sant'Elena and the Biennale pavilions.

San Giorgio dei Greci; beside it in the former Scuola di San Nicolò (1678) is the Byzantine Art Museum

Santa Barbara *by Palma Vecchio*

MACABRE MASK
John Ruskin described the statue at the base of Santa Maria's campanile as "huge, inhuman and monstrous, leering in bestial degradation, too foul to be either pictured or described...in that head is embodied the type of the evil spirit to which Venice was aban-done...[the] delight in the contemplation of bestial vice, and the expression of low sarcasm, which is, I believe, the most hope-less state into which the human mind can fall."

▶▶ **Santa Maria Formosa**   277F5
Campo Santa Maria Formosa (Quay: Rialto; Vaporetti 1, 82)
Open: Mon–Sat 10–5. Admission: inexpensive
Santa Maria Formosa was inspired by a vision of *una Madonna formosa*, a "buxom Madonna," that appeared to San Magno in the 7th century. It was the first of eight sanctuaries—the so-called "Rialtine" churches—founded on the lagoon by Magno, a bishop who had been exiled to the Rialto from Oderzo, a town northeast of Venice. The matronly Madonna in this instance told him to follow a small white cloud and build a church wherever it settled.
The present building dominates the Campo Santa Maria Formosa, one the city's nicer public spaces. The rambling square, flanked by beautiful palazzi, buzzes with every-day Venetian life. One time venue of bullfights and alfresco theater, today it's a bustling scene of market stalls, cafés, and Venetian children, making the most of that rarity in Venice: a large open space. The church, built by Mauro Coducci in 1492, was grafted onto the foundations of an earlier 11th-century church. Its Greek cross plan, probably inherited from its predecessor, was a common feature of Byzantine (and later) churches dedicated to the

Virgin. The centralized scheme symbolized the womb, and the dome above, the Madonna's crown (Santa Maria della Salute has a similar arrangment; see pages 171–173).

The church has two facades, both beautifully set off by Campo Santa Maria Formosa. The right-hand frontage, overlooking the canal, dates from 1542, and was financed by the wealthy Cappello family. An exercise in self-glorification, it amounts to little more than a celebration of Vincenzo Cappello, a Venetian admiral and scourge of the Turks. His is the statue above the door, framed by a pair of suitably martial reliefs. Equally warlike, but more interesting, is the relief of a mortar to the right of the door. A graphic little thing streaming smoke and flame, it commemorates an Austrian incendiary bomb that destroyed the church's dome in 1916 (Coducci's original dome had already been destroyed by an earthquake in 1688). This was rebuilt in 1921.

As you walk back towards the campo, look out for the determinedly gruesome mask above the campanile's door, often described as the ugliest of all Venice's grotesques. This abomination brought Ruskin close to critical melt-down (see panel on page 156). Others have seen it as a talis-man to fend off the evil eye, or a depiction of a 16th-century victim of the same congenital condition that disfigured the "Elephant Man." The second facade, built in 1604, also features three members of the Cappello clan.

The church's interior is a unique architectural blend, merging a welter of Renaissance decoration with Coducci's ersatz collection of Byzantine cupolas, barrel vaults, and narrow-columned screens. Of most immediate interest are two fine paintings, the first Bartolomeo Vivarini's *Madonna of the Misericordia* (1473), a triptych in the first chapel on the right (south) side. It was paid for by the church's congrega-tion, whom you can see sheltering beneath the Virgin's cloak with their curate and sprucely dressed parish priest.

The second, and more famous picture, Palma Vecchio's *Santa Barbara* (1522–1524), used the artist's daughter, Violante, as the model for its saintly protagonist (the painting is an altarpiece in the south transept). The 19th-century English novelist George Eliot described the figure as "an almost unique presen-tation of a hero-woman, standing in calm preparation for martyrdom, without the slightest air of pietism, yet with the expression of a mind filled with serious conviction." Barbara was martyred by her own father, Dioscorus, who was struck by lightning as he returned from her execution. This death-dealing blow from the heavens made her the patron saint of miners and artillerymen. The Scuola dei Bombardieri paid for her chapel here, hence the cannon and the cannonballs strewn liberally around it.

Bas-relief above the door

PALAZZO QUERINI STAMPALIA

A bridge behind Santa Maria Formosa leads to the 16th-century Palazzo Querini Stampali. Its strik-ingly modern ground floor has exhibition galleries, a café, and a grassy garden. The restored third floor rooms of the Museo della Fondazione Querini-Stampalia are devoted mainly to 18th-century furnishing and paintings. The Venetian scenes by Gabriel Bella and genre paintings by Pietro and Alessandro Longhi are notable as records of contemporary Venetian life (*Open* Tue–Sun 10–1, 3–6, Fri, Sat 10–10, with con-certs from 5–8:30 included in the admission price).

One of Venice's uglier residents graces Santa Maria Formosa

"The name of a Cortezan of Venice," reported Thomas Coryat in 1611, "is famoused over all Christendom. So infinite are the allurements of these amorous Calypsoes...that the fame of them hath drawn many to contemplate their beauties, and enjoy their pleasing dalliances... Most are esteemed so loose that they are said to open their quivers to every arrow."

CARRYING ON
"Much can be done...by the help of the gondola, for that is the lady's sanctum. It has never been known that the signora's gondolier has revealed things to the signora's husband; were it known, he would be drowned the next day by his fellows." Charles de Brosses, *Letter* (1739)

COURTESANS' CHILDREN
"If any of them happen to have any children (as indeede they have but few, for according to the old proverbe the best carpenters make the fewst chips) they are bought up either at their own charge, or in a house of the citie appointed...only for the bringing up of Cortezans bastards...male children are employed in the wares, or to serve in the arsenall, or Galleys at sea ...And many of the females if they be faire doe imitate their mothers and get their living by prostituting their bodies to their favorites." Thomas Coryat, *Coryat's Crudities* (1611)

Venice has long had a reputation for loose living, and few visitors to the city were able to leave without either recording or sampling its fabled pleasures. A French commentator, Charles de Brosses, claimed in 1739 that "in no other place in the world does so much liberty and licence exist so entirely as here...Whatever is known by the name of a bad action...is allowed with impunity." Lord Byron, another well qualified in such matters, observed in 1783 that a Venetian "woman is virtuous who limits herself to her husband and one lover; those who have two, three, or more, are a little *wild*; but it is only those who are indiscriminately diffuse, and form a low connection...who are considered as overstepping the modesty of marriage."

Vittore Carpaccio's celebrated portrait of Two Women, *from the Museo Correr. The painting was long believed to depict a pair of Venetian courtesans*

Monsieur de Brosses concurred, adding that "it is the custom to have a lover; it would indeed be a disgrace were a lady known to be without one."

Venice was still more renowned for the number and virtuosity of its courtesans, a refined and courtly breed, as John Julius Norwich has pointed out, "in no way to be confused with the regiments of whores that are part and parcel of the life of any flourishing sea-port." At the end of the 16th century, the city contained 11,654 women of the night, the most dexterous 210 of whom were recorded—along with price and specialty—in the famous *Catalogue of the Chief and Most Renowned Courtesans of Venice.* Rates ranged from one to 30 *scudi,* and to enjoy the company of all 210, it was suggested, would cost the libidinous visitor 1,200 gold *scudi.* Taxes from prostitution, it was estimated, provided the state with enough revenue to run twelve galleys. The number of patrician women at the time, by contrast, was put at 2,889, the number of female burghers at 1,936, and number of nuns at 2,508.

Venice made many attempts to regularize prostitution, seeking, for example, to confine it to certain areas (notably the banking area around San Cassiano and the Rialto). Courtesans were also forbidden to wear pearls, clogs, and fine clothes, or to decorate their boudoirs too extravagantly. The rules seem to have had little effect, however. Coryat wrote that women came to him "decked like the Queene and Godesse of love"; and according to a contemporary report a Spanish ambassador was so overwhelmed by the richness of one brothel that rather than "soil the rugs and hangings around him, he chose, with a delicacy that did him credit, to spit on the face of one of his valets."

The Venetian trade in flesh, however, was not all one way. Women, too, could take their pleasures where they found them. Nuns in particular were renowned for their moral laxity. Convents, wrote de Brosses, "had the reputation of favoring assignations...Indeed, nuns are among the most attractive among all the women in Venice." Venetians also perfected the functions of the *cicisbeo,* a young male companion of ill-defined role, for in Venice the "husband married in a church," as Lady Anna Miller pointed out in a letter of 1771, "is the choice of her friends, not by any means of the lady." There was little to fear, it appears, from aggrieved spouses: "jealousy," said Byron, "is not the order of the day in Venice, and daggers are out of fashion; while duels, on love matters, are unknown—at least with the husbands."

PAYING FOR PLEASURE
Running away without paying your courtesan was not a good idea, for "she will either cause thy throat to be cut by her Ruffiano, if he can catch thee in the City, or procure thee to be arrested (if thou are to be found) and clapped in prison, where thou shalt remaine till thou hast paid her all thou didst promise her."
Coryat's Crudities (1611)

A courtesan of the early 17th century; the distinctive hairstyle was typical of her profession

The Frari's redoubtable red-brick exterior

BERNARDO'S DEMANDS
Pietro Bernardo's will demanded (to no avail) that his corpse be washed in the best vinegar and anointed with musk. His lead coffin was to be lined with aloes and enclosed in a chest of the finest cypress wood. This was to be laid in a marble tomb, the front of which was to be inscribed with eight verses telling of his life's finer achievements. Seven psalms and miscellaneous prayers were also to be sung—in perpetuity—by 20 friars in front of his tomb at daybreak on the first Sunday of every month.

▶▶▶ **Santa Maria Gloriosa dei Frari**
Campo San Rocco (Quay: San Tomà; Vaporetti 1, 82)
Open: Mon–Sat 9–6, Sun 1–6.
Admission: inexpensive, free on Sun

Santa Maria Gloriosa dei Frari, more commonly known as the Frari, narrowly beats San Zanipolo as Venice's largest and most important church. Although unprepossessing from the outside, the vast Gothic pile has more to offer inside, including two of the city's most famous paintings and a bewildering variety of monumental tombs. Founded around 1250, it was the mother church of the city's Franciscans, from whom it takes its name—*Frari* is a Venetian corruption of *Frati*, or "friars." Work on the first building was completed in 1330, but resumed almost immediately, new funds from wealthy local families allowing for the construction of an almost entirely new church. The campanile, the exterior's most prominent feature, is the second highest in the city after St. Mark's.

Rather than wandering about the interior, try to make a methodical tour of the building. Start by walking to the rear right of the church, and then follow the plan in an anti-clockwise direction. Concerts are also sometimes held in the church.

What to see
1. Monumento a Pietro Bernardo Pietro Bernardo's tomb (1538), one of Tullio Lombardo's last works, is not much to look at, but the conceit of the man and the story behind it are both remarkable. A member of a minor patrician family, Bernardo resolved to make up in death the honor that had escaped him in life. This was to be done through the extraordinary requirements for his tomb, laid out in a will of 1515 (see panel).

2. Monumento al Alvise Pasqualino Pasqualino was a Venetian Procurator (d.1528), and while his tomb (the work of Lorenzo Bregno) is a touch more modest than

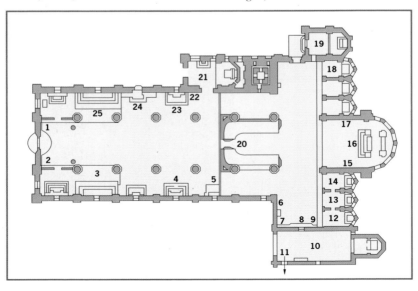

Bernardo's, it too is diminished by the mess of paintings, plumes, grubby statues, and coats-of-arms that clog the church's west wall.

3. Mausoleo Tiziano The tomb of the painter Titian was built in the mid-19th century by pupils of Canova, providing a fittingly awful partner for Canova's own monument directly opposite (which was originally earmarked for Titian—see 25 below). The artist died in the plague of 1576, aged over 90, and was buried in the Frari at his own request. His monument was a gift from Ferdinand I of Austria, who was also ruler of Lombardy and the Veneto. Look out for the pair of water stoups near the tomb (by the first pillars on each side of the nave). The

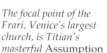

The focal point of the Frari, Venice's largest church, is Titian's masterful Assumption

Giovanni Bellini's beautiful triptych, commissioned by the Pesaro family

MIRACULOUS LETTUCE
One night in 1332, in the throes of a desperate illness, Niccolò Lion decided that the only thing that could save him was a lettuce. Servants were sent out and discovered a lettuce in the Frari's vegetable garden; their master was duly saved. Lion promptly built the Oratorio della Lattuga (the Oratory of the Lettuce) in gratitude for his deliverance. The building is now part of the complex beside the Frari housing the city's archives.

one nearer to the monument shows *St. Agnes* (1592) performing a remarkable balancing trick with a lamb, her emblem.

4. Altare San Giuseppe da Copertino This otherwise boring altar contains a statue of *St. Jerome* (1560) by Alessandro Vittoria, the face of which is said to be a portrait of Titian made just before he died. The stone in Jerome's hand recalls the saint's habit of self-castigation.

5. Altare Santa Caterina The painting here, by Palma Giovane, shows the failed martyrdom of a forlorn-looking St. Catherine. Do not miss the strange black box high up on the wall to the left of this altar, one of Venice's most bizarre anonymous tombs (see panel on page 163).

6. Monumento a Iacopo Marcello (d.1484) You will need to stand well back to admire this lovely tomb, which is attributed to Giovanni Buora. Simpler than most in the church, its Renaissance lines are enhanced by the beautifully delicate fresco that provides its background.

7. Monumento a Beato Pacifico One glance at the exquisite delicacy of this fine Gothic tomb (1437), with its intricately painted canopy and crowd of terracotta figures, is enough to discern the hand of Florentine rather than Venetian craftsmen: it was the work of Nanni di Bartolo and Michele da Firenze.

8. Monumento a Benedetto Pesaro This tomb, which provides a startling contrast to Pacifico's monument to its right, contains the remains of a Venetian admiral who died in Corfu in 1503, hence the four charming reliefs whose green and red marbles depict ships and the Ionian island fortresses of Levkas and Cephalonia.

9. Monumento a Paolo Savelli Savelli, a *condottiere* from Rome, was the first mercenary to be rewarded with a monument in Venice (he died of the plague while leading the city's army against Padua in 1405). This was also the first equestrian statue in the city (1407), though the startled-looking griffins below the tomb are more arresting than Savelli's rather tired-looking wooden horse.

10.Sacrestia The sacristy contains the most beautiful of the Frari's three great paintings, Giovanni Bellini's triptych of the *Madonna and Child between Sts. Nicholas, Peter, Mark, and Benedict* (1488). The picture was a gift from Pietro (Peter) Pesaro and his sons Niccolò, Marco, and Benedetto—hence the choice of the saints depicted. The picture is kept well away from onlookers, making it difficult to see, but even at a distance it remains ravishing. Note the tremendous perspective used to place the Madonna in her gold-coffered recess, and the manner in which the frame (the original) is carefully designed to continue the painting's perspective scheme. The picture is also still in the place Bellini intended. The illuminated work on the opposite (end) wall, almost equally sublime, is a *Madonna and Child* (1339) by Paolo Veneziano.

11.Sala del Capitolo The chapterhouse (*capitolo*) is usually only open in high summer, when you can enjoy a view of its Palladian cloister and the Tomb of Doge Dandolo (d.1339), the latter surmounted by a portrait of the doge and his wife by Paolo Veneziano (believed to be Venice's oldest surviving portrait taken from life).

12.Cappella Bernardo This chapel contains a vivid and extravagantly framed altarpiece of the *Madonna, Child, and Saints* (1482) by Bartolomeo Vivarini.

13.Ex-Cappella del Santissimo The two tombs on the opposing walls of this chapel are among the most charming in the church. The one on the left, that of Duccio degli Uberti (d.1336), contains no more than the effigy of a knight in chain mail (note the dagger at his side) and a tiny Madonna and Child hovering protectively over his head.

14.Cappella di San Giovanni Battista This chapel was devoted to Venice's Florentines and their patron saint, John the Baptist. Donatello's extraordinary statue (1438) of the saint was brought to Venice from Padua (where Donatello was then working). This is the sculptor's only work in Venice (and his earliest documented work in the Veneto).

15.Monumento al Doge Francesco Foscari Foscari died in 1457 after 34 years as doge, the longest term of office in Venice's history, his long service earning him one of the most prominent positions in the church (see panel on

MYSTERY COFFIN
In a church full of famous and grandiloquent tombs, the crude anonymity of the black box high on the wall at the end of the right nave is something of mystery. It is said to contain the ashes of a murdered Venetian noble-man, but one legend claims it was intended for the body of a *condottiere*, Carmagnola, who, having led a Venetian army to defeat in 1431, was lured back to the city, where he was charged with treason, tortured, and beheaded.

MOURNING BEARD
Niccolò Tron's effigy on his tomb to the left of the high altar sports a magnificently bushy beard. The doge began to grow it on the death of his favorite son, refusing to shave as a token of perpetual mourning.

163

St. John the Baptist, *the only work in Venice by the Florentine Donatello*

TITIAN'S *ASSUMPTION*

Despite its present fame, Titian's *Assumption* on the Frari's high altar was not always so well regarded. A 17th-century chronicler tells how the Franciscans who commissioned it criticized the artist's work. The Emperor Charles V, hearing of their dissatisfaction, offered to buy the painting. The possibility that they might lose the picture brought the friars to their senses: "art," they conceded hurriedly, "was not their profession, and use of the breviary did not convey a knowledge of painting." Later 16th-century Franciscans back-pedaled, however, and put the work into storage, where it remained until last century.

STATE ARCHIVES

Since 1815 the austere building on the north side of the Frari—once a Franciscan convent—has housed the *Archivio di Stato*. Home to almost 1,000 years' accumulation of state archives, its 280 rooms contain every scintilla of gossip collected by the Inquisition, every detail of the city's gamblers and whores, and every state secret or treaty since the 9th century. The whole lot is arranged in around 250,000 files on an estimated 45 miles of shelves. The reading rooms are open Mon and Sat 8:30–2, Tue–Fri 8:30–6.

Titian's magnificent Assumption *was initially considered too revolutionary by the Franciscan friars*

page 165). The tomb, an outstanding work, is attributed either to Antonio and Paolo Bregno or to the Florentine Nicolò di Giovanni; its nicest touch is the lightly carved marble drapes drawn back to reveal the reclining Foscari.

16. Assunta One of the most famous paintings in Venice, Titian's monumental **Assumption** (1516–1518) above the high altar is designed to attract attention from most parts of the church. Quite what you make of it depends on your attitude to the grandiose. As a painting it lacks the piety or sublimity of Bellini's altarpiece (see above), but triumphs as a piece of bravura coloring (enhanced by restoration) and as an exercise in verticality and virtuoso composition. Note in particular its powerful upward movement, of obvious importance in an *Assumption*, and quixotic details such as the cupids supporting the cloud on which the Madonna floats heavenward.

17. Monumento al Doge Niccolò Tron (d.1473). Antonio Rizzo's winsome Renaissance tomb, high up on the wall, is one of the finest such works in the city.

18. Cappella dei Milanesi Roses often lie strewn on the floor of this chapel behind its grille, poignant tributes to the composer Claudio Monteverdi (1567–1643), who lies buried beneath a simple plaque just behind the screen. The altarpiece, *St. Ambrose and Eight Saints* (1503), enclosed in one of the church's many gargantuan frames, was started by Alvise Vivarini and completed by Marco Basaiti.

19. Cappella San Marco o Corner Jacopo Sansovino's statue of *John the Baptist* (1554) on the left wall is often described as the highlight here, though the sculpture's effect is a little diminished by the Baptist's missing arm. Far better is the angel watching over the *Tomb of Federico Corner* (on the rear wall), whose face bears a clearly Florentine delicacy of touch (the Tuscan sculptor responsible is unknown). The altarpiece, clasped in yet another magnificent frame, shows *St. Mark Enthroned between Four Saints* (1474) by Bartolomeo Vivarini. A panel on the entrance wall illustrates rare 14th-century frescoes of *St. John the Baptist*, *Madonna and Child* and *St. Ambrose*. Discovered in 1990 during restoration of the roof, these decorated the church before the Corner family added the Chapel of San Marco in 1417.

20. Coro This exceptional 124-stall wooden choir, dating from 1468, is Venice's finest, full of phenomenal carving and intricate inlay, and the only one in the city (and one of only a few in Italy) to be positioned in the center of the nave. Note how its main entrance frames Titian's *Assumption* from the back of the church.

21. Cappella San Pietro As this chapel forms the church's entrance, most people hurry in to the nave and miss the 15th-century altarpiece, with the *Tomb of Bishop Miani* at the rear. The sculptor responsible for the 15 formal figures and the sour-faced Madonna is unknown.

22. Monumento a Iacopo Pesaro (d.1547). The tomb of poor old Bishop Pesaro receives little attention, being overlooked in favor of Titian's famous altarpiece to his left. Pesaro's effigy, however, is worth a look. His head is propped up nonchalantly on one hand, almost as if affecting boredom with the painting next door.

FRANCESCO FOSCARI
Venice's longest-serving doge was eventually forced by the Senate to retire. He died in 1457—apparently of a broken heart—a few days after the execution of his son for treason. For almost two centuries both his memory and his tomb were blighted by his son's shame, but in 1720 Alvise Foscari, one of his descendants, decreed that his heart should be placed in the tomb to help assuage the dishonor, an act of dynastic loyalty recorded in a plaque below the monument.

The Coro, or choir, was carved by Mauro Cozzi

MADONNA DI CA' PESARO

This is a painting in which to play "find the family." Iacopo Pesaro—father and bishop—is the figure on the left in front of a knight (who may be a self-portrait of Titian); on the right St. Francis holds his hands (note the stigmata) over Iacopo's brother, Francesco; and the boy looking out from the painting is Iacopo's nephew and heir, Lunardo. The face of the Madonna is modeled on Titian's wife, Celia, who died soon after in childbirth.

Titian's Madonna di Ca' Pesaro

Part of Giovanni Pesaro's remarkable tomb

23. Altare Madonna Ca' Pesaro Titian's *Madonna di Ca' Pesaro*, or *Madonna and Child with Saints and the Pesaro Family* (1526), is the third of the Frari's major paintings. It was commissoned in 1519 by the Bishop Pesaro buried in the tomb to its right. Pesaro led a fleet of ships against the Turks in 1502, partly in response to a request from the infamous Borgia pope, Alexander VI. Hence the man in armor behind Pesaro, shown kneeling on the painting's left, who bears a standard containing the Borgia and Pesaro coats-of-arms. The same knight is also shown leading a turbanned Turk and black slave towards St. Peter, a symbol of their conversion and the supposedly Christian spirit of the enterprise.

Although one of Titian's most important works, and one that had a lasting influence on Venetian art, the painting offers less immediate pleasure than the high altar's *Assumption*. Most fun here is to be had from identifying members of Pesaro's family (see panel). The composition, though, as ever Titian, is striking, the picture being dominated by two massive columns that bisect the painting. There are also a few questionable touches: the chubby-bottomed cherub at the top of the painting, for example, might be out of place even on a saucy vacation postcard; and the infant Jesus, who appears grossly overfed, seems so bored by proceedings that he is fiddling distractedly with his mother's veil.

24. Monumento al Doge Giovanni Pesaro (d.1659) This shockingly kitsch tomb is by far the most fun and most spectacularly vulgar in the church. Sculpted by Melchiorre Barthel in 1669, it was probably designed by Longhena, normally a fairly measured architect (he was responsible for the far more sedate Santa Maria della Salute and a brace of palaces on the Grand Canal). Four Moors support the superstructure, each equipped with padded pillows to help bear the strain. Between them languish two half-rotted cadavers, their bones sticking though blackening flesh, while above them stand two massive griffins and a figure punching the air. Pesaro, a tiny figure near the roof, seems to be holding his hands up in horror at the whole affair.

25. Monumento al Canova It is impossible to miss the tomb of sculptor Antonio Canova (1827), a bombastic pyramid of white marble originally designed by Canova as a mausoleum for Titian. In the end it was completed by pupils to act as his own tomb (see panel). Note the comically drowsy lion and the disturbing half-open door, a device borrowed from antique Roman tombs. All that remains of Canova within is his heart, enclosed in porphyry, his body having been returned to his birthplace at Possagno in the Veneto.

CANOVA'S TOMB
"The tomb of Canova by Canova," wrote John Ruskin, "cannot be missed; consummate in science, intolerable in affectation, ridiculous in conception, null and void to the uttermost in invention and feeling."
Works (1904)

The tomb of the neo-classical sculptor Antonio Canova (1757–1822); his heart lies in a porpyhry urn within

Venice not only invented the concept of the ghetto, it also introduced the word to the world. Until 1390 the Venetian enclave for Jewish people had been near a foundry, or geto. When they were moved to the Arsenale, the name was given to the remote area of Cannaregio designated as the "new" ghetto in 1516.

MUSEO EBRAICO
This museum in Campo del Ghetto Nuovo has a collection of textiles, documents, and religious silverware. It is also the starting point of impressive guided tours around three of the Ghetto's five (originally nine) surviving local synagogues, or *scuole* (those founded in the 16th century by the German, Spanish, and Levantine Jews). (*Open* Sun–Fri 10–4; closed Sat, Jewish holidays and festivals. *Admission: moderate. Guided tours* every hour 10:30–7 (5:30 in winter) *Admission: moderate.*)

Foothold It seems perhaps inevitable that Jewish people would form part of Venice's medieval melting pot of peoples and cultures. The earliest Jewish inhabitants were documented on the mainland in 1090, but by 1132 some 1,300 were operating in the city itself, free to trade and practice medicine—but not, it seems, to settle. It was only around 1381, following the Battle of Chioggia, when refugees fled to Venice from the mainland, that Jewish people were first officially allowed to live in the city. Even then they had to pay a five-yearly fee for the privilege, and were allowed only usury and trade in secondhand textiles as a means of earning a living.

Consolidation Thus was established a pattern of "tolerance" that would prevail for around 500 years. Jewish people would be "tolerated" for their business acumen and wealth, but at the same time kept in a position where their activities could be monitored—and heavily taxed. Even then their position remained precarious. In 1394, for example, a decree was issued threatening Jewish people with expulsion. Another soon after permitted residency of just 15 days a year. More insidious persecutions began about the same time, notably the compulsory wearing of identifying emblems (a yellow hat) and a complete injunction against owning property.

Turning point The screw was turned still further following the League of Cambrai at the beginning of the 16th century. Venice's defeat at Agnadello in 1509 drove thousands of refugees, Jewish among them, into the city. Here they joined refugees from recent persecutions—Jewish people displaced by the Turks, for example, and those expelled by Spain and Portugal in the 1490s. To its credit, Venice welcomed them—with one eye, pragmatic as ever, on profit. None the less, they were probably physically safer here than anywhere in Europe, and Venice stood apart as one of the few places to allow them freedom of religious worship.

Ghetto Venice's attitude to Jewish people remained ambiguous, however. In 1516 the Senate voted to create the world's first ghetto (the move had been motivated by increasing numbers of refugees). They were given just ten days to repair to the chosen spot, a small island almost completely cut off from the rest of the city (the Giudecca and Murano had been rejected as possible locations). Its outer walls and houses remained windowless, and its canal—crossed by just two bridges—was sealed at night

and guarded by four Christian soldiers (paid for by a tax levied on Jewish people). They could move freely during the day (but still had to wear their hats—red by this time) and remained restricted as to the number of trades they could follow (which is why the Campo del Ghetto Nuovo once supported some 60 tailors' shops).

To the present At its peak the Ghetto's population numbered 5,000, its inhabitants crammed into high, seven-story tenements (a few of which survive today). It was expanded twice, in 1541 (into the *Ghetto Nuovo*) and in 1633 (into the *Ghetto Nuovissimo*). Abolished by Napoléon in 1797, it was reintroduced by the Austrians before finally disappearing at Italian unification. Today only a few of the city's 600-strong Jewish population live in the area, which has become a forlorn and slightly run-down neigh-borhood. A museum (see panel) and two synagogues survive, however, together with a Jewish school and nursery, a handful of Jewish shops and restaurants, and several moving memorials to the 200 Venetian Jews murdered in concentration camps in 1943 and 1944.

Venice's Jewish population is only a fraction of its former levels

DISEASED DISTRICT
In 1852 Théophile Gautier was distressed to find the Ghetto a "fetid and puru-lent district...which had preserved the character-istic squalor of the Middle Ages." Its alleyways "got narrower and narrower; the houses rose like towers of Babel, hovels stacked one on top of another to reach for a little air and light above the darkness and filth... All the forgotten diseases of the leprosies of the Orient seemed to gnaw these blistered walls; the damp stained them with black marks like gangrene; the efflorescence of the salts caused eruptions in the plaster that looked like boils and plague spots; the roughcast, flaking like diseased skin, peeled away in scaly pieces." *Voyage en Italie* (1852)

A 19th-century depiction of Shylock, from Shakespeare's Merchant of Venice

Santa Maria dei Miracoli

MIRACLES
The Miracoli was built for an image of the Virgin, painted in 1409 to be placed on the outside of a house (a common practice in Venice). Miracles began to issue from it in 1480: a man was found alive, for example, after spending half an hour underwater in a canal; and a woman survived unmarked after being stabbed by robbers and left for dead. Votive gifts poured in, including 1,000 ducats from a Milanese merchant cured of liver disease. The sum exactly covered Lombardo's fee for the design, execution and materials of the church.

The Miracoli has one of Venice's most elegant facades

►► Santa Maria dei Miracoli
274B5
Calle delle Erbe (Quay: Rialto; Vaporetti 1, 82)
Open: Mon–Sat 10–5. Admission: inexpensive

Venice has many sudden surprises around sharp corners, but none so pretty as the first view of the Miracoli's exuberant marble-clad exterior. Largely eschewing sculpture, the church relies for its impact almost entirely on color, and on the moat-like canal that provides a shimmering mirror for its multi-hued marbles. Yellow-white stone and jewel-like medallions sit alongside red porphyry panels and serpentine inlays, many of them sliced like salami from antique columns. Legend claims most of the decorations were leftovers salvaged from the Basilica.

The work of Pietro Lombardo, the church was built between 1481 and 1489, originally to enshrine a miraculous image of the Virgin (hence *Miracoli*, or "Miracles"). Its cramped site demanded a range of architectural tricks (see panel on page 171), as well as the subtle interplay of color the sculptor was later to lavish on the Palazzo Dario (the tone of the marble appears to vary, for example, depending upon whether it faces land or water).

Lombardo's inspired use of marble continues in the interior, along with an array of sculpture executed in collaboration with his sons, Antonio and Tullio. Some of the best carving is found on the two pillars supporting the nuns' choir (near the entrance), on the half-figures of the balustrade fronting the raised choir, and—best of all—among the mermaids and assorted exotica at the base of the choir's pillars. The raised choir, often a feature of Romanesque churches, is rare in Venice (though as a means of creating a crypt in a water-logged city it might have been more common). Nicolò di Pietro's *Mother and Child*, the "miraculous" image for which the church was built, sits on the high altar (see panel). The most striking single-vaulted ceiling has been decorated with Pennacchi's fifty *Saints and Prophets* (1528).

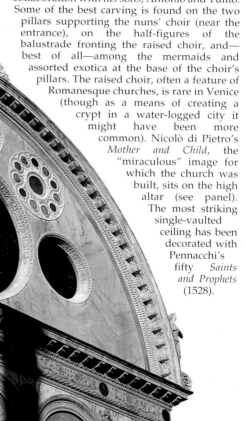

▶▶ Santa Maria della Salute

277D2

Fondamente Salute (Quay: Salute; Vaporetto 1)
Open: daily 9–12, 3–5.
Admission to the Sacristy: inexpensive

You will probably see the Salute many times before you pay it a visit, as its vast white dome and smaller cupola are key features of the Venetian skyline. Sitting proudly at the mouth of the Grand Canal, it provides a grand baroque introduction to the city from the sea—"like some great lady on the threshold of her salon," in the words of Henry James. In truth, the church becomes less appealing the

The Salute and the Grand Canal

TRICKS WITH PILLARS
Lombardo used more pillars than necessary on the Miracoli's exterior, their cramped arrangement creating a false perspective designed to make the church appear larger.

Santa Maria della Salute

AMPLE PRAISE
Henry James describes the Salute: "She is more ample and serene, more seated at her door, than all the copyists have told us, with her domes and scrolls, her scolloped buttresses and statues forming a pompous crown, and her wide steps disposed on the ground like the train of a robe." *The Grand Canal* (1892)

PUNNING PLAQUE
The plaque at the center of the Salute's marble floor is inscribed *Unde Origo, Inde Salus* ("from the origins comes health and salvation"), simultaneously recalling the reason for the church's foundation (a plague), its dedication to the Virgin, and the legend that Venice was originally founded under the protection of the Madonna. This last stems from the notion that the city was founded in AD 421 on 25 March, the feast day of the Virgin, after a vision of the Madonna had led the people of Altinum to the Venetian lagoon (see page 26).

BALDASSARE LONGHENA
The Salute's Venetian-born designer (1598–1682) was to be one of the foremost architects of his day. A pupil of Scamozzi, Palladio's closest follower, he was heavily influenced, at least in early works, by Sansovino and Palladio. His projects in the city display tremendous variety, from the baroque restraint of the Salute to the Palladian-inspired Palazzo Giustinian-Lolin on the Grand Canal. More exuberant baroque works include the Scalzi and the facade of the Ospedaletto. Three of his most famous buildings are the Grand Canal's Ca' Pesaro, Ca' Rezzonico, and Palazzo Battagia-Belloni.

closer you are: irreplaceable as a distant prospect, dazzling in its exterior detail, but a trifle dull in its interior austerity.

Background In October 1630 the Venetian Senate promised to build a church in honor of the Virgin if she could save the city from the ravages of plague. In the previous year the pestilence had claimed over 45,000 lives, about a third of the city's population. Within weeks the bubonic siege was lifted (the disease was probably choked off by the advent of cold weather) and a church was duly initiated. Christened the *Salute*, which in Italian has the twin meaning of "health" and "salvation," its first stone was laid on April 1, 1631. Countless buildings were razed to make way for the newcomer, and 1,156,627 wooden piles driven into the mud to provide its foundations. A competition was organized to choose a design, but only two of the 11 entries complied with the Senate's architectural and financial criteria, chief of which was that the church should "make a good impression without costing too much."

Design Responsibility for the church's design was eventually given to the 32-year-old Baldassare Longhena (it was his first major commission), who promised a building that would be "strange, worthy and beautiful... [and] in the shape of a round 'machine,' such as had never been seen or invented, either in its whole or in part, in any other church in the city." In achieving this marvel, Longhena mixed influences and prevailing trends to create a wholly unique building. Thus while the dome was derived from St. Peter's in Rome, the smaller cupola and the two campaniles adhered firmly to Venetian-Byzantine tradition. And while a church with a central dome was hardly a novelty, Longhena was the first architect in centuries to create an octagonal temple as the basis of a centralized plan. By far the greatest influence, however, was Palladio, most noticeably in the facade—you need only walk a couple of minutes around the headland to see the Salute's similarities with Palladio's San Giorgio (see pages 140–141). The master's legacy is also visible in the interior's gray-white décor, and in the almost separate sanctuary (the area around the high altar), which had featured in Palladio's Redentore on the Giudecca (see page 136). The result was to influence baroque architects for decades, and to provide an alternative to the baroque deliberations of Rome, where—at the time of the Salute's conception—that city's baroque masters, Bernini and Borromini, were yet to undertake a major commission.

Interior Entry to the church is via a side door, a poor substitute for the main portal, now opened only once a year during the Festa della Salute (held on November 21). Longhena's original grand entrance can be simulated by walking a few steps to the left, where, with the door at your back, you can survey the intended view to the high altar across the church's fine marble floor. Continue walking to the left and the third of the three altars on this side of the church has an early painting by Titian, the *Descent of the Holy Spirit* (ca1550). The paintings in the three altars on the opposite side are lesser works by the Neapolitan artist Luca Giordano.

Stop at the high altar to admire *The Virgin Casting out the Plague* (1670), designed by Longhena and carved by Juste le Court. The supplicant figure on the left of the Virgin represents Venice, while the old harridan scuttling off to the right symbolizes the plague: Sts. Mark and Lorenzo Giustiniani look on from below. It is worth paying to see the sacristy (the entrance is left of the high altar), which has a dozen or so well-labeled paintings: the best are Tintoretto's *Feast at Cana* (1561), its food-laden table caught in a shaft of sunlight; the Titians on the ceiling—*Cain and Abel, David and Goliath* and *Sacrifice of Abraham* (1542–1544) —each distinguished by bold perspective and powerful muscular figures; and Titian's *St. Mark Enthroned between Sts. Cosmas, Damian, Roch, and Sebastian* (1510), a youthful work painted to celebrate the passing of an earlier plague. Its protagonists are apposite choices for a plague painting, Cosmas and Damian being doctors, and St. Roch the saint invoked against infectious diseases (see pages 194–199). Notice the latter pointing to the plague sore on his right thigh, a common motif in paintings of this saint.

MARY AS MARINER

The statue of the Virgin on top of the Salute's main dome depicts the Madonna as the *capitana del mare* (ruler of the sea), clutching the baton of command of a Venetian admiral of the fleet.

BIG EARS

The huge scrolls, or *volutes*, that form the buttresses for the Salute's main dome are known to the Venetians as *orrecchioni*, or big ears.

Longhena's high altar supports statuary by Juste le Court (1670)

173

San Pantalon (San Pantaleone)

▶ San Pantalon (San Pantaleone)   *279D4*

Campo San Pantalon (Quay: San Tomà; Vaporetti 1, 82)
Open: daily 8–11:30, 4:30–7

San Pantalon is known for the gloomy but muscular epic that spreads across its vaults, a colossal painting whose vertiginous *trompe l'œil* and remarkable perspective are probably unequaled throughout the length and breadth of Italy. The work of little-known artist Gian Antonio Fumiani, it depicts *The Miracles and Martyrdom of St. Pantaleone* (1680–1704). The rather thin story covers the world's largest area of painted canvas, some 60 panels cleverly engineered so as to make the joins invisible. The project consumed 24 years of Fumiani's life—though the hapless artist never saw his masterpiece finished, having fallen to his death while working on the painting (he was buried in the church under a seat).

The painting's 4th-century protagonist, Pantaleone, whose name means "all-compassionate," was a physician to the Emperor Galerius. A convert to Christianity martyred for his pains, his legendary healing powers made him an object of veneration in plague-torn Venice. Evidence of his medicinal acumen is shown in Veronese's last painting, *St. Pantaleone Healing a Boy* (1587), originally intended for the church's high altar (but now located in the second chapel on the right). Seeking to emphasize the saint's divinely inspired powers, the picture shows Pantaleone refusing a proffered box of potions. The inefficacy of pagan remedies, by contrast, is demonstrated by the limbless (and thus ineffectual) figure of Asclepius, the Greek god of medicine.

Two further works by Veronese—both depicting St. Bernard of Siena—grace the chapel to the left (the altarpiece and the picture on the left wall). The church's most notable treasure, however, is a *Coronation of the Virgin* (1444), located in the Cappella del Sacro Chiodo (Chapel of the Holy Nail). A timeworn but attractive work, it shows tier upon tier of saints by Antonio Vivarini and his frequent collaborator, Giovanni d'Alemagna. The chapel is to the left of the chancel, and the painting is on its right-hand wall.

Fumiani's epic creation covers the largest area of painted canvas in the world

▶ San Polo (San Paolo)   276B5

Campo San Polo (Quay: San Silvestro; Vaporetto 1)
Open: Mon–Sat 10–5. Admission: inexpensive

One of Venice's oldest churches, San Polo was founded in 837 but has been much altered since. Perhaps the least appealing of its later embellishments is the set of neo-classical columns added in the 19th century, which are less than complementary additions to the Gothic rose window and artfully bowed wooden ceiling. Other fragments surviving from earlier incarnations include the quaintly worded plaque on the apse's exterior wall (see panel) and the detached campanile (1362–1365), the latter famous for the pair of worn lions at its base. One of these clutches a serpent, the other a man's head, reputedly an allegorical representation of the death sentence passed on Doge Falier.

A lovely Gothic portal, topped by a faded fresco and chubby figure, ushers you into the interior, where a simple plan indicates various points of interest around the church. Immediately to the right, in a kitsch little touch, the *Salute* altar is covered in red flock wallpaper, a hangover from the Byzantine decorative habits still to be seen in several of the city's churches. To the left, the high altar boasts bronze statues by Alessandro Vittoria, while the apse chapel, to its left again, contains Veronese's *Marriage of the Virgin*. The second altar on the left on the north wall features a *Virgin Appearing to a Saint* by Giovanni Battista Tiepolo.

Tintoretto's turbulent *Last Supper* (1547) hangs to the left of the door (on the west wall), shadowing the entrance to the sacristy, home to the church's highlight, Giandomenico Tiepolo's *Via Crucis*, or *Stations of the Cross* (1747). Painted when the artist (the son of the more famous Giovanni Battista, whose style he largely imitated) was just 20, the 18-panel cycle is a little careworn—the canvases are unframed—and suffers from the proximity of the sacristy's unprepossessing jumble of bric-à-brac and peeling plaster. The paintings manage to retain their allure, however, each being filled—for all their supposed religious content—with some finely observed vignettes of Venetian high society.

Three of Giandomenico Tiepolo's Via Crucis

SESTIERE DI SAN POLO
Campo San Polo is the largest square in Venice after Piazza San Marco, but sits at the heart of the smallest of the city's six *sestieri*. Once the scene of bullfights, mass sermons, and masked balls, it is now used for screenings during the film festival and as one of the main Carnival locations:

PROHIBITIVE PLAQUE
A small plaque on the rear of San Polo (opposite the newspaper kiosk) carries an injunction issued in 1611 by the *Esecutori contra la biastema*, special magistrates appointed to root out blasphemy, swearing and other moral lapses. "All games whatsoever are prohibited," it reads, "also the sale of goods, or the erection of shops, around this church, by order of the most excellent *esecutori contra la biastema*, with the penalty of prison, the galleys, exile and also 300 lire de' piccoli, to be divided between the accuser and captor."

176

Veronese's ceiling

SENSUOUS DELIGHT
"Vasari called one of
Veronese's pictures
'joyous, beautiful and well-
conceived.' And joyous is
perhaps the best way to
describe [San
Sebastiano's] paintings
which manifest an uninhib-
ited sensuous delight in
the beauty of the world…"
Hugh Honour, The
Companion Guide (1965)

▶▶ **San Sebastiano**   *278B2*
Campo San Sebastiano (Quay: San Basilio; Vaporetto 82)
Open: Mon–Sat 10–5. Admission: inexpensive
After years of restoration and erratic opening times, the
church is now open all day and many of the works of art
have been restored to their former glory. It is well worth a
detour to the eastern end of the church, not only for the
sake of one of Venice's most spectacular ceilings, but also
to enjoy the city's finest collection of paintings by
Veronese. These works decorate the ceiling of the sacristy
and nave, the chancel, the frieze, altarpiece, and the east
end of the choir. Born in Verona, the artist moved to
Venice in his twenties. There he lived at 3338 Salizzada
San Samuele, close to San Sebastiano, which in time

became his parish church. It was probably his friendship with the prior of San Samuele, however, a fellow native of Verona, that earned him his first shot at painting in San Sebastiano. Commissioned to decorate the sacristy, he completed its *Four Evangelists* and *Coronation of the Virgin* in 1555, just two years after arriving in the city (though restorations currently mean you stand little chance of seeing the sacristy).

He was then given free rein on the church's ceiling (1555–1556), a fantastic confection of gilt and knobbly stucco dominated by three large paintings (and a dozen smaller ones) describing scenes from the Old Testament story of Esther, chosen for it symbolic parallels with the stories of Eve and the Virgin Mary. *The Repudiation of Vashti* links Vashti, an outcast Persian queen, with Eve, exiled from the Garden of Eden. *Esther Crowned by Ahasuerus* suggests the link between a young Jewish girl chosen as queen and Mary, the Queen of Heaven, while *The Triumph of Mordecai* joins Esther, who rescued her cousin Mordecai and his companions, with Mary, who rescued, or redeemed humanity. Much of the vault's incidental decoration is by Veronese's brother, Benedetto Caliari.

To the rear stands the Nuns' Choir, an unusual gallery around the church's rear (west) wall. It, too, features frescoes by Veronese, *The Trial and Martyrdom of St. Sebastian*, but access has been restricted for years. If you look carefully, however, you might make out an archer on one side, positioned so that he appears to be shooting his arrows at St. Sebastian on the other. Just beyond the ticket office, Titian's *St. Nicholas* (1563), painted when the artist was in his eighties, decorates the first altar. On the second altar of the right aisle, contrast Tommaso Lombardo's charming 16th-century marble group with (two altars further down) Sansovino's gracelesss *Tomb of Archbishop Podocattaro of Cyprus* (d.1555).

Veronese makes a reappearance in the choir, where he was responsible not only for the design of the high altar, but also for the execution of its altarpiece, a *Madonna and Child with Sts. Sebastian, Peter, Francis and Catherine* (1570). He also contributed the two vast canvases on the side walls (ca1565), both far easier to appreciate than his ceiling paintings: *Sts. Mark and Marcellinus Led to Martyrdom and Comforted by St. Sebastian* and *The Second Martyrdom of St. Sebastian*. The second picture refers to Sebastian's little-known survival from his first "martyrdom"—the more famous one with the arrows. A Roman centurion turned Christian, he was ultimately killed by being pummelled to death (although he remains the patron saint of archers). Note the paintings' backgrounds (idealized visions of Rome) and the big skies, vast dogs, and bright clothes—all vintage Veronese motifs.

Given Veronese's monopoly of San Sebastiano—he even designed the organ and painted its door panels—it seems fitting that he should be buried in the church (along with his brother Benedetto). The tombs sit in front of the chapel to the left of the choir, marked by a simple pavement slab and the legend "*Paolo Caliario Veron. Pictori Celeberr.*" The chapel to the rear, again often closed, contains a fine 16th-century majolica pavement. The tiles come from Urbino, in the Marche.

ST. SEBASTIAN

San Sebastiano was one of Venice's five plague churches (commissioned after an epidemic in 1464). Why Sebastian should be invoked against plague is a mystery. Some say he was successfully invoked during a particular epidemic. Others suggest his courage in facing arrows in some way fortified his devotees. The reason for his popularity with Renaissance painters is more easily explained: he allowed them to portray a male nude—rare or prohibited in earlier devotional paint-ings—in a "respectable" religious context.

St. Sebastian looks down from the top of his Venetian church

FITTING DEATH

Veronese loved Venice and all it stood for, at one point rejecting a lucrative offer to work in Spain. He was also highly success-ful, owning a large house in the city and a country estate near Treviso. His sumptuous paintings suggest a zest for life; fittingly he is said to have died after becoming over-excited during an Easter procession.

CAMPO SANTO STEFANO

With Santa Margherita and San Polo this is one of the nicest neighborhood *campi* in Venice. Until 1802 it was used for bullfights, during which bulls (or oxen) were tied to a stake and baited by dogs. In 1807 Piazza San Marco's centuries-old market was moved here for just two years. For years the square was grassy, all except for a stone avenue known as the *liston*. This became such a popular place to stroll that it led to a Venetian expression *andare al liston*, meaning "to go for a walk."

The quiet beauty of Santo Stefano belies its bloody past

Far right: Gothic Santo Stefano and its campo, a pleasant place from where to watch Venice go by

▶▶ Santo Stefano (San Stin)   276C3

Campo Santo Stefano (Quay: San Samuele; Vaporetto 82)
Open: Mon–Sat 10–5. Admission: inexpensive

Santo Stefano's calm Gothic interior is one of the prettiest in Venice. Its ship's keel ceiling, an exquisite piece of work, catches the eye first, followed by the roof's delicate tie beams, some intricately patterned brickwork and the *trompe l'œil* foliage that festoons the arches of the nave. Pillars of Greek and red Veronese marble stride down the aisles, often concealed below a covering of maroon brocade. The Byzantine habit of covering church surfaces has survived in many Venetian churches.

Santo Stefano belonged to the Augustinians, an order who usually eschewed such displays, favoring simple churches that could be used for preaching without decorative distractions. Such austerity clearly cut no ice with Bartolomeo Bon, responsible for the florid but age-blackened statues on the portal, nor with the men whose tombs provide the interior's main points of historic interest. Doge Francesco Morosini (1619–1694), for example, is buried under the largest tomb slab in Venice (at the center of the nave), a suitably bombastic memorial to a man renowned for recapturing the Peloponnese and for blowing up the Parthenon with a single shot (the Turks had been using it as a powder store). He also plundered the lions to be seen outside the Arsenale (see panel on page 113). The first altar on the left frames the tomb of Giovanni Gabriele (1557–1612), an organist at San Marco and renowned pioneer of early baroque music. On the wall to the right of the door stands Pietro Lombardo's lovely *Monument to Giacomo Surian* (d.1493), an eminent physician from Rimini.

The church's best paintings clog the gloomy sacristy at the end of the right nave. On the right wall are a *Last Supper*, *Washing of the Feet*, and *Prayer in the Garden*, three paintings by Tintoretto executed around 1580. To their left is an often overlooked *Crucifixion* by Paolo Veneziano. The left wall has portraits of four Augustinian cardinals and Veronese's more famous *Madonna and Child with Saints* (on the extreme right). The altar wall features Bartolomeo Vivarini's easily missed *Saints*, contained in two narrow, gilt-framed panels. Note, too, the recessed 13th-century Byzantine icon to their right.

Move across the church to the top of the left nave, where a door leads into the baptistery, home to Canova's much-imitated *Monument to Giovanni Falier* (ca1808), the sculptor's first patron. It stands to the left of another door that gives a tantalizing glimpse of Santo Stefano's cloister. Now part of Venice's tax department, the courtyard was once home to Canova's studio (some of his earliest works were carved here) and to the Pordenone frescoes now displayed in the Ca' d'Oro (see page 77). Pordenone, once Titian's main artistic rival, is said to have so feared attacks from the painter and his henchmen that he was never without a sword while working in the cloister.

Santo Stefano is the only church in Venice built directly over the canal: the waterway was left intact when the church's apse was extended over it in the 15th century. It now runs under the high altar, making it almost impossible to see, though gondolas are reputed to be able to pass through at low tide.

Santo Stefano (San Stin)

Somewhere in the church—no one knows where—is buried Novello Carrara of Padua, an enemy of Venice who was captured in battle in 1406. He was buried with great pomp, despite the fact that he had been secretly strangled—along with his two sons—in the Palazzo Ducale the day before.

Before or after visiting Santo Stefano be certain to visit Paolin, a bar reputed to have some of the best ice cream in the city (you'll find it just outside the church on the corner of Campo Santo Stefano). You might then wander into the nearby Campo Novo, once Santo Stefano's churchyard and cemetery. During the tumultuous plague of 1630 (the one that led to the building of the Salute) it was used as a mass grave (even today its level is well above the height of surrounding streets). So many bodies were buried here that it remained closed as a health hazard until 1838.

COMFY CHURCH

"For sheer comfort and pleasure I think S. Stefano is the first church in Venice."
E V Lucas, *A Wanderer in Venice* (1914)

BLOODY WALLS

When contemplating Santo Stefano's peaceful interior, it is hard to believe that it has been reconsecrated six times in order to wash away the stain of blood spilled within its walls.

True Venetian food can be excellent, particularly away from the tourist areas. As well as pasta and risotto, you will find a strong emphasis on seafood and fresh produce. However prices in the city are higher than the rest of Italy, due in part to the problems of shipping food in from elsewhere.

180

COMMON COMPLAINT
The comments on Venetian food made by Englishman Samuel Sharp, a surgeon at Guy's Hospital, were typical of visitors to the city during the 18th century: "...this is almost constantly the fare. A soop like wash, with pieces of liver swimming in it; a plate full of brains, fired in the shape of fritters; a dish of livers and gizzards; a couple of fowls (always killed after your arrival) boiled to rags, without any the least kind of sauce, or herbage...The bread all the way exceedingly bad, and the butter so rancid, it cannot be touched, or even borne within the reach of our smell."
Letters from Italy (1767)

*On a stall at the
Rialto market*

Starters Venice's single most famous hors d'oeuvre is *sard in saor*, Adriatic sardines served cold in a marinade of vinegar and onions (*acciughe marinate*, or marinated anchovies, is a similar dish). Other seafood delicacies include Murano crabs (*granseole*), oysters from Chioggia (*ostriche*), and variations on squid (*calamari*), prawns, (*gamberi*) and octopus (*polipi*). A mixed seafood starter, *antipasto di mare,* is also common. *Soppressa* is a type of Venetian sausage, while *prosciutto San Daniele* is the region's most prized ham.

Less local but still widely available starters include salamis (*salame*), tuna (*tonno*), cured beef (*bresaola*), and raw vegetables (*verdura cruda*). Vegetables marinated in olive oil (*verdura sott' olio*) are also common, particularly mushrooms (*funghi*), peppers (*pepperoni*), and artichokes (*carciofi*). Venetian starters (*antipasti*) also often mirror the small snacks (*cichetti*) served up by wine bars to accompany the early evening *ombra* (see page 183).

First courses Pasta is naturally widely available in Venice, but any self-respecting Venetian is more likely to plump for a *risotto*, the bestknown of which is *risi e bisi*, a classic Venetian dish of rice, peas, *prosciutto* (ham), and Parmesan. Close behind comes *risotto del mare*, a seafood risotto sometimes known as *risotto dei pescatori*, *de peoci* or *de cape*. Vegetables with chicken and *prosciutto* may also feature (*alla sbirraglia*), together with mushrooms (*risotto ai funghi*), and exotica such as tripe, snails, and baby quails. *Risotto in nero* uses squid ink to flavor the rice.

Soups also make full use of the sea, particularly the mixed fish classic known as *brodetto*. Other *zuppe* include *broèto* (eel soup), *pasta e fasioi* (pasta and beans), *sopa de peoci* (mussels, garlic, and parsley), and *risi e luganega* (rice and pork sausages). Another traditional stomach-filler is *polenta,* maize flour boiled in water (also known locally as *tecia*). Once a staple of the poorest of the poor, it is now often served with great ceremony in the company of meat and tomato sauces.

Common pastas include *bigoli in salsa*, a type of thick spaghetti with onions, butter, and anchovies; *gnocchi* (little potato-based dumplings); and seafood classics such as *spaghetti alle vongole* (pasta and clams).

Main courses Venice's most famous main course is calf's liver and onions (*fegato alla veneziana*), but otherwise fish and seafood form the city's culinary staples. Mussels (*cozze* or *peoci*) are cultivated all over the

lagoon (from ropes suspended in the water), while the distinctive hoop nets and wicker baskets (*vieri*) strung from fishing boats provide crabs, eels, and a huge range of fish for Venetian tables. Sole (*sogliola*) are caught at night using lights, then speared or netted, as are cuttle-fish (*seppie*), the only member of the squid family found in the lagoon (though if it rains the lagoon's reduced salt content sends them out to the open sea). Eels move into the lagoon in autumn, and if not caught remain there for anything between six and 12 years before returning to the open sea to reproduce. Eels with tuna and lemon (*anguille alla veneziana*) is a classic Venetian dish.

Other local fish, often best eaten grilled (*alla griglia* or *ai ferri*), include *orata* (sea bream), present in the lagoon from November to March; *triglia* (red mullet), often eaten with rice; *cefalo* (mullet); *sgombro* (mackerel); *coda di rospo* (monkfish), and *dentice* (dentex), a fish similar to sea bass. To sample a variety of fish and seafood opt for a *fritto di pesce* or *fritto misto di mare*, a plate of mixed fried fish and seafood.

To round things off, try one of Italy's mouthwatering desserts, such as *tiramisù* ("pick me up"), a coffee and liqueur-laced concoction of spongecake, mascarpone cheese, eggs, and chocolate.

COURTESY AND CUISINE
Fourteen of Venice's more forward-looking restaurants have formed the *Ristoranti della Buona Accoglienza*, whose aims are to "guide the visitor towards genuine Venetian courtesy and cuisine…to create an atmosphere where food is more than a commercial consideration …and where sitting down to the pleasures of the table is an integral part of the life and culture of the city." The cost of a meal averages around L80,000, excluding drinks. For a list of participating restaurants tel: 041-5239896; fax: 041-5285521.

The range of fish in Venetian restaurants—and at the Pescheria—is usually excellent

Venice boasts no wine of its own (for obvious reasons) but the hills and plains of the Veneto produce some of the most famous names in Italian viticulture—Soave, Valpolicella, and Bardolino—as well as a variety of more prized wines that can be enjoyed in old-fashioned wine bars around the city.

HARRY'S BAR
This famous bar-restaurant was founded in 1931 when a now forgotten American ("Harry") remarked to hotel barman Giuseppe Cipriani that Venice lacked nothing except a good bar. Cipriani sought financial backing, found an old rope storeroom near San Marco (at Calle Vallaresso 1323) and Harry's Bar was born. It is now a place of high prices, good food, great cocktails, and—in the words of Gore Vidal—a "babble of barbaric voices ...the only place for Americans in acute distress to go for comfort and advice..."

182

Superlatives Although it ranks third in Italy in terms of output (after Sicily and Apulia), no other region produces as much quality-controlled wine as the Veneto (227 million bottles, or a fifth of the country's output). Two-thirds comes from one province alone (around Verona), an area which out-produces the more renowned wine regions of Tuscany and Piedmont. The most well-known, Soave, is the best-selling wine in the United States (outselling even Chianti), whilst a major producer, Zonin, is currently one of Europe's largest private vineyards. Around 80 varieties of grape grow in the region, scattered across some 116,000 vineyards. And this is without the increasingly fine wines of the regions bordering the Veneto: Trentino-Alto Adige and Friuli-Venezia-Giulia.

Reds Red wine in the Veneto has traditionally meant Valpolicella and Bardolino, two unexceptional and often mass-produced table wines from the area around Verona and Lake Garda (the best varieties are the *Ripasso* or *Classico* denominations from producers like Masi and Guerrieri-Rizzardi). Equally workaday versions of Merlot and Cabernet, French imports of long standing, are also common, along with the native Tocai Rosso. Efforts to revitalize what have become over-standardized wines include Bardolino Novello (an attempt to emulate the success of Beaujolais Nouveau), and a renewed emphasis on two excellent dessert wines, Recioto della Valpolicella and the highly prized Amarone (fine versions of the last two wines are made by Bolla, Bertini, Masi, and Allegrini). Other interesting reds you should find in Venice's bars and supermarkets are Raboso, made from the eponymous grape along the banks of the Piave river, and the well-made wines of the Lison-Pramaggiore and Colle Berici regions.

Whites While red wines are widely drunk in Venice, the Veneto's lighter white wines are closer to the city's heart. The most famous is the ubiquitous Soave, at its best in the

Cocktail hour at the world famous Harry's Bar

Classico and single-vineyard versions of producers such as Anselmi, Bolla, Masi, and Pieropan. Gambellara and Durella, close cousins of Soave, take second place to Bianco di Custoza and the increasingly fine wines of the Breganze region (those of the highly respected Fausto Maculan in particular). Other widely available names include Vespaiolo, Tocai, and Garganola, together with wines made from long-established imports such as Pinot Grigio and Pinot Bianco.

Perhaps the best white, however, is Prosecco, an inexpensive and ever more popular sparkling wine from the eastern Veneto (and one favored as an aperitif and evening *ombra*—see below). Most bars sell passable versions by the glass, but the best varieties are from Cartizze, a specially delimited region to the north of Venice around Cornegliano.

Wine bars One of Venice's more civilized habits is the custom of breaking up the day with an *ombra* ("shadow"), a small glass of wine that takes its name from the idea of escaping the heat of the sun for a restorative tipple (see page 230). The nicest places in which to indulge this habit are old-fashioned wine bars known as bacari, a vital and ritualistic feature of the Venetian working day. They are found tucked away in most areas, but a particularly large number cluster in the *sestiere* of San Polo (see page 268–269 for addresses).

A small snack, or *cichetto*, usually accompanies the wine —anything from meatballs, baby squid, and hard-boiled egg to anchovies, artichoke hearts, and oil-soaked vegetables. For better wines, and a more refined ambience, you might hunt out an *enoteca*, a place with a greater range of wines and more serious attitude to their consumption.

Wine by the (plastic) bottle cuts prices…

FLORIAN
Florian, the oldest, prettiest and most expensive of Venice's big-league cafés, is much as it was 100 years ago when Henry James described it in *The Aspern Papers*: "…the immense cluster of chairs stretches like a promontory into the smooth lake of the piazza. The whole place, of a summer's evening, under the stars…is like an open-air saloon dedicated to cooling drinks and to a still finer degustation."

EVILS OF DRINK
The 19th-century inventor of the package tour, Thomas Cook, a teetotaller, was upset by his clients' taste for cheap wine: "Wine drinking in Italy was then…one of the prevailing torments of the people…and I was sometimes grieved to see my parties…purchase large quantities of common drinks…I remonstrated with them and said… '*Gentlemen, do not invest your money in diarrhoea*'."

Walk

The Accademia to the Frari (pages 278–279)

Start at the Accademia. Take Calle Gambara and Calle Contarini Corfù to Fondamenta Priuli-Nani. Look at the boatyard and then cross the bridge to see San Trovaso. Follow the canal on Fondamenta Sangiantoffetti. Turn left into Calle della Toletta and proceed to Campo San Barnaba.

The picturesque **boatyard**, or *squero*, at San Trovaso is one of the few yards in the city still making and repairing gondolas. **San Trovaso** was founded in the 10th century, but the present church—the fourth on the site—dates from 1584. Myth claims it was the only neutral ground in the disputes between two local clans, the Nicolotti and the Castellani (who during services would enter and leave by separate doors). Tintoretto's two last works hang to either side of the choir: *The Adoration of the Magi* and *The Expulsion from the Temple* (1594). The elaborate picture in the chapel to the right of the altar is Michele Giambono's *St. Chrysogonus on Horseback* (ca1450). **San Barnaba**, a dull church, fronts a lively little *campo* at the heart of the student district (note the shop selling hand-carved wooden angels in its northeastern corner). In the past the square was known for the *Barnabotti*, poverty-stricken patricians who monopolized the area's cheap housing.

Follow Fondamenta Gherardini and at the second bridge turn left on Calle

Left: The church of San Trovaso with the boatyard in the foreground

delle Pazienze (a right turn offers a short cut to the Carmini, see below). Turn right on Calle Lunga San Barnaba and Calle Avogaria to San Sebastiano. If you are short of time make for the Carmini on Fondamenta del Soccorso. Otherwise walk through the square behind San Sebastiano and follow Fondamenta di Pescaria and Fondamenta di Lissa west to San Nicolò dei Mendicoli.

On leaving Campo San Barnaba walk on to the first bridge off Fondamenta Gherardini, the **Ponte dei Pugni** (the "Bridge of Fists"), and note its pair of marked footprints. These indicated where contestants stood at the start of vast fistfights between members of the rival Castellani and Nicolotti clans. Losers were pitched into the canal. The fights became so violent they were banned during the 18th century. Next to the bridge is a famous and very pretty grocery barge. **San Sebastiano** has one of the city's most extravagant ceilings, as well as many fine paintings by Veronese (see pages 176–177).

The area beyond the church is one of Venice's more moribund quarters, often deathly quiet and deserted. Look into the church of Angelo Raffaele, if it is open, to see the painted organ parapet. **San Nicolò dei Mendicoli**, despite its peripheral position, is a must. One of the city's oldest churches (only San Giacomo di Rialto is said to be older), it has been superbly restored by the Venice in Peril fund. The vast building opposite the entrance is an old tobacco factory.

Double back to Fondamenta Barbarigo and Fondamenta Briati. Follow them to the Palazzo Foscarini and then cross the canal to the Carmini. Linger in Campo Santa Margherita and then cross the Rio Foscari to see San Pantalon. Cut through Calle del Scalater to emerge in Campo San Rocco.

San Nicolò dei Mendicoli; its name may derive from beggars who once peopled this poorer part of the city

The church of the **Carmini** is worth a few minutes for its pleasing interior and a pair of fine paintings by Lorenzo Lotto and Cima da Conegliano (see panel page 192). The **Scuola Grande dei Carmini** is only for fans of Tiepolo and his pallid ceiling frescoes (see pages 192–193). Outside, note the building's facade (designed by Longhena) and the old wine shop opposite the entrance. **Campo Santa Margherita** is one of the city's most relaxed squares, full of little bars, fruit stalls and a small fish market. **San Pantalon** has a painting of awe-inspiring size and a lovely half-hidden altarpiece by Gian Antonio Vivarini (see page 174). Allow plenty of time to see both the **Frari**, one of Venice's top two churches (see pages 160–167), and the Tintorettos of the **Scuola Grande di San Rocco** (see pages 194–199).

185

▶▶ San Zaccaria 274C3

*Campo San Zaccaria (Quay: San Zaccaria; Vaporetti 1, 82;
Motoscafi 41, 42, 51, 52)
Open: 10–12, 4–6.
Admission to the Cappella di San Tarasio: inexpensive*

History San Zaccaria not only shelters one of Venice's
most beautiful altarpieces, but also provides an object
lesson in how the Renaissance gradually encroached on
the city's earlier Byzantine and Gothic architecture.
Founded in the 9th century as a Byzantine basilica, the
church received a Romanesque veneer a century later,
and was overhauled between 1170 and 1174, when the
present campanile was added. Rebuilding began again in
the 14th century, when the church acquired a more Gothic
flavor. Scarcely had work finished, however, than it was
decided to build yet another new church. Old and new
versions are both still visible, the brick facade of the
former on the right behind a little garden, and the white-
marbled front of the latter towering to its left.

Exterior The newer facade is among the most important
in Venice, capturing a moment of architectural transition
from Gothic to Renaissance. The epochs' contrasting
styles are clearly mirrored in the pink-orange marble and
bas-reliefs up to door level (ca1440)—the work of Gothic
master Antonio Gambello—and the Renaissance lunettes
and scallop shells of the upper facade, added by Mauro

Giovanni Bellini's
Madonna with Saints *is
one of the city's greatest
altarpieces*

Coducci on Gambello's death in 1481. Before going into the church, note, too, the yellow-fronted houses to the left, cleverly squashed into the arcades of the church's former cloister.

Zaccharias, the father of St. John the Baptist

The nave Gothic has the upper hand in the interior, a tall, rather narrow space, and particularly in the rib-vaulted ambulatory (round the high altar), whose collection of northern European pointed arches and windows is the only one of its kind in Venice. The nave's second altar on the left contains what everyone is here to see, Bellini's glorious *Madonna with Saints* (1505), described by John Ruskin as the city's second greatest Bellini (after that in San Giovanni Crisostomo). Ruskin complained that the priests were "burning [the picture] to pieces with their candles," a fate it seems to have avoided, for the painting is now pristine after being restored. Note the exquisite coloring of the cloaks, and how the frame matches the columns of the painting to create a powerful perspective effect.

Continue walking down the left-hand side of the nave. On the left as you climb the two low steps stands the tomb of the sculptor Alessandro Vittoria (1595). Two of his works grace the church: one a self-portrait (on the tomb), the other the headless statue of San Zaccaria on the facade. As you wander behind the ambulatory, notice the columns on the left, octagonal and Gothic low down, round, Corinthian and Renaissance higher up—a graphic illustration of the compromise produced in the church by two styles grappling for architectural supremacy.

Before paying the custodian to enter the "museum" off the right aisle, walk back towards the main door, where the second altar contains the relics of San Zaccaria (Zachery or Zacchariss), the father of John the Baptist.

WELL-WISHING
The well in Campo San Zaccaria features in a popular Venetian legend. One Michaelmas morning, so the story goes, the devil came and tried to woo the bride of Sebastiano Morosini. Seeing his love being tempted away, Morosini dropped to his hands and knees and started roaring at the top of his voice. The devil, fooled into thinking Morosini was the Lion of St. Mark, promptly vanished. Thereafter, every man about to be married in Venice came to the square on Michaelmas morning and crawled once around the well, roaring as he went. The idea was to ensure constant fidelity in the wife, who would come with her parents to watch the ceremony.

San Zaccaria

*Bas-relief from
San Zaccaria*

SHABBY SQUARE

Writing of Campo San
Zaccaria, Max Beerbohm
noted: "Nowhere in Venice
is a more Venetian thing
than this little, melancholy
shabby Campo; this work
of so many periods; this
garment woven by so
many cunning weavers,
and worn threadbare, and
patched again, and at
length discarded." *A
Stranger in Venice* (1906)

LOOSE MORALS

San Zaccaria was not
alone in its wayward
nuns. In 1509 the
novices of Santa Maria
Celeste held a mixed ball
for the city's young
bloods, dancing until
dawn to the music of fifes
and trumpets. The Mother
Superior of Santa Maria
Maggiore was banished
to Cyprus for having an
affair with a priest. The
confessor to the 400
Convertite nuns on the
Giudecca organized nude
bathing parties; novices
who caught his eye where
whisked off to bed, and
tortured if they failed to
yield to his wishes.
   In 1681, San Lorenzo's
nuns threatened to burn
down their convent rather
than let it be closed. The
Senate prevailed upon the
Patriarch of Venice to
keep it open.

"The museum" The museum occupies two linked
chapels, both part of the earlier 12th-century church.
The first, the Cappella di Sant'Atanasio, has an
impressive, if battered choir and an early Tintoretto, *The
Birth of John the Baptist* (hanging over the main altar
directly ahead of the entrance). A door to the left takes
you into the Cappella di San Tarasio, where steps on the
left lead into the dank 9th-century crypt, final home to
eight of the city's early doges.
   The vaults above the chapel's main altar contain
damaged frescoes (1442) by Andrea del Castagno,
among the first artists to introduce the Venetians to the
ways of Renaissance Florence. Just how much notice the
Venetians took of the new wave can be gauged from the
chapel's three altarpieces (1443), which remain
resolutely Gothic despite being painted a year *after* the
vaults. They are the work of Antonio Vivarini and his
brother-in-law, Giovanni d'Alemagna. Note the little
seven-paneled predella below the main altarpiece,
attributed to Paolo Veneziano. The mosaic floor around
the main altar is a survival from the 12th-century church;
the glass panel in the floor at the chapel's rear offers a
glimpse of the 9th-century pavement.

Naughty nuns San Zaccaria was linked from earliest times
to its neighboring Benedictine convent (see panel). Many
of its novices were incarcerated against their will, usually
because their fathers were unable (or unwilling) to
provide them with dowries. As a result, the girls, who
came from some of the city's best families, often behaved
with less than nun-like decorum. Men were openly entertained, nuns produced children, and the convent's *parlato-
rio* became the focus of a fashionable salon. Nuns'
partners, with nice irony, were nicknamed *monachini*, or
"little monks." In the 14th century laws were passed to
discourage fraternization. Convent chaplains, for
example, had to be over 50, while confessors—a nice
touch—had to be over 60. During the 1730s San Zaccaria
was one of three convents openly competing to supply a
mistress to the new papal nuncio. By the 18th century,
balls, theatrical events, and mixed masquerades were
taking place within its walls.

▶ Scalzi, Chiesa degli
(Santa Maria di Nazaretta)   280C2

Fondamenta degli Scalzi (Quay: Ferrovia; Vaporetti 1, 82, Motoscafi 41, 42, 51, 52). Open: daily 7–noon, 4–7

In its position close to the bedlam surrounding the station, the Scalzi is a place you might unknowingly miss in the rush to escape elsewhere.

The Scalzi (see panel) arrived in Venice in 1633, having endeared themselves to the Venetians, through their charitable work in the Peloponnese during the Greek wars. Competition to finance their new church was fierce. The tussle was eventually won by Conte Geromalo Cavazza, who had just bought himself a place in the Golden Book.

Much of his 70,000-ducat subsidy to the church went towards the facade (begun in 1672); money not terribly well spent, for it became notorious for falling masonry and for years was fenced off to protect passersby. Only recently has the facade been restored. The finished church, built by Baldassare Longhena and consecrated around 1680, took its official name from an image of the Virgin, *Santa Maria di Nazaretta*, brought by the Scalzi from Lazzaretto Vecchio, an island in the lagoon.

The eerie interior is an orgy of baroque excess, all the more striking for its contrast to the bustle outside. Until World War I it had more than just curiosity value, as it boasted a ceiling fresco by Tiepolo; the work was reduced to fragments in 1915 by an Austrian bomb intended for the railroad station (a couple of surviving fragments, together with Tiepolo's original drawings, are preserved in the Accademia). Only the tomb of Venice's last doge Lodovico Manin and two limp frescoes by Tiepolo will detain you: the latter are in the vaults of the first chapel on the left and the second chapel on the right.

THE SCALZI

The church takes its name from the Scalzi, an ultra-strict branch of the Carmelites, popularly believed to have wandered around barefoot—or *scalzi* (literally "without shoes"). In fact they wore sandals like other religious orders.

DOGE MANIN

The melancholy character of Lodovico Manin, Venice's last doge (1789–1797), made him suited to preside over the pathetic events that saw the Republic surrendered to the French. Even his calling card suggested passivity—a picture of a nude Adonis asleep beneath an oak tree. Worse, his family were Florentines, having bought their way into the Venetian nobility during the wars against Genoa. As a result, his tomb in the Scalzi is a stark slab with the simple epitaph *Cineres Manini*— "the ashes of Manin."

189

The baroque Scalzi

Guilds and their wealthy members played key roles in countless medieval cities, their common interests providing a degree of social cohesion, and their riches the wherewithal for new churches and artistic patronage. It is unlikely, however, that any such bodies played quite such a vital a part in the life of a city as the countless scuole *of Venice.*

DOGES' MELONS
The fruiterers' *scuola* enjoyed the ancient annual honor of awarding the doge their prize melons.

LATIN ROOTS
Venice's *scuole* were never schools, but took their name from the Latin word *schola*, meaning "guild" or "corporation."

SIZE
Scuole varied in size from the 600 men of the Scuola Grande di San Rocco to the 20 members of the sand-merchants' *scuola*. Despite the latter's small size, it was still able to commission an altarpiece by Bartolomeo Vivarini for its chapel in San Giovanni in Bragora.

PAINTINGS
A remarkable number of pictures and painting cycles in Venice were commissioned not by individuals—as often happened in Florence and elsewhere—but by the *scuole*. The best-known are the Accademia's *Miracles of the True Cross* (painted by Gentile Bellini for the Scuola di San Giovanni Evangelista) and Carpaccio's *Life of St. Ursula* (for the Scuola di Sant'Orsola); the 54 paintings by Tintoretto in the Scuola Grande di San Rocco; and Carpaccio's cycle in the Scuola di San Giorgio degli Schiavoni.

Origins *Scuole* have their origins in the Flagellants, a fundamentalist (and eventually outlawed) sect who around 1260 began to wander Italy, wailing and scourging themselves in expiation for the sins of the world. Such behavior struck a chord among mendicant orders, notably the Franciscans, and led to the formation of religious confraternites sympathetic to the Flagellants' aims. Venice's first *scuola*, Santa Maria della Carità, drew up its statutes in the year of the Flagellants' first appearance. Another, San Giovanni Evangelista, was founded in 1307 expressly to serve a group of Flagellants.

In time the *scuole* inevitably broadened their intake and increased the range of their activities. Many became tremendously wealthy. By the time of the fall of the Republic in 1797 there were over 300 in Venice. Six of the more prosperous acquired the title *Scuola Grande*, one being promoted by the Council of Ten in 1552 (San Teodoro), and the rest by the Senate at the beginning of the 16th century (San Rocco, San Marco, Valleverde, the Carità, and San Giovanni Evangelista).

Make-up Most *scuole* had a common bond of membership. Some were designed to unite groups of expatriates, such as the Scuola dei Greci (Greeks) and Scuola degli Schiavoni (Dalmatians). Others pursued a specific charitable endeavor, such as visiting prisoners or tending to the sick. A few owed allegiance to religious orders, such as the Carmelites' Scuola dei Carmini. Most were also guilds, representing professions such as the goldsmiths and silk merchants (the Scuola Grande di San Marco).

Organization Despite their religious associations, *scuole* were lay organizations, and deliberately excluded both priests and patricians from their hierarchies. Each was bound by a constitution and administered by an elected committee (the *banca*) and president (the *gastaldo*). Committees settled everything from pay awards and internal disputes to codes of behavior and standards of workmanship. Annual subscriptions, calculated according to an individual's ability to pay, funded a *scuola*'s many activities. *Scuole* had their own patron saints, and often their own churches, but would also commission meeting places of their own. These were usually two-story buildings, with the ground floor reserved for workaday activities, and the upper story divided into an *Albergo* and *Sala del Capitolo*. The former served as a committee room, the latter as a hall for services and ceremonies.

Function A *scuola*'s main purposes were charitable works and mutual assistance. They might provide free accommodations for destitute members or dowries for daughters, pay for doctors, or distribute alms to the poor. As such they bridged several social classes, often providing a political voice to those disenfranchised by Venice's patrician structure. Some became almost states within a state, acquiring a role that overlapped that of the state itself. Many financed military adventures, for example, or recruited men to row the Venetian galleys.

Importance Venice's lack of civic strife was remarkable, particularly given the fact that after 1297 and the closing of the "Book of Gold" (see page 32) the majority of its population was excluded from even nominal democratic involvement in the Republic's affairs. The social mingling and civic services promoted by the *scuole*, not to mention their many artistic commissions, go a long way towards explaining the city's calm passage through almost five centuries of narrowly focused patrician rule.

The trompe l'œil *exterior of the Scuola Grande di San Marco*

LEGACY
The *scuole*'s main historical legacy and chief attraction for visitors are their often remarkable buildings and the works of art commissioned to decorate them. Their monuments were designed to reflect both the greater glory of God and the stature of an individual *scuola*. They were paid for by subscriptions, donations, and bequests accumulated by the confraternities over the centuries.

SANTA MARIA DEL CARMELO

The 14th-century basilica church adjacent to the scuola is best known for Lorenzo Lotto's *St. Nicolas of Bari* (ca.1529), located immediately to the left of the entrance (second altar). The landscape depicted in it was described by Bernard Berenson in *The Venetian Painters of the Renaissance* (1894) as "one of the most captivating in Italian painting." Another fine canvas, Cima da Conegliano's *Nativity* (ca.1509), occupies the second altar on the opposite (south) wall.

The facade of the Scuola Grande dei Carmini

TALL STORY

In 1756 the Carmini's campanile was apparently struck by lightning—which then began to sway gently —causing the monks who were ringing the bells at the time to leave in such panic that one ran headlong into a brick wall and was killed.

▶ Scuola Grande dei Carmini   278C3

Campo Santa Margherita (Quay: Ca' Rezzonico; Vaporetto 1)
Open: Apr–Oct Mon–Sat 9–6, Sun 9–4; Nov–Mar Mon–Sat 10–1, 3–6, closed Sun. Admission: moderate

The Carmini is far less grand than its name suggests. Its interior is only really worth seeing if you are a fan of Giovanni Battista Tiepolo, whose 18th-century frescoes form its main attraction.

You might make the visit more worthwhile by popping into the Carmini church (Santa Maria del Carmelo) or by taking a break in nearby **Campo Santa Margherita**, which, with its sun-drenched bars, children at play, and a handful of market stalls, is one of Venice's nicest squares, and one of the best places to sit with a cappuccino and watch the world go by.

The Carmelites The Carmelites (*Carmini*) or Order of Our Lady of Mount Carmel, originated in Palestine, spreading to Italy in 1235, where its confraternity of women members became known as *pinzochere dei Carmini*, or Carmelite zealots. Where the Franciscans might be recognized by their habits or triple-knotted belts, the Carmelites were known by their scapulars: two pieces of white cloth joined by strings.

The garment became a feature of Carmelite life after the Virgin appeared to the Blessed Simon Stock, scapular in hand, in the unlikely English surroundings of Cambridge. She assured him of the order's continuing good health, a reassurance that allowed its previously female bastions to be opened to men in 1595. A papal bull issued in the aftermath of the vision promised the scapular's wearers relief from the pains of purgatory "on the first Sunday after death," or failing that, "as soon as possible." Additional impetus was given to the Carmelite cause during the Counter Reformation, when the cult of the Virgin—much celebrated by female-dominated movements like the Carmelites—was built up as a bulwark against the rising tide of Protestantism. By 1675 the order boasted some 75,000 members.

The Scuola Having originally been stationed in Santa Maria del Carmelo (see panel), the Carmelites' Venetian chapter bought several buildings near the church in 1625 to serve as a new headquarters. In 1667, turning property speculators once more, they purchased a building opposite the church, employing Baldassare Longhena to convert it into a still more prestigious base for their operations (Longhena is best known for Santa Maria della Salute and several Grand Canal palaces—see pages 171–173).

The resulting facade receives high praise, but in truth is quite grubby and cramped. If you do step back to admire it, notice its rigorous symmetry and the panoply of masks and projections, all elements favored by architects of the period. Note, too, the old-fashioned wine store opposite, where you can take bottles to be filled straight from the barrel (see picture on page 183).

The ground floor features forgettable 18th-century *chiaroscuro* works, together with boards listing the Scuola's current (and still predominantly female) membership. The Salone on the first floor, reached by a staircase with amazing stucco decorations, contains Tiepolo's nine noted ceiling paintings (1739–1744). The central panel depicts Simon Stock's vision (in surroundings far removed from Cambridge), the scapular (handled by a cherub-like acolyte rather than the Madonna), and scenes of the purgatorial darkness from which the scapular was to save Simon and his ilk.

The other panels depict angels and female allegories, many of them bursting with alarmingly large and decidedly un-Carmelite visions of naked flesh. The best is a scene to the left of the main panel, a dramatic account of the Virgin saving a workman tumbling from his scaffolding.

Two smaller rooms lead off the Salone, the Albergo and Archivio, each distinguished by a heavy-handed wooden ceiling. Both are smothered in paintings, only one of which stands out, Piazzetta's *Judith and Holofernes* (ca1743), immediately on the right as you pass from the Albergo to the Archivio.

LEANING TOWER
The wobbling campanile of the Carmini was saved by an engineer who in 1688 straightened it by drilling holes into the brickwork on three sides (but not the side under the lean). He then drove wooden wedges into the holes, adding acid to dissolve the wood so that the tower settled gently into the resulting cavities.

Tiepolo's Simon Stock receiving the scapular

THE SALA GRANDE

See the plan, below:

1 Moses strikes water from the rocks
2 Adam and Eve
3 God appears to Moses
4 The pillar of fire
5 Jonah emerges from the whale
6 The miracle of the bronze serpent
7 The vision of the prophet Ezekiel
8 Jacob's ladder
9 The sacrifice of Isaac
10 The fall of manna in the desert
11 Elisha distributes bread
12 Elijah is fed by the angels
13 The Passover
I St. Roch
II St. Sebastian
III Adoration of the shepherds
IV The Baptism
V The Resurrection
VI The Agony in the Garden
VII The Last Supper
VIII The feeding of the five thousand
IX The raising of Lazarus
X The Ascension
XI Christ heals the paralytic
XII Christ tempted by Satan
XIII The vision of St. Roch

▶▶▶ Scuola Grande di San Rocco   *279D4*

Campo San Rocco (Quay: San Tomà; Vaporetti 1, 82)
Open: Apr–Oct, daily 9–5:30; Nov–Mar, daily 10–4.
Admission: moderate

Many painters have left their mark on Venice, but none so firmly as Tintoretto, an artist whose works grace churches and palaces all over the city. Nowhere are they more thickly clustered than in the Scuola Grande di San Rocco, where over a period of 25 years, the painter created 54 pictures which even the sternest critics have found hard to resist. John Ruskin called the scuola "one of the three most precious buildings in Italy" (Rome's Sistine Chapel and the Campo Santo at Pisa were the other two), a sentiment echoed by Henry James, who wrote that "we shall scarcely find four walls elsewhere that inclose within a like area an equal quantity of genius."

San Rocco The Scuola di San Rocco was founded in 1478 in honor of St. Roch, a saint whose efficacy against disease made him an obvious favorite in a pestilence-ridden city like Venice. He was also the obvious patron for a body dedicated to healing the sick, so much so that the scuola, one of the richest in the city, went to great lengths to secure his relics (paying 600 ducats for his head, hands and feet).

Born in Montpellier in 1295, the saint abandoned his career as a doctor at the age of 20 in order to visit Italy as a pilgrim. There he helped the plague victims of Rome, Rimini, Cesena, Forlì, and Piacenza, before falling sick himself (paintings of Roch often show him pointing to a plague sore on his thigh). Miraculous recovery arrived in the shape of a divinely sent dog, which brought bread to his forest lair and licked clean the sores on his leg (the dog is another feature of Roch-inspired paintings). On his return to Montpellier,

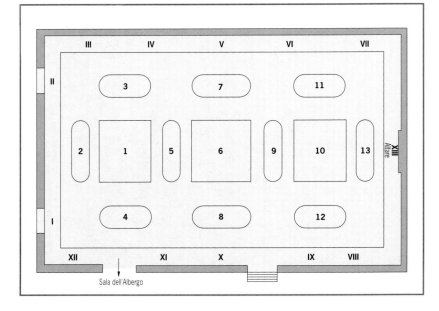

The Scuola Grande
di San Rocco (left) and
the church of San
Rocco (right)

however, he was shunned by his family, who failed to recognize him in his reduced state. Rejected as an imposter, he died in prison in 1327, aged just 32. Once his deeds were recognized he received widespread veneration, and was canonized in 1414. His relics were whisked off to Germany before being brought back to Venice in 1485 (just seven years after the foundation of the scuola). So great was the cult of St. Roch that in 1576 (after a great plague) he was declared co-patron of the city with St. Mark, the doge himself attending the ceremony to commemorate his feast day (August 16). The *Tendon del Doge*, or doge's canopy, is still erected in Campo San Rocco during the present-day *festa*.

The Scuola The Scuola di San Rocco was originally based in San Giuliano, near the Frari, and then in nearby San Silvestro. With the arrival of Roch's body, however, and the cascade of donations that accompanied it, the scuola felt able to commission a new headquarters from Bartolomeo Bon the Younger (in 1516). Another flood of donations generated by the plague of 1527 financed a second bout of building, this time under Scarpagnino, the architect responsible for the present building's distinctive asymmetrical facade. San Rocco was the only *scuola* spared when Napoléon closed the city's religious houses in 1806, and still survives as a working confraternity, with about 350 members.

Tintoretto's trick For almost a century after its foundation the scuola's interior decorations consisted of a series of moveable and undistinguished paintings. In 1564, however, it was decided to commission a fixed painting for the Sala dell'Albergo, the meeting place of the confraternity's ruling general council. Four of Venice's leading painters were invited to submit

REDUCED TO LAUGHTER
John Ruskin wrote to his father after visiting the Scuola Grande di San Rocco: "I have had a draught of pictures today enough to drown me. I never was so utterly crushed to the earth before any human intellect as I was today, before Tintoret. Just be so good as to take my list of painters, and put him in the school of art at the top, top, top of everything, with a great big black line underneath him to stop him off from everybody— and put him in the school of Intellect, next after Michel Angelo. He took it so entirely out of me today that I could do nothing at last but lie on a bench and laugh." *Letter* (1845)

Scuola Grande di San Rocco

Tintoretto's vast Crucifixion *dominates the Sala dell'Albergo*

THE CRUCIFIXION

"At the Scuola di San Rocco," wrote Henry James, "there is scarcely anything at all adequately visible save the immense 'Crucifixion' in the upper story. It is true that in looking at this huge composition you look at many pictures; it has not only a multitude of figures but a wealth of episodes; and you pass from one of these to the other as if you were 'doing' a gallery...It is one of the greatest things of art; it is always interesting. There are works of the artist which contain touches more exquisite, revelations of beauty more radiant, but there is no other vision of so intense a reality, an execution so splendid."
Italian Hours (1909)

designs for the picture, to represent a vision of St. Roch in Glory. The ruse by which Tintoretto won the commission, and outwitted Veronese, Salviati, and Zuccari in the process, is one of the most oft-told of Venetian tales. While his rivals worked on sketches for the painting, as per instructions, Tintoretto not only produced a finished canvas, but also managed to have it installed behind a veil on the Albergo's ceiling. On the day of judgement, as the others submitted their drawings, Tintoretto tugged on a string to reveal St. Roch in all his ready-installed glory. Howls of protest ensued, all to no avail, for the scuola plumped for Tintoretto, swayed, no doubt, by his offer of the finished picture as a gift and—more to the point—his readiness to complete any further paintings for nothing (perhaps as a mark of devotion, for he eventually became a member of the scuola).

Sala dell'Albergo A vast hall-full of paintings greets you upon entering the scuola's gloomy interior, but to follow the chronological order of Tintoretto's 25-year association with the building, avert your eyes and climb the monumental staircase on the right. Keep them averted as you march through the upper hall (the Sala Grande), then turn left into the Sala dell'Albergo, decorated by Tintoretto between 1564 and 1567. The enormous *Crucifixion* (1565) that confronts you is one of Italy's greatest paintings, if only it were possible to make out more of its detail in the gloomy surroundings. Tongue-tied wonder was Ruskin's understandably bewildered reaction to the work, his habitual eloquence deserting him as he observed simply: "I must leave this picture to work its will on the spectator, for it is beyond all analysis and above all praise." Henry James was scarcely less moved: "Surely no single picture in the world contains more of human life," he wrote, "there is everything in it."

The opposite wall contains (from left to right) the *Ascent to Calvary, The Crowning with Thorns* and *Christ before Pontius Pilate.* The central ceiling panel depicts *St. Roch in Glory*, the winning picture in the competition. The smaller and gloom-obscured figures around it are mostly ineffectual allegories. The two easel paintings in the room are a *Pietà*, possibly by a pupil of Giorgione (near left-hand corner), and *Christ Carrying*

The Sala Grande

the Cross, attributed to either Titian or Giorgione (far left-hand corner). Until 1955 the latter hung in the church of San Rocco, where it was once believed to have miraculous properties.

Sala Grande (Chapter House) The main upper hall contains the meat of Tintoretto's work in the Scuola, painted eight years after the Albergo, between 1575 and 1581. The paintings on the ceiling—the first to be tackled—depict scenes from the Old Testament, with virtually every subject, however obscure, carefully chosen to draw some allusion to the scuola's charitable or curative aims. *Christ Heals the Paralytic*, for example, and the *Raising of Lazarus*, have obvious relevance, as do the *Feeding of the Five Thousand* and *Samson drawing Water from the Jawbone of an Ass*.

The ten paintings on the walls, all episodes fom the New Testament, are some of the scuola's most compelling, packed with the features for which Tintoretto was famed: narrative originality, dramatic fore-shortening, obsession with the human form, bizarre use of color, and the use of light to reinforce action or emphasize spiritual content. This iconoclastic approach is best observed in the *Last Supper*, and in the *Adoration of the Shepherds*, where the Virgin and Child occupy the raised bier of a two-story stable—a novel

SECOND THOUGHTS
Tintoretto originally painted most of the countless figures in his great *Crucifixion* as nudes. Later, however, he changed his mind and added various clothes and draperies.

EASEL PAINTINGS
Around the altar of the Sala Grande are a number of free-standing paintings: an *Annunciation* by Tintoretto; a *Visitation* by Tintoretto; and two early works by G. B. Tiepolo, *Abraham and the Angels* and *Hagar and the Angels*.

The ceiling of the Sala Grande

COBBLERS
Not all of Venice's *scuole* were as majestic as the Scuola Grande di San Rocco. To see a more humble *scuola* walk one block east to Campo San Tomà: the building at its western end is the simple Scuola dei Calegheri, the headquarters of the shoe-makers' guild. A faded relief (1478) above the door by Pietro Lombardo shows St. Mark healing the cobbler Annanius, later to become Bishop of Alexandria and the patron saint of shoemakers. The building is now used for temporary exhibitions.

conceit—with the straw falling in tufts through the rafters and a dirty orange sky (anything but realistic) appearing through the ruined roof.

It is well worth taking the time to look at the sala's easel paintings (see panel on page 197), and at the series of extraordinary wooden carvings that provide a cartoon-like counterpoint to Tintoretto's more mystical works. Ranged around the room under the New Testament pictures, these are 17th-century works by the little-known sculptor Francesco Pianta. The best, which occupy the long wall opposite the staircase, are the *Painter*, a caricature of Tintoretto complete with brushes (near the altar), and *Curiosity*, a sinister, spy-like figure in Cuban-heeled boots and cocked hat, with one shifty eye peering over his cloak (left and below Tintoretto's *Resurrection*).

As you walk down the stairs, be sure to notice the figure of *Mercury* on the left. He is armed with a long scroll on which Pianta has very thoughtfully listed the carvings' allegorical meaning. The two canvases flanking the staircase, by Antonio Zanchi and Pietro Negri, were painted to commemorate the ending of a plague in 1630.

Ground floor The eight paintings in the Lower Hall were Tintoretto's last in the scuola, painted between 1583 and 1587, when the artist was in his late sixties. Critics laud the landscapes of *The Flight into Egypt*, but it is the *Annunciation* that offers the most startling spectacle. Note how the left of the painting is filled with an excessively realistic confusion of shattered timbers and exposed brickwork, and the top with a great squadron of cherubs spilling in arched formation towards an understandably startled-looking Virgin.

Church of San Rocco The church of San Rocco in the campo outside the scuola is a bright and airy experience after the all-pervading gloom and exhausting intensity of the scuola. Built between 1489 and 1508 by Bartolomeo Bon, the scuola's first architect, and then rebuilt in 1725, it contains a handful of works by Tintoretto. These paintings might have had rather more impact if you had not just seen over 50 similar paintings next door.

The interior is something of a mishmash, its paintings eccentrically arranged, and none more so than the lonely little fresco on the ceiling. The best pictures sit in the apse to either side of the high altar: all, sadly, are difficult to see. On the left are *St. Roch Cures Sick Animals* and *St. Roch Comforted by an Angel in Prison*; to the right *St. Roch Heals Plague Victims* and *St. Roch in the Desert*. The urn above the altar contains St. Roch's remains (the statue is by Bon). Other works by Tintoretto hang on the right of the nave between the two altars (the *Pool of Purification* and *St. Roch Captured at the Battle of Montpellier*) and on the rear (west) wall, on either side of the entrance (*Annunciation* and *St. Roch Presented to the Pope*).

The Annunciation *from the Lower Hall of the scuola*

199

SHABBY BUT WONDERFUL

Henry James was captivated by Carpaccio's painting of St. Augustine: "...who has it well in his memory," he writes, "will never hear the name of Carpaccio without a throb of almost personal affection. Such indeed is the feeling that descends upon you in this wonderful little chapel...where this most sociable of artists has expressed all the sweetness of his imagination. The place is small and incommodious, the pictures are out of sight and ill-lighted...the visitors are mutually intolerable, but the shabby little chapel is a place of art."
Venice (1882)

Tucked away in an alley, the Scuola is still home to Carpaccio's cycle paintings

TRIUMPH OF ST. GEORGE

The white-turbanned king and his daughter in the Triumph of St. George raised Ruskin to a fever-pitch of praise: "I tell you, through all this round world of ours, searching what the best of life has done...you shall not find another piece quite the like of that little piece of work, for supreme, serene, unassuming, unfaltering sweetness of the painter's perfect art. Over every other precious thing...it rises in the compass of its simplicity; in being able to gather the perfections of the joy of extreme childhood, and the joy of a hermit's age, with the strength and sunshine of mid-life, all in one."
Works, Vol. XXIV (1904)

▶▶ Scuola di San Giorgio degli Schiavoni 275D3

Calle dei Furlani (Quay: San Zaccaria; Vaporetti 1, 52, 82)
Open: Apr–Oct, Tue–Sat 9:30–12:30, 3:30–6:30,
Sun 10–12:30; Nov–Mar, Tue–Sat 10–12:30, 3–6,
Sun 10–12:30. Admission: moderate

Venice has few sights as charming and unexpected as Carpaccio's cycle of paintings in the Scuola di San Giorgio, a confraternity founded in 1451 to look after the city's Dalmatian, or Slav (*Schiavoni*), population. Dalmatia (roughly present-day Croatia) was among the first territories absorbed by the new Republic, having been seized in the 9th century, allegedly in retaliation for the harrying of Venetian shipping by Dalmatian "pirates." Although captured Slavs initially found themselves traded as slaves, by the 15th century a nucleus of sailors, artisans, and merchants involved in Levantine trade formed the core of a large—and better received—expatriate community.

The Scuola The Slavs' first confraternity, founded in 1451, was shared with the Knights of Malta, in whose hospice (San Giovanni di Malta) they were allowed to raise an altar. In time this was replaced by a simple structure on Fondamenta San Antonin, and it was the walls of this latter building that Carpaccio was commissioned to decorate in 1502. His paintings were to detail events from the lives of Dalmatia's three patron saints, George, Tryphon, and Jerome. On completion (in 1508) they were installed in the scuola's upper gallery, only to be removed to their present

position when the scuola was rebuilt on a grander scale in 1551. This makes San Giorgio among the few Venetian *scuole* to have retained its artistic heritage intact, and the paintings the only one of Carpaccio's five painting cycles to remain in the *scuola* for which it was painted.

Paintings One modest door and a curtain and you are immediately in the scuola, a far smaller place than you might have expected. Sit for a moment to take in the room's air of calm, and to let your eyes become accustomed to the light. The rosey-yellow glow that

bathes the paintings also illuminates one of the most beautiful and intricately decorated ceilings imaginable. Below it sit nine paintings in all, plus an altarpiece of the Madonna and Child by Carpaccio's son, Benedetto. The cycle begins on the left-hand wall.

St. George and the dragon The story of St. George is told in the *Golden Legend*, a medieval compendium of tall tales first published in Venice in 1475. According to its unlikely narrative, the saint passed through "Silcha, a provincial town in Libya" and saved Selene, daughter of the local king, from a deranged local dragon (see panel). Carpaccio's depiction of the episode is one of Venice's most memorable paintings, if only for the explicit gore of its foreground, littered with severed hands, partly devoured corpses, skulls, jawbones, and half-gnawed forearms.

On a more technical level, notice how the saint's lance, rammed into the dragon's gullet, forms a diagonal dividing the painting into two of its four compositional triangles. Each triangle has its own predominant color and narrative preoccupation—the dragon and the city, St. George and Selene, the sky, and the human debris of the foreground. Carpaccio's (and Venice's) taste for the exotic finds expression in the outlandish tower behind the dragon, and in the gateway to its left, probably derived by the artist from an engraving of Bab al-Futuh in Cairo.

St. George finishes off the dragon in peremptory fashion in the adjacent *Triumph of St. George,* converting the entire town to Christianity in the process (see panel). In *St. George Baptizing the Gentiles,* typical Carpaccian details—a vermilion parrot, eye-catching dogs—distract from the baptism of Selene's royal parents, the painting's main action. The diversion was perhaps a sop to the Venetian penchant for pomp and ceremony—note, for example, the carpets hung from the windows, long a custom in the city during processions and ceremonials.

In the Miracle of the Lion *Carpaccio makes the most of the comedy of the scene by accentuating the billowing habits of the fleeing monks*

GEORGE'S DRAGON
Myth relates how the dragon in the famous story of St. George terrorized an entire country, killing with its poisoned breath anyone who approached it. For a time it was kept quiet with a daily offering of two sheep, but when these ran out a human sacrifice, chosen by lot, was substituted. In time the lot fell on the king's daughter, who walked to her doom dressed as a bride. In the event George tames the beast, leading it into captivity with the princess's girdle. The price paid by the 15,000 locals was conversion and mass baptism.

Scuola di San Giorgio degli Schiavoni

HANGED AND QUARTERED

Corte Coppo, the first alley on the left to the south of the scuola on Fondamenta dei Furlani, was the 16th-century home of a certain Bernardina, the first woman in Venice to be hanged and quartered. Having beaten her husband to death (after 22 years of marriage), she forced her daughter and a cousin to bury him, telling neighbors curious as to her spouse's whereabouts that he was on a pilgrimage to Loreto (home to the House of the Virgin Mary). The crime came to light after relatives made fruitless inquiries in Loreto, and when Bernardina tried to con a guest into digging up her husband to rebury him elsewhere.

Tryphon, protagonist of the next picture, *The Miracle of Tryphon* was an obscure boy-saint born in Bithynia, Asia Minor. One of his miracles before his early martyrdom was the exorcising of a demon from the daughter of the Roman Emperor Gordian. The offending devil is the innocuous-looking little basilisk in the center of the painting. Neither of the following pictures, *The Agony in the Garden* and *The Calling of St. Matthew*, relates to the saints of Carpaccio's brief, though the artist secured Venetian sympathies by setting the latter in the Ghetto.

The last three paintings deal with St. Jerome, a reformer of Church liturgy and the driving force behind the Vulgate Latin translation of the Bible. Neither achievement offered much in the way of pictorial inspiration, which is perhaps why Carpaccio plumped for more modest but infinitely more graphic episodes from the saint's life. In the *Miracle of the Lion*, Jerome points at the paw (from which he has previously removed a thorn) of a decidedly tame lion, his comically terrified companions scattering in all directions (see page 201). The picture's more robust group of Turks suggests an eastern location, which would tie in with the story's traditional setting. The background, however, depicts the Schiavoni's original scuola and the hospice of the Knights of Malta, San Giovanni di Malta (the building with the wooden porch).

The Vision of St. Augustine *portrays an early 16th-century Venetian interior and—something of a Carpaccio trademark— an engaging dog*

The Funeral of St. Jerome is followed by one of the city's most praised paintings, *The Vision of St. Augustine* (its famous little white dog seems to attract most attention). Its almost obsessive precision, however, makes it somewhat stilted alongside the earlier paintings. St. Augustine related how he was writing to Jerome, debating a point of doctrinal trivia, when his study was flooded with light and a voice told him of the saint's death (in some versions the voice is divine, in others it is that of the dead Jerome). Carpaccio's Augustine is actually a portrait of Cardinal Bessarion, the scuola's first patron, and his study clearly that of a latter-day Venetian.

Few names are as redolent of mystery and romance as that of Marco Polo, a Venetian merchant who journeyed vast distances across Asia and the Middle East during the 13th century. His life's adventures were collected in Il Milione, *a book that for centuries contained Europe's finest description of the Orient.*

Absent father Born around 1254, Marco Polo was the son of a merchant adventurer, Niccolò, and scion of a family who had long traded in the Middle East with great success. Niccolò and Marco's uncle, Maffeo, had set off on their first epic journey in 1260, traveling east via the Volga and Black Sea to reach Shang-tu, summer capital of the Mongol Empire, in 1265 (Shang-tu was the Xanadu of the English poet Coleridge; Ta-tu, the Empire's winter capital, was modern-day Beijing). Here they befriended the great Kublai Khan, who sent them back to Europe as ambassadors to the pope (with requests for oil from Jerusalem's Holy Sepulchre and a hundred intelligent men "acquainted with the Seven Arts"). No sooner had they returned to Venice (around 1269) than they embarked on fresh adventures, this time taking the young Marco with them.

Travels Proceeding first to Palestine, the family voyaged east, passing through Turkey and northern Iran (in the early part of 1272) before reaching Hormuz on the Persian Gulf. Here they decided against a perilous sea crossing to India, settling instead for an overland route that was to take them through the deserts of eastern Iran and Afghanistan, where they remained for a year (apparently to recover from a serious illness, possibly malaria). Hereafter the route becomes hazy, Marco's later accounts making it difficult to discover which places he had actually seen, and which he described from information picked up along the way. In time, though, the family probably joined the old Silk Road, crossing into present-day China to arrive at the court of Kublai Khan in 1274 or 1275.

China Marco and his companions were to remain in China for 17 years, though the details of what they did and where they traveled to have tantalized scholars for centuries. All three probably spoke some of the

DEATHBED ASSERTION
So fantastic were Marco Polo's tales that he was asked on his deathbed to salve his conscience and retract the "fables and fairy stories" of his tales. He replied that, far from exaggerating, he had barely told half of the things he had actually seen.

203

Jacopo Bassano's 16th-century portrait of Marco Polo

Marco Polo

A 14th-century manuscript illumination of Venice at the time of Marco Polo; it may also show the departure of the explorer's vessels

TALL TALES

No one knows the origin of *Il Milione*, the popular name of Marco Polo's book (and of the courtyard in front of his house).

A 16th-century biographer claimed the traveler repeatedly used the word "millions" (*milioni*) in an attempt to suggest the wealth of the Orient. Other sources claim it refers to Polo's million lies and tall tales. Whatever the origin, the name stuck, for records of Venice's Great Council refer to Polo as *Messer Marco Milioni*.

Empire's several languages—Mongol, Persian, and Turkish—and undoubtedly served the government in some offical capacity (foreigners were often used by the Mongol state, which deeply mistrusted Chinese officials). Marco Polo also became a favorite of Kublai Khan, who apparently delighted in hearing tales of distant lands, and who sent him on fact-finding missions to far-flung parts of the Empire.

Homeward bound Around 1292, perhaps because they were homesick, or concerned at the chaos expected after Kublai Khan's death (the emperor was then in his 80th year), Marco and his companions decided to make for home. *En route* they offered to accompany a Mongol princess and 600 courtiers bound for a dynastic marriage in Persia. Packed into 14 boats, the party traveled via Champa (modern Vietnam) and the Malay peninsula, halting to avoid monsoon storms for five months in Sumatra (where Marco recorded in wonder the fact that the North Star dipped below the horizon—a sign that he had unwittingly crossed the Equator).

Following landfall in Sri Lanka and on the Indian coast, the fleet finally docked at Hormuz, where the Polos left the princess and proceeded on land to Venice (arriving around 1295). After a flurry of excitement as his family failed to recognize their prodigal son (see panel on page 205), Marco settled into a relatively uneventful middle age. He died in 1324, and was buried in the church of San Lorenzo.

His former house, marked by a plaque, can be seen in Corta Seconda del Milion (from *Il Milione*), a courtyard off the Salizzada di San Giovanni beside the church of San Giovanni Crisostomo. (As you leave the courtyard to return towards the church, look out for some fine bas-reliefs above the *sottoportego*.)

Fact or fiction History might never have heard of Marco Polo but for his capture by the Genoese in 1298 at the Battle of Curzola. During the year which he then spent in jail he met a scholar named Rusticello di Pisa, a writer of historical romance and an expert on chivalry and its lore (then much in vogue). Page by page, Polo dictated his 25 years in Asia to Rusticello, recounting each detail in Franco-Italiano, a strange composite language fashionable in the 13th and 14th centuries (after so long abroad, Marco, by all accounts, barely spoke his mother tongue, perhaps the reason he failed to write a personal account of his travels).

The resulting epic, now known as *Il Milione*, but originally titled *Divisament dou Monde* (Description of the World), was a runaway success. "In a few months it spread throughout Italy," wrote Polo's 16th-century biographer, the geographer Giovanni Ramusio. People read the book not as fact, however, but as romance, with Kublai Khan as its chivalric hero. Worse, from posterity's point of view, it was published before the advent of printing, with the result that each subsequent copying of the book saw scribes add countless embellishments. Over 140 known manuscript versions of the text survive, in a dozen languages and dialects, but no original or authentic text exists. As a result, controversy has obscured Marco Polo's reputation for more than seven centuries.

HOMECOMING
Marco and his father had to persuade their family of their true identity after returning to Venice. This they did, according to Marco's 16th-century biographer, by sitting them down—in true Italian fashion—to a big meal. They then presented the shabby Tartar clothes in which they had returned: "Straightaway they took sharp knives and began to rip up some of the seams and welts, and to take out of them jewels of the greatest value in vast quantities, such as rubies, sapphires, carbuncles, diamonds, and emeralds, which they had stitched up in so artful a fashion that nobody could have suspected the fact." Giovanni Ramusio, *Ser Marco Polo*

205

This Catalan world map from 1375 is thought to include a portrait of Marco Polo

GETTING THERE
Take one of the hourly No 12 boats from the Fondamente Nuove (try for the first boat of the day to avoid the crowds). ACTV single or return tickets, travel cards or *Biglietti turistici* for Murano (see page 102), Burano (page 72), and Torcello (page 102) are valid. Murano, however, is best seen as a separate trip. At Torcello's single quay follow the path along the canal ahead of you to the hamlet (no more than a five-minute walk).

Torcello, the most peaceful of the lagoon's islands

206

►►► Torcello, Isola di   *271B3*

Torcello is the trip you should make into the lagoon if you make no other: the island presents a remarkable contrast to the city, and its open fields and peaceful backwaters would be worthy of a visit even without the beautiful church—the best in Venice—sitting at the heart of its single hamlet.

Venice's birthplace, the island was the first spot settled by refugees fleeing the mainland during the 5th or 6th centuries. Its cathedral, the lagoon's (and Venice's) oldest building, became the focus of a thriving city with its own laws, palaces, shipyards, and booming population. Long after the Rialto developed, it continued to be the center of Venetian trade.

From its 12th-century heyday, however, when its citizens numbered upwards of 20,000, it went into decline, held back by the ravages of malaria and the silting up of its canals. Instead Venice prospered, better placed as it was at the mouth of the Brenta for trading, and free of the mud that clogged Torcello's waterways. Over the years the city's builders rifled the island's palaces for stone and statuary, leaving only the pair of churches and huddle of houses that cluster around today's grassy village square.

Santa Maria Assunta (*Open* daily 10–12:30, 2–5. Campanile *open* daily 10:30–5:30, closed winter. *Admission for both: inexpensive*) Santa Fosca, an atmospheric if heavily restored Byzantine church, has its charms, but unless you treat yourself to a meal in the pleasant (but wildly expensive) Locanda Cipriani, the cathedral of Santa Maria Assunta is the real reason to visit Torcello. Founded in 639, it is the finest piece of Veneto-Byzantine architecture in Italy, and its breathtakingly simple interior is likely to provide one of your most abiding Venetian memories. Only the crypt and a few foundations survive from the

MUSEO DI TORCELLO
The small but well-presented museum opposite Santa Maria Assunta contains a miscellany of exhibits relating to the area's history. (*Open* Apr–Sep Tue–Sun 10:30–6; Oct–Mar Tue–Sun 10–5)

"A RECLAIMED WILDERNESS"
"Torcello is a reclaimed wilderness. Through copses of water-willow and hibiscus bushes run salt-water streams where petrel and teal delight to stalk. Here and there a marble capital, a fragment of…sculpture or a lovely, shattered Greek cross emerges from the long grass. Nature's eternal youth smiles in the midst of these ruins. The air was balmy, and only the song of the cicadas disturbed the religious hush of the morning." Georges Sand, *Lettres d'un voyageur* (1837)

A detail from the Last Judgement *in Santa Maria Assunta*

Attila's Throne: the link with the Hun, and even its date, is unknown

ATTILA'S THRONE
In the shade beneath the olive tree outside Torcello's museum stands a stone throne known as Attila's Throne. This was perhaps originally used by the island's early consuls or magistrates. According to tradition, anyone sitting on it will be married within the year.

earliest church, the facade and portico dating from around 864, the main body of the church from 1008 (when it was rebuilt by Bishop—later Doge—Otto Orseolo, prompted, it is said, by the fear that the world was to end at the millennium). For breathtaking views of the whole lagoon, climb up the Campanile (belltower), which has reopened after 30 years.

Every element in the interior is matchless, from the 11th-century marble pavement and simple wooden ceiling to the apse's 12th-century mosaic of the Madonna and Child. The last, in the words of Jan Morris, is "the noblest memorial of the lagoon…the Venetians, through all their epochs of splendor and success, never created anything quite so beautiful." The 11th-century frieze below it depicts the Apostles, together with a square mosaic portrait of St. Heliodorus, first Bishop of Altinium, whence Torcello's settlers had fled. Heliodorus's relics were brought to the island, and lie buried under the 7th-century high altar. His original tomb, a recycled Roman sarcophagus, stands to the left, close to the church's foundation stone. To its left you can glimpse the waterlogged crypt.

The chapel to the right of the altar has more outstanding mosaics, mainly 11th-century depictions of Christ and the Lamb of God studded with 7th- or 8th-century fragments. A few steps back down the right nave, lift the four small planks to see the church's original stone floor. The rood screen and choir are also superb, the former supporting a painted balcony of the *Virgin and Apostles* on beautifully toned 11th-century pillars. Most diverting of all is the vivid 12th-century mosaic of *Christ's Apotheosis* and the *Last Judgement* on the rear wall. The best of its tiers is the lowest, which depicts the sinners and the saved, the former consumed by red flames from Christ's feet. Hell is a graphic black hole, full of skulls with snakes winding in and out of their empty sockets.

Death and Venice go hand in hand. From Thomas Mann's Death in Venice *to the deaths of Wagner and Robert Browning, the city's crumbling grandeur and melancholic air have provided an apt and atmospheric backdrop for untimely ends both in fact and in fiction.*

Above and below: San Michele memorials

DISEASED CITY
Plague came to Venice with the merchant ships of the Levant, killing vast numbers on countless occasions— 70,000 in 1576, 45,000 in 1630. As late as 1848, cholera victims were loaded into barges for mass burials in the lagoon. Malaria also ravaged Murano and Torcello, reducing the latter to a virtually deserted shell.

WINTER FUNERAL
"Marvelously evocative is a winter funeral in Venice. A kind of trolley, like a hospital carriage, brings the coffin to the quayside, the priest shivering in his wind-ruffled surplice, the bereaved relatives desperately muffled; and presently the death-boat chugs away through the mist down the Grand Canal, with a glimpse of flowers and a little train of mourning gondolas." Jan Morris, *Venice* (1960)

Death and decay It requires little imagination to find metaphors for death in Venice's moribund palaces and all-pervasive decay. For Jan Morris the city's "tall tottering palaces" seem "like grey symbols of the grave," its sadness "a wistful sense of wasted purpose and lost nobility." Even Venice's gondolas carry intimations of mortality: "moths of which coffins might have been the chrysalis," according to the poet Shelley; "black as nothing else on earth except a coffin" in the words of Thomas Mann. Literature is full of Venice's imminent or imagined decay. "Her palaces are crumbling to the shore," laments Byron in *Childe Harold's Pilgrimage*, "and silent rows the songless Gondolier." To Shelley's "Sun-girt City" must come a "darker day," a day of "drear ruin" when all will be in "its ancient state." William Wordsworth's "maiden City, bright and free" must some day "espouse the everlasting Sea" and watch her "glories fade," her "titles vanish" and her "strength decay."

Many writers have sent their fictional protagonists to die in the city. Dark portents quickly gather around Thomas Mann's von Aschenbach in *Death in Venice*: "The sky was grey, the wind humid...all sight of land soon vanished in the mist...beyond the somber dome of the sky stretched the vast plain of empty sea." Shakespeare's Bolingbroke, "retir'd himself to Italy; and there at Venice gave his body to that pleasant country's earth and his pure soul unto his captain's Christ."

Fictional demises were inspired not only by Venice's literal decay, but also by the aura of death that clung to the city, a ghostly shroud woven by the thousands killed

A Venetian hearse

by disease over the centuries; by cholera, plague, malaria, and the chilling vapors of the lagoon. Richard Wagner expired in a palace on the Grand Canal, as did the poet Robert Browning. Shelley's daughter Clara died here ("We had scarcely arrived at Venice," wrote her mother, "before life fled from the little sufferer"). Dante died in Ravenna from a fever contracted in the city. Diaghilev breathed his last here, as did Verrocchio, carried off before he could finish the famous Colleoni statue (see pages 152–153).

San Michele Until 1807 Venetians were buried in cemeteries around the city, but in that year the Napoleonic authorities decreed that burials should hence-forth be confined to the island of San Cristoforo. In time the small canal separating the island from its neighbor, San Michele, was filled in, and by 1870 the two islands between Murano and the Fondamente Nuove had become one. Until recently, San Michele's walled redoubt was Venice's island cemetery (there is now no more room for fresh graves). Having been brought here, the deceased, depending on wealth and previous social standing, were either allowed to remain in perpetuity or removed after a decade for reburial on the mainland.

Although the island has had a church since the 10th century, the present building, San Michele in Isola, dates from 1469. Designed by Mauro Coducci, it was among the first Renaissance buildings in the city, and one of the first to use white Istrian stone to face its gleaming facade. To its left is the Cappella Emiliana, an appealing hexagonal chapel built around 1530 by Guglielmo dei Grigi.

Wandering the rows of tombs, tended by Franciscan monks, the visitor gains a strange insight into the Italian way of death (cemetery *open* daily in summer 8–6, in winter 8–4). Pick up the small plan at the entrance to trace the graves of the more famous inmates, particularly those of the unkempt Protestant section, whose walk-ways contain the bodies of Stravinsky, Diaghilev, and Ezra Pound, among others.

DECAY
"This Venice, which was a haughty, invincible, magnificent Republic... is fallen prey to poverty, neglect and melancholy decay...her piers are deserted, her warehouses are empty, her merchant fleets are vanished, her armies and navies are but memories. Her glory is departed, and with her crumbling grandeur of wharves and palaces about her she sits among her stagnant lagoons, forlorn and beggared... She that in her palmy days commanded the commerce of a hemisphere...is become the humblest among the peoples of the Earth—a peddler of glass-beads for women, and trifling toys and trinkets for school-girls and children." Mark Twain, *The Innocents Abroad* (1869)

Venice   Excursions

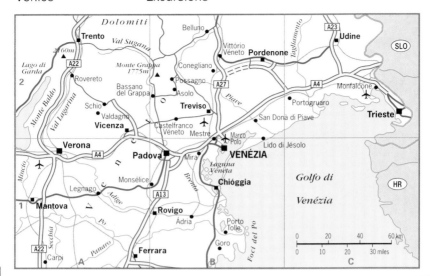

210

AVOID MESTRE
Heed Jan Morris's
warning, and think twice
before taking a room in
Mestre: "Administratively
Mestre is part of Venice,
and many of the guide
books list its hotels
together with those of the
Serenissima. There are no
sadder people on earth
than those unfortunates
who inadvertently book
rooms there, or accept
some claptrap advice
about its advantages,
and are to be seen emerg-
ing from their hotel
lobbies, spruced and
primped for an evening's
gaiety, into the hubbub,
traffic jams, half-complete
streets and dowdy villas of
this dismal conurbation."
Venice (1960)

*The Arena in Verona
is the third-largest
Roman amphitheater
in the world*

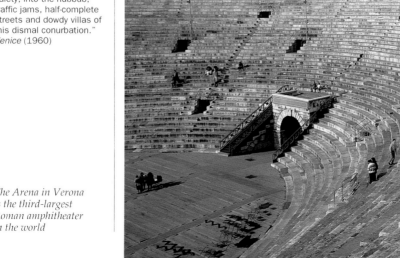

Excursions

ESCAPING THE CITY With arguably the world's most beautiful city at your disposal it might seem perverse to consider spending time on the Venetian mainland. Venice's environs abound with interest, however, and can make a welcome change from a wearying round of sights or the crowds and clamor of a Venetian summer. Among the countless trips possible, only three really stand out—to Verona, Padua, and Vicenza. All, with the possible exception of Verona, can be managed as day trips, and all are easily accessible by train from Venice. Trips to islands such as Burano and Torcello (see pages 72–73 and 206–207) offer more of a contrast to the city than you might expect, and if island retreats appeal, other smaller islets such as San Lazzaro degli Armeni lie dotted around the lagoon (see page 213).

THE VENETO Venice's prosperous hinterland takes its name from the Venetii, its pre-Roman inhabitants, and corresponds roughly to the city's medieval mainland empire (the lion of St. Mark still lords it over many of the

PLEASANT VERONA
Charles Dickens' words on Verona are as true today as they were 150 years ago: "Pleasant Verona," he wrote "with its beautiful old palaces, and charming country in the distance…With its Roman gates, still spanning the fair street, and casting, on the sunlight of today, the shade of fifteen hundred years ago. With its marble-fitted churches, lofty towers, rich architecture, and quaint old thoroughfares …with its fast-rushing river…great castle…and prospect so delightful, and so cheerful! Pleasant Verona!"
Pictures from Italy (1846)

211

The magnificent facade of Verona's Duomo

region's towns and villages). Its considerable prosperity has been bought at some cost, however, notably the drab industrial suburbs that blight many historic towns. None are worse than those of Mestre and Marghera, Venice's near neighbors (the photograph on page 14 shows how close the belching chimneys have come to *La Serenissima*). These two towns should really be avoided at all costs. **Padua**, by contrast, just 30 minutes or so from Venice by train, boasts one of Italy's foremost fresco cycles, a stunning art gallery and a tight historical core dominated by one of the country's most celebrated religious shrines. **Vicenza**, roughly another half an hour beyond Padua, boasts not only Italy's prettiest theatre and another fine gallery, but also a Palladian-inspired center that ranks as one of the most urbane in all Europe.

Verona, among the most captivating of Italian cities, perhaps offers more of historical interest than the rest of the region put together. Beautiful and romantic—it is of course the city of Shakespeare's *Romeo and Juliet*—its broad appeal encompasses atmospheric streets, medieval squares, grand sculpture, tiny churches, first-rate galleries, and a magnificently preserved Roman amphitheater. Indeed, Verona has so much to offer that a day trip may not do it justice, particularly as the train journey from city to city takes about two hours. If you are going to spend a night away from Venice, this might be the place to do it.

VILLAS OF THE BRENTA One of the best-known excursions from Venice is the boat trip inland to survey the villas of the Brenta, the southernmost of the three rivers that empty into the Venetian lagoon. Some 80 villas, originally built as summer retreats by wealthy Venetians, lie on or close to the river and the canal of the same name (the latter built during the 14th century to prevent flooding and the silting up of Venice's waterways). In times past, villa owners made their way inland on the *Burchiello*, a stately boat

On board the modern-day Burchiello

whose modern and far less elegant namesake today conveys visitors along much the same route. Be warned, though, that the journey is not as pretty now as it must have been in the past.

Services leave Venice at 9 AM on Tuesday, Thursday, and Saturday (March–October) from the quay in front of the old Zecca building (located on the waterfront immediately to the west of Piazza San Marco). The cost is L110,000, plus L43,000 for an optional lunch at the Ristorante Burchiello at Oriago. The price also includes the return trip to Venice from Padua by bus or train and entry to the villas Pisani, Grimani-Valmarana, and Foscari (or Malcontenta). Reservation is obligatory and can be made through travel agents. For more information contact the San Marco tourist office or tel: 041/5298740.

SAN LAZZARO DEGLI ARMENI The most rewarding of the smaller islands on the lagoon, this was originally a 15th-century leper colony, hence *Lazzaro*, the Italian for Lazarus, patron saint of lepers. Deserted for years thereafter, it was given in 1717 to the Armenians, who had been in Venice since the 13th century. Their monastery (*Open* 3–5 only. *Admission: expensive*) became—and remains—an important center of Armenian culture, and its monks have long been noted for their skill as linguists. Byron spent happy winter days here, immured in the monastery's library helping to prepare the first English-Armenian dictionary. Visitors must catch the No 20 boat from the San Zaccaria stop on the Riva degli Schiavoni and join one of the fascinating guided tours conducted by the multilingual monks. The tours visit: the ancient library whose 150,000 volumes include many beautiful illuminated manuscripts; the cell of the monastery's founding monk; the art gallery; museum; Byron's study; and the wonderful flower- and peacock-filled gardens.

San Lazzaro degli Armeni: the cloisters (top) and the library (above)

From left to right, the Basilica di Sant'Antonio's bas-reliefs show Antony as he receives the Franciscan habit; revives a woman stabbed by a jealous husband; raises a man from the dead; revives a drowned woman (by Sansovino); revives a drowned baby (Sansovino); directs mourners to the heart of a miser (Tullio Lombardo); and restores a boy's severed foot (Lombardo). The last panels portray separate miracles: a heretic throwing a glass which fails to break; and a baby describing its mother's innocence (both by Antonio Lombardo).

214

Santa Giustina

▶ Padova (Padua)   *210B1*

The World War II bombing that devastated Padua seems at first glance to have left the city a rebuilt sprawl of factories and modern suburbs. Two major monuments, however, together with the bulk of a tight medieval center, escaped the bombs. Giotto's paintings in the **Cappella degli Scrovegni** (which can now only be visited by advance reservation) are one of Italy's most famous fresco cycles, while the **Basilica di Sant'Antonio**—among the country's most visited shrines—features some of the Veneto's finest sculpture. The rest of the city center contains a handful of sights easily seen in a morning. This account assumes a walking tour starting and finishing at the railroad station.

Museo Civico Eremitani▶▶▶ A dispiriting walk down Corso del Popolo takes you across the river to a lovely park on the left, home to Padua's main museum complex and the Cappella degli Scrovegni (the entrance is at Piazza Eremitani 8, beyond the park on the left). The old monastery of the adjoining church of the Eremitani incorporates a superb medley of galleries. The **Museo d'Arte Mediovale e Moderna**, or art gallery, is outstanding, its modern displays—with polished floors and matt-gray

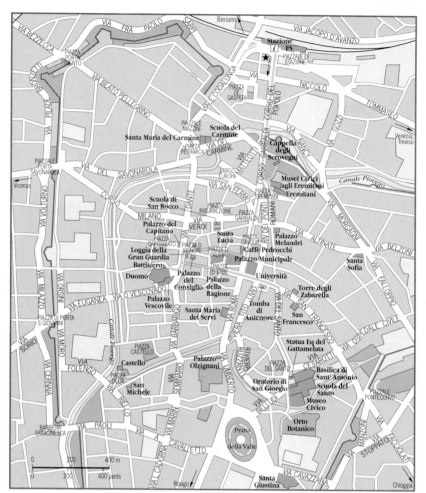

Central Padua

walls—among the most sophisticated in Europe. Among its 3,000 paintings are works by Giotto, Jacopo Bellini, Alvise Vivarini, Giorgione, Titian, Veronese, Piazzetta, Squarcione, and the prolific local painter Guariento.

The **Museo Bottacini** contains some 50,000 coins, medals and seals, and the **Museo Archeologico** a range of finds from Padua's Roman and Etruscan past. Be sure to pick up the multilingual guides to the museum and Padua's other sights at the museum entrance: a desk here also serves as a tourist information point.

Cappella degli Scrovegni▶▶▶ Padua's famous chapel formed part of a now-vanished palace on the former site of the Roman arena. Built by Paduan nobleman Enrico Scrovegni, it was intended to atone for the usurious sins of his father, Reginaldo (which were so extreme that he was not only denied a Christian burial but also singled out for his miserliness in Dante's *Inferno*). Enrico had seen Giotto at work in the city's basilica (see below), and

215

CHILLY HUMILIATION
The Salone contains a black stone block just inside its door known as the *pietra del vituperio*. A debtor could redeem some of his debts by sitting on this variation of the medieval pillory, in the words of a chronicler, "with his naked buttocks three times in some public assembly."

PRACTICALITIES

Trains run twice hourly to Padua from Venice and the travel time is 30 minutes. Buy a return ticket (*andata e ritorno*) and remember to validate your outward and return portions in the yellow platform machines at Venice and Padua. For the city center in Padua take Corso del Popolo (straight ahead and a little to the right) from the station forecourt (a 5-minute walk). Padua's main tourist office is at the railroad station (*Open* summer, Mon–Sat 9–7, Sun 9–noon; winter, Mon–Sat 9–5:30, Sun 9–noon; tel: 049/8752077). It has plenty of maps and pamphlets, and sells a L15,000 combined ticket (*Padova Arte*) to the following monuments and museums: Cappella degli Scrovegni, Museo Civico Eremitani, Palazzo della Ragione, Scoletta del Santo, Museo Antonieri, and Oratorio di San Giorgio. The ticket can also be purchased at any of the museums. The ticket does not include the reservation fee to the Scrovegni chapel. For a reservation (now compulsory) tel: 049/8204550. The chapel and Museo Civico Eremitari are *open* summer, Tue–Sun 9–7; winter, Tue–Sun 9–6. *Admission: expensive.*

Giotto's Last Judgement, *on the west wall of the Cappella degli Scrovegni (ca1305)*

commissioned the chapel's frescoes from him between 1303 and 1306.

Although smaller than you might expect, the chapel is bathed in a cool blue light which creates an air of calm even when the place is crowded with people. Its paintings are arranged in three bands, spread over the altar wall and two side walls. On the right, from top to bottom, the tiers depict the *History of Joachim*, the *Childhood of Christ*, and the *Passion of Christ*. On the left they portray scenes from the *Life of the Virgin*, *Christ's Public Life*, and *Christ's Death and Resurrection*. The marble panels on the lower part of the walls show the *Vices* (left) and *Virtues* (right). The best of the scenes is the *Last Judgement* on the rear (door) wall, which includes a portrait of Scrovegni presenting his chapel (immediately above the door).

Central Padua Outside the museums, look into the church of the **Eremitani▶** (*Open* summer Mon–Sat 8:15–noon, 4–6, Sun 9:30–12:15, 4–6; winter Mon–Sat 8:15–noon, 4–6, Sun 9:30–noon, 4–6 in winter), rebuilt after being bombed during an Allied raid in 1944. It once held countless Mantegna frescoes, the loss of which is considered one of the greatest blows ever to befall Italy's artistic patrimony. Only a few sad fragments survive, in the chapel to the right of the altar.

Walking southwards on the main street, past the vast UPIM supermarket, you come to the recently refurbished **Caffè Pedrocchi**, a famous neoclassical bar (once renowned for having no doors and being open 24 hours a day). Its *piano nobile*, where temporary exhibitions and concerts are held, is Padua's choicest spot for a drink and a snack, though it is no longer the famous haunt of intellectuals. Turn right after the café to walk through the town's main squares, **Piazza della Frutta** and **Piazza dei Signori**. The former is the site of a fruit and general market; the latter contains Italy's oldest astronomical clock, on the **Torre dell'Orologio**, and the former residence of Padua's Venetian commander, the Palazzo del Capitano (the city fell to Venice in 1405).

Bearing left, you come quickly to the **Duomo**, surely one of Italy's dullest, and to the **Baptistery**►► (*Open* daily 10–6. *Admission: inexpensive*), one of the city's more unexpected treats. The interior is completely covered in vivid frescoes (ca1376) by Giusto de' Menabuoi, a follower of Giotto commissioned by the Carrara family, Padua's ruling noble dynasty before the city's capitulation to Venice.

From the piazza's northern corner take Via de Manin, a pleasantly arcaded street, and at the end pause to admire the redoubtable **Palazzo della Ragione**►► (*Open* summer, Tue–Sun 9–7; winter, Tue–Sun 9–6. *Admission: moderate*), or Salone, built as law courts in 1218 and once painted with frescoes by Giotto (they were lost in a fire in 1420). One of Italy's largest medieval halls, it is worth a look inside for its comic stone horse and prodigiously endowed wooden version (built for jousts). There are also some 300 modest frescoes (1425–1440) by Niccolò Miretto.

Basilica di Sant'Antonio (Il Santo)►►► (*Open* daily 6:30 AM–8 PM in summer; 6:30 AM–7 PM in winter) Two blocks after the Salone, turn right on to Via del Santo and walk to the Piazza del Santo, home to Donatello's statue (1453) of the mercenary captain of the Venetian army known as the Gattamelata ("the Honeyed Cat"). The finest of the Renaissance equestrian statues, it slightly predates Verrocchio's similar Venetian statue of Bartolomeo Colleoni (see pages 152–153). The vast building to its rear is the bizarre 14th-century basilica built to house the body of St. Antony, who died in Padua in 1231. The faithful troop past his tomb (contained in a chapel on the left), touching and kissing its polished stone, or studying its poignant votive offerings—anything from pictures of car crashes to missing children and even the syringes of reformed drug addicts.

The nine bas-reliefs (1505–1577) round the chapel's side and rear walls show a series of scenes from the life of St. Antony and are the basilica's artistic highlight (see panel page 214). While many of the church's frescoes are comparatively recent, the high altar has a series of reliefs depicting the miracles of St. Anthony and bronze statues by Donatello. Do not miss the extraordinary collection of relics at the rear of the apse, including parts of the saint's larynx, tongue, lower jaw, and the beard which grew after his death.

ST. ANTONY
One of Catholicism's best-loved saints—as Padua's cohorts of pilgrims demonstrate—Antony (1193–1231) was a Portuguese missionary who joined the Franciscans in 1220 after being shipwrecked off Italy. He attended one of the order's first General Chapters in Assisi, while Francis himself was still alive (he was close to Francis in both spirit and outlook). Sent to preach in Bologna and Padua, he became renowned for his sermons (described in Rome as a "jewel case of the Bible"). His humility, gentleness, and devotion to the poor earned him a considerable following that survives to this day. He is also invoked to help find lost articles. Sainthood was bestowed upon him within just a year of his death.

217

Excursions

PRACTICALITIES

Fast trains from Venice run roughly hourly to Verona's Porta Nuova station and take about an hour and a half. At the station take buses from Bay A (tickets from *tabacchi* in the station) to Piazza Brà. The main APT office is at Via Leoncino 61, just off Piazza Brà (tel: 045/8003638). The tourist office website is: www.tourism.verona.it. Entry to the Arena, the Museo at the Castelvecchio, and the Teatro Romano is free on the first Sun of every month.

▶▶ Verona   270A1

Verona is the most distant but also the most alluring of the excursions that are realistically feasible from Venice. Clustered around the fast-flowing Adige River, the historic core—a simple bus ride from the station—is crammed with Roman and medieval remains, and interspersed with churches, monuments, picturesque piazzas, and rambling old streets. Much of the center is pedestrianized, and most of the sights are within walking distance of one another.

City center Start your exploration in Piazza Brà, Verona's mammoth main square, dominated by the truncated remains of the **Arena**▶▶▶ (*Open* daily 9–6, during opera season 8–3:30. *Admission: moderate*), one of the world's largest surviving Roman amphitheaters (only Capua's and the Colosseum are larger). Built during the 1st century AD, it still hosts the city's famous summer opera festival. During the day you can clamber up to the top of its 44 tiers to savor fine views of the city.

*Verona's busy
Piazza Brà*

Verona's elegant main street, Via Mazzini, leads to **Piazza delle Erbe►►**, an intimate square that has long been the city's social hub (it was the site of the Roman forum). Lined with cafés, stores, and medieval palaces, it makes a good place for coffee or just to browse around its market. Then walk under **Arco della Costa**, the "Arch of the Rib," named after the whale bone that hangs here. According to myth, the rib will fall if an adult virgin walks beneath it.

Next door lies one of Italy's most magical squares, **Piazza dei Signori►►►**, once the city's chief civic square, hence its trio of 12th-century civic buildings: the Palazzo del Governo, seat of Verona's medieval rulers; the Loggia del Consiglio, a council meeting chamber; and the Palazzo della Ragione, a rugged Gothic ensemble. The latter's 272-feet-tall **Torre dei Lamberti►►** (*Open* Tue–Sun 9–6, shorter hours in winter. *Admission: moderate*) offers vertiginous views of the city.

Excursions

An attractive window from Verona

A GLASS OF WINE

Verona is known for its wine—Italy's biggest wine fair, *Vinitaly*, takes place here every April—and for its historic *osterie*: old-fashioned wine stores, popular for a glass of sparkling Prosecco, Soave or one of the inexpensive local Bardolino or Valpolicella reds (see pages 182–183). Places to try include the Bottega dei Vini, Vicolo Scudo di Francia (off Via Mazzini); Osteria del Duomo, Via Duomo; or Osteria delle Vecete, Via Pellicciai (near Piazza delle Erbe).

Drinking Prosecco in Verona

A statue of a stern-looking Dante commands the center of the square, surveying the **Arche Scaligere▶▶**, the tombs of Verona's medieval overlords and the poet's erstwhile patrons. The family reposes in some of Italy's most remarkable Gothic funerary monuments, the finest being that of Cangrande I ("The Big Dog"), whose grinning figure looks down from the equestrian statue atop his tomb. Other clan members lie in canopied graves behind a wrought-iron palisade (decorated with ladder motifs, the family's emblem and a pun on their name—*scala* means "ladder" or "steps").

Going north This is a good point to make the slight detour to see the so-called **Casa di Giulietta▶** (*Open* daily 9–6:30; closed Mon. *Admission: moderate*; courtyard *free*), or Juliet's House, in Via Cappello, the reputed home of Shakespeare's heroine. While the Bard's Capulets and Montagues were based on real families (the Cappello and Montecchi—although no record exists of the two feuding), the characters of Romeo and Juliet are almost certainly fictitious. Nonetheless, the house—once an inn known as the Cappello—remains hard to resist. Both building and courtyard are extremely pretty, and there is even a balcony, although as Arnold Bennett once pointed out, it is "too high for love, unless Juliet was a trapeze

artist, accustomed to hanging downwards by her toes."
According to legend, Juliet was buried in the Church of
Francesco al Corse on Via Pallone. The (empty) tomb has
an evocative setting in a crypt below the cloister.

Not far away from the Casa di Giulietta looms
Sant'Anastasia▶, Verona's largest church (1290–1481).
The facade was never completed but has a fine portal with
frescoes and reliefs of St. Peter Martyr. The interior has a
mix of frescoes (the best is Pisanello's *St. George and the
Princess* in the sacristy). A few streets to the northwest
stands the **Duomo▶**, known for its exterior carvings and
Titian's *Assumption*, painted in 1540 and hanging in the
first chapel on the left.

Cross the river behind the church to see the **Teatro
Romano▶** (*Open* Tue–Sun 9–6:30 in summer; Tue–Sun 9–3
in winter. *Admission: moderate*), a ruined Roman theater,
and the modest Museo Archeologico. Climb the steps
above the museum to the Castel San Pietro to enjoy one of
the city's best viewpoints. Rich in art works, **San Giorgio
in Braida▶**, just to the west, is worth a brief stop to see
Veronese's *Martyrdom of St. George*.

ROMEO AND JULIET

"There is no world without
 Verona's walls,
But purgatory, torture,
 hell itself.
Hence—banished is
 banish'd from the
 world—
And world's exile is
 death…"
William Shakespeare,
Romeo and Juliet (1594)

OPERA IN THE AMPHITHEATER

A performance in Verona's
arena is an unforgettable
experience, whether or not
you are a fan of opera.
The season runs through-
out July and August. You
can buy tickets
(L28,000–290,000) from
the box office (arches 8–9
of the Arena); from the
Fondazione Arena di
Verona, Piazza Brà 28
(who also sell tickets in
advance by mail or over
the phone: tel:
045/8005151). Most
seats are unnumbered, so
arrive early—the build-up
is fun anyway—and be
sure to rent a cushion and
bring a sweater.

221

OPENING TIMES

Eight of Verona's churches
charge visitors a moderate
admission, and have—
to a limited extent—
standardized their opening
hours. These include the
Duomo (Mon–Sat 9:30–6,
Sun 1:30–6), San Zeno
Maggiore (Mon–Sat 9–6,
Sun 1–6) and Sant'
Anastasia (Mon–Sat 9–6,
Sun 1:30–6). A *Biglietto
Unico* gives admission to
all these churches.

*The clock tower which
looks down upon the
Piazza delle Erbe*

Excursions

One of the 12th-century bronze panels on the door of San Zeno Maggiore

ST. ZENO
Bishop of Verona in 362, Zeno was known for his sermons, almsgiving, and enthusiam for new churches. He was particularly opposed to the loud wailing and lamentations that used to interrupt masses for the dead. His symbol is a fish, a reference either to the rite of baptism or to the saint's well-documented passion for angling.

The Piazza Duomo from above

Going west Head off for the **Castelvecchio▶▶▶** (*Open Tue–Sun 7:30–7:15; closed Mon. Admission: moderate*), the former fortress home of the Scaligeri, now the seat of the city's Museo Civico d'Arte. The best of its many paintings are Madonnas by Pisanello, Carlo Crivelli, Mantegna, and Giovanni Bellini; Tiepolo's *Heliodorus*; and Tintoretto's *Nativity* and *Concert in the Open*. Almost as appealing is the castle's maze of chambers and courtyards, an attraction in its own right. Behind the museum the evocatively fortified Ponte Scaligero crosses the river to Piazza Arsenale, heart of Verona's main park, a drowsy spot for picnics and afternoon siestas. Wander north and recross the river to reach **San Zeno Maggiore▶▶▶**, widely regarded as northern Italy's finest Romanesque church. Eye-catching exterior details include the ivory-colored facade; the reliefs around the main portal; the huge rose window with its wheel of fortune: and the 12th-century bronze panels of the main door. Inside, frescoes cover many of the surfaces, but all of them are overshadowed by Mantegna's compelling *Madonna and Saints* on the high altar.

►► Vicenza   270A2

A morning is enough to breeze round wealthy Vicenza, city of Palladio, but its urbane charm and intimate atmosphere (not to mention some good shopping) may well keep you in town for the best part of a day. More attractive than Padua, though perhaps without such impressive sights, it has had a similar history, evolving from a Roman colony and Lombard vassal to become a city state and Venetian satellite (like Padua, it was also bombed by the Allies in the Second World War). Follow the rough itinerary below (starting and finishing at the railroad station) to see the best of the sights, all of which are within easy walking distance of one another.

Corso Andrea Palladio►► A walk down Vicenza's main street gives you a good idea of both the city's wealth and its elegance, and a first chance to glimpse some of the buildings that have made it famous (many of the best shops and cafés are also to be found under its civilized arcades). See the panel on page 225.

Teatro Olimpico►►► (*Open* mid-Jun–end Aug, Tue–Sun 9–7; Sep–mid-Jun, Tue–Sun 9–5. *Admission: moderate.* A combined ticket costing L12,000 is available for the Museo Naturalistico-Archeologico, Museo Civico, Teatro Olimpico, and old Palazzo Barbaran da Porto). Look into the tourist office at the end of the corso, then walk through

PRACTICALITIES
Trains leave Venice roughly hourly and take between 45 minutes and one hour to reach Vicenza. From the station which is south of the city center, walk on Viale Roma (the road straight ahead of you) and turn right up Via Gorizia to reach Piazza del Castello (a 10-minute stroll). Remember to validate your ticket in the yellow platform machines before your return train journey to Venice. The tourist office is next to the Teatro Olimpico at Piazza Matteotti 12 (tel: 0444/320854; www.ascom.vi.it/ aptvicenza).

223

The Teatro Olimpico; the liberal use of classical statues is typical Palladio

Vicenza's needle-like Torre di Piazza—one of several sights clustered in and around the Piazza dei Signori. Others include Palladio's magnificent basilica and the Loggia del Capitaniato

224

the graceful green courtyard to its left, an attractive if unlikely prelude to the most winsome of all Palladio's buildings, the Teatro Olimpico. Begun by Palladio in 1580, just months before his death, it was completed by Scamozzi in 1584 and inaugurated with a performance of Sophocles' *Oedipus Rex* in 1585 (making it Europe's oldest surviving indoor theater). It was commissioned by the humanist Accademia Olimpica, which was founded in 1555 and is still going strong (it meets in the second of the rooms you walk through before reaching the theater). Palladio was among its 21 founder members.

The stage's breathtaking facade, admired from the creaking boards of a semicircular amphitheater, would be impressive on a church or palace, never mind in a theater: you can only sympathize with the players who have to compete with one of the world's finest sets. Equally startling are the vertiginously foreshortened "streets" to its rear, Scamozzi's reconstruction of an idealized "Greek city" (it was modeled on Thebes); there is even a frescoed sky above to give an added touch of verisimilitude. The toga-clad figures at the back, another suitably classical touch, are said to represent members of the original Accademia.

Museo Civico►►► (*Open* summer, Tue–Sun 9–7; winter, Tue–Sun 9–5. *Admission: moderate*) Outside the theater, cross the piazza to the Palazzo Chiericati, Palladio's most impressive Vicentine palace and home to the art gallery and civic museum. Here art and archeology have been brilliantly combined in a state-of-the-art gallery on the upper floor (to reach it turn left after the ticket hall and climb the stairs). The gallery is arranged chronologically, so at the top of the stairs turn right and follow the left-hand set of rooms first. Many of the pictures are by local painters, and there are also fine paintings by more familiar names such as Paolo Veneziano, Cima da Conegliano, Memling, Tintoretto, Veronese, Longhi, G. B. Tiepolo, van Dyck, and others.

Santa Corona►► (*Open* Mon 3–6, Tue–Sun 8:30–noon, 3–6) A few steps back up the Corso and a right turn bring you to what is probably the city's most important church, a Dominican foundation built to house a thorn from Christ's crown (*corona*) of thorns. The star turns are Veronese's *Adoration of the Magi* (1573) (fourth chapel on the right) and Giovanni Bellini's *Baptism of Christ* (1500) (fifth chapel on the left). Also look at Palladio's eerie and echoing crypt, and the *Madonna delle Stelle* (left of the

An embellishment to one of the great brick surfaces of Palladio's basilica, now used for art exhibitions

225

CORSO PALLADIO

Palaces to note here include Palazzo Thiene Bonin-Longhare (No 13), attributed to Palladio and executed by his follower, Scamozzi; Palazzo Pagello (Nos 38–40); Palazzo Thiene (No 47); Palazzo Brashi-Brunello (No 67); Scamozzi's Palazzo Trissono-Baston (No 98), now the town hall (rather spoiled by the supermarket opposite); and the star of the show, the Palazzo da Schio (No 147), also known as the Ca' d'Oro after its former gilt-swathed resemblance to Venice's "House of Gold" (see pages 74–77).

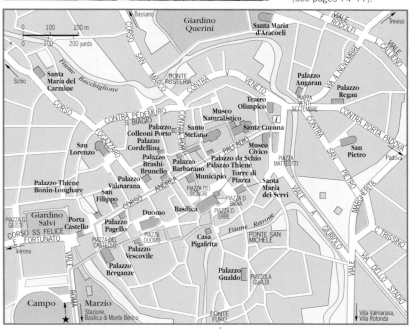

ROMEO AND JULIET

A plaque on the wall of Contrà Porti 15 records the death there in May 1529 of Luigi da Porto, the author of *Giulietta e Romeo*, the likely inspiration for Shakespeare's *Romeo and Juliet*.

WEALTH

Vicenza is among Italy's wealthiest cities. As well as being one of Europe's biggest textiles center, it is Italy's "silicon valley" (Federico Faggin, inventor of the silicon chip, was born here). It also has a huge jewelery trade (over 700 producers) and a large leatherwear and printing sector.

Palladio in Vicenza, the town of his birth

Bellini), whose lower foreground features a smudged view of late 16th-century Vicenza. To the left of the church is a run-of-the-mill natural history museum, the **Museo Naturalistico-Archeologico** (same hours as the Museo Civico). At the end of the street the fine baroque **Palazzo Leoni Montanari** (*Open* Fri–Sun 10–6. *Admission: moderate*) houses a museum devoted to Russian icons from the 13th–19th centuries and Venetian art, including works by Canaletto, Guardi, and Longhi.

Contrà Porti►► Walk down Contrà Santo Stefano opposite Santa Corona, looking into **Santo Stefano** (*Open* Mon–Sat 8:30–10, 5:30–7) to see Palma Vecchio's fine *Madonna and Child with Saints* (if you are lucky enough to find the church open). Then continue westwards to join Contrà Porti, a surprisingly well-integrated showcase of palace architecture spanning several centuries. On your left as you meet the street is the Palazzo Thiene (No 12), its frescoed and pink-brick facade dazzling amid the grimy Gothic and Palladian piles to either side. Turn right to see Palladio's recently restored Palazzo Barbaran Da Porto (No 11) (*Open* Tue–Sun 10–6. *Admission: expensive, but combined ticket with Musei Civici—see page 223*), the nicely balconied Palazzo Trissino-Sperotti (No 14), the similarly

Gothic Palazzo Colleoni Porto (No 19) and Palladio's big, bright, white Palazzo Iseppo Porto, next door at No 21.

Piazza dei Signori►►► Retrace your steps up Contrà Porti towards the corso. Then cross over to Piazza dei Signori, Vicenza's Roman, medieval and modern heart, a vast square dominated by Palladio's first major triumph, the Palazzo della Ragione, better known as the **Basilica** (ca1540–1620). The green-roofed, multi-arcaded monster is no more than a shell, a beautiful work of buttressing dreamed up by Palladio to provide support for an older civic *palazzo* that had been in danger of collapse.

Look for the plaque at the base of its slender **Torre di Piazza**, informing you, among other things, that you are 3 minutes and 44 seconds ahead of the time in Rome. To its left stand columns topped with a statue of Christ the Redeemer and Venice's inevitable Lion of St. Mark. Opposite the basilica stands the handsome brick-columned **Loggia del Capitaniato** (1571), a late and unfinished Palladian enterprise, decorated with reliefs celebrating the victory of the Battle of Lepanto. To its left is the large and soulless terrace of the Gran Caffè Garibaldi, a good suntrap and coffee-stop, but not as nice as the old-fashioned Bar Sorarù in the piazza's southern corner (Piazzetta Andrea Palladio).

From here you can drop behind the basilica to enjoy the small but colorful fruit and vegetable market, or walk a few paces to the **Casa Pigafetta** at Contrà Pigafetta 8. This tawny-stoned and Spanish-influenced oddity was built for Antonio Pigafetta, a chronicler and companion of the explorer Magellan. The **Palazzo Valmarana**, back across the corso would round off a Palladian tour, but it is one of the very few Vicentine buildings in a poor state: the partially finished courtyard—just eight pillars—looks like a bomb-site and is now used as a parking lot. The pinkish-green **duomo**, by contrast, which indeed *was* a bombsite (it was virtually destroyed in 1944 and rebuilt) is immensely handsome, looking rather like a pink and green-topped salt cellar. Inside, though, it is disappointingly bland and cold, with only a beautiful and complex polyptych by Lorenzo Veneziano to warrant a visit (fifth chapel on the right). It is close to the basilica, however, and if you are returning to Venice by train, it leaves you well placed for the walk to the railroad station.

The statue of Christ the Redeemer in Piazza dei Signori; the other of this pair of columns supports a winged lion of St. Mark

227

The entrance ticket to Vicenza's Teatro Olimpico

SUMMER NIGHTS

Mosquitoes can still be a nuisance, as they obviously were in Théophile Gautier's day: "The great business before going to bed," he lamented, "is the hunt for insects, vicious mosquitoes that particularly torment foreigners, on whom they hurl themselves with the sensual appetite of a gourmet savoring some rare and exotic dish." *Voyage en Italie* (1852)

FINDING A ROOM

Italian state tourist offices abroad (see page 258) can provide you with a list of hotels in Venice, detailing prices and facilities. Either reserve direct or telephone AVA (Venetian Hoteliers' Association) who will reserve a hotel for you free of charge (tel: 041/715016 or 715288).

LAST-MINUTE BOOKING

If you arrive in Venice without a room, head straight for one of the tourist offices run by the AVA (the Venetian Hoteliers' Association). Expect long lines and be prepared to accept rooms on the mainland in July and August. There are offices at the train station at the Tronchetto parking lot (*open* in season 8 AM–10 PM) (tel: 041/5222264); at Piazzale Roma; at Marco Polo airport; and at the Mestre–Marghera exit of the A4 motorway.

Accommodation

Venice has been accommodating visitors for hundreds of years, but never so many as the hordes that have visited the city over the last couple of decades. The increasing numbers have both strained its 200 or so hotels to capacity, and brought about a slide in standards among the city's more cynical hoteliers (who know they are guaranteed customers however grim their hotels). Prices are generally higher than in the rest of Italy, and reservations are now a virtual necessity all year round. Although it may not be an ideal arrangement, you might consider staying in Padua or Treviso (but *not* Mestre; see panel page 210), both less than half an hour by train from Venice.

BOOKING It is now almost essential to reserve a room in advance for July and August, and wise to do so in the rest of high season. Officially this runs from March 15 to November 15 and from December 21 to January 6, but it now also effectively includes the period of Carnevale in February. While some hotels charge the same prices throughout the year, others still drop their rates in winter to two-thirds, or in some cases nearly half the summer rates. If you are going to Venice independently, telephone the hotel with your reservations well in advance (nearly all hotel staff speak English). You can fax or write with your enquiry, but don't expect a prompt reply. Some hotels, if they are fully booked up for the dates you require, probably won't reply at all. Most hotels accept credit cards as a deposit over the telephone. An increasing number of hotels can now be booked online.

CATEGORIES Italy's hotels, including those in Venice, are classified into five categories, from basic one-star establishments to luxury five-star accommodations. The prices charged in each category are set by law and should be displayed on the door of each hotel room. If they are not, complain first to the hotel, then to the tourist office, and ultimately to the Questura (see page 254). Although the E.U. has outlawed the practice as "price-fixing," most hotels seem for the moment to be adhering to the old system. Prices vary according to the size and outlook of the room. Single rooms cost about 70 percent of the price of a double, and adding an extra bed increases the rate by 35 percent. Rooms without private bathrooms can cost around 20–30 percent less than a standard double. Taxes and service charges should be included in the room rate. It is also difficult to avoid paying for breakfast—since it is

included in the room rate—and in high season many hotels with restaurants will even insist on your taking half-board (*mezza pensione*).

LOCATION Venice's best hotels line the Grand Canal near San Marco or overlook the lagoon on the Riva degli Schiavoni; the cheapest lie in the somewhat grubby streets around the station and the Lista di Spagna. Touts at the station invariably work for over-priced hotels near by. Other concentrations of hotels are to be found near the Rialto and in Dorsoduro, the latter being one of the city's less touristy locations (though there is no "undiscovered gem" in Venice). In a city as compact as Venice, hotels are rarely far from the sights. Wherever your hotel, be certain when reserving to find its exact location— which means a street name as well as a number and *sestiere*. Also remember you may need to carry your luggage a long distance.

Above: inside the Danieli, one of Venice's top hotels
Left: the Gabrielli, Riva degli Schiavoni

NOISE
Although Venice is a remarkably quiet city, it still has its share of nocturnal traffic—even without cars. Church bells clatter through the night, and pedestrian chatter can reverberate noisily in narrow streets. Traffic on the larger canals can also be surprisingly noisy.

Eating out on the Riva del Vin by the Rialto; the view is superb, but beware the prices

THE *OMBRA*

There are several theories as to how Venice's *ombra*, or shadow, got its name. One suggests it derived from the idea of coming in from the sun to take a refreshing drink. Another claims it refers to a "shadow of a liter," another way of saying a small drink. The best recalls the days when wine was sold from barrels at the foot of the Campanile: as the sun moved across the sky the barrels had to be constantly moved into the shade to keep the wine cool.

SMOKING

Italians smoke more than most, and Italy has only recently acquired an anti-smoking lobby. As a result, few Venetian bars and restaurants have non-smoking sections.

Food and drink

EATING OUT Great food abounds in places like the Rialto and San Marco, and even average food can be worth enduring for the beauty of the setting. You will still find dire food, especially around the touristy areas, and the prices can make your eyes water. Fish, one of Venice's specialities, is always expensive—but here, too, the city's poor reputation is not always borne out on the ground, despite guide after guide suggesting that visitors are likely to be given sub-standard food, indifferent service and sky-high prices. Stay away from San Marco, shop around, and read menus carefully, and eating out in Venice will be a pleasure.

STYLES These days there is little to choose between a *ristorante* and a *trattoria* (a *ristorante* used to be nicer), and equally little to distinguish either from the once-humble *osteria*, now likely to be a chic and expensive option. Pizzerias are still as straightforward as ever, though their pizzas are often complemented by pastas, risottos, and simple main courses. A *rosticceria* and *tavola calda* serve hot snacks, usually to take out; they are now something of a rarity, their role in Venice having been taken by wine bars offering hot lunch and supper dishes (which are usually eaten standing up). A *gelateria* serves ice cream, a *pasticceria* cakes and pastries (for which Venice is rather unjustifiably famed).

MEALS The Venetian breakfast (*prima colazione*) is a straightforward stand-up event of cappuccino and plain, cream- or jam-filled croissants (*brioches* or *cornetti*). Lunch (*pranzo*) starts at around 12:30, but it is no longer, for locals at least, the extended blow-out of days gone by—this might be a good time to save money by having a bar snack instead, or making up a picnic with market-bought produce. Any time of day is right for an *ombra*, or "shadow" (see panel), but particularly around 5 PM, when bars and *bacari* perk up with people taking a glass of wine and snacks known as *cicheti*. Dinner (*cena*) starts a little earlier than elsewhere in Italy—usually around 7 PM.

MENUS Venetian menus (*la lista*) start with *antipasti* (starters), typically *prosciutto* (ham), salami, and seafood, followed by a *primo* (first course) of soup, risotto, polenta, or pasta. Main courses (*il secondo*) usually involve fish (meat usually comes a poor second in Venice), with salad and vegetables (*insalata* or *contorni*) served separately. Desserts (*dolci*), cheese (*formaggio*), and fruit (*frutta*) round things off, often followed by coffee, liqueurs, and *digestivi*. Few people wade through every course, so in all but the smartest restaurants feel free to stick to pasta, salad, and a glass of wine. When ordering fish or more expensive cuts of meat (such as filet), payment is usually by the *etto* (3.5oz) or *hectogram* (14oz). Items thus priced are usually marked *S.Q.* or *hg*.

PAYING The bill (*il conto*) invariably includes a cover charge per person (*pane e coperto*) and a 10–15 percent service charge (*servizio*). Tip around the same amount if service is not included. Remember that bars and restaurants are required by law to give you a proper receipt (*una ricevuta*). Always check the bill carefully, especially if—as sometimes still happens—the *ricevuta* is a semi-legible scrawl on a scrap of paper.

Costs can be kept down by skipping *antipasti* and desserts (go to a *gelateria* for an ice cream instead), or by opting for a fixed-price (but lower quality) *menù turistico*. Fixed-price menus usually include a basic pasta, main course, and simple dessert; wine or water is occasionally included. Beware of the slightly different *prezzo fisso* combination, a set-price menu that usually excludes cover and service charges. In more serious restaurants look out for the *menù degustazione*, a set-price gourmet menu which usually costs less than eating *à la carte*.

SNACKS Wine bars offer the best-value hot snacks, usually a plate of pasta or risotto, while most ordinary bars also serve a variety of *panini* (filled rolls) and *tramezzini* (crustless sandwiches), often with very generous fillings. Slices of pizza (*pizza a taglio*) can also be good value, but make sure the topping is more than a token smear of tomato. A *rosticceria* will provide

TRATTORIA
DONA ONESTA

DORSODURO 3922 - VENEZIA
Tel. 041-5229586

231

GRAPPA
Italy's most famous spirit is a clear firewater made from the mulch of skins and stalks left over after winemaking. The best varieties come from Bassano del Grappa, a town in the Veneto not far from Venice. Traditionally you drink the clear, neat original, but fruit- and herb-flavored versions—invariably foul—are also available. It is usually drunk after a meal, or added to an espresso (*un caffè corretto*).

A traditional cake baked for the feast day of St. Martin (November 11)

Food and drink

COFFEE
The first recorded mention of coffee by an Italian was by Francesco Morini, the doge's ambassador to Constantinople between 1582 and 1585. "In Turkey," he reported, "they drink a black water… which, so they say, has the ability of keeping people awake." Regarded as a medicinal drug when it first appeared in Venice in 1640, it only assumed its status as a focus for fashionable banter when the city's first coffee house opened in 1683. The fledgling café occupied the site now filled by Florian (which opened in 1720).

APERITIFS
Fortified wines such as Martini, Cinzano, and Campari are some of the most common Italian aperitifs. Campari Soda comes ready-mixed in its own distinctive bottle (see below). Artichoke-based Cynar is also popular.

anything from fries to a whole roasted chicken, while a *tavola calda* confines itself to a few soups and simple pastas. Picnic provisions can be bought from corner stores (*alimentari*), or from the Rialto markets and food stalls in some of the larger *campi*.

BARS The majority of Venetian bars are functional places for coffee, snacks, and an after-work *ombra* or *aperitivo*. In most you pay a premium to sit down and enjoy waiter service, and this is considerable in many places. However, a single purchase allows you to sit and watch the world go by almost indefinitely. Standing up, the procedure is to pay for what you want at the cash desk (*la cassa*) and take your receipt (*lo scontrino*) to the bar, where a L200 tip slapped down should work wonders with the service. Wherever possible, take breakfast in bars (better and cheaper than in hotels) and use cafés for lunchtime snacks.

COFFEE Breakfast means a milky cappuccino, named after the brown robes and white cowls of Capuchin monks. At other times the coffee of choice is the kick-start of caffeine known as an *espresso* or *un caffè*. Decaffeinated coffee is *un caffè Hag*, iced coffee *caffè freddo*, and American-style coffee (large and watery) *un caffè americano*. Other varieties include *caffè corretto* (with a dash of grappa or brandy), *caffè latte* (tall, milky, and non-frothy), and *caffè macchiato* (an *espresso* "stained" with a drop of milk). The mark of a good bar is the use of fresh (not UHT) milk. Italians never drink tea or coffee with meals, and rarely touch *cappuccino* after midday—*never* after a meal, when they opt for an *espresso* or camomile tea (*una camomilla*).

WINE Most better restaurants should have a selection of local wines from the Veneto and Friuli (see pages 182–183), together with a variety of vintages drawn from further afield in Italy (and perhaps France and Germany). Cheaper places may have only a house wine (*vino della casa*), usually a Valpolicella, Bardolino, or one of the Veneto's many innocuous whites. Ask for a bottle (*una bottiglia*), half-bottle (*mezza bottiglia*) or quarter-liter (7oz) flask (*un quartino*). The smartest places often have a dazzling selection of vintages, but be prepared for some stratospheric prices. At the other extreme, you could adopt the *ombra*-habit and enjoy an inexpensive glass of local wine—preferably the sparkling Prosecco—in almost any bar (ask for it by name, or *un bicchiere di vino rosso* or *bianco*).

BEER The cheapest way to buy beer (*birra*) is from the keg (*una birra alla spina*). Be sure to specify the size you want—*piccola* (25cl) or *media* (50cl). A *grande* (liter) is getting serious. Yellow, light-colored beer is the most common, though dark British-type ale (*birra scura*) is gaining in popularity. Italian bottled beer (*birra nazionale*) is reasonably priced, with Dreher and Peroni's Nastro Azzurro the most common brands. The 25cl Peroncino ("Little Peroni") is a particularly good thirstquencher. Foreign beers, by contrast, are fashionable, and consequently expensive.

WATER Venice's water is perfectly safe to drink, even if it is often hard and over-chlorinated, though Venetians, in line with all Italians, prefer to drink mineral water (*acqua minerale*)—either sparkling (*gassata*) or flat (*liscia, naturale* or *non gassata*). Ask for a liter (*un litro*), half a liter (*mezzo litro*), or a glass (*un bicchiere*).

SOFT DRINKS A wonderful accompaniment to breakfast is freshly squeezed orange juice (*una spremuta*), particularly in spring or early summer when Sicily's oranges are in season. Lemon (*limone*) and grapefruit (*pompelmo*) juice are usually also available. Alternatively, ask for bottled fruit juices (*un succo di frutta*), available in flavors such as pear (*pera*), peach (*pesca*), and apricot (*albicocca*). Lemon soda, a bitter lemon drink, is popular and widely available. Also be sure to try a fresh milk shake (*un frullato* or *un frappé* if made with ice cream). *Granita* is crushed ice covered in a syrup (usually coffee). Colas, of course, are ubiquitous. *Crodino*, a non-alcoholic aperitif, has also recently become popular. Ice is *ghiaccio*; a slice of lemon *uno spicchio di limone*. Tea with lemon (*tè al limone*) is common in Italy.

Tea with milk is still a combination that raises eyebrows, so be sure to ask for it specifically (*un tè con latte*). Make sure the milk is cold (*latte freddo*). Camomile (*camomilla*) is popular before bed, and iced tea (*tè freddo*) is widely available in summer.

A wide choice…

COCKTAILS

Many people are familiar with Venice's better-known cocktails—the Bellini (champagne and peach juice) and the Tiziano (champagne, grape, and pomegranate). Fewer are acquainted with the *Bucintoro*, a mixture of champagne (or Prosecco) and strawberry juice, or the remarkable strawberry-flavored wine made from the grape variety known as *una fragola*.

LIQUEURS AND BRANDIES

The best-known Italian liqueurs outside Italy are Sambuca, a sweet aniseed-based drink, and Amaretto, a sweet almond-flavored concoction. In Italy itself, however, the most common after-dinner tipple is *amaro*, a bitter medicinal brew of herbs, wines, and secret ingredients. The best brands (in ascending order of bitterness) are Montenegro, Ramazotti, Averna, and Fernet-Branca. The best Italian brandies, both widely drunk, are Vecchia Romagna and the second-ranked Stock.

San Maurizio's flea market turns up the occasional bargain

PASTA
For attractively packaged dried pasta, in all shapes and sizes, try Giacomo Rizzo at Salizzada S. Giovanni Crisostomo, San Polo 5778, not far from the Rialto. Unusual varieties include beet, squid, curry, and cocoa.

ARTISTS' MATERIALS
For paints, pigments, paper, pens, and other materials—often sold in nice old-fashioned stores—visit Testolini, Fondamenta Orseolo, San Marco; Seguso, Calle dei Fabbri, San Marco; Cartoleria Accademia, Rio Terrà della Carità 1044, Dorsoduro; and (for pigments in particular) Renato Burelli, Calle Lunga San Barnaba, Dorsoduro.

Shopping

ANTIQUES Bric-à-brac and antique bargains are few and far between in a city acutely aware of its past and the value of its objets d'art. If you have the resources, however, the choice of beautiful things in Venice is almost unlimited. Antiques stores dot the city, but the best (and most expensive) gather around San Maurizio and Santa Maria Zobenigo, in the *sestiere* of San Marco (just east of Campo Santo Stefano). Campo San Maurizio, in front of the former, hosts occasional flea markets, on whose stalls you should find more reasonably priced books, paintings, and bric-à-brac (contact tourist offices for details of forthcoming markets—the biggest are held around Easter and All Saints' Day). Somewhere worth seeing whether or not you are buying is **Pietro Scarpa**, whose outlet at Campo della Carità 1023, Dorsoduro (next to the Accademia) is more like a museum than a shop. Somewhere else you might like to browse is Venice's auction house, **Franco Semenzato** (tel: 041/721811), Palazzo Giovanelli (near Santa Fosca) Cannaregio 2292.

BOOKS For the non-Italian-speaking or casual bibliophile Venice offers a handful of stores selling books in English, a selection of high-quality art bookstores and others that specialize in tomes on Venice itself (most ordinary bookstores also keep a small stock of English-language paperbacks if you find yourself stuck for holiday reading). The best of the art bookstore is **Fantoni**, Salizzada San Luca 4119, San Marco, crammed with beautiful (and expensive) coffee-table books on a huge range of art and artists. **Sansovino**, just outside the Procuratie Vecchie at Bacino Orseolo 84, San Marco, is almost as good, and also has an impressive collection of art books. The best bookstore for English-speaking customers is **Libreria Studium**, Calle de la Canonica 337a, off Piazza San Marco, with an excellent selection of guides and other books on Venice. **Filippi Editore Venezia**, Calle della Casselleria 5284, Castello, is famous for its vast collection of books about all aspects of Venice. It also produces countless facsimile editions of old books, the originals of which may still be lurking in **Libreria Cassini**, Calle Larga XXII Marzo 2424, San Marco, one of many shops in the city specializing in old prints and antique books.

GLASS At times it seems that every other store in Venice sells glassware, one of the city's most famous traditional products. The biggest selection, and some of the most kitsch pieces, are to be found on Murano, the main center of production, and home to some of the best-known names (see pages 102–103). **Venini**, Piazzetta dei Leoncini 314, San Marco and Fondamenta dei Vetrai 47, Murano, has been an institution since the 1930s, attracting some of the foremost names in glass design. **Archimede Seguso**, Ponte Longo (Ponte Vivarini) 138, Murano, dates from about the same era, and also has an outlet in Piazza San Marco. **Salviati**, founded in 1866, also has outlets on Murano (Fondamenta Radi 16) and in the city itself in Piazza San Marco. The oldest firm of all, claiming to trace its roots back to the 14th century, is **Barovier e Toso**, Fondamenta dei Vetrai 28, Murano, whose current products draw for inspiration on the firm's historic 26,000-piece collection. For more modern work visit **Galleria Marina Barovier** at Salizzada San Samuele 3216, San Marco, an art gallery exhibiting contemporary and early 20th-century glass, or **Lucio Bubacco**, Rughetta del Ravano 1077a, San Polo (just east of Campo San Aponal), whose innovative pieces have found their way into museums all over the world.

CLOTHES The biggest names in Italian fashion cluster together within a few streets of Piazza San Marco. **Valentino** is at Salizzada San Moisè 1473, San Marco; **Giorgio Armani** at Calle Goldoni 4412, San Polo; the less expensive **Emporio Armani** at Calle dei Fabbri 989, San Marco; **Missoni** (for knitwear) at Calle Vallaresso 1312, San Marco;

SCENTS
L'Artisan Parfumeur at Campo Santa Maria Formosa specializes in exotic perfumes and toilet waters made from old-fashioned recipes.

COFFEE
The coffee shop Caffè Costarica has been in the same family for three generations, and is the place to buy fresh coffee to take home. They also sell gift-boxes and run a mail order service.

235

Lace and glass—from Burano and Murano respectively

LACE
With the advent of foreign and machine-made lace, genuine Venetian and Burano lace is now hard to come by (see pages 72–73). One of the places where you will still find the genuine article is Jesurum, one of the biggest and best names in the city. There are branches at the Merceria del Capitello 4857, San Marco and Piazza San Marco 60–61.

Shopping

LEATHER

Venice's best leather goods are sold in stores ranged along Calle Larga XXII Marzo and Calle dell'Ascensione. The most famous of all is Vogini at Salizzada San Moisé, 1257/a San Marco.

Kenzo at Ramo Fuseri, San Marco 1814; **Versace** at Campo San Moisé, San Marco 1462; **La Conpole** at Calle Larga XXII Marzo No 2366 and No 2031: and **Laura Biagiotti** at Via XXII Marzo 2400a, San Marco. Other high-fashion clothes and accessories shops congregate around La Fenice, the Mercerie, the Frezzeria, and on Calle Larga XXII Marzo. The best place to go for more reasonably priced clothes is the **COIN** department store, located just west of the Rialto bridge at Rio Terrà San Leonardo 5788, Cannaregio. Cheaper and more youth-orientated stores line the streets around the Rialto market, notably in Ruga Vecchia San Giovanni. Venice's wittiest store window is **Fiorella**, at the southern end of Campo Santo Stefano, where the clothes are modeled by mannequins of former doges in drag (complete with skirts and high heels).

FABRICS Venice's former trade in silks, damasks, and other exotic materials is still reflected in stores selling a host of fine fabrics. Perhaps the best known is **Trois**, Campo San Maurizio 2666, San Marco, whose specialization in old fabrics includes exclusive rights to some of Fortuny's famous silks (see panel on page 236): many are still made to old specifications in Fortuny's 1919 factory on the Giudecca. The crêpe and silk scarves at **Venetia Studium**, San Polo 3006 by the Frari Church, and on the Mercerie at San Marco 723, also take their inspiration from Fortuny's distinctive pleated, or *plissé* techniques. **Bevilacqua**, with branches at Campo S Maria del Giglio 2520 and Fondamenta Canonica 337/b, both in San Marco, has been making its brocades and velvets on hand looms since 1875.

Venetians share the Italian ability to create superb window displays

MASKS The revival of the Venetian Carnival means Venice now has almost as many stores selling masks as there are stores selling glass. Most are much the same, but for something a cut above the rest visit **Mondo Novo Maschere**, Rio Terrà Canal 3063, Dorsoduro (south of Campo Santa Margherita); the **Laboratorio Artigiano Maschere**, Barbaria delle Tolle 3063, Castello (near San Zanipolo), home to Giorgio Clanetti, the man credited with starting the current revival in maskmaking; and **Tragicomica**, Calle Nomboli, San Polo 2800, where you can both buy masks and watch them being made. These intriguing creations range from Commedia dell'Arte characters (Harlequin, Punch, etc.) to allegorical masks of the artist's own creation.

PAPER Marbled paper provides, along with masks and fabrics, some of the nicest and most distinctive souvenirs you can take home from Venice. The craft is almost a thousand years old, and spread from Japan to Persia and the Arab world during the Middle Ages. It reached Europe in about the 15th century, but largely vanished as an art until its reappearance in Venice in the 1970s. Alberto Valese, the man at the cutting edge of its revival, has a workshop called **Ebrù** at Campo Santo Stefano, San Marco 3471 that still produces some of the city's most innovative work. Also at the forefront of the craft's resurgence is **Paolo Olbi**, whose store at Calle della Mandola 3653, San Marco, sells a wide range of marbled stationery. **Legatoria Piazzesi**, Campiello della Feltrina 2511, San Marco is the last Venetian paper maker still using old hand- and wood-block-printing techniques. Other good stores include **Il Papiro** at Calle del Piovan, San Marco 2764 and Calle delle Bande, Castello 5275 (just off Santa Maria Formosa) selling marbled stationery and hand-embossed cards, and the beautiful little **Polliero**, an old-fashioned store right next to the church of the Frari in Campo dei Frari 2995, San Polo. It sells paper, plus a selection of leather-bound books and marbled-paper stationery.

OPENING TIMES Stores usually open Monday to Saturday 8 or 9–1 and 3:30 or 4–7:30 or 8. Many stores close on Monday morning (except food stores and bakeries). Markets, grocers, and bakers close on Wednesday afternoon. An increasing number of stores are open all day every day, including Sunday.

They're not necessarily to everyone's taste, but in Venice there's no chance of avoiding masks

MARIANO FORTUNY
Born in Catalonia in 1871, the son of a painter and fabric collector, Fortuny moved to Venice in 1889, quickly establishing himself as a gifted physicist, chemist, inventor, painter, photographer, architect, engraver, sculptor, couturier, and theater designer. It is for his fabrics that he is best remembered, however, and in particular the pleated silk dresses so fine they could be rolled up and threaded through a wedding ring. The pleating technique, patented in 1909, involved folding the pleats by hand into wet material, sewing them in place, and then sealing the folds with a hot iron. Among his wide-ranging designs were patterns taken from Carpaccio paintings. Sadly, none of the famous dresses feature amongst the eclectic personal ephemera collected in the Museo Fortuny, housed in the Palazzo Pesaro in Campo San Benedetto 3780, San Marco (closed for restoration).

238

WHAT'S ON
Details of films, concerts, and exhibitions can be found in daily editions of local newspapers such as *Il Gazzettino* and *La Nuova Venezia. Un Ospite di Venezia*, a free Italian/English magazine available from hotels and tourist offices, also contains detailed listings and is published weekly in high season (monthly in winter). Tourist offices always have plenty of posters and leaflets on current events. Also keep an eye open for posters in the streets. The monthly *Venice News*, in Italian and English, gives details of bars, clubs, and restaurants.

The winter home of the Casino, on the Grand Canal

THE CASINO
Venice's Casinò Municipale (*Open* Oct–Mar, daily 8:15 PM–2:45 AM), is at the Grand Canal's Palazzo Vendramin-Calergi, Calle Larga Vendramin, off Rio Terrà della Maddalena, Cannaregio (tel: 041/529711). Between April and mid-September it moves to the Lido (same hours) at the Palazzo del Casinò, Piazzale del Casinò, Lungomare G Marconi (tel: 041/5297111). Dress is reasonably elegant and you should take your passport. The minimum age is 18.

OPERA AND CLASSICAL MUSIC The **Fenice** theater was severely damaged by fire in January 1996 (see page 96) and until the completion of its restoration (possibly 2003), performances of opera, ballet, and concerts are being held at the **Palafenice** on Tronchetto island. Tickets are available from the box office in the Cassa di Risparmio bank on Campo San Luca. Performances are still expensive (concerts L25,000–50,000, opera L40,000–200,000) and tickets are quickly snapped up. Postal applications for tickets should be made to the Biglietteria del Teatro del Fenice, Campo San Fantin, San Marco 30124 Venezia (tel: 041/5210161; fax: 041/786580). Or you can book tickets online with major credit cards at www.tin.it/fenice.

Concerts are also performed in lesser venues all over the city, notably in the **churches** of San Stae, Santo Stefano and the Frari, and at the Palazzo Prigioni Vecchie, the Palasport dell'Arsenale, and the Scuola Grande di San Giovanni Evangelista. Two foundations also organize regular musical evenings: the **Cini Foundation**, based at San Giorgio Maggiore, which specializes in modern composers, and the more eclectic **Ugo and Olga Levi Foundation**, based at the Palazzo Giustinian-Lolin (almost opposite the Accademia on the Grand Canal). The state radio network (RAI) allows the public into recordings of its concerts at the **Palazzo Labia**, Campo San Geremia (just east of the railway station off the Lista di Spagna). Tickets must be booked in advance (tel: 041/5242812).

The best-known (and commercialized) of the occasional concert cycles are the regular performances of Vivaldi's

music in the church of **La Pietà** (tel: 041/5231096) on the Riva degli Schiavoni. Tickets are expensive, and often pricier than the performance merits. The **Amici della Musica Classica** (tel: 041/5230616) is a "club" next to the Miracoli which holds small concerts, art exhibitions, and readings of prose and poetry (nightly 5 PM–midnight; closed Tue).

CLUBS AND LIVE MUSIC Venice has a reputation as a city that goes to bed early. Young Venetians lament the lack of nightlife, most of the city's student population returning home to the mainland after lessons have finished. All the big discos and clubs are in Mestre—and hardly worth crossing the water for—while the nearest that big bands come to the city is Padua or Verona. Nevertheless, there are things to do after dark, thanks to a smattering of small clubs, the occasional disco, and a handful of excellent and smoochy late-night bars (see pages 268–269).

One of only a few discos is the **Il Piccolo Mondo** (*Closed* Wed; tel: 041/5200371), just west of the Accademia at Calle Contarini Corfù 1056a (bar 10 AM–8 PM; disco 10 PM–4 AM). More popular among the young is the longer-established and more expensive **Paradiso Perduto** (*Closed* Wed; tel: 041/720581), an atmospheric late-night restaurant and bar with jazz and piano bar at Fondamenta della Misericordia 2540, Cannaregio. **Da Codroma** (*Closed* Mon and Sun; tel: 041/5246789) at Fondamenta Briati 2540, Dorsoduro (near the Ponte del Soccorso) is an *osteria* with live jazz every Tue, chess, backgammon, and other games. A recent addition is **Casanova** (*Open* nightly 6 PM–4 AM; tel: 041/2750199) at 158/a Lista di Spagna, Cannaregio, which combines a disco, a snack restaurant, and internet café. On the Giudecca, in more sedate mode, **Harry's Dolci** (*Open* daily 10:30 AM–3 PM and 7:30–10:30 PM; closed Tue Nov–Mar; tel: 041/5224844) at Fondamenta Sant'Eufemia 773 has occasional concerts of Dixieland jazz to accompany cakes and pastries.

Florian, the most Venetian of cafés

CINEMA
Venice has just six cinemas, a risible number given that the city hosts one of Europe's leading film festivals. Art-house, classic, or original language films are screened only at the so-called "Cinemas d'Essai," for example, Giorgione Movie d'Essai at Rio Terra dei Franceschi, Santi Apostoli, Cannargio 4612 (tel: 041/5226298). The best films are shown at the old-fashioned Accademia, immediately west of the Accademia at Calle Contarini Corfù, 1018, Dorsoduro (tel: 041/528 7706).

STROLL
Many Venetians content themselves with a stroll, happy to end up at a little bar to round off the evening: one of the best places to sit and watch the shadows lengthen is Campo Santa Margherita, a square full of easy-going bars and cafés in the student district of Dorsoduro. Other similar squares include Campo San Polo, Campo Santo Stefano, Campo San Barnaba, and Campo Santa Maria Formosa.

Venice

FINDING YOUR WAY

Despite Venice's plethora of signs, finding your way around the city has not become any easier since Shakespeare's day. Here are Launcelot's instructions to Gobbo on how to find Shylock's home: "Turn up on your right hand, at the next turning, but at the very next turning of all, on your left; marry, at the very next turning, turn of no hand, but turn down indirectly to the Jew's house." "By God's sonties," replies Gobbo, "'twill be a hard way to hit." *The Merchant of Venice*

NIGHT SERVICES

ACTV runs a special night service (N) which is a combination of the main No 1 and No 82 routes: from the Lido to San Zaccaria, San Marco, Grand Canal, Piazzale Roma, Tronchetto, Zattere, Guidecca, and San Giorgio; then back again.

Practical details

INFORMATION The main tourist information offices in Venice are at Piazza San Marco 71c, under the arch just west of the square (*Open* Mon–Sat 9:30–3:15; tel: 041/5298740) and at the Venice Pavilion, Palazzina del Santi by the Giardinetti Reali, San Marco (*Open* daily 10–6; tel: 041/5225150). This new office has a bookstore, sells waterbus tickets and rents equipment for audio tours of the city. There are smaller offices at the station on the left beside the bank before you leave the main concourse (*Open* Mon–Sat 8–7; tel: 041/2411499); at Marco Polo Airport (Mon–Sat 9:30–6); and on the Lido (daily Apr–Sep 10–1), on the right as you disembark at Gran Viale Santa Maria Elisabetta 6 (tel: 041/5265721). All offices provide a basic map or a more detailed one if you persevere. Also useful is the list of current opening hours of monuments and museums and the free *Un Ospite di Venezia* listings and information magazine for visitors. The central line for information is 041/5298711 and the website www.turismovenezia.it.

Information on the city's public transportation system (see below) is available from the ACTV office on the northern side of Piazzale Roma (tel: 041/5287886, *Open* Apr–Oct Mon–Fri 8–6:30; Nov–Mar 8–2:30), the booth on the Fondamente Nuove, or the Venice Pavilion (see above).

ADDRESSES Conventionally written Venetian addresses —with a *sestiere* and street number (but without a street name) as in Hotel Perduto, San Marco 3310—are intelligible only to the city's postal service. Houses in any one of the six *sestieri* are simply labeled from 1 upwards until you cross into another *sestiere*. San Marco, for example, begins at 1, the Palazzo Ducale, and ends 5562 buildings later near the Rialto. There are a total of 29,254 numbers within the city. This makes it impossible to find an address unless it also includes a street name (as in Hotel Perduto, Calle della Confusione 3310, San Marco). Slightly different conventions are sometimes used, with the number often following the *sestiere* rather than the street name. Numbers are also sometimes omitted in squares (*campi*) or small alleys, where the hotel, store or *palazzo* in question is so large as to be obvious. Remember to make a careful note of the *sestiere*, for streets of the same name are often found in more than one district.

PUBLIC TRANSPORT As Venice is a very compact city, the occasions when you need to use its public transport system will be surprisingly few. This said, while walking in so beautiful a place is an obvious pleasure, so too is the experience of taking a boat, particularly along the Grand Canal or out to the Giudecca and the islands.

The city's transport company, ACTV, runs two basic types of boat: the plodding, general purpose *vaporetto*, and the faster, smaller *motoscafo* (mostly used for longer trips out to the islands). Both follow set routes and are numbered (look for the number at the front of the boat). As the same number boat may run in two directions

(up and down the Grand Canal, for example), you should check at the quays to make sure you board a boat heading the right way. While this is usually obvious, it can be less clear at stops along the Giudecca, and at San Zaccaria, a busy terminus for several routes.

CANAL ROUTES The spider's web of routes in and around Venice is not as confusing as it first appears. The basic route, and the one you will use most, is No 1 from Piazzale Roma to San Marco (and back) along the Grand Canal (an unbeatable sightseeing trip). As the No 1 halts at every stop, however, the No 82 may also be useful—it runs along the same route with fewer stops. Note that the No 82 has two routes: Piazzale Roma to San Marco and back, and from San Zaccaria to Piazzale Roma by way of the Giudecca. Other boats you might use are the 41, 42, 51 and 52, circular routes providing scenic tours around the periphery of the city, and the No 12, the larger *motonave* which runs to Murano, Burano, and Torcello from the Fondamente Nuove.

TICKETS Tickets can be bought at most landing stages, on board boats, at stores displaying an ACTV sticker, and at *tabacchi* (tobacconists displaying a sign with a white "T" against a blue background). There is a large on-the-spot fine if you are caught traveling without a ticket, though you can buy one on boarding the boat. One-way tickets at L6,000 and return tickets at L10,000 are an expensive way of traveling, though there are slight reductions for families or groups of three, four, and five people. Better value is the *Biglietto a Tempo*, a ticket which allows an unlimited number of trips on all boats (except the Alilaguna, Clodia, and Fusina-Zattere lines). Tickets are available for 24 hours (L18,000), three days (L35,000), and a week (L60,000). For groups of three, four, or five the cost is L45,000, L60,000 and L75,000 respectively. *Biglietto Itinerario*, valid for 12 hours, cost L15,000 and are available for the Grand Canal, Murano, Burano, and Torcello and the route between Venice, the Lido, and Chioggia.

Venetian transport: a motoscafo in the foreground, a vaporetto in the background and a water taxi coming into view on the right

WATER TAXIS
Venice's water taxis are quick but exorbitantly expensive. The ride between the airport and San Marco, for example, costs L150,000. Hefty surcharges are also levied for each piece of luggage; for trips between 10 PM and 7 AM; and for each additional passenger over a maximum of four. Although it is possible to hail a taxi on a canal, it is usually easier to call by phone—which means there will be around L10,000 on the clock before you start (tel: 041/5235775, 041/716124, 041/723112 or 041/5229450).

TAXIS
For journeys to and from the mainland there are taxi ranks at Piazzale Roma and at the airport. To call or reserve a taxi tel: 041/5232473 or 041/5228538

With endless bridges to negotiate, Venetian porters clearly earn their fees

PORTERS

Given Venice's lack of cars, and the inflated price of water taxis, the licensed porter (look out for the badge) is an invaluable way of moving heavy luggage around the city. Porters operate mainly from the railroad station and from Piazzale Roma, levying fixed tariffs according to time, distance and pieces of luggage. Always ensure that you agree to the price, nevertheless, before hiring one.

TRAGHETTI With only three bridges across the Grand Canal, Venice's *traghetti* (literally "ferries") provide an invaluable service. Using gondolas that are too old for more arduous work, they ply back and forth at seven strategic points across the Canal (daily 6–7 or 8; shorter hours in winter). Quays are often obscure, so look out for the little yellow "Traghetto" signs.

Moving from west to east along the Grand Canal, services run between the following points: the railway station to Fondamenta San Simeon Piccolo; San Marcuola to Fondaco dei Turchi; Santa Sofia (by the Ca' d'Oro) to Pescheria; Riva del Carbon to San Silvestro; Sant'Angelo to San Tomà (one of the most useful services, linking the Frari and San Rocco with Campo Santo Stefano and San Marco); San Samuele to Ca' Rezzonico; and Campo Santa Maria del Giglio to Santa Maria della Salute.

The fare is just L700 (which you hand to one of the ferrymen as you board) a small price to pay for a service that can save a lot of walking as you become more familiar with the city's geography. Venetians invariably stand for the short crossing (see picture on page 24), but no one minds too much if you sit down (except when the boat is crowded). Be especially careful with small children, and watch your balance when the boat pushes off from the bank with a sudden lurch.

GONDOLAS Hiring a gondola, with or without singers and accordionists, is an enchanting but expensive business. In theory the official tariff is around L120,000 for a 50-minute ride for up to six passengers, rising to L150,000 for the same trip between 8 PM and 8 AM. An extra L70,000 is levied for each additional 25 minutes, and more for any musical accompaniment. In practice, however, rates are somewhat negotiable—usually in the gondoliers' favor—so it is essential to confirm the price *and* duration of a trip before departure. Most gondoliers also have set routes, so if you want to see a particular part of the city you may want to discuss this before agreeing to a price.

To be still surer of not being ripped off, and if you want to make reservations, take gondolas only from official stands. These are located at Bacino Orseolo, northwest of Piazza San Marco (tel: 041/5289316); outside the Hotel Danieli (tel: 041/5222254); Calle Vallaressa, west of Piazza San Marco (tel: 041/5206120); at the railroad station (tel: 041/718543); Santa Maria del Giglio (tel: 041/5222073); San Tomà (tel: 041/5205275); Campo San Moisè (tel: 041/5231837); and Riva del Carbon, near the Rialto (tel: 041/5224904).

WATER TAXIS For the phenomenally expensive business of using a water taxi, see the panel on page 241.

see the panel on page 241.

CARTA v

Visitors return .
Venice after a nui..
years and hoping to bu
Carta Venezia, a discount
card for travel on *vaporetti*
and *motoscafi*, will find
that it is now reserved for
residents only. The
confusing array of cheaper
prices advertised at the
ACTV ticket offices and
in the timetables are
available only to people
holding the card.

*Water taxis moored on
the Grand Canal beneath
the Ponte di Rialto*

243

244

ght

che
list on
setting
out. ...   e to visit
a church c.   .Sunday,
remember that it is primarily a place of worship,
and only incidentally a
tourist attraction.

PEACE AND QUIET
Sun-drenched bars,
children at play and a few
market stalls make
Campo Santa Margherita
one of Venice's nicest
squares, much as they
did over 30 years ago
when Jan Morris described
it as "an unsophisticated
place ...No elegant
socialites sit at its cafés.
No actresses cross their
legs revealingly on the
steps of its war
memorial...but there is no
better way to taste the
temper of Venice than to
sit for an hour or two...
drinking a cheap white
wine, and watching this
particular small world go
by." *Venice* (1960)

THE CAMPANILE'S BELLS
Each of the Campanile's
bells had a function: the
smallest, Il Maleficio,
tolled at executions; the
Nona rang the hour of
nones, or noon; the Pregadi
summoned senators to
the Palazzo Ducale; the
Trotteria brought magis-
trates to the palace; and
the Marangona, the largest
(from the word for carpen-
ter, then synonymous with
worker in Venice), tolled
the beginning and end of
the working day. All the
bells were rung when a new
doge or pope was elected.
Traditionally the
Campanile's bell is the only
one in the city allowed to
toll the hour of midnight.

Day One
Breakfast — Campo Santa Margherita
Morning — Chiesa dei Carmini
(Scuola Grande dei Carmini)
San Pantalon
Santa Maria Gloriosa dei Frari
Afternoon — Scuola Grande di San Rocco
Chiesa di San Rocco

Day Two
Breakfast — Campo San Barnaba
Morning — Ca' Rezzonico
Accademia
Afternoon — Collezione Guggenheim
(walk, pages 184–185)
Santa Maria della Salute

Day Three
Morning — ascent of the Campanile
Basilica di San Marco
Museo Civico Correr
(Museo Storico Navale)
Afternoon — Boat to the Giudecca
San Giorgio Maggiore
Campanile di San Giorgio Maggiore
(Redentore)
boat ride from the Giudecca to the Ferrovia

Day Four
Morning — Ca' d'Oro
traghetto to San Giovanni in Bragora
San Polo
traghetto from San Tomà to Santo Stefano
Lunch — Campo Santo Stefano
Afternoon — Palazzo Ducale

Day Five
Morning — Scalzi
San Giobbe
Ghetto
Madonna dell'Orto
Afternoon — excursion to Padua
or — shopping
walk, pages 82–83
boat ride down the Grand Canal

Day Six
Breakfast — Campo Santa Maria Formosa
Morning — (walk, pages 154–155)
Santa Maria Formosa
San Zaccaria
San Giorgio dei Greci
(San Francesco della Vigna)
Scuola Grande di San Giorgio degli Schiavoni
(San Giovanni in Bragora)
Afternoon — *motoscafo* (41) from Arsenale to Murano
Murano (boat from Arsenale or Fondamente Nuove)
(San Michele)
I Gesuiti
Santi Giovanni e Paolo
statue of Colleoni
Santa Maria dei Miracoli

Day Seven
Morning — Burano and Torcello
Afternoon — excursion to Vicenza
or — shopping
walk, pages 106–107
boat ride down the Grand Canal

_ommonwealth and
_ire a passport for
echnically, an identity
_s licence will suffice for
_uropean Union (E.U.)
_ut in practice a passport
_s_ _al at immigration and for
check_._ g into hotels and changing
money. Visas are usually required
for nationals of other countries and
for stays exceeding three months.

By air Scheduled internal and
international flights (plus a few
charters) arrive at Venice's Marco Polo
airport (tel: 041/2609260 or
041/2606111), 6 miles north of the city
center. There are several options for
getting to Piazzale Roma from the
airport. Taxis cost around L50,000 and
take 30 minutes; ATVO blue buses cost
L5,000, take 30–40 minutes and depart
on the hour (tickets can be bought on
the bus). The ACTV No 5 orange
city buses cost L1,500,
take 50 minutes and
leave every half hour
(buy tickets from the
newsagent in the termi-
nal). The most dramatic
entry to Venice is by
water, however. Alilaguna
waterbuses run two
services, one to Fondamente
Nuove, Riva degli Schiavoni,
and San Marco, the other to

Murano, the Lido, Arsenale, San
Marco, and Zattere. Tickets are bought
at the Alilaguna desk inside the
airport. Alternatively there are expensive water taxis (L150,000 to San
Marco). The airport has a small tourist
office (tel: 041/5415887) and a room-
finding service, Associazione
Veneziana Albergatori (AVA) (tel:
041/5415133).

Charter flights usually arrive at
Treviso, 18 miles from Venice. If you
have no organized connection, a shut-
tle bus (No 6) runs from the terminal
into the center of Treviso, from where
there are regular bus and train
connections to Venice. The airport is
also used by Ryanair from the U.K.,
and an ATVO bus service to Venice
connects with their flights. Journey
time is 65 minutes.

By train Direct trains to Venice arrive
at Venezia Santa Lucia station,
often abbreviated to Venezia S L
(tel: 041/888088). The station
has two banks, a buffet, left
luggage facilities, a lost property office (tel: 041/785238).
and a busy information
office (tel: 041/888088). It is
at the head of the Grand
Canal, five minutes' walk
from Piazzale Roma, with

Marco Polo airport
borders the lagoon

frequent waterbus services to the rest of the city.

Many through trains stop on the mainland at Mestre station, confusingly called Venezia Mestre (Venezia M), without proceeding to Venezia Santa Lucia (most Santa Lucia trains also stop at Mestre). Check your train is for Santa Lucia, and if not catch a connecting service at Mestre for the 15-minute trip across the causeway.

By car This is an expensive and potentially frustrating way to arrive. After crossing from the mainland all vehicles must be left in one of the busy multi-story parking lots at Tronchetto (linked by boat No 82 to the rest of the city) or the more central Piazzale Roma (from where you can walk or catch boats Nos 1, 41, 42, 51, 52, or 82). Rates start at about L17,000 a day. There are *no* free parking lots and *no* other parking places (cars will be towed away). Lines stretch back across the causeway during the summer, so it is easier to use Mestre's open-air San Giuliano parking lot and then take a bus or train.

Customs "Duty free" has now been phased out in Europe. In theory there is no limit on goods imported from one E.U. country to another, provided tax has been paid and they are for personal use. Authorities have issued "guide-

Venice's few parking lots are busy

Venezia Santa Lucia station

lines," however, as follows: 10 liters of spirits, 20 liters of fortified wines, 90 liters of wine, 110 liters of beer, 800 cigarettes, 400 cigarillos, 200 cigars, 1kg pipe tobacco, no limit on perfume. Duty-free limits for visitors travelling to/from a non-E.U. country are:

- 200 cigarettes or 100 cigarillos or 50 cigars or 250g of tobacco.

- 1 liter of spirits or 2 liters of fortified wine or sparkling wine.

- 2 liters of still table wine.

- 60ml of perfume and 250ml of toilet water.

- Gifts, souvenirs, and other goods up to a value of about $200.

Travel insurance It is highly recommended that you take out fully comprehensive travel insurance before traveling to Italy.

Climate Despite its generally mild winters and warm summers, Venice has a varied and sometimes extreme climate. Summers can be uncomfortably hot and oppressive, while winter temperatures often match those of northern European cities. Rainfall can be high until well after Easter, and tumultuous summer thunderstorms are fairly common (particularly in September). A chill easterly wind known as the *bora* often brings down temperatures in spring and autumn. Outside the summer months, fog is an almost constant phenomenon. Flooding (the *acqua alta*) can occur any time, but particularly between November and March. Also be prepared for foul-smelling canals in high summer.

When to go If possible, avoid July and August, and plan a visit for April,

Good weather cannot be guaranteed

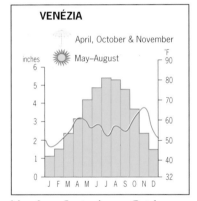

VENÉZIA

April, October & November

May–August

May, June, September, or October. Hotels will be busy throughout the period from Easter to October (and in February during Carnevale). Despite the weather (and occasional flooding), winter can be a delightful time to see the city.

National holidays Stores, banks, offices, and schools close on the following national holidays: January 1 (New Year's Day); January 6 (Epiphany); Easter Sunday; Easter Monday; April 25 (Liberation Day); May 1 (Labour Day); August 15 (Assumption); November 1 (All Saints' Day); December 8 (Immaculate Conception); Christmas Day;

December 26 (Santo Stefano). Stores and businesses may also close or work shorter hours during the *Festa della Salute* on November 21. Note that Good Friday is *not* a holiday.

Accommodations are in especially short supply around public holidays, and roads and railroads will be busier than usual. The causeway can be jammed solid, and it is not unknown for the city to be "closed" to reduce numbers. When a holiday falls on a Tuesday or a Thursday it is customary to make a *ponte* (bridge) to the weekend and take the Monday or Friday off as well.

Time differences Italy is one hour ahead of British (and Irish) time, but for a brief period in October when they are the same. U.S. Eastern Standard Time is six hours behind Italy; Sydney is eight hours ahead in summer. Note that these time differences may vary by an hour for short periods in spring and autumn, as the seasonal time change takes place on different dates in different countries.

Money matters The Italian *lira* and the Euro are both legal tender until 1 July 2002, when the *lira* will cease to function. However, Euro coins (1–50 cents, EUR1 and EUR2) and

banknotes (EUR5–500 will not be available until 1 July 2002. One Euro will be the equivalent of L1,936. The *lira* (plural *lire* and abbreviated "L") is issued in the following denominations:
• Notes—L1,000; L2,000; L5,000; L10,000; L50,000; L100,000; L500,000.
• Coins—L50; L100; L200; L500; L1,000. Italy no longer has acute change problems, but presenting a L100,000 or L500,000 note can still cause difficulties. All the zeros of Italy's currency can be confusing, so check change and all monetary transactions carefully.

Foreign exchange Many Venetian banks offer over-the-counter exchange (*cambio*) facilities (see page 256 for opening times). Many have external ATMs (*Bancomat* in Italy) for obtaining cash with a major credit card, also for exchanging major foreign banknotes and *lire*. Exchange booths are also reasonably common. The Exact Change Booth at the train station is *open* 8:20–7:40. Thomas Cook has offices at Piazza San Marco 142

Carnevale *celebrations in February*

(tel: 041/2775057) and Riva del Ferro 5126, Rialto (tel: 041/5287358). American Express is at San Moisè 1471, San Marco (*Open* Mon–Sat 9–7:30, Sun 9–5:30; tel: 041/5200844).

Credit cards Major credit cards are now widely accepted in hotels, restaurants, and stores, but there may be more reluctance in smaller establishments. The most commonly recognized cards are Mastercard, Visa, American Express, and Diner's Club.

By car

Car rental To rent a car you must be over 21 and hold a valid driver's license. The larger firms have offices at Piazzale Roma, Mestre railway station, and Marco Polo airport. Enquire about fly-drive deals at travel agents before leaving home. All agencies are listed in the Yellow Pages (*Pagine Gialle*) under *Autonoleggio*. Be sure to read the small print, and to satisfy yourself that insurance cover is adequate. Check all extra charges carefully (accident waiver, additional insurance) and note that VAT (IVA) will be added to the final bill.

Car breakdown If your car breaks down, switch on the hazard warning lights and place a warning triangle 54 yards behind your car. Then call the Automobile Club d'Italia (ACI) emergency number (tel: 116) and give the operator your location and the car's make and registration. The car will be towed to the nearest ACI-affiliated garage. This service is free for foreign-registered cars if you belong to a touring club (such as the AA, RAC, or AAA) affiliated to the ACI. The ACI office in Venice is at Fondamenta Santa Chiara, Piazzale Roma 518/A (tel: 041/5200300). For Venice's traffic police (Polizia Stradale) tel: 041/5343232 or 5343434.

Documents Visitors bringing their own (foreign-registered) cars to Italy must be at least 18 years of age and carry the vehicle's registration documents (logbook), an international green card (maximum 45 days' cover) or equivalent insurance, and a full driving license (*patente* in Italian). The pink and green E.U. driving licenses and the new photocard licenses are accepted throughout Europe.

Rules of the road Italian traffic rules are allied to the Geneva Convention and Italy uses European standard road signs (motorway signs are green, others blue). Driving is on the right, and you should give way to traffic from the right unless there are signs to the contrary. Tolls are payable on almost all freeways (*autostrade*). The speed limit in built-up areas is 50kph (31mph); outside urban areas it is 110kph (70mph) on dual carriageways and 90kph (56mph) on secondary roads. The limit on freeways is 130kph (81mph) for vehicles over 1100cc. The wearing of front seat belts is compulsory. Police can levy heavy on-the-spot fines for many offences.

Accidents If you have an accident (*un incidente*), place a warning triangle 54 yards behind your car. Call either the ACI (tel: 116) or the emergency services (tel: 112 or 113). Do not admit liability or make statements which might incriminate you later. Ask any witnesses to remain. Make a statement to the police and exchange names, addresses, car details, and insurance companies' names and addresses with any other drivers involved.

Gasoline Gasoline (*benzina*) in Italy is some of the most expensive in Europe. Diesel (*gasolio*) is cheaper. Gas stations follow normal store hours (*Closed* 12:30–3:30 or 1–4 PM and after 7 PM) and most close all day Sunday, except on motorways, when they are open 24 hours. Those that look closed may well have automatic self-serve pumps that take banknotes. The majority of service stations now take credit cards.

By train

The best way to see towns like Padua, Vicenza, and Verona on the Venetian mainland is by train from Venice's Santa Lucia station.

• **Network** Except for a few private lines the Italian rail network—cheap, comprehensive, and increasingly efficient—is run by the Ferrovie dello Stato (FS).
• **Trains** There are several basic train categories: Fastest of all is the international *Eurostar*, which links Venice with major Italian cities (and beyond), followed by *Eurocity* and the national *InterCity* service—for which reservations are

250

Buy your vaporetto *tickets here*

may also be labeled *Regionali* or *Inter-regionali*.

• **Tickets** (*biglietti*) Both single (*andata*) and return (*andata e ritorno*) tickets are available in either first (*prima*) or second class (*seconda classe*). All tickets including return halves should be date-validated on platform machines before travel. Failure to do so can result in a high on-the-spot fine. Tickets can be bought on the train from the conductor, but this normally incurs a 20 percent premium.

• **Fares** Fares are calculated on a kilometric basis and are among the cheapest in western Europe. Return tickets represent a 15 percent discount on distances up to 250km (154 miles).

• **Reservations** On some of the faster *InterCity* trains reservations are compulsory. These can be made at the ticket offices at stations.

recommended. A supplement of up to 30 percent on top of the basic cost of the ticket is normally required on these fast trains. *Espressi* and *diretti* make more stops, while *locali* halt at every station. Services

Italian trains are cheap and usually reliable

Media

Venice's two local newspapers (*giornali*) are *Il Gazzettino* and *La Nuova Venezia*. Both contain listings for the city. The other widely read quality national papers are the center-left *La Repubblica* and center-right *Corriere della Sera*. Two exclusively sports-based papers are also popular, the *Gazzetta dello Sport* and *Corriere dello Sport*. News magazines (*riviste*) also enjoy a large readership, notably *L'Espresso* and *Panorama*.

Foreign newspapers and magazines are readily available in Venice, usually from late afternoon on the day of issue (the railroad station newsstands are the most reliable source). European editions of the *Financial Times* and the *International Herald Tribune* are also widely available.

Italian radio and television are both deregulated, and offer a vast range of national and local stations, often of pitifully low standard. National

The Italian press, a fair sprinkling of European titles and a selection of souvenirs are all available from this newsstand in Piazzale Roma

stations are a little better, dividing equally between the three channels of the state RAI network and the stable of channels owned by Silvio Berlusconi (Canale 5, Rete 4, and Italia Uno). Telemontecarlo has CNN and regional channels with programs on Venice and the Veneto.

Post offices Venice's central post office (*posta* or *ufficio postale*) is near the Rialto at Palazzo delle Poste, Fondaco dei Tedeschi (*Open* Mon–Fri 8:15–5:30, Sat 8:15–1; tel: 041/2717111). Small post offices on the Zattere and off Piazza San Marco in Calle dell'Ascensione (tel: 041/5285949) are open Monday–Saturday 8:15–2.

Post offices close at noon on the last working day of each month.
• **Stamps** (*francobolli*) These can be bought either from post offices or from tobacconists (*tabacchi*) displaying a blue "T" sign.
• **Postboxes** These are small, red, and marked *Poste* or *Lettere*. Usually they have two slots—one for local mail (marked *Città*), the other for further afield (marked *Altre Destinazioni*).
• **International mail** Mail sent to and from Italy can take anything up to three weeks to arrive. You can speed matters by sending it *espresso* (express) or *posta prioritaria* (priority post).
• **Poste restante** Letters can be sent poste restante to the main post office by addressing them Fermo Posta, Fondaco dei Tedeschi, 80100 Venezia. They can be collected Monday–Friday 8:15–5:30, Saturday 8:15–1. Take a passport or some other form of identification when collecting mail and be prepared to pay a small fee.

Telephones
The majority of public pay phones only accept cards (*schede telefoniche*). You can buy the cards (values of L5,000, L10,000 and L15,000) at post offices, tobacconists, bars, and telephone offices. Pay phones accepting coins (L500, L200 and L100) are fast disappearing. Remember to tear the corner off the card before using it.
• **Timing of calls** For calls within Italy, cheap rates apply Monday–Friday 6:30 PM–8 AM, Saturday after 1 PM and all day Sunday. The cheaper international rate applies 10 PM–8 AM and all day Sunday.
• **Tones** The dialing tone is alternating long and short beeps. A series of rapid beeps means you are being connected, while a series of long beeps indicates a ringing telephone at the other end.

More rapid beeps mean "engaged."
• **International calls** Direct international calls can be made from public telephones using a phonecard. Dial 00 for an international line followed by the country code: 44 for the U.K.; 1 for the U.S. and so on. The code for Italy when calling from abroad is 39.
• **Reversing the charges** To make a reverse-charge (collect) call, dial 15 (Europe) or 170 (international).
• **Area codes** The Italian telephone system changed in 1998. All numbers are now prefixed with the full area code. If you are calling a Venice number, even from within the city, you must dial the code 041 first. If dialling from abroad, remember to insert the 0 which formerly would have been omitted.

Fax
Faxes can be sent from the main post office or from any of the city's internet connection sites (see below).

Internet and email
There are currently a dozen internet connection sites in the city, including The Net House, Campo S Stefano, San Marco 2967; Café Noir, Calle dei Preti Crosera Dorsoduro 3805, (*open* 7 AM–2 AM); Play the Game (a computer games store) at Calle Lunga Santa Maria Formosa, Castello 6187 and Calle Lunga S Pantalon, Dorsoduro, and Internet Café at Chioverette de S Simon at Santa Croce 644/c. An hour online costs around L15,000. Those that are not cafés have the same opening hours as stores (see page 257).
• **Internet resources** The official APT site for Venice is www.turismovenezia.it. For general information try www.italiantourism.com (the Italian State Tourist Board site), www.initaly.com or www.excite.com/travel/countries/italy/venice.

Crime and the police The sheer number of visitors to Venice makes them an obvious target for the unscrupulous thief. But by using common sense and taking a few precautions you should be able to keep both yourself and your possessions safe.

Report any theft to your hotel and then to the police at the main police station, the Questura, Fondamenta San Lorenzo, Castello (tel: 041/2705500). They will also issue you with a special document (*una denuncia*) to forward with any insurance claims. Report lost passports to the police and your nearest consulate or embassy.

• To contact the police in an emergency, telephone 112 or 113.
• Always carry cash in a belt or pouch—never in a pocket.
• Do not carry large amounts of cash. Where possible, use credit cards or travelers' checks.
• Wear your camera around your neck, and never put it down on café tables. Beware of strap-cutting thieves.
• Do not flaunt valuables. Better still, leave them at home.

• Leave jewelery in the hotel safe (not in rooms), especially items like chains and earrings which can easily be snatched.
• Women should hold bags across their front as the Venetians do—not hung over one shoulder where they can be rifled or grabbed.
• Be careful of pickpockets on crowded buses, in street markets or anywhere where large groups of tourists congregate.
• After dark, avoid non-commercial parts of the city, parks, and the area around the railroad station.
• When driving always lock your car, and never leave luggage, cameras, or valuables inside.

Consulates
Austria Santa Croce 251
(tel: 041/5240556)
Australia Via Borgogna 22, Milan
(tel: 02/777041)
Belgium San Marco 1470
(tel: 041/5224124)
Canada Riviera Ruzzante 25, Padua
(tel: 049/878147)

All Venice's emergency services are adapted to the demands of the city

Denmark Santa Croce 466/g
(tel: 041/5200822)
France Castello 6140
(tel: 041/5224319)
Netherlands San Marco 2888
(tel: 041/5283416)
New Zealand Via Zara 28, Rome
(tel: 06/4417171)
Norway Santa Croce 466/b
tel: 041/5231345)
Republic of Ireland Piazza Campitelli
3, Rome (tel: 06/6979121)
Switzerland Zattere 810, Dorsoduro
(tel: 041/5225996)
U.K. Dorsoduro 1051 (tel:
041/5227207)
U.S.A. Via Principe Amedeo 2/10,
Milan (tel: 02/290351)

Emergency telephone numbers
Police (*Carabinieri*) 112
Emergency services (Police, Fire,
Ambulance) 113
Fire (*Vigili di Fuoco*) 115
Car breakdowns 116
Questura (Venice Police Station)
271 5511
Ambulance 118
Hospital and first aid (Ospedale
Civile, Venice) 529 4517

Lost property
If you lose something in the city
contact the Comune di Venezia
(tel: 041/5208844). For losses on buses
or boats (*vaporetti* or *motoscafi*) try the
ACTV office (tel: 041/5287886).
Report general losses to the police at
the Questura, Fondamenta San
Lorenzo, Castello (tel: 041/2705500).

Health
The chief everyday health hazards
which you are likely to encounter
are: too much sun; air pollution
(especially a problem for asthma
and allergy sufferers); biting insects,
and snakes. Water is safe to drink
unless the tap is marked *acqua
non potabile.*
  Be certain to take out health
insurance before traveling (and
keep all receipts for medicine and
treatment). Free treatment is available to citizens of E.U. countries, but
to be eligible you must bring
the necessary documentation
(Form E111) to Italy with you from
your country of origin.

*The green cross—international symbol
for a pharmacy*

Pharmacies Drug stores (*farmacie*),
identified by a green cross, have
the same opening hours as other
stores, but take turns to stay open
late and all night (the rota is
displayed on pharmacy doors).
Staff are well qualified to
give advice on minor ailments,
and can dispense many medicines
over the counter. Remember to
bring any prescriptions or doctor's
notes that might be required to
obtain medicine. Better still, bring
with you from home enough
medication to last the duration of
your stay.

Doctors If you need a doctor (*un
medico*) ask first at your hotel. For
first aid (*pronto soccorso*), which is
often given free, or hospital treatment visit the Ospedale Civile,
Campo Santi Giovanni e Paolo,
Castello (tel: 041/5294516/7
or 5205622).

Vaccinations Vaccinations are not
necessary for entry into Italy unless
you are traveling from a known
infected area. Check current
requirements if you are traveling
from Southeast Asia, Africa, South
America, or the Middle East.

Camping and self-catering

The closest campsites to Venice are near the airport, in the unattractive surroundings of Mestre and Marghera. Others can be found on the coast to the north at Punta Sabbioni, Cavallino, and the Lido di Jesolo; and to the south at Chioggia and Sottomarina. Most open seasonally (typically June to September) and are extremely busy during the peak months of July and August, when usually you must reserve ahead or arrive before 10 AM to have any hope of finding a place. Tourist offices have lists of sites and current prices. You might also invest in the widely available *Campeggi e Villaggi Turistici*, an exhaustive list of sites published by the Touring Club of Italy.

Many agencies rent flats and villas in Venice and the Veneto; most advertize in Sunday newspapers. Agencies and local tourist offices in Italy can also be helpful. Prices are considerably higher than for similar properties elsewhere in Italy. It is essential to know exactly what is included in the rental price (water, electricity, maid service, cleaning, and linen can all be extra).

Visitors with disabilities

Matters are improving, but with its narrow streets, numerous bridges, and antiquated hotels and galleries, Venice is still not the easiest of cities for visitors with disabilities. Lists of hotels from tourist offices usually indicate places suitable for the disabled. Italian state tourist offices abroad also provide lists of appropriate hotels and the addresses of Italian associations for the disabled in various towns and cities.

New public buildings in Italy must all be wheelchair accessible, and museums generally are gradually improving their accessibility. A few intercity trains now have special wheelchair facilities. Staff at airports, stations, and in galleries are usually helpful. Restaurants present few problems, though it is advisable to call ahead to reserve a convenient table.

In Venice the *vaporetti* allow wheelchair access, but the narrow *motoscafi* are not well designed for wheelchair users. On the main tourist office map, the yellow zones indicate the most interesting areas of the city with *vaporetti* access and no bridges. Note, however, that these yellow zones are not marked on the basic map of the city given to most visitors.

Opening times

Opening hours can be a thorny problem in Venice, where most of the "sights" are churches, museums, and galleries. Be sure to obtain a list of current opening times (*orario di apertura*) from one of the city's tourist offices. See also page 270.

• **Banks** Open weekdays 8:30–1:30. Some larger branches may also open 2:35–3:35 PM or 3–4 PM.

• **Churches** Opening times of Venetian churches have always varied, but thanks to a program called Chorus there are now 13 major churches which are open all day from Monday to Saturday: S Maria del Giglio, S Stefano, Frari, S Sebastiano, S Polo, S Giacomo dell'Orio, S Stae, Madonna dell'Orto, Sant'Alvise, Miracoli, S Maria Formosa, S Pietro di Castello, and SS Redentore. A Chorus Pass (L15,000) enables you to visit all 13; the fee for a single church is L3,000. Other churches are generally open Monday to Saturday at 7 or 8 AM, close at noon or 12:30 and reopen from 3 or 4 to 6 or 7:30. A notable exception is the Basilica di San Marco (see page 60 for opening times).

• **Museums and galleries** Opening hours change all the time, and there are normally at least three or four sights closed for restoration at any given time. City-run museums such as the Correr, the Palazzo Ducale are usually open all day. The Accademia closes on Monday afternoon, and the Guggenheim all day Tuesday.

Some of the other museums tend to open in the morning and perhaps also in the afternoon and some close an hour or two earlier in the afternoon between about October and March. Closing days of the smaller museums vary.

• **Post offices** Open Monday to Saturday 8–2. Smaller post offices may not open on Saturday. Main post offices often stay open for some

services until 8 PM. All post offices close at noon on the last working day of the month.
• **Restaurants** Most restaurants close for one day a week, varying from place to place. Most close for all or part of August (sometimes July).
• **Stores and offices** These are usually open Monday to Saturday from 8:30 or 9 AM to 1 PM and reopen between 3 and 4 PM, closing at 7:30 or 8 PM. Most of the year food stores close on Wednesday afternoon. Most other stores are shut on Monday morning (except between mid-June and mid-September, when many close on Saturday afternoon). Gas

stations close on Sundays (except on freeways). Supermarkets and department stores usually open Monday to Saturday 9–8, and some are also open on Sunday.

Places of worship
• **Anglican** St. George's, Campo San Vio, Dorsoduro 870.
• **Catholic** San Moisè, Campo di San Moisè, San Marco (English readings Sunday 6 PM). Confessions are heard in English on Sunday mornings at San Marco, the Gesuiti, Scalzi, San Zanipolo, the Redentore, and San Giorgio Maggiore.
• **Evangelical/Methodist** Campo Santa Maria Formosa 5170 Sunday 11 AM)
• **Jewish** Ghetto Vecchio (tel: 041/715012)

Restrooms
Public conveniences can be found at Piazzale Roma, the railroad station, on the west side of the Accademia bridge, off Campo San Bartolomeo, by the Giardinetti Reali, in the *Albergo Diurno* (Day Hotel) behind the Ala Napoleonica on Ramo Primo a Ascensione, and on Calle Erizzo near the church of San Martino. Otherwise you will have little choice but to use museum restrooms or the grim facilities in bars or cafés. These are free but intended for the use of customers, so you will be more welcome if you buy something first. Ask for *il gabinetto* or *il bagno*, and remember not to confuse the rather similar *signori* (men) with *signore* (women).

Photography
There are countless stores always ready to serve Venice's innumerable visitors with film and various items of photography paraphernalia. In Italian a print film is *una pellicola*, while slides are *diapositive*.

Tipping
A 10–15 percent service charge (*servizio*) is usually included in restaurant bills, but waiters expect a small tip on top. For quick service in bars, do as the locals do and slap down a coin or two with your till receipt when ordering. It is a good idea to give around L1,000– 2,000 per visitor to custodians or sacristans who open up churches or museums out of hours. In taxis, round the fare up or give a tip of about 10 percent.

Electricity
Current in Italy is 220 volts AC (50 cycles). Plugs are of the two round-pin variety. Some sockets have a third (central) earth socket, but still accommodate the standard two-pin plug. In older hotels you may find two-pin plugs of a different type. Here you will need an Italian adaptor.

257

CONVERSION CHARTS

FROM	TO	MULTIPLY BY
Inches	Centimeters	2.54
Centimeters	Inches	0.3937
Feet	Meters	0.3048
Meters	Feet	3.2810
Yards	Meters	0.9144
Meters	Yards	1.0940
Miles	Kilometers	1.6090
Kilometers	Miles	0.6214
Acres	Hectares	0.4047
Hectares	Acres	2.4710
Gallons	Liters	4.5460
Liters	Gallons	0.2200
Ounces	Grams	28.35
Grams	Ounces	0.0353
Pounds	Grams	453.6
Grams	Pounds	0.0022
Pounds	Kilograms	0.4536
Kilograms	Pounds	2.205
Tons	Tonnes	1.0160
Tonnes	Tons	0.9842

MEN'S SUITS

UK	36	38	40	42	44	46	48
Rest of Europe	46	48	50	52	54	56	58
US	36	38	40	42	44	46	48

DRESS SIZES

UK	8	10	12	14	16	18
France	36	38	40	42	44	46
Italy	38	40	42	44	46	48
Rest of Europe	34	36	38	40	42	44
US	6	8	10	12	14	16

MEN'S SHIRTS

UK	14	14.5	15	15.5	16	16.5	17
Rest of Europe	36	37	38	39/40	41	42	43
US	14	14.5	15	15.5	16	16.5	17

MEN'S SHOES

UK	7	7.5	8.5	9.5	10.5	11
Rest of Europe	41	42	43	44	45	46
US	8	8.5	9.5	10.5	11.5	12

WOMEN'S SHOES

UK	4.5	5	5.5	6	6.5	7
Rest of Europe	38	38	39	39	40	41
US	6	6.5	7	7.5	8	8.5

Etiquette

- **Churches** When visiting churches you should dress modestly, covering your arms and legs, and do not intrude while services are in progress. Check before using your camera, as many churches and galleries forbid the use of flash, and some ban photography altogether.
- **Smoking** There are still very few non-smoking areas in restaurants or public places, but smoking is banned on public transport.
- **Bargaining** This is no longer appropriate in stores, though in markets (with the exception of food markets) and budget hotels you may be able to negotiate lower rates.
- **Hotels, restaurants, and bars** As elsewhere in Venice, children are more than welcome in most hotels, bars, and restaurants.

Tourist offices

Visit a tourist office early in your stay to collect free information (such as maps, lists of events, museum opening hours, and charges) which will be invaluable in planning your sightseeing. The most convenient tourist office in the city is the Venice Pavilion by the Giardinetti Reali, San Marco (*Open* daily 10–6; tel: 041/5225150). Details of other tourist offices in the city appear on page 240, and details of offices in other Veneto towns appear on the relevant pages of the Excursions section (pages 210–227).

Italian State Tourist Offices abroad

Australia Level 26, 44 Market Street Sydney, NSW 2000 (tel: 2/9262166; email: enitour@ihug.com.au)

Canada 175 Bloor Street East, Suite 907, South Tower, M4W Toronto (tel: 416/925 4882; www.italiantourism.com; email: enit.canada@on.aibn.com)

Irish Republic Contact the Italian Embassy (tel: 00 353 1 660 1744)

United Kingdom 1 Princes Street, London W1R 8AY (tel: 020 7408 1254; email: enitlond@globalnet.co.uk)

United States 630 5th Avenue, Suite 1565, Rockefeller Center, New York NY 10111 (tel: 212/245 4822; www.italiantourism.com

Italians respond well to foreigners who make an effort to speak their language (however badly). Many Italians speak at least some English, and most nice hotels and restaurants have multilingual staff.

All Italian words are pronounced as written, with each vowel and consonant sounded. The letter c is hard, as in English "cat," except when followed by "i" or "e," when it becomes the soft ch of "children." The same applies to g when followed by "i" or "e"—soft in *giardino* as in the English "giant"; hard in *gatto*, as in "gate." Words ending in o are almost always masculine in gender (plural ending—i); those ending in "a" are feminine (plural—e).

Use the polite second person (*lei*) to speak to strangers: use the familiar second person (*tu*) to friends or to children.

Courtesies

good morning	buon giorno
good afternoon/ good evening	buona sera
good night	buona notte
hello/goodbye (informal)	ciao
hello (answering the telephone)	pronto
goodbye	arrivederci
please	per favore
thank you (very much)	grazie (mille)
you're welcome	prego
how are you? (polite/informal)	come sta/stai?
I'm fine	sto bene
I'm sorry	mi dispiace
excuse me/I beg your pardon	mi scusi
excuse me (in a crowd)	permesso

Basic vocabulary

yes	sì
no	no
I do not understand	non ho capito
left/right	sinistra/destra
entrance	entrata
exit	uscita
open/closed	aperto/chiuso
good/bad	buono/cattivo
big/small	grande/piccolo
with/without	con/senza
more/less	più/meno
near/far	vicino/lontano
hot/cold	caldo/freddo
early/late	presto/ritardo
here/there	qui/là
now/later	adesso/più tardi
today/tomorrow	oggi/domani
yesterday	ieri
how much is it	quant'è?
when	quando
do you have …?	avete …?

Emergencies

help!	aiuto!
Where is the nearest telephone?	Dov'è il telefono più vicino?
There has been an accident.	C'è stato un incidente.
Call the police.	Chiamate la polizia.
Call a doctor/an ambulance.	Chiamate un medico/ un'ambulanza.
first aid	pronto soccorso.
Where is the nearest hospital?	Dov'è l'ospedale più vicino?

Some of Venice's nicer hotels have their own water taxis

Glossary of artistic and architectural terms

aedicule	decorative niche framed by simple medieval columns
ambo	simple medieval pulpit, often with marble inlay
anfiteatro	amphitheater
apse	semicircular recess behind church altar
architrave	a supporting beam above a column
atrium	inner entrance court of early house or church
baldacchino	a canopy on columns, usually over a church altar
battistero	baptistery
campanile	bell tower
campo	square
camposanto	cemetery
cantoria	choir-loft
capital	top of a column
cappella	chapel
cartoon	full-size preliminary sketch for a fresco or painting
caryatid	carved female figure used as a column
chancel	part of church containing altar
chiaroscuro	exaggerated light and shade effects in a painting
chiesa	church
chiostro	cloister
ciborium	tabernacle or casket for the eucharist on or behind the altar
columbarium	part of a tomb, with wall niches for the dead
comune	administrative department of an Italian town, city or village
confessio	crypt beneath a church's high altar
cornice	top of a classical facade
cortile	courtyard
crypt	burial place of a church, usually under the altar
cupola	dome

diptych	painting on two panels
duomo	cathedral
fresco	wall painting on wet plaster
graffito	incised decoration on a building or wall
intarsia	mosaic or inlay work in wood or stone
loggia	roofed gallery or outside balcony
lunette	semicircular space above door, window or vaulting
maestà	image of the Madonna and Child in majesty
matroneum	women's gallery in early churches
narthex	vestibule of a church
nave	central space of a church
palazzo	palace, large house or apartment block
pendentives	four curved triangular elements on piers supporting a dome or cupola
peristyle	courtyard surrounded by colonnades
piano nobile	main floor of a palace
pietà	image of the Madonna mourning the dead Christ
pietre dure	semi-precious stones such as agate and amethyst
pinacoteca	picture gallery
porta	gate
portico	covered doorway
predella	small panel below main part of an altarpiece
presepio	Christmas crib
putto	cherubic child in painting or sculpture
sinopia	wall sketch for a fresco
stele	vertical headstone
teatro	theater
tempio	temple
terme	baths
tondo	round painting or relief
torre	tower
transept	transverse arms of a church
tribune	raised gallery in a church or the apse of a basilica
triptych	painting on three panels
trompe l'œil	tricks using perspective to create the illusion of depth in a painting

Accommoations & Restaurants

ACCOMMODATIONS

The accommodations recommended in this section have been divided into three categories, with prices given for a double room with private bathroom (where appropriate). Note that prices may vary considerably within the same hotel, depending on the views:

- inexpensive ($), under L200,000/EUR100
- moderate ($$), from L200,000–350,000/ EUR100–180
- expensive ($$$), over L350,000/EUR180

Telephone numbers are given in the form you would use if phoning from Venice. If you telephone from outside Italy use the country code plus the number you are dialing.

San Marco

Ai Do Mori ($)
Calle Larga San Marco 658 tel: 041/5204817
Located almost alongside Piazza San Marco, with eleven 1-star rooms (eight with bathrooms). Prices vary quite considerably for different rooms. The best have views over the Basilica and Torre dell'Orologio. Amiable owners.

Al Gambero ($)
Calle dei Fabbri 4687 tel: 041/5224384
A large, plain 1-star hotel just north of Piazza San Marco.

Boston ($–$$)
Calle dei Fabbri 848 tel: 041/5287665
This large 42-room 3-star hotel is on one of the main shopping streets close to the Piazza. Rooms vary: the best are furnished with antiques and have balconies overlooking the canals.

Casanova ($–$$)
Frezzeria 1284 tel: 041/5206855
A comfortable 3-star hotel very close to Piazza San Marco and the shopping district.

Casa Petrarca ($)
Calle delle Colonne 4394 tel: 041/5200430
Among the cheapest of the hotels close to the Piazza. Just seven rooms (five bathrooms).

Do Pozzi ($$)
Corte do Pozzi 2373 tel: 041/5207855
A 3-star hotel with 29 quiet rooms, each with a private bathroom. Do Pozzi is in a peaceful small square close to the Piazza.

Europa & Regina CIGA ($$$)
*Calle Larga XXII Marzo 2159
tel: 041/5200477*
This CIGA-owned luxury 5-star hotel tends to be overlooked in favor of the Gritti, Danieli (also CIGA-owned), or Cipriani, but its prices compare favorably, some of the reception areas are stupendous and the rooms are large—many have views over the Grand Canal or look out on a garden courtyard. Very expensive.

Flora ($$)
Calle Bergamaschi, 2283a tel: 041/5205844
Handy for the Piazza, this large 44-room 3-star hotel has a pleasant garden, but some of the rooms are small for the price.

Gritti Palace ($$$)
Santa Maria del Giglio 2467 tel: 041/794611
One of Venice's grandest and most celebrated old-world hotels. Very expensive.

Kette ($$–$$$)
Piscina San Moisè 2053 tel: 041/5207766
A good mid-range hotel in a tranquil location near the Fenice theater. Some of the 44 rooms are rather small. Popular with up-scale tour operators.

La Fenice et des Artistes ($$–$$$)
Campiello Fenice 1936 tel: 041/5232333
This nice, old-world 3-star hotel, with 70 rooms, is close to the Fenice theater. It was once the home of painter Lorenzo Lotto.

Locanda Fiorita ($)
Campiello Nuovo 3457 tel: 041/5234754
This very pretty little 1-star hotel is in a quaint square. Nine rooms (eight with private bathroom). Very popular, so reserve well ahead.

San Fantin ($–$$)
Campiello Fenice 1930a tel: 041/5231401
This modern and functional 2-star hotel is close to the Fenice theater. It has 13 rooms, ten of which have private bathrooms.

San Samuele ($)
Piscina San Samuele 3358 tel: 041/5228045
Some of the 10 rooms are basic, and only six have bathrooms, but the general quality is better than many places in this price range. Excellently located, and the owner is welcoming.

San Zulian ($$)
*off Campo San Zulian 534/5
tel: 041/5225872*
This comfortable 19-room 3-star hotel lies behind San Marco in the heart of the city, but off the beaten tourist track. San Zulian has been fully remodeled and has attractive furnishings and air-conditioning throughout.

Saturnia & Internazionale ($$–$$$)
*Calle Larga XXII Marzo 2398
tel: 041/5208377*
Each of the 95 rooms is slightly different, but all share a romantic, old-fashioned feel. The best of the rooms look out on to the garden courtyard.

San Polo and Santa Croce

Alex ($)
Rio Terrà Frari 2606 tel: 041/5231341
An inexpensive 1-star hotel conveniently placed for the Frari, but the 11 rooms suffer from slightly garish 1960s-style décor. Five bathrooms.

Al Sole ($–$$)
*Fondamenta Minotto, Santa Croce 136
tel: 041/710844*
This big 62-room 3-star hotel is known for its tranquil canal location and vast 16th-century Gothic *palazzo* setting.

Falier ($–$$)
*Salizzada San Pantalon, Santa Croce 130
tel: 041/710882*
While some of the 19 rooms in this well-located 2-star hotel are small, they are all elegant, clean, and neat. The flower-filled terraces and common areas are very nice, and the management efficient and helpful.

Locanda Sturion ($–$$)
Calle dello Sturion, San Polo 679
tel: 041/5236243
This 3-star hotel is highly popular because of its position on the Grand Canal. The 11 rooms, each with bathroom, vary in price.

Pantalon ($$)
Crosera San Pantalon, Dorsoduro 3942
tel: 041/5223646
A 3-star hotel on the edge of San Polo; convenient for the Accademia, Frari, San Rocco, and nice squares like San Polo and Santa Margherita.

San Cassiano-Ca' Favretto ($–$$)
Calle della Rosa 2232 tel: 041/5241768
This elegant and old-world 3-star hotel occupies a converted 14th-century palazzo on the Grand Canal opposite the Ca' d'Oro (the nearest *vaporetto* stop is San Stae). Only half the rooms overlook the Canal (others look on to a side canal), but all have TV, minibar, and air-conditioning.

Dorsoduro

Accademia-Villa Maravege ($$–$$$)
Fondamenta Bollani 1058 tel: 041/5210188
This 17th-century palazzo once housed the Russian embassy. Its 27 3-star rooms, each individually appointed, retain something of their former antique grandeur. Convenient for the Accademia and Grand Canal, with a lovely garden. Much in demand, so remember to reserve well ahead.

Agli Alboretti ($$)
Rio Terrà Foscarini 882/4 tel: 041/5230058
A very popular 2-star, 20-room hotel (all rooms have private bathroom) with a fine restaurant below. On a tree-lined street close to the Accademia and the Zattere.

American ($$–$$$)
San Vio 628 tel: 041/5204733
A 3-star, 28-room hotel close to the Accademia, but on a small canal away from the hurly-burly.

Antico Capon ($)
Campo Santa Margherita 3004b
tel: 041/5285292
Seven simple rooms (with bathrooms) above a good pizzeria-restaurant on one of Venice's nicest and most lively squares.

Antica Locanda Montin ($)
Fondamenta di Borgo 1147 tel: 041/5227151
An 11-room 1-star hotel which owes much of its popularity to the famous co-owned restaurant below—see page 266.

La Calcina ($$)
Zattere ai Gesuati 780 tel: 041/5206466
A comfortable 29-room, 3-star hotel, recently refurbished using original furniture. Its position on the Zattere can make it seem off the beaten track. Fine views across the Canale della Giudecca from some rooms. Best known as the house where John Ruskin spent much of his time in Venice.

Locanda Ca' Foscari ($)
Calle della Frescada 3888 tel: 041/710401
This easy-going and nicely appointed 1-star hotel has 11 rooms (none with private bathroom) secreted away in a tiny alley close to San Tomà and the Frari. There is often a good chance of finding space here when other places are full.

Locanda San Barnaba ($$)
Calle del Traghetto 2486 tel: 041/2411233
Attractive and small, this 3-star place is near the Ca' Rezzonico *vaporetto* stop. Each of its 14 rooms is individually decorated with antiques and has a different theme.

Messner ($$)
Rio Terrà dei Catacumeni 216
tel: 041/5227443
A romantic location near the Salute and Guggenheim Gallery. Fine garden and modernized rooms, but aim to stay in the main hotel rather than the nearby annexe, or *dipendenza*.

Seguso ($–$$)
Zattere ai Gesuati 779 tel: 041/5286858
Characterful and very popular 2-star hotel, all of whose 36 rooms (19 with private bathroom) have a canal view. Essential to reserve well ahead.

Castello

Bisanzio ($$–$$$)
Calle della Pietà 3651 tel: 041/5203100
This quiet and unassuming Best Western 3-star hotel (the former home of sculptor Alessandro Vittoria) lies just off the busy Riva degli Schiavoni, close to Vivaldi's old church.

Canada ($–$$)
Campo San Lio 5659 tel: 041/5229912
An immaculately kept 2-star hotel with plenty of single rooms if you are traveling alone. The nicest double has its own roof terrace, but you will need to reserve well in advance to be sure of securing it.

Casa Fontana ($$)
Campo San Provolo 4701 tel: 041/5220579
Prices are rather high for what is only a 2-star hotel, but this is a good and relatively little-known place with just 16 rooms close to the church of San Zaccaria.

Casa Verardo ($–$$)
Ruga Giuffa 4765 tel: 041/5286127
A friendly and extremely good value 1-star hotel with nine rooms (all with private bathroom) that is extremely handy for Piazza San Marco.

Colombina ($$$)
Calle del Remedio 4416 tel: 041/2770525
A nicely refurbished 4-star hotel in an ancient palazzo by the Bridge of Sighs. Seventeen of its 32 rooms have canal views.

Da Bruno ($–$$)
Salizzada San Lio 5726a tel: 041/5230452
Many of the 32 rooms in this 2-star hotel are very small, but its position close to the Rialto is a major plus.

Danieli ($$$)
Riva degli Schiavoni 4196 tel: 041/5226480
Perhaps the grandest (though not costliest) of Venice's big three luxury hotels (the Gritti and Cipriani are the others). Very expensive.

Doni ($)
Fondamenta del Vin 4656 tel: 041/5224267
A cosy 1-star hotel just away from the crowds of the Rialto, but still in a central and picturesque setting. The best of the 13 rooms (none with private bathroom) overlook the Riva del Vin; the others face on to a quiet courtyard.

263

Accommodations and Restaurants

Metropole ($$$)
Riva degli Schiavoni 4149 tel: 041/5205044
One of the elegant hotels facing onto the Grand Canal, the Metropole was once the orphanage in which Vivaldi taught. It stands out for its stylish interiors and relatively modest prices.

Paganelli ($$)
Riva degli Schiavoni 4182 tel: 041/5224324
This charming 2-star hotel's word-of-mouth reputation is high, but in truth some of the 22 rooms are quite small; be certain to secure one with a lagoon view—not one in the far less exalted annexe, or *dipendenza*.

Santa Marina ($$)
Campo Santa Marina 6068 tel: 041/5239202
Opened in 1990, this intimate and comfortable 20-room 3-star hotel is one of Venice's newest hotels (rooms in the annexe are newer still). Two rooms on the first floor are specially adapted for visitors with physical disabilities. Located by Santa Maria Formosa, and so convenient for San Marco and San Zanipolo.

Scandinavia ($–$$$)
Campo Santa Maria Formosa 5240
tel: 041/5223507
A considerable range of rooms is to be found in this 34-room 3-star hotel whose biggest draw is the large and lively *campo* outside.

Silva ($)
Fondamenta Rimedio 4423 tel: 041/5227643
It is well worth seeking out this welcoming 24-room 1-star hotel (16 bathrooms) between San Zaccaria and Santa Maria Formosa on one of the city's prettiest canals.

Cannaregio

Abbazia ($–$$)
Calle Priuli detta dei Cavalletti 68
tel: 041/717333
If you need to be near the railroad station this 39-room 3-star hotel is far nicer than many others in the area. Located on the first street on the left after the Scalzi church.

Bernardi Semenzato ($)
Calle dell'Oca 4366 tel: 041/5227257
Rooms here have been renovated. The patron is helpful and friendly, and speaks reasonable English.

Casa Carettoni ($)
Lista di Spagna 130 tel: 041/716231
The best of the numerous cheap 1-star hotels—many of them of dubious repute—that cluster close to the station: only 15 rooms (three bathrooms), so be sure to reserve ahead.

Casa Martini ($$)
Calle del Magazen 1314, off Rio Terrà San Leonardo tel: 041/717512
A truly charming five-room hotel in a converted private palazzo, with tasteful antique furnishings and an intimate atmosphere.

Club Cristal ($$)
Cannaregio (for enquiries and reservations, tel Liz Heavenstone, London: 020 7722 5060)
A friendly bed and breakfast in a 19th-century Venetian townhouse in a residential area, whose five bedrooms are furnished with antiques.

Eden ($–$$)
Rio Terrà della Maddalena 2357
tel: 041/5244003/5
This tiny, eight-room 3-star hotel is located between the railroad station and the Rialto.

Giorgione ($$–$$$)
Campo SS Apostoli, 4587 tel: 041/5225810
A large hotel with 72-rooms with modern facilities. It offers good value in the 4-star category.

Guerrini ($–$$)
Lista di Spagna 265 tel: 041/715333
Convenient for the railroad station, this 28-room 2-star hotel is the best of the mid-price hotels found on or just off the busy Lista di Spagna.

The Islands

Cipriani ($$$)
Giudecca 10 tel: 041/5207744
Venice's most famous luxury hotel and the choice of well-heeled honeymooners the world over. It is worth remembering, however, that while enjoying every comfort you will be stationed on the Giudecca, which can feel well away from the sights and action of the city proper. Very expensive.

Locanda Cipriani ($$)
Piazza Santa Fosca 29, Isola di Torcello
tel: 041/730150
With just five rooms, this tiny but luxurious hotel—the only place to stay on the magical but far-away island of Torcello—is almost more exclusive than its famous namesake on the Giudecca.

Ostello Venezia ($)
Fondamenta delle Zitelle, Giudecca 86
tel: 041/5238211
Venice's extremely busy youth hostel requires reservations for places in July and August—lines can start at dawn. Apply in person or in writing. IYHF membership required (available at the hostel).

Padova

Donatello ($$)
Via del Santo 102 tel: 049/8750634
This large 4-star hotel is situated almost alongside the Basilica. It is the best of Padua's up-scale, central hotels.

Verona

Due Torri ($$$)
Piazza Sant'Anastasia 4 tel: 045/595044
Far and away Verona's most prestigious and expensive luxury hotel.

Il Torcolo ($)
Vicolo Listone 3 tel: 045/8007512
An amiable and popular 2-star hotel, within a stone's throw of Piazza Brà.

Victoria ($$$)
Via Adua 6 tel: 045/590566
A quiet, calm, and very tasteful 4-star hotel with good service in a central position: as with all Verona's hotels, it is essential to reserve many months in advance during the July and August opera season.

Vicenza

Cristina ($)
Corso SS Felice e Fortunato 32
tel: 0444/324297
A nice, mid-priced 3-star hotel, centrally located.
Due Mori ($)
Contrà Do Rode 26 tel: 0444/321 886
This medium-sized refurbished 2-star hotel is in
the historic center of Vicenza.

RESTAURANTS

It is usually worth reserving a table at all but
the cheapest ($) restaurants, especially during
Carnevale and high season. Few restaurants
have any form of dress code, but a jacket (and
sometimes a tie) is certainly in order at most
expensive places. See the panel on page 181
for details of the *Ristoranti della Buona
Accoglienza,* an excellent independent
association of Venice's better and more fairly
priced restaurants.

San Marco

Ai Mercanti ($$$)
Calle dei Fuseri 4346 tel: 041/5238269
Just a few steps from Campo San Lucca, this mainly
fish restaurant offers the courteous service and
high-quality cooking (Venetian with a twist) you can
rely on from a member of the *Buona Accoglienza.*
Set-price menus are available to help keep tabs on
spending. Closed Sunday and Monday lunchtimes.
Al Bacareto ($)
Calle Crosera 3347 tel: 041/5289336
Off Salizzada San Samuele near the Palazzo
Grassi and Campo Santo Stefano. An inexpensive
and authentic place where you stand to eat hot
snacks with a glass of wine (downstairs). A full
meal eaten sitting down costs more. Closed
Saturday evening and Sunday.
Al Teatro ($–$$)
Campo San Fantin 1916
tel: 041/5221052
A venerable bar-restaurant that also serves pizzas.
Convenient for the Fenice theater (currently closed
for restoration), so can be busy. Outside tables.
Closed Monday.
Antico Martini ($$$)
Campo San Fantin 1980 tel: 041/5237027
Founded as a coffee house in the 18th century,
this has long been one of the most elegant and
romantic places to eat (at a price) in the city. The
cooking has recently returned to classic Venetian
cuisine (with seafood, as ever, well to the fore),
although there are also more "international"
dishes. Excellent wine list. One of the *Buona
Accoglienza* restaurants. Closed Tuesday and
Wednesday lunchtime.
Da Ivo ($$$)
Ramo dei Fuseri 1809 tel: 041/5285004
This pleasant restaurant serves plenty of Venetian
staples, but is better known for its range of Tuscan
specialties. Closed Sunday and January.

Do Forni ($$$)
Calle dei Specchieri 468 tel: 041/5230663
This is known among both Venetians and visitors
as one of the best places to eat in the upper price
bracket. In a maze of small rooms and salons
there are two main dining rooms, one in rustic
"farmhouse style," the other decked out in the
manner of an opulent *Orient Express* cabin
(travelers on the famous train often use the
restaurant). The number of covers has grown with
Do Forni's success, as has the menu (now listing
over 100 *primi* and *secondi*), but despite the size
and slightly (but pleasantly) chaotic air, the cook-
ing remains good, particularly the fish, which is
wonderfully fresh—though never as exceptional as
the invariably enormous bill really requires. Closed
Thursday in winter.
Fiore ($–$$)
Calle delle Botteghe 3460 tel: 041/5235310
Not be confused with the better-known, and more
up-scale, Da Fiore in San Polo, Fiore is a
thoroughly Venetian *trattoria* still full of locals
and local color. Located just off Campo Santo
Stefano, it has a bar on the left full of friends
eating snacks with a glass of wine, and a
romantic intimate restaurant on the right. There
are only 50 covers, so reservation is essential.
Closed Tuesday and January or February.
Harry's Bar ($$$)
Calle Vallaresso 1323 tel: 041/5285777
A legendary institution—at least among
foreigners—known as much for its celebrity
status as for its food and famous cocktails.
Menus in the upstairs restaurant (the bar area
downstairs for snacks and sandwiches is a little
less formal) have barely changed in decades, and
though the food is always reliable—and can still
be excellent—many now think its quality is not
quite what it was. However, it remains a good
place to dress up and treat yourself. Restaurant
and bar open daily.
Rosticceria San Bartolomeo ($)
Calle della Bissa 5424 tel: 041/5223569
An inexpensive self-service place near the Rialto
(off Campo San Bartolomeo). Good for snacks and
light meals: sit at the long window tables down-
stairs—the food in the restaurant upstairs is
almost the same, but more expensive. Closed
Monday and the week before Carnevale.
Vino Vino ($)
Ponte delle Veste 2007a tel: 041/5237027
This wine bar-cum-glorified snack bar, close to the
Fenice theater, is run as an offshoot of the far
more expensive Antico Martini (see above).
Excellent for quick hot snacks and a glass of wine
at a fair price. Closed Tuesday.

San Polo and Santa Croce

Al Bancogiro ($)
Campo San Giacomo di Rialto 122
tel: 041/5232061
This small but trendy *osteria* is in a disused
food warehouse by the Rialto marketplace.
Great for home-made snacks and fine wines,
with a few tables upstairs and in the courtyard
for light meals.

Accommodations and Restaurants

Alla Madonna ($$)
*Calle della Madonna (near the Rialto bridge),
San Polo 594 tel: 041/5233824*
One of Venice's most traditional restaurants, in
both food and ambience: a popular favorite for
informal business meetings and with Venetian
families celebrating a special occasion. Roomy,
lively and efficient, though with 600–700 meals
served a day, the atmosphere may be too chaotic
and the service too brusque for some: the mainly
fish cuisine, however, is good and reliable. Without
a reservation you may well have to line up for a
table. Closed Wednesday and two weeks in August.

Alle Oche ($)
Calle Tintor, San Polo 1459 tel: 041/5241161
Arrive early to secure one of the outside tables at
this popular pizzeria, with over 50 varieties of pizza
on the menu. Just south of Campo San Giacomo
dell'Orio, one of Venice's quietest and most
attractive little squares. Closed Monday.

Antica Trattoria Poste Vecie ($$)
Pescheria, San Polo 1608 tel: 041/721822
The seafood could hardly be fresher at this noted
fish restaurant, located in an old post house
across its own little bridge alongside the Pescheria
fish market. This is one of the oldest restaurants
in Venice, having reputedly been founded in 1500.
Fine cooking and a good wine list. Closed Tuesday.

Da Fiore ($$$)
*Calle dello Scaleter, San Polo 2202
tel: 041/721308*
This intimate and pretty temple to Venetian
alta cucina is one of the most exalted and well-
patronized restaurants in the city. Exquisite
food—even the bread is home-made. Self-taught
owners, Mara and Maurizio, offer a different menu
each day. Book well in advance—and study the map
carefully to find its well-hidden location (just north of
Campo San Polo). A *Buona Accoglienza* member.
Closed Sunday, Monday and three weeks in August.

Da Ignazio ($$)
*Calle Saoneri, San Polo 2749
tel: 041/5234852*
An unspoiled and old-fashioned family fish
restaurant with garden, just east of San Tomà on
the way to San Polo. A *Buona Accoglienza*
member. Closed Saturday.

La Zucca ($–$$)
Ponte del Megio 1762 tel: 041/5241570
An easy-going trattoria whose cooking centers
around vegetables. Popular with Venetians looking
for a change from traditional seafood cuisine.

Pizzeria San Tomà ($)
*Campo San Tomà, San Polo 2864
tel: 041/710586*
Good pizzas and reasonable trattoria food with
tables outside on a pretty little piazza. One minute
from the Frari and San Rocco in the shadow of the
church of San Tomà. Closed Tuesday.

Vivaldi ($)
*Calle della Madonetta, San Polo 1457
tel: 041/5238185*
A wonderfully informal place for simple hot food
and a glass of wine, either standing at the front or
sitting at one of the few tables to the rear (where
more ambitious and expensive dishes are also
available). Roughly midway between Campo San
Polo and the Rialto. Closed Sunday and August.

Dorsoduro

Agli Alboretti ($$–$$$)
*Rio Terrà Antonio Foscarini– Sant'Agnese 882
tel: 041/5230058*
This attractive restaurant takes its name from the
trees (*alberi*) outside. It is conveniently located for
the Accademia, which is just two minutes' walk
away. The dining rooms are pretty inside and out—
in summer you can eat in the shaded courtyard.
Closed Wednesday and Thursday lunchtimes.

Ai Gondolieri ($$$)
*Fondamenta Ospetaleto 366
tel: 041/5286396*
Unique among Venetian restaurants as it serves
no fish, Ai Gondolieri offers a rich menu of meat,
vegetable, and cheese dishes from the Veneto.
Great wines too in this *Buona Accoglienza* member.

Al Profeta ($)
*Calle Lunga San Barnaba 2671
tel: 041/5237466*
Inexpensive, cheerful, and popular pizzeria located
close to the student quarter. Closed Monday.

Antica Montin ($$)
Fondamenta di Borgo 1147 tel: 041/5227151
The Montin has been well known for decades—
Hemingway, Ezra Pound, and Peggy Guggenheim
all came here to eat—and it trades somewhat on
its former reputation. The food no longer merits
the prices charged, but it remains an evocative
place to eat, especially if you manage to reserve a
table in the lovely rear garden. Closed Tuesday
evening and Wednesday.

Antico Capon ($)
*Campo Santa Margherita 3004B
tel: 041/5285292*
An excellent pizzeria with wood-fired ovens—a
rarity in fire-conscious Venice—in one of the city's
nicest squares. Outside tables are occasionally
available for *al fresco* eating. Closed Wednesday.

Crepizza ($)
Calle San Pantalon 3757 tel: 041/5242236
This standard-looking pizzeria-trattoria serves
excellent pizzas, and is well placed for the Frari
and San Rocco. Closed Tuesday.

Dona Onesta ($–$$)
*Calle della Madonna Onesta 3922
tel: 041/5242236*
Overlooking a little canal midway between San
Pantalon and San Tomà, the "Honest Woman"
offers good basic Venetian food at reasonable
prices. Closed Sunday.

Museum Café –
Peggy Guggenheim Collection ($–$$)
Palazzo Venier dei Leoni tel: 041/5228688
More of a restaurant than a snack bar, the stylish
Museum Café serves sandwiches, salads, and meat
dishes, overlooking the tranquil sculpture garden.

Castello

Aciugheta ($–$$)
*Campo SS Filippo e Giacomo 4357
tel: 041/5224292*
The best reasonably priced place to eat or drink
near Piazza San Marco, this pizzeria-trattoria also
serves *cicheti* from the bar. Closed Wednesday.

Al Covo ($$–$$$)
Campiello della Pescaria 3968
tel: 041/5223812
Like all restaurants belonging to the *Buona Accoglienza*, this is an excellent choice for a memorable meal. The setting is calm, romantic, and tasteful (some tables outside), and the service warm and civilized. Plenty of fish and seafood, but also meats and game in season, particularly in autumn, when you can expect a range of unusual dishes. Closed Wednesday and Thursday, mid-December–mid-January and August 1–15.

Al Milion ($)
Corte del Milion 5841 tel: 041/5229302
A trattoria at its best at lunchtime for inexpensive *cicheti*, hot snacks, and good selection of local Veneto wines. Located in the backstreets a short distance from the Rialto. Closed Wednesday.

Alla Rivetta ($)
Ponte San Provolo, Campo SS Filippo e Giacomo 4625 tel: 041/5287302
Reasonably priced, good quality trattoria, invariably busy with boisterous locals. Closed Monday and August.

Canaletto ($$)
Calle della Malvasia 5450 tel: 041/5212661
A large, welcoming restaurant serving grilled meats and Venetian specialities, with an enterprising wine list. A few minutes from Rialto bridge.

Corte Sconta ($$$)
Calle del Pestrin 3886 tel: 041/5227024
Many Venetians and visitors alike rank this as their favorite restaurant. It is always busy, but the cooking and seafood are never less than excellent, especially the imaginative *antipasti*. A member of the *Buona Accoglienza*. Closed Sunday, Monday, and two weeks in summer.

Da Remigio ($–$$)
Salizzada dei Greci 3416 tel: 041/5230089
You will definitely need to reserve or arrive early to share a table with the locals who pack this outstanding neighborhood trattoria. Closed Monday evening and Tuesday.

Testiere ($$–$$$)
Calle del Mondo Nuovo 5801
tel: 041/5227220
A tiny restaurant that has earned a reputation for some of Venice's finest fish dishes, paired with a great wine list. It only seats 22, so book ahead at this *Buona Accoglienza* member.

Cannaregio

Ai Promessi Sposi ($)
Calle dell'Oca 4367 tel: 041/5228609
Young and amiable bar-restaurant offering some of the city's cheapest food (predominantly fish) and largest portions. Excellent, and even more reasonably priced, stand-up snacks and *cicheti* are available from the bar. Closed Wednesday.

Al Bacco ($–$$)
Fondamenta Capuzine 3054 tel: 041/717493
Close to the Ghetto, this restaurant retains the pleasing and slightly rustic feel of the humble trattoria it once was. The food is good at the price. Closed Monday.

Bentigodi ($)
Calesele 1423, off Rio Terrà Farsetti
tel: 041/716269
An easy-going *osteria* for simple snacks or meals in a traditional-style room popular with the locals. Good wines, and tables outside.

Casa Mia ($)
Calle dell'Oca 4430 tel: 041/5285590
Popular pizzeria near SS Apostoli. Closed Tuesday.

Fiaschetteria Toscana ($$–$$$)
Salizzada San Giovanni Grisostomo 5719
tel: 041/5285281
Deservedly the best-known of the Cannaregio restaurants, and among the most frequented since it opened in 1956, so reservations are essential. Classic Venetian and fish cuisine, despite the "Toscana" of the name, and an excellent wine list. Tables out on the square during summer. A member of the *Buona Accoglienza*. Closed Monday, Tuesday, and two weeks in summer.

Gam-Gam-Kosher Restaurant ($)
Sottoportico di Ghetto Vecchio 1122
tel: 041/715284
Venice's only Kosher restaurant and bar offers a wide range of Jewish and Israeli dishes—many also vegetarian. A friendly and informal atmosphere adds to the appeal.

Il Melograno ($–$$)
Calle Riello 458B tel: 041/5242553
A simple but elegant and sophisticated place well away from the tourist beat. Food, service, and setting are all very pleasant. Closed Sunday.

Paradiso Perduto ($)
Fondamenta della Misericordia 2540
tel: 041/720581
More of a club, with a lively bar and occasional live music, the food and easy-going ambience draw in a young and varied crowd. Closed Wednesday.

Vesuvio ($)
Rio Terrà Farsetti 1837 tel: 041/718968
Busy pizzeria with pizzas from a wood-fired oven. Closed Wednesday.

Vini Da Gigio ($$–$$$)
Calle de la Stua, Fondamenta San Felice
tel: 041/5285140
Traditional dishes from a family kitchen, plus an exceptional wine list, make this one of Venice's gastronomic finds. Book well ahead for this *Buona Accoglienza* member situated on a pretty canal.

The Islands

Al Gatto Nero ($–$$)
Fondamenta della Giudecca, Burano 88
tel: 041/730120
A simple trattoria with tables outside on the canal looking across to Burano's old fish market. Located slightly away from the bustle of the island's main streets, and the best place for a reasonably priced meal. Closed Monday.

All'Artigliere ($$)
Via Sandro Gallo 83, Lido tel: 041/5265480
This classic family-run trattoria, situated beside a pretty canal, serves traditional Venetian seafood (some meats as well) accompanied by a hand-picked wine list. The same owners run the **Da Valentino** (tel: 041/5260128) next door.

267

Accommodations and Restaurants

Altanella ($$)
Calle delle Erbe, off Fondamenta di Ponte Piccolo, Giudecca 270 tel: 041/5227780
Excellent fish and seafood, and a tremendous position overlooking the Giudecca's broadest canal. Reservation recommended. Closed Monday evening and Tuesday.

Busa alla Torre ($$)
*Campo Santo Stefano 3, Murano
tel: 041/739662*
The best fish restaurant on Murano, and in one of the island's nicest corners. During the summer there is the added attraction of outside tables. Closed Monday.

Cip's Club, Hotel Cipriani ($$–$$$)
*Giudecca 10—al Palazzetto
tel: 041/5207744*
This fine hotel offers two dining options: the formal, elegant restaurant Cipriani, and this more relaxed pizzeria-restaurant with great views across the canal to San Marco's. Tables outdoors in summer also make it a romantic option.

Locanda Cipriani ($$$)
Torcello tel: 041/730150
Nothing to which Cipriani adds its name is inexpensive, but the food in this slightly pretentious mock-rustic restaurant is top quality, while the setting—looking over broad gardens to Torcello's two lovely churches—is one of the best in Venice. Reservation necessary. Closed Monday, Tuesday, and November to March.

Osteria ai Cacciatori ($–$$)
Fondamenta dei Vetrai 69, Murano
A good old-fashioned place for a fairly priced meal away from the crowds of day trippers.

Da Romano ($–$$)
Via Galuppi 221, Burano tel: 041/730030
A large and atmospheric restaurant right on the island's main street, which is famed less for its food than for the collection of "Burano School" art that covers its walls.

Padova

Antico Brolo ($$–$$$)
Corso Milano 22 tel: 049/664555
Among the finest restaurants in northern Italy, the Antico is long-established, and the cooking, service, and fine wines are the result of years of experience and experiment. Closed Monday.

Verona

Il Desco ($$$)
Via Dietro San Sebastiano 7 tel: 045/595358
Verona is blessed with two superlative top-class restaurants. There is really nothing to choose between here and Le Arche. Closed Sunday and two weeks in June.

Le Arche ($$$)
Via Arche Scaligere 6 tel: 045/8007415
Along with its rival Il Desco, Le Arche has been voted among the top restaurants in Italy. The food and service are what you would expect, given its reputation and prices. Closed Sunday and lunchtime on Monday.

Maffei ($$–$$$)
Piazza delle Erbe 38 tel: 045/8010015
A long-established restaurant that is now enjoying something of a renaissance. Closed Sunday and Monday lunchtime in summer.

Vicenza

Agli Schioppi ($$)
*Contrà Piazza del Castello 26
tel: 0444/543701*
A restaurant with a reputation for good traditional local cooking. Closed Saturday evening, Sunday, and two weeks in August.

Le Due Volpi ($–$$)
Viale X Giugno tel: 0444/323363
A popular place with locals for a special night out. Closed Monday.

CAFÉS, BARS, AND GELATERIE

San Marco

Al Volto
Calle Cavalli 4081
A genuine old *enoteca* with good light snacks and over 1300 varieties of wine. Closed Sunday.

Florian
Piazza San Marco 56–9
Venice's most famous café, in business since 1720. Expensive, but worth visiting at least once for a little bit of Venetian history. Closed Wednesday.

Harry's Bar
Calle Vallaresso
Dress up for (expensive) cocktails in this Venetian institution. Closed Monday.

Leon Bianco
Salizzada San Luca 4153, between Campo Manin and Campo San Luca
Great spot for light snacks, sandwiches, and simple hot meals (noon–3 only). Closed Sunday.

Marchini
Ponte San Maurizio 2769
A wonderful *pasticceria* with a reputation for the city's best cakes and pastries.

Osteria agli Assassini
Rio Terrà degli Assassini 3695
Good wine bar with a fine selection of wines, light snacks, and simple meals. Closed Sunday.

Osteria alle Botteghe
Calle delle Botteghe 3454
Lively place for snacks, sandwiches, and light meals. Closed Sunday.

Paolin
Campo Santo Stefano 2962
Perhaps the city's best ice cream. Tables outside on a pretty square from which to admire the street life. Closed Monday in winter.

Quadri
Piazza San Marco 120–4
Not as old or as pretty as Florian, but the prices are in the same league. Closed Monday.

San Polo and Santa Croce

Antico Dolo
Ruga Vecchia San Giovanni 778, San Polo
This osteria is a good alternative to the pricey snack bars found around the nearby Rialto. Closed Sunday.

Caffè dei Frari
Fondamenta dei Frari 2564
A lively bar, popular with students and locals, just over the bridge in front of the Frari's main facade. Closed Sunday.

Ciak
Campo San Tomà 2807
Nice, easy-going bar (with food) to the left of San Tomà used by everyone from gondoliers to society ladies. It is particularly good for a snack lunch, and stays open late in the evening, when there is occasional live music.

Da Elio
Campo delle Becarie 317
One of Venice's greatest providers of *cicheti* and sandwiches is on the corner of the fish market-place. Go for a stand-up, mid-morning break.

Do Mori
Calle do Mori 429, north of Ruga Vecchia San Giovanni
The best, busiest, and most atmospheric of the old-style bars in the Rialto area, in business since 1462. Good snacks and a choice of 350 wines. If you visit just one typical Venetian bàcaro, come here. Open 8:30–8:30. Closed Sunday.

Do Spade
Sottoportego delle Do Spade 860
Not as rumbustious and dark as Do Mori, but otherwise similarly authentic. Hard to find—look for the two lanterns at No 860. Open 9–2:30, 5–11. Closed Sunday and Thursday evening.

Dorsoduro

Caffè Causin
Campo Santa Margherita 2996
Open since 1928 for coffee and ice cream, and just one of several nice bars on this enchanting piazza. Plenty of outdoor tables. Closed Sunday.

Cantina del Vino
Fondamenta Nani 992
Authentically fusty wine bar directly across the canal from San Trovaso and the famous gondola boatyard. A good place to come if you wish to buy a good wine to take home. Closed Sunday.

Il Caffè
Campo Santa Margherita 2963
Another appealing and photogenic little bar on Campo Santa Margherita. Its outside tables are a favorite place to soak up the sun and streetlife.

Nico
Zattere ai Gesuati 922
Runs Paolin a close second as the producer of Venice's best ice cream. Try the famous house praline speciality, *gianduiotto*. Closed Thursday.

Tonolo
Salizzada San Pantalon 3764
Very popular among the locals who crowd this *pasticceria* for calorie-oozing cakes, coffee, and snacks.

Castello

Cip Ciap
Calle del Mondo Nuovo 5799/a
Nowhere in Venice does *calzone* and take-out sliced pizza better than this busy little place off Campo Santa Maria Formosa. Closed Wednesday.

Enoteca Mascareta
Calle Lunga Santa Maria Formosa 5183
A very popular wine bar serving selected fine wines and a range of good accompanying snacks. Open until late.

Il Golosone
Salizzada San Lio
A bar and *pasticceria* with an excellent choice of cakes and pastries.

Pasticceria Ponte delle Paste
Ponte delle Paste 5991, off Calle del Pistor
A charming pastry store with tea room serving home-baked cakes. Good for an afternoon break in the town center. Affordable prices.

Cannaregio

Boldrin
Salizzada San Cancian 5550
Excellent wine bar with hot snacks and wine by the glass. Closed Sunday.

Caffè Costarica
Rio Terrà di San Leonardo
One of Venice's older and better coffee bars. Known for its iced coffee. Note there are no seats.

Ca' d'Oro
Calle del Pistor and Ramo Ca' d'Oro 3912–3952
Known to all as La Vedova "The Widow," this little place has been serving simple hot meals (and owned by the same family) for 120 years. Closed Sunday lunchtime and Thursday.

Due Colonne
Calle del Cristo and Rio Terrà del Cristo
Busy and enjoyably bustling *enoteca* with a large range of wines and beers.

Paradiso Perduto
Fondamenta della Misericordia 2540
Boisterous and popular late-night bar with live music. Closed Wednesday.

Pub Da Aldo
Fondamenta degli Ormesini 2710
A popular late-night bar with lots of good beer and even more atmosphere. In the center of the Fondamenta della Misericordia "strip" of nightlife in Cannaregio.

The Islands (Giudecca and Lido)

Harry's Dolci
Fondamenta San Biagio, Giudecca 773
An offshoot of Harry's Bar (see page 265). An up-scale but not intimidating oasis for coffee, cakes, and pastries.

Bar Gelateria Maleti
Gran Viale Maria Elisabetta 45–7, Lido
A great place for an after-dinner ice cream or drink, with tables outside on the avenue for those who want to people-watch.

Opening times

Page	Attraction	Weekdays	Sundays	Closed
52	Accademia	8:30–7:30	9–7	Monday
60	Basilica di San Marco (St. Mark's)	10–4:30	2–4:30	—
73	Scuola dei Merletti (Burano)	10–5	10–5	Tuesday
74	Ca' d'Oro	9–2	9–2	—
78	Ca' Pesaro	closed for restoration		
79	Ca' Rezzonico	closed for restoration		
84	Campanile	9:30–7 (winter 9:30–3:30)	9:30–7 (winter 9:30–3:30)	—
94	Collezione Guggenheim	10–6	10–6	Tuesday
97	I Gesuiti	10–noon, 4–6		—
100	Madonna dell'Orto	9:30–noon, 4–6 (winter 9:30–noon, 3:30–5:30)	9;30–noon, 4–6 (winter 9:30–noon, 3:30–5:30)	—
108	Museo Civico Correr	9–7	9–7	—
168	Museo Ebraico (Ghetto)	10–7 (winter 10–5:30)	10–7 (winter 10–5:30)	Saturday
237	Museo Fortuny	closed for restoration		
115	Museo Storico Navale	9–1:30	—	Sunday
78	Museo Orientale	9–2	—	Monday
105	Museo Vetrario (Murano)	10–5	10–5	Wednesday
118	Palazzo Ducale (Doge's Palace)	9–7 (winter 9–5)	9–7 (winter 9–5)	
136	Il Redentore	10–5	Services only Sunday	
137	San Francesco della Vigna	8–12:30, 3–7		
138	San Giacomo dell'Orio	10–5	Services only Sunday	
139	San Giobbe	10–noon, 4–6	Services only Sunday	
140	San Giorgio Maggiore	9:30–noon, 2:30–6 (4 in winter)		
142	San Giovanni in Bragora	9:30–11, 5–7	Saturday afternoon	
146	Santi Giovanni e Paolo	9–noon, 2:30–6	Sunday afternoon	
206	Santa Maria Assunta (Torcello)	10–12:30, 2–5		
103	Santi Maria e Donato (Murano)	9–noon, 4–6	9–noon, 4–6	
156	Santa Maria Formosa	10–5	Services only Sunday	
160	Santa Maria Gloriosa (I Frari)	9–6	1–6	
170	Santa Maria dei Miracoli	10–5	Services only Sunday	
171	Santa Maria della Salute	9–noon, 3–5		
174	San Pantalon	8–11:30, 4:30–7		
175	San Polo	10–5	Services only Sunday	
102	San Pietro (Murano)	8–noon, 3–6:30	8–noon, 3–6:30	
176	San Sebastiano	10–5	Services only Sunday	
178	Santo Stefano	10–5	Services only Sunday	
186	San Zaccaria	10–noon, 4–6		
189	Scalzi	7–noon, 4–7		
192	Scuola Grande dei Carmini	9–noon, 3–6	—	Sunday
194	Scuola Grande di San Rocco	9–5:30 (winter 10–4)		
200	Scuola Grande di San Giorgio degli Schiavoni	Tue–Sat 9:30–12:30, 3:30–6:30 (winter Tue–Sat 10–12:30, 3–6)		Sunday afternoon and Monday

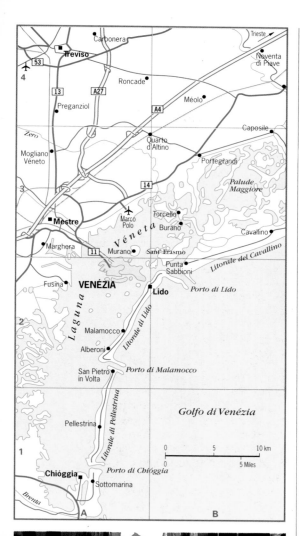

Carbonera

Treviso

53

Noventa
di Piave

4

13   A27

Roncade

Preganziol

Méolo

A4

Caposile

Zero

Quarto
d'Altino

Mogliano
Véneto

Portegrandi

3

14

*Palude
Maggiore*

Mestre

Marco
Polo

Torcello

Burano

Cavallino

Marghera

11   Murano

Sant' Erasmo

V é n e t a

Punta
Sabbioni

Litorale del Cavallino

Fusina

VENÉZIA

Lido

Porto di Lido

L a g u n a

2

Malamocco

Litorale di Lido

Alberoni

San Pietro
in Volta

Porto di Malamocco

Golfo di Venézia

Pellestrina

Litorale di Pellestrina

1

0   5   10 km

0   5 Miles

Chióggia

Porto di Chióggia

Sottomarina

Brenta

A   B

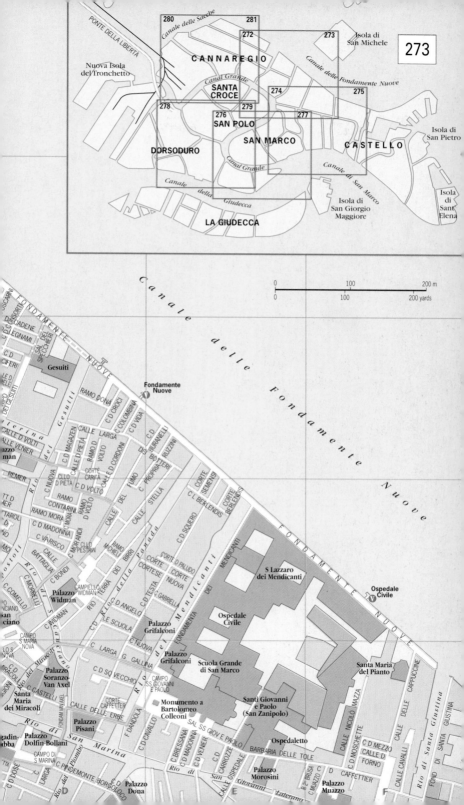

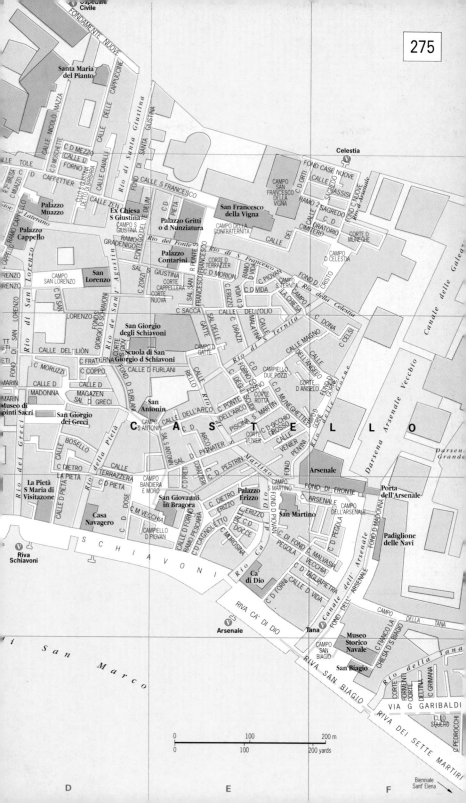

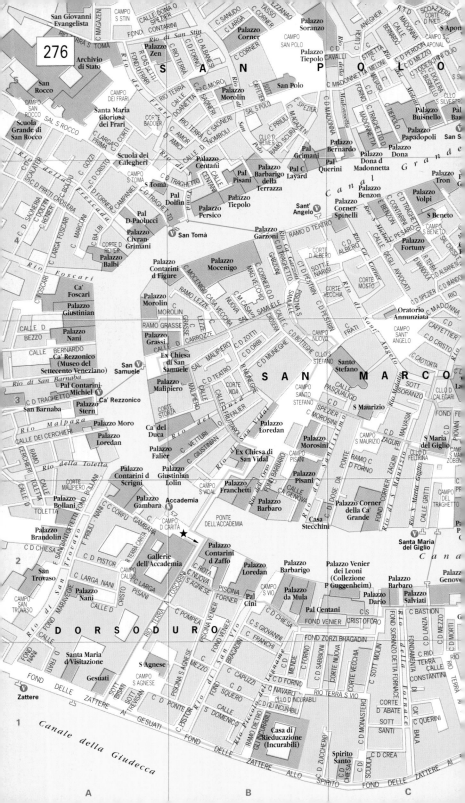

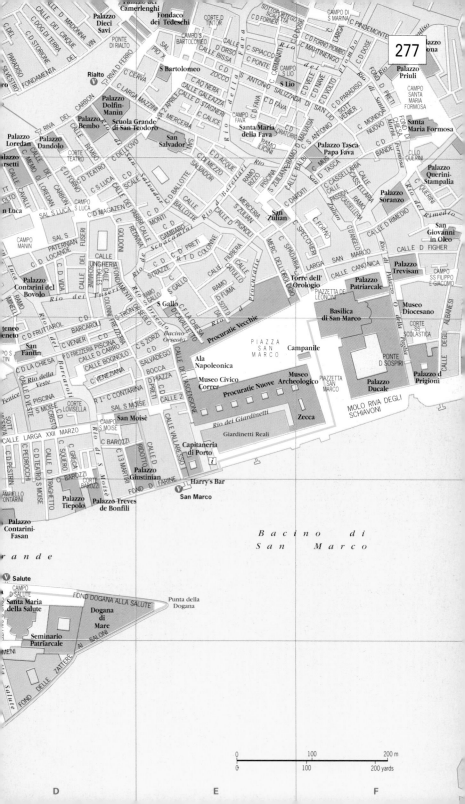

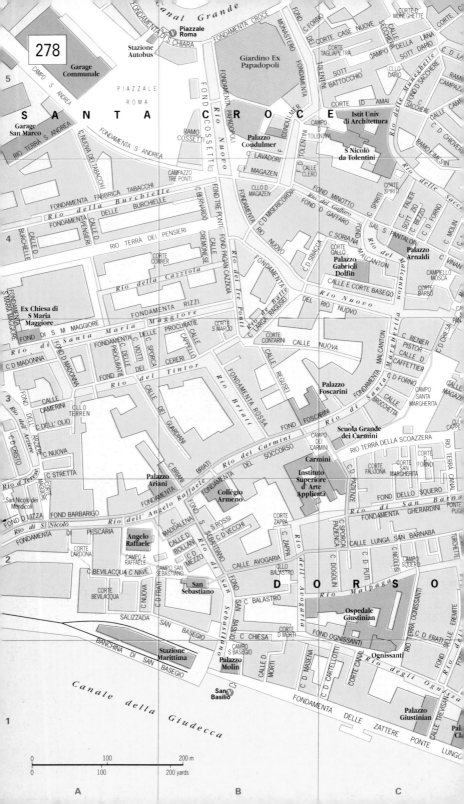

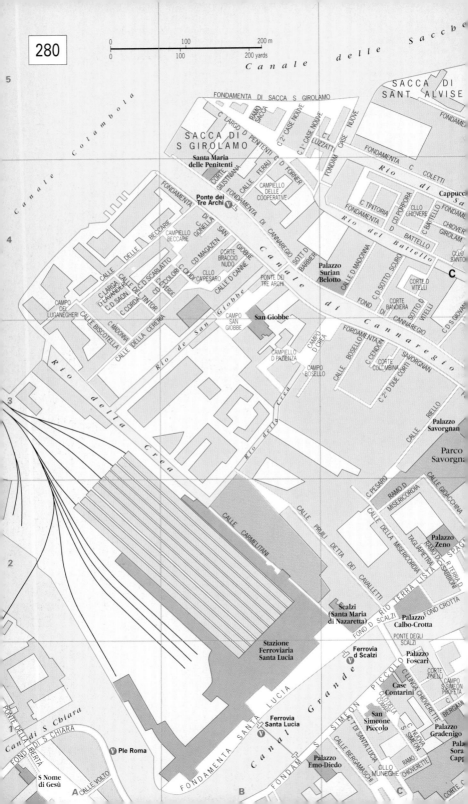

280

Canale delle Sacche

5

SACCA DI
SANT'ALVISE

Canale Colambola

FONDAMENTA DI SACCA S GIROLAMO

C LARGO D PENITENTI E D FORNER

C² CASE NUOVE

C L CASE NUOVE

C L LUZZATTI

FONDAM CASE NUOVE

RAMO SACCA

SACCA DI
S GIROLAMO

Santa Maria
delle Penitenti

FONDAMENTA

Canale

CORTE
GIUSTINIAN

CALLE FERAU

CAMPIELLO
DELLE
COOPERATIVE

FONDAMENTA

FONDAMENTA C COLETTI

Rio di

Cappucci

4

Ponte dei
Tre Archi Ⓥ

CAMPIELLO
BECCARIE

CALLE DELLE BECCARIE

CALLE DI GONELLA

C² DI

CALLE SAN

FONDAMENTA DI CANNAREGIO

SOTT D BARBIER

Canale di

C TINTORIA

CLLO PORPORA

CLLO CHIOVERE

Rio del Battello

C BATTELLO

CHIOVER
GIROLAM

CLLO SANTO

C

CALLE DELLE

C LARGA
D LAVANDERE

C D SAON

CALLE DEL TINTOR

CD MAGAZEN

C D SCARLATTO

C CORDAROLI

C D CHIODI

C D VERDE

CORTE
BRACCIO
NUDO

CLLO CAPESARO

CALLE D CANNE

PONTE DEI
TRE ARCHI

Palazzo
Surian
Belotto

C D MADONNA

C D SOTTO

CORTE D
VITELLI

FOND

CORTE
DI SOTTO
VITELLI

C DS GIOVA

CAMPO DEL
LUGANEGHERI

C MADONNA

C D CORDA

CALLE BISCOTELLA

CALLE DELLA CERERIA

Rio de San Giobbe

CAMPO SAN
GIOBBE

San Giobbe

CAMPO
D CREA

CORTE
BANDIERA

FONDAMENTA SAVORGNAN

CORTE
COLDIMINA

CORTE
C² D DUE CORTI

Cannaregio

CALLE BOSELLO

C CENDON

3

Rio della Crea

CAMPIELLO
D PAZIENZA

CAMPO
BOSELLO

Rio della Crea

RIELLO

CALLE

Palazzo
Savorgnan

Parco
Savorgna

CALLE GIOACCHINA

2

CALLE CARMELITANI

CALLE PRIULI DETTA DEI CAVALLETTI

CALLE PESARO

RAMO D
MISERICORDIA

CALLE DELLA MISERICORDIA

TAGLIAPIETRA

RAMO DI CABRION

RAMO D

SPAG

Palazzo
Zeno

Stazione
Ferroviaria
Santa Lucia

Scalzi
(Santa Maria
di Nazareta)

FOND SCALZI

Rio Terra Lista

Ⓥ

Rio Scalzi

Palazzo
Calbo-Crotta

FOND CROTTA

PONTE DEGLI
SCALZI

Palazzo
Foscari

CORTE
ZINELLI

1

Ponte della libertà

FOND DI S CHIARA

Canal di S Chiara

Ferrovia
d Scalzi Ⓥ

Canal Grande

PISCINA

C LUNGA CHIOVERETTE

CAMPO
SIMEON
PROFETA

C BERGAM

CALLE VOLTO

Ferrovia
Santa Lucia Ⓥ

Ⓥ Ple Roma

FONDAMENTA SANTA LUCIA

Canal Santa Lucia

FONDAM

SIMEON

San
Simeone
Piccolo

C SIMEON

CALLE BERGAMASCHI

C NUOVA SIMEON

RAMO
CHIOVERETTE

Palazzo
Gradenigo

Pala
Sora
Capp

S Nome
di Gesù

Palazzo
Emo-Diedo

CLLO
MUNEGHE

CORTE

A   **B**   **C**

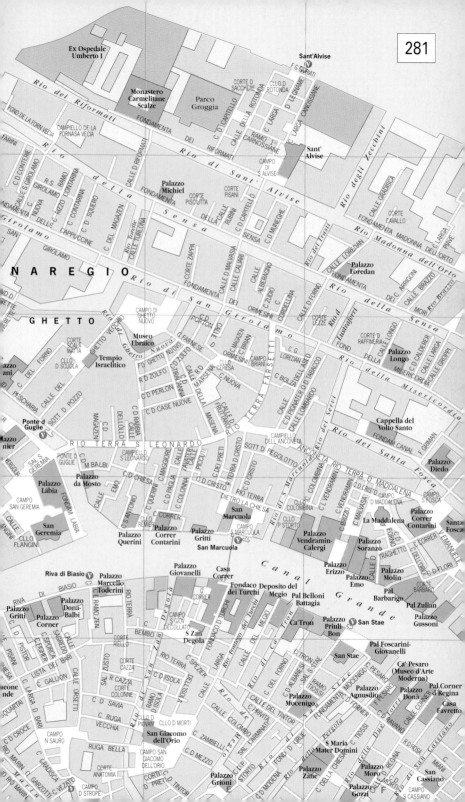

Index

All entries beginning with San, Santa, Santo, or Santi are indexed as though they began with San, and then alphabetically by the *second* element of their name. This reflects the sequence in the book, and dictates, for example, that Santa Maria precedes San Polo. **Bold** figures denote the main entry of a particular subject, rather than an incidental mention.

Index

Index

Acknowledgments

The Automobile Association would like to thank the following photographers, libraries and associations for their assistance in the preparation of this book.

BRIDGEMAN ART LIBRARY 33 *The Room of the Council of Ten, Doge's Palace, Venice* by Gabriele Bella (*fl.*1700–1750) Galleria Querini-Stampalia Venice, 39 *The Coronation of the Virgin* by Stefano Veneziano (*fl.*1353–1381) Galleria dell'Accademia, Venice, 41 *Madonna and Child Enthroned, St. John the Baptist as a boy, St. Joseph, St. Jerome, St. Justinia and St. Francis* by Paolo Veronese (1528–1588) Galleria dell'Accademia, 53 *The Tempest* by Giorgione (ca1476–1510) Galleria dell'Accademia, 54 *The Stealing of the Body of St. Mark* by Jacopo Tintoretto (1518–1594) Galleria dell'Accademia, 55 *Madonna and Child with St. John the Baptist and a Female Saint* by Giovanni Bellini (ca 1430–1516), 56 *Procession in Piazza San Marco* by Gentile Bellini (ca1429–1507) Galleria dell'Accademia, 57 *The Miracle of the Cross on Ponte San Lorenzo* by Gentile Bellini (ca1429–1507) Galleria dell'Accademia, 58/9 *The Meeting of Etherius and Ursula and the Departure of the Pilgrims*, from the St. Ursula Cycle (originally in the Scuola di Sant'Orsola) by Vittore Carpaccio (ca1460–ca1525) Galleria dell'Accademia, 74 *The Ca' d'Oro* by Friedrich Nerly (1807–1878) Christopher Wood Gallery, London, 75 Ceramic jug decorated with a profile portrait of a man, Venetian, 15th–17th century, Ca' d'Oro, 76 *Hercules Wrestling with Achelous* by Stefano Maderno (1576–1636) Ca' d'Oro, 77 *Portrait of the Procurator Nicolò Priuli* by Jacopo Tintoretto (1518–1594) Franchetti Gallery, Ca' d'Oro, 110 *Daedalus and Icarus* by Antonio Canova (1757–1822) Museo Correr, 111 *Pietà* by Cosimo Tura (1430–1495) Museo Correr, 143 *The Baptism of Christ* by Giovanni Battista Cima da Conegliano (ca1459–1517) San Giovanni in Bragora, 164 *The Assumption of the Virgin* by Titian (1485–1576) Santa Maria Gloriosa dei Frari, 201 *St. Jerome and Lion in the Monastery*, 1507–1509, by Vittore Carpaccio (ca1460–ca1525) Scuola Grande di San Giorgio degli Schiavoni, 216 *The Last Judgement*, ca1305, by Giotto (ca1266–1337), 216 Scrovegni Chapel, Padua **BRUCE COLEMAN COLLECTION** F/cover (b). **HUGH and TESSA CHEVALLIER** 9a Calle del Carbon, 24b traghetto from Santa Sofia to the Pescheria, 177 San Sebastiano, 231 St. Martin's Day cake, 246 boats at Marco Polo airport, 251a ticket machine, 252 newsstand, 253 telephone. **STEVE DAY** 36a the Dolomites at Trentino. **MARY EVANS PICTURE LIBRARY** 26b Attila, 28b Paulucco Anafesto, 98 Lido, 113a The Arsenale, 129b Casanova, 144b Antonio Vivaldi, 153 Scuola Grande di San Marco, 158/9 courtesans. **GETTY ONE/STONE** f/cover (a). **RUPERT GORDON** 5b reflection of Santi Apostoli. **RONALD GRANT ARCHIVES** 99 *Death in Venice*, 129a *Casanova*. **J HESELTINE** 26a Torcello; view of the lagoon, 88b Ca' Foscari. **HULTON DEUTSCH COLLECTION** 94 Peggy Guggenheim. **IMAGES COLOUR LIBRARY** B/cover. **THE MANSELL COLLECTION LTD** 29a medal showing turreted vessel, 31 Doge Gradenigo, 34/5 Crusades, 34b Wedding of the Adriatic, 34/5c Knights of the Holy Ghost, 45a Napoléon, 45c Manin, 46b tourists in the Piazza San Marco, 84a collapse of the Campanile, 112b Arsènale and shipyards, 128 Casanova, 130a Piazza San Marco, 145b Claudio Monteverdi, 152a 15th-century Italian warriors, 169b *The Merchant of Venice*, 203, 205a Marco Polo map, 203b Marco Polo, 204 departure of Marco Polo. **THE NATIONAL GALLERY** 25a *Doge Leonardo Loredan* by Giovanni Bellini, 31 *Doge Andrea Gritti* by Catena. **THE NATIONAL MARITIME MUSEUM** 42/3 *The Battle of Lepanto* by Letter. **PICTOR INTERNATIONAL LTD** f/cover (c). **SPECTRUM COLOUR LIBRARY** 160 Santa Maria Gloriosa dei Frari, 214 Santa Giustina, Padua, 222a San Zeno, Verona, 223 Teatro Olimpico, Vicenza, 226 Palladio and Palladian architecture, Vicenza. **ZEFA PICTURES** 22a Vogalonga Festival, 23 festival.

The remaining photographs are held in the Automobile Association's own photo library (AA PHOTO LIBRARY) and were taken by Clive Sawyer, with the exception of the spine and page 87d which was taken by Simon McBride, pages 8a, 13a, 14c, 16/7, 16, 22b, 30b, 36b, 44b, 68, 95, 96b, 101, 107, 108, 109, 135, 136, 144a, 146, 185, 154, 156, 158, 161, 163, 186, 200, 202, 213a, 213b, 229, 249a, 260 and 271b which were taken by Dario Mitidieri, pages 6/7, 42a, 83a, 93a, 97, 150, 245, 248 and 261b which were taken by R Newton, and page 10b which was taken by A Souter.

288

Contributors

Revision copy editor: Sarah Hudson   **Original copy editor:** Barbara Mellor
Revision verifier: Susie Boulton